MONCKTON MILNES

The Flight of Youth: 1851–1885

RICHARD MONCKTON MILNES, CIRCA 1851

James Pope-Hennessy

MONCKTON MILNES

The Flight of Youth
1851–1885

NEW YORK
FARRAR, STRAUS & CUDAHY, INC.

CAPE TOWN   NAIROBI

First published 1951

Contents

List of Illustrations

vii

List of Illustrations

Preface

This sequel to the study of the earlier life and times of Richard Monckton Milnes, Lord Houghton, published in 1950 as *Monckton Milnes: The Years of Promise 1809–1851*, is based like its companion volume upon the great quantity of material—chiefly in the form of letters—preserved in the collection of the Houghton Papers. *The Years of Promise* was an attempt to recreate the first forty-two years of Richard Monckton Milnes' long, full life, from his birth in 1809 to his proposal of marriage accepted by Miss Annabel Crewe at Madeley Manor, Staffordshire, in June 1851, the year of the Great Exhibition. The present book traces Milnes' career from his engagement and marriage up to his death at Vichy in August 1885. In this second part of my study of Lord Houghton I have again intended to present him as he must have seemed in life, surrounded by a throng of friends and acquaintances of many nationalities and of every class and creed. The very wide range of Lord Houghton's interests, as well as his unflagging curiosity and zest for living, meant that he touched the life of his century at many varied points; until, by a paradox which he would himself have relished, this least representative of mid-Victorians provides us with a clear, close understanding of many typically Victorian characters and ways of life. By keeping so many of the day-to-day letters and papers which he received at Fryston or in Upper Brook Street, Lord Houghton has enabled us to peer as through a window into a world now dead and gone. I have sometimes felt that my function in preparing these two volumes has been to pull up the blind and let in the light.

As recorded in the preface to *The Years of Promise*, this study of Lord Houghton could not have been written but for the kindness of the late Lord Crewe who placed all his father's papers at my disposal, and of Lady Crewe who has since implemented his intentions. I must again repeat the sense of obligation which I feel to Lord Houghton's biographer, Sir Thomas Wemyss Reid, whose book was published by Cassell & Co. in 1890, although as I suggested in my earlier preface my selection of material from the Houghton Papers has been less hampered by personal considerations than Reid's could at that moment be. I have also, in the course of my researches for the present volume, come upon a mahogany chest, apparently unopened since the period of the Franco-Prussian war, and containing upwards of four thousand letters which Wemyss Reid could not have seen.

I wish also to thank Miss Gertrude Ireland Blackburne, for the personal recollections of Lord Houghton which she has been good enough to send me; the late Mrs. Laurence Cannon of Oxon Hoath who, through her great-grandmother Emma Blackburne, had inherited the pretty Richmond drawing of Miss Annabel Crewe reproduced in this book; Lord Houghton's granddaughter, Lady Cynthia Colville, who has helped me by her reminiscences of Fryston Hall, a house which no longer exists; Major Hugh Crewe of Madeley Manor, who has helped me in a variety of ways; Capt. Guy Langham for allowing me to make use of the unpublished journals of his grandfather, Henry Spencer Ashbee; Messrs. Heinemann for giving me permission to print unpublished Swinburne material; Mr. John Lehmann; Mr. Angus Wilson, of the Department of Printed Books, British Museum; and Mrs. Woodham-Smith, the author of the *Life of Florence Nightingale*. To Mrs. Gordon Waterfield, who has combined the task of making the fair copy of the book and of many hundreds of the Houghton letters with shrewd and helpful criticisms of the text, and to my brother John Pope-Hennessy for his indispensable, attentive critical assistance, I owe thanks that are not easy to express. Sir Edward Marsh and Mr. C. E. Vulliamy have both done me the kindness of reading the text in proof form, and of making valuable corrections to its grammar and its sense. In this context I may add that no attempt has been made in this or the preceding volume to improve the grammar of the French and German anecdotes transcribed from Lord Houghton's commonplace-books. Lord Houghton's French, German and Italian were fluent rather than correct.

The sub-title of this volume *The Flight of Youth* is one which every contemporary of Lord Houghton's would have recognised, for it is the name of one of his most widely known youthful poems. *The Flight of Youth*, which Lord Houghton perhaps rightly considered his best effort in verse, laments the swift transition from Youth to Age. As it is not inappropriate to the theme of this second volume, I have ventured to apply its title to the book.

March 1951   J. P.-H.

Chapter One

1851

I

The day after Miss Crewe had accepted his offer of marriage, Richard Monckton Milnes left the manor-house at Madeley to address a public meeting in Leeds. The fly to take him to the station was late, so he borrowed his hostess's small pony trap, and hurried away in that, a plump, middle-aged figure with his valet and his valise. It was ten o'clock in the morning. From the garden the scent of honeysuckle and June roses mingled with the pungent aromatic smell of the evergreens that flank the Madeley drive, hot and damp from Monday's rain. Retiring to her upstairs sitting-room, Miss Annabel Crewe settled down at her desk to pen a long, 'more coherent' account of Milnes' proposal in a letter to her only sister Henriett, who resided at a Catholic convent in the South.

They had agreed that no one but Henriett and Richard Milnes' father should be told of the engagement until it had been decided how best to break the news to Miss Crewe's brother, Hungerford Lord Crewe. 'I hope and think Hungerford will be really gratified,' Miss Crewe wrote to her sister, 'after the *first shock* is *over.*'[1] Richard's aunt Louisa, the eldest of his father's three maiden sisters, put it another way:

Don't be surprised if Lord Crewe should rather dislike the marriage [she wrote some days later, when the engagement had been announced];[2] brothers don't care for their sisters marrying and often don't fancy the man they choose—& if this should be so with you, take it quietly and meekly, & by due deference and forbearance prejudice may be removed.

Miss Louisa Milnes in her villa at Torquay now saw her nephew rarely, but she had known him long enough to think that he was seldom quiet and almost never meek; nor was he noted for his deference to any but leading statesmen, and not always to these. The plain fact was that although a number of parents—Lord and Lady Carlisle, the Nightingales, possibly also Lady Stanley of

---

[1] A.C. to her sister, 11 June 1851.
[2] Louisa Milnes to R.M.M., Fryston Lodge, Torquay, 21 June 1851.

Alderley and perhaps the Wyndhams—were supposed to favour Milnes as husband for some daughter, he was not everyone's ideal of a prospective son- or brother-in-law. Henriett Crewe herself harboured doubts as to how so notoriously sociable a man would suit her grave and sensitive sister. Henriett knew Monckton Milnes by repute only, but since he rejoiced in a variety of reputations, any one of them bizarre enough to justify a doting sister's qualms, this was sufficient. The true qualities of heart which Milnes possessed, his warmth, sensibility, humour and touching charm were still unknown to her. Annabel's own faith in Milnes alone reconciled her sister to a marriage of which she felt that she could not spontaneously approve. Like her sister's other confidante Emma Blackburne, Henriett Crewe thought Milnes had been a long time (some eighteen months) in coming to the point. She had written several sympathetic letters to Annabel, and one of these was shown to Monckton Milnes: this letter 'delighted him—he laughed when I told him the doubts, & said, "they must have all thought me quite a brute! did they?"'[1]

Lord Crewe's approval of the match was deemed essential. It seemed unlikely that this moody and unstable nobleman would ever marry, and it was obvious that Henriett, a religious invalid, would not do so either. In consequence, their considerable fortunes and, in Lord Crewe's case, estates, might be expected to devolve in time upon the children of their sister's marriage. The Crewes of Crewe could trace their ancestry back into the twelfth century, whereas the Milneses, who a couple of generations ago had been Methodist mill-owners at Wakefield, were not of ancient stock. They were not noble. They were not rich.[2] These were important considerations in the English society of that epoch. The pre-eminence of breeding was still taken for granted, and birth usually connoted wealth, property and at least local political power. In 1854 the Crimean War caused the first widespread attack upon these assumptions,[3] but in 1851 they were questioned only in advanced radical circles—those of the Grotes, Sir William Molesworth or Roebuck. It can hardly have 'gratified' Hungerford Crewe to realise that his future brother-in-law was publicly known to be at one with these.

---

[1] A.C. to her sister, Madeley Manor, 11 June 1851.

[2] 'We shall not be rich. But she is a person of simple tastes, and will, I trust, accomodate herself to a less luxurious life than she has been accustomed to.' R.M.M. to C. J. MacCarthy, 18 July 1851.

[3] 'This war has given the country a vast impulse towards democracy . . . At this moment it would be an absurdity in the nobles to pretend to the position which was quietly conceded to them, a year ago. This one year has done the work of fifty ordinary ones:—or more accurately, perhaps, it has made apparent what has long been preparing itself.' Nathaniel Hawthorne's *English Notebooks* (ed. Randall Stewart, Oxford University Press, 1941), p. 99, dated January 3rd, 1855.

The Milneses, on the other hand, were much pleased at Richard's engagement, for he had dallied as a bachelor on to the verge of middle-age, and had indeed proposed to Miss Crewe a week before his forty-second birthday. Since his wife's death in 1847, Robert Pemberton Milnes had led a solitary life at Bawtry, sometimes visiting his daughter Lady Galway at neighbouring Serlby or his sisters at Torquay, occasionally coming up to London to see his son. The prospect of a daughter-in-law was delightful to him, and he sent an entirely characteristic answer to Richard's letter about Miss Crewe: 'You know my quiet habits,' he wrote; 'you could not get me to Holland House, you can't get me to Lady Ashburton's but I would go to Madeley if Miss Crewe wished it.' 'He *is* charming,' Annabel Crewe told her sister after Mr. Milnes' visit to Madeley that June: 'Mr. Milnes,' she declared, 'is like a Man in a Book.' It soon transpired that old Mr. Milnes' retiring and unworldly nature, a contrast to the more erratic character of his son, had found a perfect complement in his daughter-in-law's ways and point of view. From 1851 until his death in 1858 he drew pleasure from her company, and when she was away in London with her husband, or paying interminable visits to country houses, he would write to her, and expect an answer, almost every day.

II

Richard Milnes and his father easily persuaded Miss Crewe to cross the country to Bawtry and on to Serlby, the Galways' Nottinghamshire house, with a daytime expedition to see Fryston, her future home. Milnes' political interests in Pontefract precluded their living at 'sweet Madeley' as Miss Crewe would have preferred, and it was with some apprehension that she went to inspect Fryston on 27 June. She did not care for what she saw. 'I have taken a positive *dislike* to Fryston, with its great dismal park,' she wrote immediately to her sister. Later, as Mrs. Monckton Milnes, she became reconciled to her husband's gaunt house on the banks of the murky river Aire, but she always missed the village interests of Madeley and the garden she and her aunt had loved. Fryston Hall had no flower garden to speak of, though an 'unusually large' area was given over to vegetables and fruit. Its only beauty was its woods with long grassy rides leading through them. In 1850 Mr. Pemberton Milnes had sown broom in all the vacant spaces of these woods: 'It will give them quite a savage aspect,' he wrote happily to Richard, adding that the land under plantation at Fryston was 'absolutely worthless, except for wild grapes & broom & gorse' and that his new farmer 'could not make it grow wheat by any admixture—the decomposed magnesia under the inch of soil destroys all profitable crops.' Richard Milnes did not like Fryston himself, and would describe the bleak countryside round Ferrybridge as 'the English Thrace.'[1] The indoor comfort of Fryston compensated, however, for the smoky and exposed landscape outside its windows:

There was such a bright fire & the house felt so much warmer than any we have been in lately [wrote Annabel Milnes of a return from Ampthill in January 1852], & our room is so airy with the sun streaming through it next morning that I am growing *quite fond* of Fryston! Then I see it is a house & place full of capabilities & in doors & out might furnish plenty of interesting employment to render all pretty & enjoyable.

Both before and after her marriage Annabel Milnes was delicate and often ailing, subject to prolonged headaches and susceptible to every chill. Her weak health made her very conscious of the cold which was then an even more noticeable feature of English country-house existence than it is to-day. Houses were either too cold, like Ampthill and Broadlands, or, like Mr. Milnes' house at Bawtry, too hot: 'a catch-cold house to move about in—the rooms being very hot & the passages full of cold mixed draughts.' At the Grange Mrs. Milnes found that alone among her husband's friends the formidable and luxury-loving Lady Ashburton knew how to warm a house. In common with many of her contemporaries, Mrs. Milnes really thought a chill and level indoor temperature the healthiest one. 'I think it better,' she wrote from her brother's freezing apartments at Crewe Hall, 'than the heated atmosphere of my father-in-law's rooms.'

Monckton Milnes' engagement and marriage did not modify his habit of scampering hither and thither. He still trotted from party to party, from house to house. His wife's health, as well as her distinct preference for domesticity, rendered her unwilling to take part in all of these activities, though she cordially entertained her husband's guests in London and at Fryston and, in the first years of her marriage, went the round of country houses with him too. Richard was 'beginning to understand that society to women is often a fatigue, not a *refreshment* as *he* rather takes it to be,' she wrote to her sister during her short engagement, and again: 'with

[1] 'I do not know why you call your country the English Thrace. Three hundred years ago Thomas Cromwell told Henry the Eighth that the country round Ferrybridge was the most flourishing part of the whole realm of England; and, for my own part, though I have seen finer scenery, I have never seen a more thriving population than that among which you live.' (T. B. Macaulay to R.M.M., dated Albany, London, 2 December 1843.)

his untiring energies I dare say it is difficult to understand how comparatively little any woman *can* do.' At first Miss Crewe fancied that she could change Milnes' ways: 'By degrees I shall trust to wean him from his love of society' she told Henriett in that summer of 1851, and she nicknamed him 'the Genius of Locomotiveness.' Her letters abound in references to his care and solicitude, all the more remarkable because Milnes' dislike of illness was almost as great as his dislike of age. Years before, staying at Castle Ashby, he had shocked a girl by remarking at breakfast that he was always 'perfectly miserable' when he was ill: 'life in its best form is burdensome enough, with pain it would be intolerable, particularly when that pain may lead to a state of which we know nothing and have all to fear.'[1]

Every marriage is a private relationship which cannot be truly judged or evaluated from outside. Some of the published letters and memoirs of Milnes' acquaintances contain gossip about the obvious contrasts between his wife's quiet tastes and his own inexhaustible curiosity and activity. 'Dicky Milnes goes on Monday to Brougham, leaving his oppressed wife at Crewe' runs a typical comment. 'He eats enormously, will soon be ill again & also complains of his throat.'[2] Against these snap judgements of London society we may balance three collections of letters preserved amongst the Houghton Papers—Monckton Milnes' own ample correspondence with his wife, her numerous letters to him, and, most revealing of all, her detailed letters to her sister covering the twenty-three years of her married life. In Richard Milnes she found an ideal focus for what she herself termed her *besoin d'aimer*. Her father-in-law, who had warned her that marriage was full of 'cares' and 'oppression' and might well prove 'irksome' to her, was astonished to find how well she adapted herself to her new state:

If indeed there be an exception [he wrote in 1852 to Mrs. Blackburne (his subject human unhappiness)], & anyone has an unalloyed felicity, I think it is Annabel—From the mopy creature

---

[1] Conversation reported in a letter from Alice Spring-Rice (later Mrs. Henry Taylor) to Aubrey de Vere, quoted in Una Taylor's *Guests and Memories: Annals of a Seaside Villa* (Oxford University Press, 1924) without date. 'Tell me that he was not speaking seriously,' Miss Spring-Rice continued. '. . . You know he could not mean it seriously, but still his eyes frightened me, and I cannot forget the words.'

[2] Lord Stanley to his wife, Broadlands 15 January 1864 (*The Stanleys of Alderley* 1851–1865, ed. Nancy Mitford, Chapman & Hall 1939). Other references to Milnes' marriage in this volume (notably that dated from the Grange, 22 November 1851) exemplify Stanley's notorious spite, of which Milnes was well aware, as an impromptu couplet of his own in his 1851 commonplace-book shows:

Ben Stanley's poisoned! gossip what a song!
How did it happen? did he bite his tongue?

as I saw her first at Madeley she has sprung into a youth & freshness beyond belief—younger by at least some dozen years—& in the highest spirits & enjoyment.

Milnes' oldest friends were much impressed by the care he lavished on his wife:

Mrs. Procter . . . spoke of Mr. Milnes with the most hearty admiration [Miss Williams Wynn told Annabel][1] though she based it on facts which perhaps did not seem heroic enough to deserve such unmeasured eulogium—'He never forgot your luncheon at Fryston, but popped the bottle of soda-water in his pocket, & took you the tray himself'. Oh dear! how long would it be before a crumb of praise would be thrown to the wife for not *forgetting* her Husband's food!!!!

On his side Milnes found comfort and stability in the marriage: 'Annabel is even more of a companion than I had ever anticipated,' he wrote three weeks after the wedding, 'and so wise and reasonable that, even in the most calm and prudential point of view, I must look upon myself as a very fortunate man.'[2] 'She was a perfect woman', he told another friend on the day, twenty-three years later, that she died.

Again and again, years afterwards, one noticed the softening of his tones, the break in his voice, when by any chance her name was mentioned. A man of his peculiarities of temperament—to say nothing of his intellectual endowments—was not one who could easily have found a wife suited to him in every respect.[3]

Although Milnes lived with a restless zeal and denied himself no pleasure, he at times found the process of existence as unbearable as all sensitive and reflective persons must often do. 'There are moments when I feel that nothing is real but evil, nothing true but pain,' he had noted in his commonplace-book a few years earlier. 'I hardly know the morning when I have been *glad* to wake,' he added on another page of the same volume. His marriage formed an antidote to these recurrent moods of disillusion. Some short and simple lines addressed by Milnes to his wife, and dated New Year's Day 1854, best serve to indicate the tone and atmosphere of their relationship:

[1] Undated letter '27 North Audley Street, Tuesday night,' probably 1852.
[2] R.M.M. to C. J. MacCarthy, 16 August 1851.
[3] Reid, vol. ii, p. 291.

Thou Gleaner of the sunny hours
Harvested in the home of God,
Gild me the future summer's bowers,
Revive the present ice-bound sod!

Thou Gleaner from the darkest hours
Of scattered good, I could not see,
Preserve thy dear remedial powers,
And shed them as I need o'er me.

III

The news of Milnes' engagement delighted his family, and aroused the sympathetic attention of his friends. 'I believe you will make the best husband in the world,' wrote a hopeful relative from Cowes. 'I always thought Miss Crewe a particularly nice girl, with such pleasant and agreeable gentle manners,' was Lady Palmerston's comment: 'Lord P. desires to unite his congratulations with mine.' Lady Harriet Baring, by then Lady Ashburton, told Milnes that she could not pretend to have read his letter 'with unmixed feelings':

Independently of all that could be said of the Lady—for I do not know her—I am sure that married you will be a much happier— even—a better man—tho' I daresay you don't think *this*.

He would also, she concluded be 'less of a vagrant.' We may safely fancy that Lady Ashburton did not much like her male friends marrying; the only women she cared for were those she hoped that she could patronise—Mrs. Brookfield, Mrs. Henry Taylor or Mrs. Carlyle. An ornate but frank letter came from Milnes' old Paris friend, the journalist F. O. Ward.

It argues, I think, a happy frame of mind when a man in middle age has a well-considered desire for marriage. It shows him minded to forego the hasty plucking of pleasure's blossoms, rootless and fading, and content patiently to cultivate the whole plant of happiness.

Milnes cannot have cared for the emphasis on middle-age; already in 1843, when he was only thirty-four, he had been publicly ridiculed in the *Morning Chronicle* for always referring to himself as young. In one of his most popular early poems, *The Flight of Youth*, he had expounded the theory that Love alone could compensate for the loss of youth:

We are cold, very cold,—
All our blood is drying old,
And a terrible heart-dearth
Reigns for us in heaven and earth:
Forth we stretch our chilly fingers
In poor effort to attain
Tepid embers, where still lingers
Some preserving warmth, in vain.
Oh! if Love, the Sister dear
Of Youth that we have lost,
Come not in swift pity here,
Come not, with a host
Of Affections, strong and kind,
To hold up our sinking mind,
If she will not, of her grace,
Take her brother's holy place,
And be to us, at least, a part
Of what he was, in Life and Heart,
The faintness that is on our breath
Can have no other end but Death.

He was now about to put this theory into practice. While Disraeli and certain other of Milnes' acquaintances considered him conceited, Milnes was not in fact especially so. At the time of his engagement—disturbed perhaps by Miss Crewe's patent admiration for himself—he jotted this reflection down in his commonplace-book: 'How often must the woman be undeceived as to the worth of her husband by the treatment he receives from others; how many a love-delusion must be thus dispelled.' 'I only hope,' he wrote in a 'quasi-brotherly' letter to Miss Crewe's sister in June 1851, 'that her example may so work on me as to enable me to be all she can desire.'

Since Milnes and his bride felt 'much repugnance to the pomp of "St. George's,"' they planned that the marriage should take place at Madeley on the last day of July. To prepare for this they proceeded severally to London, Miss Crewe to stay at her brother's stuffy Hill Street house, Richard Milnes to dismantle his famous rooms at 26 Pall Mall.

Henceforth, to me, your number 26 will have something funereal about it [wrote his old Cambridge tutor, the Bishop of St. Davids]. I am sure that I shall never enjoy a breakfast again in that room, . . . It is very likely—nay, certain—that you will still collect agreeable people about your wife's breakfast table; but can I ever sit down there without the certainty that I shall meet with none but respectable persons?[1]

[1] Letter from Bishop Thirlwall, dated June 1851.

'I get on quicker than most people with the Trousseau I imagine,' Miss Crewe reported to her sister, 'having the knack of making up my mind promptly.' What she called 'the cadeaux' were soon pouring into Hill Street—a string of oriental pearls with a ruby and diamond locket from her brother ('very lovely but I think he means to give something more'), a massive gold bracelet from Henriett ('so useful to wear both morning & evening—always handsome without being smart, emblematic, too, I trust of the chains of Love, binding us all together!'), a 'parure in perfect taste' from a Greville cousin ('three brooches to go down the body of the gown of blue enamel, diamonds and pearls') and from Emma Blackburne a bracelet of her own hair with (in memory of the primrose woods at Madeley) '*a primrose* in gold on the clasp.' Richard Milnes gave her a 'handsome dressing-case' and told her they would buy some 'fine jewels' in Vienna, where they were to spend their honeymoon. It was the summer of the Great Exhibition, and though there were fewer foreign visitors than had been expected, London was busy and cabs were hard to find. They went often to the Crystal Palace, where Milnes placed orders lavishly—'lace shawls &c . . . so I have rather to restrain his ardour.' The pernicious influence of the Great Exhibition was also evident in some of the gifts that other friends sent Miss Crewe—'a blotting-book with electro-silver embossed figures on it,' for instance, and a gold penholder set with stones. The month in London proved tiring, for apart from the business of the trousseau and the frequent tours of the Crystal Palace, Miss Crewe had to face innumerable entertainments offered her by the Milneses as well as by her brother Crewe—dinner-parties, opera boxes, luncheons at the new restaurant, Soyer's Symposium, which the famous chef had opened in May 1851 in the former residence of Lady Blessington, Gore House. She was not sorry to return to the rural solitude of Madeley.

IV

The weather of 31 July proved 'unpropitious' and the wedding party, which had assembled at Madeley Manor that morning, proceeded to the village Church in a line of carriages through summer rain. The Madeley bells had been pealing all morning, festoons and triumphal arches decorated the route, and streamers from the village windows bore fervent mottoes: 'Long Life and Happiness to Mr. and Mrs. Milnes,' 'Let No Alloy Mix with their Joy,' 'The Blessings of the Poor are Yours.' The bride wore a dress of glacé silk (silver-white and covered with old point lace), an orange-blossom wreath and large lace veil. She was attended by four bridesmaids in white dresses and blue mantles and sashes, with transparent white bonnets adorned with convolvulus upon their heads. As the bride, small, elegant and smiling, with bright blue eyes and dark golden-brown hair, alighted from her carriage and walked through the churchyard crowded with well-wishers from Madeley and all the neighbouring villages, she was met by eight of the principal tenants' daughters, 'who performed the grateful and pleasing ceremony of strewing her path with flowers.' In 1851 the English aristocracy was still treated in a manner which seems incredible to-day. In this remote part of Staffordshire social distinctions were as black and white as the old beamed manor-house at Madeley itself, and the local attitude to the Crewe family was feudal. Leaning on the arm of her tall, stiff-backed brother,[1] Miss Crewe entered the roomy medieval church of Madeley to be greeted by a hymn of praise chanted by the children of the endowed school:

> Hail, hail to those
>   Who raised these walls,
> Whose liberal bounty ne'er doth fail
>   When sacred duty calls.
>
> .   .   .   .   .   .
>
> Kind patrons and true friends,
>   Where'er your feet may roam,
> Our heartfelt prayers to God ascend
>   To bless you and your home.

The Milneses were heartily cheered on leaving the church, and all the way from Madeley to Crewe, six miles distant, the roads were packed and the villages festive. The tenantry of Madeley and of Mucklestone dined, one hundred and twenty of them, at the Crewe Arms, and then repaired to meet their wives and daughters at Madeley for a tea-party which lasted, with dancing, until midnight. Celebrations continued in the Madeley countryside for three whole days, and beef and ale were liberally distributed to the poorer cottagers. Meanwhile the wedding luncheon had been given at Crewe Hall, accompanied by a good deal to drink and a series of felicitous family speeches. The bridegroom distinguished himself by alluding 'to the noble old hall & its owner—in quite poetical terms'[2] while his father spoke of the bride's admirable character—
'& how she was beloved by relations and friends of the highest rank, but what was still better her goodness was told in stronger language by the tears of the poor of Madeley.'[3] Late in the afternoon the

---

[1] 'That great walking-stick Crewe' Milnes had written to Charles MacCarthy in a letter of January 1838, adding that Crewe had 'grown to be an *absolute* idiot.'

[2] Emma Blackburne to Henriett Crewe, 31 July 1851.

[3] *Idem.* A hay-fever victim, Henriett did not go to the wedding.

THE HONOURABLE ANNABEL CREWE

newly-married couple managed to escape from their numerous relatives to Teddesley Park, the nearby seat of Lord Hatherton, a middle-aged Whig widower who re-married in February 1852 and became Lord-Lieutenant of Staffordshire in 1854. After three days at Teddesley they went via Clifton to Torquay, the new, fashionable resort where Richard's aunts lent them the little yellow, gabled cottage called Fryston Lodge. After a visit from Henriett Crewe they returned, in mid-August, to London, dined at the Palmerstons' where they met the Duchess of Inverness and some French people who included one of Milnes' earliest friends, the Comte de Circourt, and set out for Vienna, via Ostend, Cologne, Bonn and Frankfurt.

'Richard Milnes is married, about two weeks ago,' wrote Carlyle from Great Malvern, where he was doing a cure, to his New England correspondent Emerson, 'and gone to Vienna for a jaunt. His wife, a Miss Crewe (Lord Crewe's sister), about forty, pleasant, intelligent and rather rich : that is the end of Richard's long first act.'[1]

---

[1] Correspondence of Thomas Carlyle and Ralph Waldo Emerson 1834–1872, vol. II; (Chatto and Windus 1883), letter of 25 August 1851. Carlyle had retired to Malvern after correcting the proofs of the *Life of John Sterling* (Chapman and Hall 1851).

Chapter Two

1851   *1852*

I

Milnes' choice of a honeymoon tour in Germany and Austria rather than through France to Italy was determined by several factors. In the summer of 1851 France, on the verge of the Second Empire, was viewed with distrust amounting to alarm by most English people; and though Milnes, in spite of his liberalism, was still slightly inclined to favour his 'old friend' the Prince-President, he had no special wish to pass through Paris just then. Italy he and his wife both knew; melancholy memories of his lost exuberant youth would have awaited him in Venice, Milan, Florence or Rome. Vienna, on the other hand, was a place to which 'by some odd *combinazione*' neither he nor Annabel had ever been. The journey that he planned, down the Rhine by steamboat from Bonn to Mainz, on to Frankfurt (once again the seat of the Federal Parliament), across to Linz and down the Danube to Vienna with Hungary as the final goal, was an instructive as well as a romantic one, though his father pretended not to admit this. Mr. Milnes wrote to warn his daughter-in-law of the discomforts of the projected tour:

I think that [the Ostend] passage is most disagreeable. . . . Nor am I in better humour when I get to Ostend—it lasts all up the Rhine. I dislike it all. That would be a noble river, if it ran, as Nature designed it, thro' forests—but those hills, stript as they are to sticks of a yard for their grapes, is it not a profanation? With us the trees are felled for contested elections (that of Richard's with Sir Culling Eardley cost the best forty acres of oaks I had)—it was not so there, & shows that Metternich & those guzzling Germans think more of their sour wines than of all the beauty of creation. I don't feel at home up that river [continued Mr. Milnes] till I get on to Basle, & thence all on to Italy, which is my proper domicile.

He also teased his daughter-in-law about possible dangers in her journey:

It is right you should be cautious. Are you aware, in Protestant Germany, how easily you may be divorc'd? They don't require, as with us, any thing serious—only some incompatibility, & almost any will do. A difference between you & Richard about your white dog would be quite enough.[1]

Milnes' passion for Germany and German things, dating from his student months at Bonn in 1830, had been nourished during his visits to Berlin in 1845 and 1850, as well as by his friendship with the Bunsen family, with Varnhagen von Ense and with Bettina von Arnim. A devotee of Goethe, a friend of Heine, and always ready to help exiled poets like Ferdinand Freiligrath and Moritz Hartmann, Milnes had acquired and kept up a very wide knowledge of German books: 'One of the men most interested in, and best acquainted with, our literature is Monckton Milnes,' wrote Amely Bolte to the novelist Fanny Lewald in June 1849.

The political condition of Prussia, Austria and the German States in 1851 was not encouraging to a man of Milnes' liberal mind. The hasty outbreaks of 1848 and '49 had been neutralised in Germany and in the Empire by successful reactionary regimes. English people were struck by the sharp change in the political atmosphere of the German States. Miss Charlotte Williams Wynn, an astute observer with a long experience of Germany, noticed it in July 1851: '. . . the difference I find since six years ago I was last on the Rhine is astonishing,' wrote this cousin of Mrs. Milnes to her French friend Rio, from Schwalbach.

All seem discontented, and the apparent quiet is the gathering before the storm. There is a general feeling of hatred to the aristocracy and to royalty, and I may say they have well deserved the hatred, for the wanton acts of despotism which one comes across at every turn make one only wonder that any nation can bear them so long. At Frankfort the people are completely soldier-ruled . . .[2]

Things had gone even farther in the heart of the Empire, as Milnes and his wife discovered to their surprise. 'You will be amused, by the bye, to hear that Annabel and I were thought too dangerous to be admitted into Hungary,' Milnes wrote to MacCarthy,[3] 'Schwarzenberg personally forbidding it: how childish and unwise.' Milnes' pronouncements on foreign politics—his speech in 1847 on the suppression of the Free State of Cracow, his *Letter to the Marquess of Lansdowne on the Events of 1848*—had received moderate attention in London, but had caused sharp irritation at Vienna, where Princess Metternich's view of Milnes as 'one of the most advanced

---

[1] Letter dated from Seaton, 23 August 1851.
[2] *Memorials of Charlotte Williams Wynn*, ed. by her sister (Longmans, Green 1877).
[3] Undated detached sheet from a letter.

democrats in England' and in league with the Hungarian exiles was evidently shared by Prince Felix zu Schwarzenberg, the absolutist minister of the young Emperor Franz Josef. Milnes had always been taken more seriously abroad than at home.[1]

The hotels of German spas and cities were filled with English summer visitors, many of them friends or acquaintances of Monckton Milnes. From Ostend to Cologne the Milneses travelled with Sir Frederick Thesiger, a handsome Tory lawyer who became Lord Chancellor in 1858; on the Rhine boat from Bonn they foun Lady St. Maur and her daughters Lady Hermione and Lad Ulrica; at Frankfurt there were Lord Cowley, English minister to the Confederation, and his 'engaging' wife, as well as Milnes' Yorkshire neighbour Mexborough. They made special journeys to Homburg to see Lord and Lady Ashburton and to Wiesbaden to see Miss Charlotte Williams Wynn and her pet dog; at Wildbad they met the Elys, and at Baden the Greville cousins of Milnes' wife. English people of fashion were cordially received by the numerous German royalties, some of whom spoke English fluently while others did not. At Baden the Milneses were presented to the Grand Duchess Stéphanie, while at Homburg they saw the Duke and Duchess of Augustenburg. The Augustenburg daughter, who piqued herself on her English, amused Milnes considerably. 'Are you going to Baden?' she asked a Miss Stanley, who had just been introduced to her. 'Yes, next week.' 'Good God! Gracious Heavens! Then we shall meet again!' the Princess disconcertingly replied.

Mrs. Milnes bore all the rushing about, and the succession of new acquaintances, better than she had expected, better indeed than her husband, who was often upset by the great August heat, the Rhine wines and the early meals. In four weeks they slept in seventeen different hotels, as well as making daytime expeditions to sights such as Schwalbach and Schlangenbad. They bought jewellery and old books, visited curiosity shops and moonlit cathedrals, admired the autumn woods at sunset or the floral garlands with which South German village girls would decorate their cows. The nine-hour journey down the Danube to Vienna was accomplished in pouring rain, and when she finally reached the haven of the Hotel Erzherzog Karl Mrs. Milnes retired to bed with influenza. 'If you marry the wind,' Harriet Ashburton had said to her at Homburg, 'you must take the consequences.'

---

[1] Schwarzenberg, who gave a ball to celebrate Palmerston's dismissal from office in December 1851, must have known of Milnes as an ardent Palmerstonian and perhaps suspected him of some political mission from the English Foreign Secretary to Hungarian dissidents.

II

'We were neither of us charmed with Vienna,' Mrs. Milnes told her sister. They stayed a fortnight in that capital, going to the opera (*Oberon, Lucrezia Borgia*) and to hear Strauss's band in the Volks-Garten, and visiting Schoenbrunn, Klosterneuburg, the Liechtenstein and Prince Esterhazy's collections. Annabel Milnes had more knowledge of painting than her husband, who was only intent upon the 'subject' of any work of art. She particularly admired the Giorgiones and Guercinos in the Imperial Gallery, and the Cuyps, Ruysdaels and Murillos at Prince Esterhazy's. Milnes noted one or two of her remarks with a certain awe:

What is the use of niggling for hours at a representation of so-called trees, but which in the end are not the least like trees at all? [she asked him one day in the Vienna gallery]. De Wint's vaguest sketches suggest as much to the imagination as the most elaborate leaf-work.

It is probable that Mrs. Milnes did not then share her husband's nascent fondness for Pre-Raphaelite art.

The technique of Turner's oil painting was one of the subjects which Mrs. Milnes discussed with a new English friend, Mr. Thomson, 'a charming Oxford Tutor, a fellow of Queen's College' with whom she had got into conversation during the long but beautiful journey up the Danube from Vienna back to Linz. Mr. Thomson, ever afterwards a welcome guest at Fryston, ended his life as Archbishop of York. He became their constant companion in Munich, which the Milneses preferred to Vienna, a city where they had known few people. In Munich, which Mrs. Milnes called 'this airy bright capital . . . this seat of modern art which is to be seen here to perfection,' they were dazzled by the new churches and palaces, the frescoes and statuary. Kleuze, the architect of the Valhalla and the Glyptothek, personally took them over the palace built by the 'old king.'[1] Lady Byron's nephew, Sir John Milbanke, was then Minister to Bavaria, and he and his wife, a pretty woman whom Mrs. Milnes already knew, showed them courtesy. On one afternoon in early October, when they had been to the studio of Raulbach's nephew to see his painting of the Milbankes' progeny, Mrs. Milnes went shopping with Lady Milbanke and returned for tea at the Legation. Here she was deeply interested to meet the

---

[1] Ludwig I, who had abdicated in March 1848 in favour of his son Maximilian II.

English novelist Baroness Tautphoeus,[1] authoress of *The Initials*, a book which she remembered as having made 'some noise' in England when it appeared in 1850 and which she, her brother Crewe, Miss Williams Wynn and Richard Milnes had all greatly enjoyed. Three days later they were invited to visit the house of the authoress, who won Mrs. Milnes' heart by explaining that though she 'scarcely ever' entered 'society' she had been 'bribed' to go to Lady Milbanke's by being told she was to meet Richard Monckton Milnes. 'After this, of course, the Poet's Wife could no less than send her the next day a Vol. of his Verses,' Mrs. Milnes added.

The steamboat from Bonn to Mainz had served to remind Richard Milnes of his student days in that Rhenish town. At Munich, to his pleasure and surprise, he recognised, in the Archbishop's Vicar-General, a man who had been one of the most intimate friends of that joyful period of his youth. Monsignor Windischmann and Milnes had not met for twenty years, though they had corresponded for a certain time after Milnes' departure from Bonn in September 1830 to join his father, his mother and his sister Harriette in Milan. Fritz Windischmann was one of those youths who had immediately succumbed to Milnes' charm, and who himself exemplified that emotionalism, that unashamed sentimentality which had first attracted Milnes towards the German race. Windischmann's letters had been passionate, high-minded and, ultimately, somewhat wistful. Sometimes in German, sometimes in English, he implored Milnes to return to Bonn 'the little town where there are people who love you so much,' and would describe himself as standing 'like a sentinel looking for you there.' 'I have a beautiful letter from Windischmann, telling me he is just going into orders and is to have a cure in the mountains near Munich,' Milnes had written in a letter of November 1835, and when his sister had gone with her husband Galway to Germany in 1838 he told her to buy him any books 'that Windischmann recommends.' Now, after twenty years of separation, their youth a memory, they met again. If Windischmann had changed we cannot know it; in twenty years Milnes had altered in appearance and importance, but in little else.

Windischmann had once written to him, in a long German letter from Munich, dated 4 July 1835:

---

[1] Jemima Montgomery, Baroness Tautphoeus (1807–1893) was of Irish origin and had married in 1838 the chamberlain of the King of Bavaria. She wrote several novels of German life, of which the diverting *Initials* (Richard Bentley, 1850) was the first; the others were *Quits* (1857), *Cyrilla* (1854) and *At Odds* (1863). Justly praised in their day, the writings of this clever woman have been forgotten since.

. . . I am so often troubled on your account. I know, without your telling me, that you have no peace of mind. You see the world and all its beauty, you are now here now there on the earth, now here now there in science, now here now there amidst the pleasures of life: you mean to attain peace, you arrive at some belief, you discover some new thought that fills your soul, you are inspired, encouraged— and then, again, cold, cast down: and the highest philosophy with which you console yourself is still 'vanitatum vanitas.'

It is revealing to compare this just analysis of Milnes' character as a youth of nineteen with the comments on him of Herbert Spencer,[1] who first made his acquaintance in the year of his marriage, 1851. Spencer declared that you could form but 'an undecided impression' of Milnes' views, that he was mentally restless, ready 'to listen to ideas of all kinds, however extreme' and consequently in 'an un-settled state of opinion upon most things.' 'Even in his later years,' Spencer continued, 'when increasing age might have been expected to have a sedative influence, he was ever moving hither and thither . . .' The Archbishop's Vicar-General can have had small difficulty in rediscovering Monckton Milnes.

In mid-October the Milneses turned north through Nuremberg, Bamberg, Dresden (where they lingered some days, going to the theatre and visiting the poet Berthold Auerbach whom Milnes had met the previous year), Leipzig, Brunswick and Cologne to Calais and across to Dover. Welcomed in London, where the bride was pronounced to be '*so* fat and blooming' and the bridegroom 'thinner and fresher,' they then 'railed' up to Crewe before going on to Fryston. Richard Milnes wrote to his sister-in-law that his 'Yorkshire friends' wished

to get up some inauguration for Annabel: I fear it will not be com-parable to Kossuth's[2]—but then, you know, she could not make such long speeches. She has however got a white waistcoat just like mine, which her brother approves of, but which I think quite a Bloomer[3] & no one can say what the consequence of this might be . . . I have often thought [he told Henriett Crewe in the same missive] that the rationale of sending new-married people on a tour is, that if they stand that kind of life well together, they will put up with almost any other.

[1] In the second volume of his *Autobiography* (1904). This passage is quoted at some length in *Monckton Milnes: The Years of Promise*, p. 4 and n.

[2] Kossuth, refused permission to cross France by the Prince-President, had landed at Southampton from Marseilles on 23 October 1851 and was spending three weeks in England, as the object of wild enthusiasm. Milnes had watched him going to Guildhall on 30 October.

[3] Mrs. Amelia Bloomer (1818–1894) had launched her reformed dress for women (a short skirt over loose trousers) in 1849. In November 1851 a play about 'The Bloomers' was running at the Adelphi, and many obvious jokes upon the subject were current.

III

In the latter months of 1851 and the first weeks of 1852, that year of great alarm in England, Milnes took his wife to stay with some of the wealthiest and most powerful of his friends. Brought up to regard Crewe Hall as a house of normal size, and by nature less readily impressed than Richard Milnes, she drifted through these visits placidly. The Grange she called 'a pretty place, with a comfortable, not a grand, house with a Drawing room full of comfortable sofas & corners & strewed with all the new publications,' well ventilated and surrounded by clean gravel walks. Woburn seemed 'enormous': 'the guests depart and arrive amidst a sort of silent & stately indifference that gives me the impression of being in a large hotel.' They went also to chilly Broadlands, and in the new year to Ampthill Park. In all these houses Mrs. Milnes played her part in her unobtrusive, amiable manner, acting at need in the charades and dialogues her husband loved to organise, participating also in those tedious guessing-games which were already an integral feature of English country-house evenings. 'The Milnes ménage is in great form,' wrote Lady Ashburton to Mrs. Brookfield in November 1851 ; 'she doesn't seem the least afraid of him, and he is all the better for a little control.'[1]

The compelling personality of Harriet Ashburton did not at first please Mrs. Monckton Milnes. 'Her conversation is very clever & often amusing but with a good deal of bitterness, all giving the impression of a person not happy,' she wrote. The cult for Lady Ashburton was indeed a strictly masculine one, and though Mrs. Milnes considered herself lucky to meet 'no fine ladies' at the Grange, she may have thought it odd to find a party of nine men (including Thackeray and her old friend 'Eothen' Kinglake) and only three women. She was gratified to see what a success Richard was with his hosts

& so nice & affectionate with me, & I *must* say *I behaved beautifully*, & the last 2 days when we were the only company excepting a man or two, really had my reward, by finding it agreeable & that she & I got on better. I have no doubt our visit was a greater trial than *she* had even anticipated & at first she looked very ill & was in wretched spirits.[2]

---

[1] Letter printed in *Mrs. Brookfield and her Circle* by C. & F. Brookfield (Pitman 1906) vol. ii.
[2] This and other extracts above are from Mrs. Milnes' letters to her sister. Lady Ashburton had in fact caught a bad cold walking with Thackeray the day before the Milneses arrived (*v.* her letter to Mrs. Brookfield of 31 October).

Lady Ashburton's tone to those she thought her inferiors was sometimes positively insolent, and this was resented by Mrs. Milnes as
much as by the actual victims, intelligent bourgeois women like Mrs.
Procter and Mrs. Carlyle.

If Lady A. was affronting to Mrs. Procter I would not be introduced
to her for her weight in gold quartz! [Mr. Milnes senior wrote in
reply to a letter from his daughter-in-law.]   Women were made for
nothing but to be loved (except perhaps for cooking & attending
hospitals) & Mrs P. being to my fancy a *very* loveable woman, Ly
A's haughtiness shows that she has no heart, whatever her brains
may be.   The Devil himself is written of, as being a clever person.

Mrs. Monckton Milnes preferred on the whole the old-fashioned
good manners of the Duke and Duchess of Bedford and of Lady
Palmerston, who reminded her of her aunt.   'Ly P. was so courteous
& kind—very unlike *Ly A*,' she wrote to Henriett from Broadlands;
'Richard,' she added, 'is beginning to recover the fall of his friend
which threw him into a *frantic state* at first.'
    The fall of Palmerston, dismissed from the Foreign Office on 19
November 1851 by Lord John Russell at the instance of the Court
(following his unofficial approval, in a private conversation with the
French ambassador, Count Walewski, of Louis Napoleon's coup
d'état), had astonished many other people as well as his ardent
admirer Monckton Milnes.   Palmerston was amazed himself.

Lord Palmerston's [dismissal] [Milnes wrote to MacCarthy on 21
January 1852] could not have surprised any one more than it did
himself.   It was . . . a something which comes over Lord John
about Christmas—which one would call 'calenture' if it happened
in summer,—which made him write the Durham letter in 50
& eject his best colleague in 1851.   The cause was totally inadequate: Ld. P. has a great dislike to the Orleans family & a strong
distrust of their feeling to Eng^d. & thus he saw, without dissatis-
faction, their project of appealing to France by arms or otherwise,
put an end to.   But he said nothing official, nothing which in any
way compromised the Government . . .

As a youthful Tory and disciple of Peel, Milnes had in the past
voiced much disapprobation of Lord Palmerston; now as a middle-
aged Whig his feelings for the old statesman, to whom he applied
the adjective 'cocky,' went to lengths which made Disraeli call him
a toady and Greville call him a 'lacquey.'   What hopes of political
advancement Milnes still cherished were bound up with Palmerston,
who treated him kindly, occasionally made use of him and did not
bother to laugh at him behind his back.

Palmerston was ready to do anything for [Milnes] but give him office [Disraeli wrote in his memorandum on the characters in *Tancred*], and refused him everything on every occasion. He always went to relieve his feelings and plead his cause with Lady Palmerston, who smoothed him down, asked him to perpetual dinners, and said he was a 'social favourite.'[1]

On every count the fall of Palmerston struck Milnes as a disaster. He called it the end of his own 'dilettante officiality. . . . I retire into the modesty of private ignorance.' From a wider viewpoint he thought it bad as well.

The effect in Europe has been humiliating for Eng^d but the French coup d'état has absorbed all other subjects. . . . We were going to France this next month, but it would so worry me to see my old breakfaster L.N. in his sham Cæsarean attitude that I have not the heart for it.[2]

IV

The coup d'état of December, 1851 which made Milnes cancel his plans for going to Paris, was followed by the promulgation of the new French Constitution in January 1852. Ten months later a plebiscite upon the restoration of the Empire was arranged, and in December 1852, the Prince-President mounted the imperial throne. 'The grand theatricals in France go on,' wrote Milnes, 'I have always a feeling that 12 o'clock must strike soon, and all Cinderella's splendour vanish into air.' As busy as ever with his desultory commonplace-books, he noted down the current tales of Louis Napoleon's sexual eccentricities, together with Lady Ashburton's theories about where to get the best view when the French armies should enter London, and Carlyle's scornful reference to 'the gilt-edge Crispin-crown of Louis Napoleon.' All the same, as Milnes well knew, the danger was a real one. 'The mood of England in 1852' writes Justin McCarthy in the second volume of *A History of Our Own Times* 'was not one of idle and baseless panic.' England had had no major war since Waterloo. An inexperienced and eager generation clamoured for one, while the Government and public men, aware that England was as unprepared as usual in a time of crisis, temporised.

Tous vos hommes politiques ont eu en parlant des derniers évènements de la France un langage prudent, modéré, quasi-

---

[1] Monypenny & Buckle, vol. iii, p. 51.
[2] Letter to MacCarthy already cited.

approbateur pour le pouvoir qui achève de renverser la liberté sur le continent [wrote Tocqueville to Milnes from Paris on 19 February 1852].

It was a long time since Europe had heard such language, he added in oblique reference to Palmerstonian diplomacy.

On voit qu'il ne s'agit plus d'un Roi de Naples, mais du chef de notre nation et du maître d'une armée de 400,000 hommes. Si comme moraliste j'en ai un peu souffert, ma vanité de français en a été très flatté.

Explaining that he had no intention of standing in the forthcoming French elections, Tocqueville told Milnes what he really thought of the new regime:

Le nouveau pouvoir [he wrote] poursuit son plan de gouverner à l'aide des paysans et des soldats, n'empruntant à la démocratie que son plus mauvais principe, la force brutale des nombres, le vote universel au milieu du silence et de l'obscurité que le despotisme crée.

Further reports on French developments came to Milnes from Miss Charlotte Williams Wynn, who had quitted Wiesbaden to settle for some months in the Rue du Colisée, where she found she was in danger of becoming 'a "dame qui tient salon," a consummation devoutly to be avoided.' Cosmopolitan by experience but insular by temperament, Miss Williams Wynn was much shocked by the French love of approval, by their egotism and apparent lack of patriotic feeling. Tocqueville alone seemed sympathetic: 'He sits and cozes over the fire, nor does he expect the constant flattery which, alas! the others do.' The foolishness of English residents and visitors to Paris and their anxiety to be in the fashion provoked Miss Williams Wynn.[1] She felt it disgraceful that they should frequent the palace of the Prince-President.

The President is most cringing to the English [she wrote to Milnes in February 1852] asking young ladies if *they* want to make war upon him—&c, &c. I am sorry to say he finds plenty to go to his . . . fêtes. I am weary of being asked *why* I dont go too, & of

---

[1] 'Miss T(rotter) is taking lessons from a professor as to the best way of managing *trees*. In the present vogue for Professors nothing can be learnt without them, or one should have said that experience was the best teacher, and after she had killed one or two dwarf lilacs (the nearest approach to a tree she will have in her garden) she would learn the best management was just to let them alone.' Miss Trotter's mother, Lady Trotter, had taken a house near Paris, and had lately annoyed Miss Williams Wynn by declaring, the day after attending a ball at the Tuileries, that '*the People* are coming round to the present order of things.' (Letter to Mrs. Monckton Milnes dated 10 March (1852)).

answering 'because I think he deserves abuse therefore I intend to abuse him & *so* cannot go to his House' which seems to me both simple & logical but not a bit do they comprehend it. . . . All seem to agree on the likelihood of a European War, in three months (says M. de Tocqueville & Circourt) in which case we shall hardly be able to carry out our projected tour in the summer.

The coup d'état of 1851 brought a new batch of French political exiles to England. In the course of a few years Milnes had offered hospitality to Louis Napoleon, to the Orleans family, to Guizot and to Louis Blanc. He now wrote to welcome Adolphe Thiers, who, although he inconsistently voted for the Presidency of Louis Napoleon, had been arrested, imprisoned, and then escorted out of France. Thiers found a temporary refuge at the Clarendon Hotel. Replying to Milnes' note of welcome he told him that France just then was to be pitied more than blamed—'et pour moi elle est toujours à aimer.' 'Si vous saviez combien les classes éclaircies se dèfendent contre la violence et la corruption d'une indigne et ridicule tyrannie, vous verriez que la France est digne de l'estime des nations civilisées.'[1] 'Louis Napoleon,' Thiers remarked to Milnes at this time, 'est avant tout un esprit perplexe.'[2]

The invasion scare of 1852 involved Monckton Milnes in the absurdly unsuitable activity of military training. Milnes had held a sort of sleeping commission in the 2nd West Riding Regiment of Militia since 1840, and in the autumn of '52 he set to work drilling the Pontefract volunteers. 'I am much obliged to you for your interesting commentaries which like a great military commander of former times you have found leisure to write amidst the warlike duties which you have to perform,' wrote Palmerston from Broadlands,[3] replying no doubt to one of those political surveys which Milnes had in former times addressed to his earlier idol, Peel.

You were quite right to buckle on your armour. The sight of gentlemen joining the Militia is a great encouragement to the lower classes to do the like. I am glad to hear the good report you make of the aptness of your men, I have always considered it mere Pedantry in regular officers to contend that endless drill is needed to fit a man for duty as a soldier . . . the history of all wars shows that men may be made good fighting soldiers in a much shorter time than is now held necessary to qualify a Private of the Guards to walk up & down before a sentry box in St James's Park.

[1] Letter of 18 January 1852 (Clarendon Hotel, London).
[2] Commonplace-book 1852–1854.
[3] Letter of 2 November 1852.

22

V

For Monckton Milnes the year 1852, memorable to most people for the death of the Duke of Wellington, was marked by a personal loss which he felt as intensely as his easy-going nature would allow. Eliot Warburton, the friend of twenty years, was drowned on the 4th of January in the disaster to the new steamboat *Amazon*. Warburton, who had just bidden Milnes and his wife good-bye at his hotel in Brook Street, had sailed from Southampton for the Isthmus of Darien on the second day of the new year. When the steamer caught fire he went down with it, after gallantly rescuing as many of the women passengers as he could. A strange twist was given to the news of the disaster by the fact that Warburton (whose *The Crescent and the Cross*, dedicated to Milnes, had had a considerable success), had just produced a new novel, *Darien, or the Merchant Prince*,[1] in which he described the destruction of a ship by fire. Warburton, who had married in 1848, left a young widow and two little boys, with whose future Milnes characteristically concerned himself.

There was no man [he wrote sadly], to whom I owed a similar debt of affection, so constant and so enduring. Ever since we had been together at Cambridge he had looked to my friendship as a portion of his own inner life; &, if others had more moved my sensibilities, there was perhaps no one intimate whom I so thoroughly esteemed. He had all the good of the Irish nature, its gracefulness & its vivacity, combined with the very chivalrye of truth.

Warburton's memory was linked to many odd and charming episodes of Milnes' youth—Cambridge larks, travels in Ireland, the meeting on the Nile, and, later, the support Warburton had given him over the awkward question of Milnes' challenge to George Smythe. At times reproachful at Milnes' apparent neglect, often anxious over the way in which his old friend seemed to have frittered his talents, Warburton had still cherished a profound affection for him:

How do you feel after your London career? [he wrote to ask him in the month of Milnes' marriage] Do your

> 'Yesterdays look backwards with a smile,
> Nor wound you, like the Parthians, as they fly?'

[1] *Darien, or The Merchant Prince. An Historical Romance.* By Eliot Warburton, Colburn & Co. 1852. In three volumes. The book contains quotations from Milnes' verse.

They ought, if triumphs bought with no others' pain—if thoughtful kindness—unostentatious & unconscious self-sacrifice—memory enriched & mind exercised can avail.

'The last days . . .' Milnes recorded in January 1852, 'have been dimmed—I might say, darkened—by the awful calamity that has enveloped my dear Eliot Warburton.' Milnes had reached an age when so old and true a friendship was something to be valued as well as missed.

On August 3, nearly six months to a day after the *Amazon* tragedy, Annabel Milnes gave birth to her first child, a girl. Given the Gothic name of Amicia, after an heiress who had married into the Crewe family in the reign of Edward the First, the child was christened at St. Mark's, North Audley Street. Mrs. Milnes settled happily to the novel and exciting interests of motherhood, sewing sprigged muslin dresses and sending accounts of each new gesture of 'the sweet Amice' to Henriett Crewe at Torquay. Richard Milnes affected to be less excited by what Venables called his 'prolongation into a future generation.' The event would once, he wrote, 'have given me much pleasure, but . . . I now take (it) very philosophically.' Few of his friends understood how cold a pessimism underlay the dilettante creed by which Milnes seemed to live.

Chapter Three

1852   *1853*

I

The calm, gliding entrance of Annabel Crewe into the Milnes family had as refreshing an effect upon her father-in-law as on her husband. Old Mr. Milnes, now sixty-seven, as astringent and as positive as ever, had taken a great fancy to his son's wife, who acted as what Richard called 'quite a wholesome stimulus' upon him. He began corresponding on a pleasant scale entirely novel to his habits. 'Ever since you were my Daughter, I have discoursed with you with my pen more copiously if not eloquently than I ever did with anyone in my whole life,' he told her shortly after the marriage. When she was quietly at Fryston with him and her cousin for company he would read aloud to her, while she gummed and ironed Richard's growing collection of autographs into brown-paper albums.

Mr. Milnes reads Burke & Fox & Pitt to us, till he gets so eager he stands up, & flourishes his arms till Emma & I are in terror lest table, teacups, & candle should be in our lap.[1]

Mr. Milnes' almost daily letters to his daughter-in-law range over a very wide scope of topics. He was partly anxious to explain his own family to her—his sister Louisa 'so grave and pondering,' his sister Caroline with her 'invective fiercer than Lord Brougham's.' 'Don't write again of the "wit" of the Milnes's,' he reproved her on one occasion, 'rather say their probity—tho' I have told more *white* lies than any man, Louisa saying there isn't much difference of colour.' Two characteristics of old Mr. Milnes, the Low Church views he had inherited from his chapel-going forebears, and his distaste for London society, stood out sharply. 'It may be one of my strange phantasies, but I dislike seeing the Elements on silver,' he confided to his new correspondent, 'the Bread on a fine Waiter, the Wine in a Cambridge prize-cup—I would have them in the plainest earthenware.' He said he thought London life demoralising ' by

---

[1] Letter to Henriett Crewe, February 1852.

its extinguishing our best social affections—deadening them to conform to the formalities & exclusiveness of London fine people— our "country cousins" are no relations there.' He was sceptical about the conversation of 'wise people like Mrs. Grote & Flo:' which consisted, he declared, of a constant discussion of principles and the use of words like 'esoteric.' After the publication of Miss Nightingale's book on Deaconesses, he suggested that the authoress should henceforth be addressed as 'the Revd. Flo.' He also wrote to her about his reading—his love for Samuel Butler, his contempt for the poetry of Lamartine ('time worse than lost'). A great part of his letters was composed of domesticities, and the local gossip at Fryston, Bawtry and Serlby, while a good deal more space was devoted to acidulated comments on the politics and tenets of the Whigs. But the most constant theme of all throughout these letters was Mr. Milnes' favourite and now time-honoured one—what, in any given set of Parliamentary circumstances, Richard should, or should not, have done.

His son's recurring anxiety for office or a peerage seemed of a certain comic interest to Mr. Pemberton Milnes, who shared Disraeli's view that Palmerston did not take Richard seriously.

Evidently having no trust or admiration P[almersto]n can have no *dislike* to R., or he would not have him so frequently at his house [he wrote, somewhat maddeningly, to Annabel]. There can't be two natures & instincts, more in contrast than his & R's [he remarked on another occasion].

The fall of the Whigs (Palmerston's famous 'tit-for-tat'), in February 1852, and the establishment of Lord Derby's rickety 'Who-Who' Ministry, half-pledged to repeal the Free Trade measures of '46, sharpened the party differences that had long separated Mr. Milnes politically from his son. The Derby administration, which lasted ten months, with Lord Malmesbury at the Foreign Office and Disraeli at the Exchequer, appeared to the old man (as well as to his son-in-law Lord Galway who was appointed a Lord-in-Waiting in March '52) to be all that could be desired. Disraeli was Mr. Milnes' hero for many reasons—one of them being the fact that he never addressed him as anything but Squire (and sometimes 'dearest Squire'), and another that such open admiration must 'vex' Richard.[1] Whatever the origins of this admiration, Mr. Milnes now filled his letters with praise of all Disraeli's makeshift measures, and with blunt contradictions of all Richard's views. Yet through all the teasing and the tartness Mr.

[1] This was Disraeli's own explanation of Mr. Milnes' attachment (*v.* the memorandum already quoted).

ROBERT PEMBERTON MILNES

Milnes' common-sense remained in evidence—and in this important quality he was indubitably superior to his son. 'Your [party] I could give a vocabulary of bad names to,' he wrote in reply to some 'moralising' of Richard's upon the insincerity of the Tories.

My belief is it is just the same as to both parties, now—that if both were put in the crucible *Self* would be found as the residuum, & that no one is to look for any other return from his party but just as the party deems he may be of use to it.

On 1 July 1852 Parliament was dissolved. The Government, already in two minds about restoring Protection, presented the electorate with a muddle-headed programme, which was differently interpreted by candidates in different parts of the country. Returned as a Ministry on sufferance, the Derbyites announced through Disraeli that it was apparent that the great majority of the electors did not wish to repeal the Free Trade decisions of six years before. A number of members, Gladstone amongst them, experienced difficulty in retaining their seats. Monckton Milnes kept his at Pontefract, but he found it annoying work. Milnes had never stomached criticism. The personalities, and the monetary intrigues, of a contested election had always been hateful to him. He now minded these more than before, nor was Fryston, where across the dinner-table, his father maintained a quizzical interest in his speeches and prospects, a place in which to gather new daily confidence before setting off to face the tough self-interested burghers, the querulous Dissenters and the surly coal-operatives of his constituency.

I have hardly yet got over Richard's flustration at Pontefract—Sending the carriage with a message that I must come immediately. He could not have made more to do, if he had been on fire [her father-in-law wrote to Mrs. Milnes on 21 July]. A man is not fit for electioneering—or perhaps politics—if he cannot bear attack & abuse of all sorts however unmerited, he remaining as passive as the pavement. [However, he told her] not to fidget as to the election —He does his best to lose it, but they all say he can't & he must be a long way ahead on the poll.

Richard Milnes was in fact returned, and could, from his usual place in the House, witness the collapse of Lord Derby's Ministry in December 1853, and its replacement by Lord Aberdeen's Coalition Cabinet with Gladstone in lieu of Disraeli at the Exchequer.

Christmas 1853 was spent by the Milnes family at Serlby, Lord Galway's Nottinghamshire house. Richard was mostly in London that December:

Of course I wish for [him] here [wrote his wife], my 3 weeks visit having been passed without him excepting those 2 days last week; but the fact is Ld G[alway] is a thorough Derbyite, & so full of prejudices, which he asserts so loudly & angrily, that even Richard's temper is sorely tried, just now, when defeated,[1] he is not an agreeable companion, & so they are capital friends by not seeing too much of each other.—Ld. Palmerston having consented to join the new Govt. is a great satisfaction to my husband, as without him they would have been weak, & R. in an uncomfortable position.

If Milnes' position under the new Ministry was not exactly uncomfortable, it had not on the other hand improved. While continuing to hope for recognition, he presented a cool façade of indifference to his friends: 'I . . . am content to occupy an unambitious position as supporter of this Government we have at last got, and which we ought to have had two years ago,' he wrote in one of his news-letters to Charles MacCarthy in Ceylon.

Monckton Milnes' political ambition was not singular, nor was his passion for office more violent than that of the majority of his contemporaries in Parliament. Even the pious Gladstone thirsted for power. John Morley, in his life of that statesman, has compared the Whigs, Tories and Peelites scrambling for place in the 1853 Coalition to 'the venerable carp . . . struggling for bread in the fish-ponds of the palace of Fontainebleau.' Morley quotes a sad reflection from Sir James Graham's journal for Christmas 1853: 'It is melancholy to see how little fitness for office is regarded on all sides, and how much the public employments are treated as booty to be divided among successful combatants.'[2] The only real difference between Milnes' ambitions and those of other men lay in his recurrent failure to reach anything that he desired.

II

Under the will of her aunt, Mrs. Cunliffe Offley, who had brought her up, and had died in February 1850, Annabel Crewe inherited some money, the furnishings and pictures at Madeley, and those of Mrs. Cunliffe's convenient London house in Upper Brook Street between Park Lane and Grosvenor Square. She also inherited the remainder of the seven-year lease of this London house. Sixteen Upper Brook Street, refaced in the Edwardian epoch, has

[1] Lord Galway was replaced as a Lord-in-Waiting in January 1853, having held the appointment eleven months, during which he suffered somewhat from Prince Albert's lectures on science.

[2] *The Life of William Ewart Gladstone* (Macmillan 1903), vol. I, book iv, first chapter.

barely survived the bombing of the Second German War. It was in this house, to-day a dank and musty shell with boarded door and broken windows, that Mr. and Mrs. Monckton Milnes spent the London seasons of their married life. At the moment of their wedding, the house was let. They entered into possession of it in the spring of 1852.

Milnes' grandfather Richard Slater Milnes, the Whig politician, had taken Effingham House, Piccadilly, in the last decade of the eighteenth century, but after his sudden death in 1802 his impoverished family gave up any attempt to maintain a London establishment. In 1836 Robert Pemberton Milnes, newly returned with his wife, his son and his daughter from an Italian exile of eight years, hired what he called 'a showy house' at the junction of South Street and Park Lane. Costing eight hundred pounds for a single season, Lady Kilmaine's corner house was given up by the Milneses as soon as it had served its purpose of providing a frame for Harriette's coming-out, and launching Richard into fashionable life. In 1837 Richard Milnes took the set of rooms above a tailor's shop at 26 Pall Mall, and these he kept till his engagement—always living a little beyond his means in bachelor comfort, keeping a valet, a silk-lined carriage, and a horse for riding in the Park, and entertaining his friends, acquaintances and enemies at morning meals which became as celebrated as Samuel Rogers' breakfasts though the company was more variegated and sometimes less respectable than that encountered in the 'banker poet's' luxurious house in St. James's Place. Milnes' breakfast-parties had usually been male, though he would of course ask on occasion Mrs. Carlyle and Miss Jewsbury, the ambitious Mrs. Nightingale and her elegant daughters Florence and Parthenope, or some visiting foreign novelist like the German Jewess Fanny Lewald. Now that he had a wife, a house of his own in a Mayfair street, and a considerably increased income, Milnes could embark on more frequent and more ambitious parties than had ever been possible for him before.

Built, like other houses on the Grosvenor Estate, in the early eighteenth century, 16 Upper Brook Street was in every way typical of the smaller houses in this part of London. On the first floor it had a large front drawing-room, together with a back drawing-room from which a few steps led down into a 'middle room' probably used by the Milneses as a library. On the second floor were two big bedrooms, and a room for Dawkins the lady's maid; in the attics three other maids' rooms; and on the ground floor a dining-room at the back of the house, a 'front parlour' and an ante-room. In the street to the right of the front door tradesmen's steps led down to an 'area' protected by tall iron railings, and gave access to the dark, stone-flagged vaults (kitchen, housekeeper's room, servants' hall, etcetera) in which London domestics were expected to work and live. While the house was being got ready for its owners, Mr. Milnes senior made two 'excursions' from Boodle's Club to look at it. He wrote to his daughter-in-law that he had been 'rather amused.' 'The endless stairs & steps, slips and cupboards' (he wrote), 'desirous of making so much out of space so little, it reminded one of the Kingdom of Monaco, or the expedients of a country theatre.' The dining-room (which contained a vast circular table that made Nathaniel Hawthorne think of King Arthur and his knights), was decorated with some of the paintings Annabel Milnes had inherited, including a crowded mythological 'Rubens' and the full-length Lawrence portrait of Mrs. Cunliffe Offley which gazed down with sharp blue eyes at the dinner-parties of the newly married couple. Elsewhere in the house were portraits and portrait-drawings of Milnes and his wife.

Your fine Rubens was under gauze [Mr. Milnes wrote after his second inspection] as I wish'd that of yourself, & the conceited one of Richd, had also been—I so dislike both. I greatly admired that of Mrs. Cunliffe, could you get an artist to reconstruct the dress, which is the same as my wife's at Fryston.[1] It omits the charming-est portion of the female form, making the lower limbs join the bosom. But the picture I was most taken with is that of Tieck—of itself worth your journey to Germany. It is finely painted, tho' the expression is not remarkable. Would it be possible to obtain those of Goethe, Schiller, & Jean-Paul? Posterity would give more for them than for Sir R. Peel's gallery of our own so-called eminent men.

He added that he had looked over the stables in the mews and found the stalls too large: '& this concludes what I have to sing' (he added in mischievous reference to his son's famous lyric) 'when I wandered by the Brook side.'

Beyond repainting and re-papering the rooms, building new cupboards and most necessary bookshelves, it is not likely that the Milneses did much to change the inside of their house. The inventory made for succession duty valuation after Mrs. Cunliffe's death can thus be relied on to give us some idea of the furniture. This inventory shows that the two drawing-rooms were comfortably filled with ottomans, couches, framed settees and easy chairs with loose covers. There were many pieces of satinwood and rosewood furniture—round tables, 'loo' or card tables, fire screens, and little

[1] The fine full-length Opie of Mrs. Pemberton Milnes standing by a sunflower is now at Helperby Hall, Yorkshire. The Lawrence portrait of Mrs. Cunliffe Offley is in an American collection.

bookcases (used in Mrs. Cunliffe's day for three-volume bibles and a set of the Encyclopædia). There were also spindle chairs and 'Swiss' chairs. Brussels carpet was laid in the drawing-rooms and on the staircase, and Turkey carpet in the dining-room. At night the rooms were lit from wall-brackets, candelabra and a large eight-lustre chandelier. Drawing-room curtains of blue merino hung from gleaming brass rods, and white muslin at the windows protected the Milnes family from the enquiring gaze of their neighbours over the way. Mrs. Cunliffe had owned a normal quantity of silver, a good many plated dishes, two china breakfast sets in white and gold and blue and white, a flowered-and-gold and a white-and-flowered dessert set, some 'embossed' dinner plates, and a quantity of good cut glass. Georgian silver with the Milneses' wheatsheaf crest would have taken its place amongst this in the butler's pantry, and on their honeymoon the couple had bought silver salt-cellars and a silver filigree sugar-basin at Dresden, as well as more dessert plates, a *milieu-de-table* in *porcelaine de Saxe*, some porcelain figures and a dozen gilt teaspoons. Some of the objects they acquired must have been distressing examples of German mid-century taste—glass dishes specially frosted for them at Steigerwald's glass bazaar in Munich, some frosted alabaster ice-plates, an inkstand in blue and gilt enamel, and sets of those knobbly red and green glasses used in Bavaria for drinking Rhine-wine and Moselle. Thus equipped the Milneses settled down to entertain.

In their first season, somewhat curtailed by Mrs. Milnes' pregnancy, they gave twenty-six dinners (usually of fourteen or sixteen people), six very large and three smaller evening parties, and twelve breakfasts. Old Mr. Milnes, kept well informed of Upper Brook Street activities by his daughter Harriette Galway, declared himself shocked at Richard asking 'lords to dine' and his 'best friend' Mrs. Grote to come in afterwards. He also disapproved of entertaining on Sunday, and of Richard staying on after eleven o'clock at his own parties instead of getting down to late sessions at the House, though he was pleased to hear from Harriette that Annabel Milnes' 'dress & tournure' were handsome, and of the 'general effect as quite equalling Lady Derby's.' Mrs. Milnes thoroughly enjoyed herself in her new rôle of hostess, her husband teasing her by saying that the soup was cold and the champagne hot, and counting up the number of people who had failed to come. Although neither of them were in their first youth, they made a cheerful, rather excited impression during these initial experiments at large-scale hospitality.

Lord Frederick Hamilton has described mid-Victorian London

society in his memoirs as 'a sort of enlarged family party'; Mrs. Milnes' address books, kept by streets for purposes of leaving cards, show how close together in Mayfair everyone lived. No person in society then left London from Saturday to Monday, and indeed the week-end was the time when people met for lengthy luncheons or when those with big houses gave dinners and balls. Certain receptions occurred with solemn regularity throughout the season, like the ticking of a great clock; chief amongst these ranked Lady Palmerston's Saturdays,[1] evening parties at Cambridge House where leaders of the Government and Opposition mingled together in an atmosphere of Whiggish ease and tolerance. Men of letters, artists, and of course musicians, were rigidly excluded from Cambridge House, where fashionable and political persons gossiped the evening away while their host moved from one group to another, and old Lady Palmerston, still bearing traces of her great beauty, sat before a silver tea-kettle in an inner room to which by no means all the guests had access. Lord Redesdale, who has left the most vivid account of these entertainments (it is he who compares Lord John Russell to Holbein's *Erasmus*)[2] states that Monckton Milnes and the illustrator 'Dickie' Doyle were the only representatives of the arts admitted to Cambridge House. Lady Palmerston had long made a pet of Monckton Milnes, and she had welcomed his marriage with benevolence. She did not even mind when he protested that he and his wife had not been asked to some ball at Cambridge House—'I did not think that you and Mrs. Milnes went to balls.' Lady Palmerston was wrong, for Milnes still liked going to any great assembly. Shortly before his marriage he had appeared as Saint-Evrémond at the third of the royal Costume Balls at Buckingham Palace (devoted this time to the reign of Charles the Second), and in August 1852 he caused amusement by partnering Lady Davy, the widow of Sir Humphry Davy, 'famous for her good company and Italian Malapropism,' at Holland House. He and his wife would also figure at the fine evening parties at Lansdowne House (which Effie Ruskin so brightly described in her letters) and, naturally enough, at the glittering entertainments which Lady Ashburton would languidly offer London society. Lady Ashburton was sometimes lured from Bath House to Upper Brook Street, and sometimes she would invite herself in an imperious manner not perhaps wholly acceptable to Mrs. Milnes:

We are to be in town on Monday [she wrote to Milnes shortly after

[1] 'Will Lady Palmerston's Saturday evenings go on after she is dead'? Lady Ashburton once asked Milnes. 'One can't conceive her existing without them.' (Commonplace-book, 1855–1856).
[2] In his bulky autobiography, *Memories*, (2 vols., Hutchinson, 1915).

Easter one year], if you like to have me at dinner any day in that week with a *reasonable* number of conversible people do—for I shall not be ready at home till the week after.   But if you make an *unreasonable* number I shall vanish up the chimney.

Into this closed, grand world the parties which Milnes organised in his own house came like a gush of air.   They were as mixed and original as his Pall Mall breakfasts had been, though now the percentage of 'fashionables' was higher than in old days.   In the Milneses' first season a great many people dined in Upper Brook Street.   A very great many more passed through the house. Political personages who dined there included Lord and Lady Palmerston, the Duke of Newcastle, old Lord Lansdowne, the Stanleys and Sir James Graham, while many Whig and some Tory members of parliament came to evening receptions.   Purely social people such as the Ashburtons, the Westminsters, the Meaths, Lord and Lady George Quin, the Lytteltons, Lord de Mauley, Lady de Dunsterville, Lady William Russell and Lady Rosa Greville came fairly frequently to the house, and so did serious thinking women like Mrs. Grote and Charlotte Williams Wynn, and precarious persons on the fringe of fashion—the Reverend William Brookfield, incumbent of St. James's Piccadilly, for instance, and his rather bitter wife.   Milnes took care to mix such people up with the literary: the Carlyles, Tennyson, the Charles Dickenses, Robert and Elizabeth Browning, Arthur Clough, the poet, Sir Francis Hastings Doyle, Spedding, Thackeray, Coventry Patmore and the Angel, and Mrs. Norton.   Henry Hallam and Macaulay were also asked, as well as Delane,[1] the formidable editor of *The Times*, Henry Reeve,[2] for fifteen years in charge of that newspaper's foreign side, and the gigantic Matthew Higgins.   Foreign guests were some of them diplomats like M. Van de Weyer the Belgian minister, or Mr. Ingersoll the American one; others were exiled liberals (Thiers or Louis Blanc), old friends like George Bunsen or travel acquaintances like Baron Leopold Rothschild.   As a general rule it is only foreigners who take the trouble to record the patterns of life in a strange capital; to those accustomed to it London society did not seem odd, remarkable, or even specially interesting.   It is two American visitors to London in the 'fifties who have left the sharpest accounts of Milnes' hospitality in Upper Brook Street at that period.   One of these visitors was Mrs. Edward Twisleton.   The other was the United States consul at Liverpool, Nathaniel Hawthorne.

[1] John Delane (1817–1879) became editor of *The Times* in 1841 at the age of twenty-four and continued to edit the paper until two years before his death.
[2] Henry Reeve (1813–1895) was in charge of the *Edinburgh Review* for forty years and is remembered as the first editor of the *Greville Memoirs*, which appeared in 1865.

III

The Honourable Mrs. Edward Twisleton had been born Ellen Dwight. She was the daughter of a member for the Province of Massachusetts in the House of Representatives. A sloe-eyed, dark-headed girl she had married her husband, younger brother of the sixteenth Lord Saye and Sele in May 1852 and she died just ten years later. Edward Twisleton was the exact contemporary in age of Monckton Milnes. A scholar, archæologist and minor politician, Twisleton was said to have sat on more commissions than any man in England, had dug up temples on the coast of Asia Minor and tried to prove that Sir Philip Francis was *Junius* by an analysis of his handwriting. He was a lanky, amiable and (after his wife's death) melancholy man, 'the heart and soul of the Dilettanti Society,' and in many ways the kind of person Milnes would like:— learned, sweet-natured, with 'an old-world manner' and a 'quiet quaintness,' and he spoke 'with a laugh and little twist of the head that was humour itself.'[1] His wife was ladylike and she came from Boston. She combined that nervous anxiety then common to all Americans who had managed to penetrate into European society with a species of self-confidence and denigration peculiar to the city of her birth. She entered the drawing-rooms of Mayfair in a mood at once eager and censorious, recounting for her family's benefit, in a series of letters, anything peculiar that she saw.[2]

'. . . A mess of all characters, positions and opinions' wrote Mrs. Twisleton of dinner at the Milneses' in June 1853. Restive at being forced to meet the W. E. Forsters (for she thought the Bradford Quaker and his wife—a daughter of Doctor Arnold—socially inferior and ill-mannered), Mrs. Twisleton was delighted to find that her host's sister Lady Galway (at no time an unconventional person) shared her prejudice. 'A decidedly handsome, and decidedly clever woman, taller than her brother I should think,' she wrote enthusiastically of Harriette Galway. Mrs. Milnes passed

---

[1] Edward Turner Boyd Twisleton, born in May 1809, never recovered from his young wife's death in 1862 and committed suicide at Boulogne, shortly after a visit to Fryston, in October 1874. The suicide, concealed by the French doctor who attended him and by Lord Saye and Sele, is confirmed in a letter from Henry Reeve to Lord Houghton, dated 30 October (1874): 'There is, I believe, no doubt at all of the truth of the sad story of Twistleton's end . . . (He) lived for 3 days after the attempt for he had not divided the carotid artery . . . I have no doubt that there was pressure on the brain.' There are constant references to the Twisletons in the *Letters and Journals* of the American literary historian, George Ticknor, whose wife was Ellen Twisleton's aunt and who habitually stayed at the Twisletons' comfortable house in Rutland Gate. The Ticknors were much gratified by Mrs. Twisleton's popularity in London society.

[2] Her letters to her family were published by John Murray in 1928.

34

muster as having 'excellent, thoroughly-trained manners' and maintaining 'that admirable neutral-tinted conversation which does with everyone and offends none—and with her husband's fashion of inviting all sorts of people,' Mrs. Twistleton continued, 'if he didn't want a clever woman . . . he could not have chosen better I should say.' She thought Milnes himself 'jolly,' good-natured, unsentimental, tactful, stout and 'rather reddish in the face.' She also thought he looked as though he had 'lost his upper teeth.' We do not know the Milneses' views on Ellen Twistleton.

Nathaniel Hawthorne, with his wife and two children, had landed at Liverpool, to take up his post as United States Consul there, in July 1853. He remained in England till 1857, and in Europe till 1860. It was Hawthorne's first journey abroad. He was forty-nine years of age, famous as the author of *The Scarlet Letter*, *The House with the Seven Gables*, and *The Blithedale Romance*; before leaving for England he had just published the work by which his name more happily survives—*Tanglewood Tales*. Hawthorne's attitude to England and his reactions to English men and manners, were conditioned both by his dour, Puritanical childhood in New England, and by the fact that like most Americans of the generation that remembered the burning of the Capitol in 1812, and had been reared on tales of the American Revolution, he regarded English people as natural foes. Hawthorne's case, however, was complicated by his somewhat grudging admiration of England as 'our old home' which at times became as strong as his dislike of English arrogance, and hatred of English condescension. This ambivalence colours the numerous pages of Hawthorne's *English Notebooks*, which, first completely published in 1941, have been described by their editor as 'perhaps the fullest and richest book ever written by an American about England.'[1]

Hawthorne shared with Mrs. Twisleton a special readiness to take offence; he was, for instance, offended that old Lord Lansdowne, one of a breakfast-party at the Milneses' house in 1856, forced him to go upstairs first—'by insisting upon it, he showed his sense of condescension, much more than if . . . he had passed forward, as if the point were not worth either asserting or yielding.' Yet on the whole the touchiness of American visitors to London was not unreasonable. *Punch* and other popular papers made vulgar

---

[1] *The English Notebooks*, published from the original MSS in the Pierpont Morgan Library, and very sanely edited by Professor Randall Stewart of Brown University, were sponsored in England by the Oxford University Press. Hawthorne himself used some of this material in *Our Old Home* (1863), while in 1870 Mrs. Hawthorne published a bowdlerised volume entitled *Passages from the English Notebooks* of her husband who had died in '64. Mrs. Hawthorne even tampered with the manuscripts themselves, making erasures, some of which have defied scientific examination.

and persistent fun of American manners and speech, while even *The Times* stooped on occasions to scathing ridicule on the same subject. Milnes' commonplace-books contain many current jokes about Americans, though he himself was too amiable to repeat these in front of American visitors, a practice not infrequent in London society at that time.

I think . . . we are fast verging into Democracy and Americanism [wrote Lady Palmerston to Milnes in October 1858]. Sir Hamilton Seymour teaches his Children to speak thro' their Noses as this is what he thinks they must all come to. . . .

Incidents like that in which a West Point professor, dressed in 'frock coat, black neck-cloth, and yellow waistcoat' was refused admittance to the Queen's levée in June 1856 were given much jubilant publicity in London, and Hawthorne judged that 'this resolute quizzing of our manners' not only made Americans self-assertive but actually jockeyed them into committing blunders. 'The cold, unbelieving eye of Englishmen, expectant of solecisms in manners, contributes to produce the result which it looks for,' he wrote in *Doctor Grimshawe's Secret*. His own reaction to the cold and unbelieving eye was to adopt a very exaggerated yardstick for comparison of English and American ways. In Hawthorne's opinion no English persons possessed manners as fine as those of his compatriots. Amongst the few who nearly did so he placed Leigh Hunt, attributing 'whatever excellence' this beautiful old man had to his American blood (Hunt's mother had come from Pennsylvania), and Richard Monckton Milnes, who fortunately resembled Longfellow in personal appearance 'though of a thicker build, and (being an Englishman) with not quite so polished an address.' 'He is pleasant and sensible,' Hawthorne noted of a second meeting with Milnes in the autumn of 1854, 'but an intellectual and refined American is a higher man than he—a higher and a finer one.' To Mrs. Milnes, Hawthorne took a positive fancy: 'her manners being more like those of an American lady than those of any other Englishwoman whom I have met . . . Also,' Hawthorne asininely added, 'like so many American ladies, she appears to be in delicate health.'

Though Hawthorne did not trouble to realise it, Milnes was one of the men in England most ready to welcome Americans, and to take them as seriously as they took themselves. Back in 1839, in a review of some of Emerson's works in *The London and Westminster*, he had made an earnest attack on those who laughed at American literature, and at the American way of speaking and writing. Emerson, who met Milnes in London and in Paris in 1848, called him the 'most goodnatured man in England, made of sugar'; but it was not in Hawthorne's nature to be as warm or spontaneous as this. In consequence, much of the *English Notebooks* seems petty and carping, while some passages are downright absurd. Yet Hawthorne's great descriptive powers, his solemn observation of detail, and the untiring industry with which he worked at his English journals, which comprise more than three hundred thousand words, make him a witness of unparalleled value to anyone studying English social history in the period of the Crimean War. Hawthorne met the Milneses again in 1856, in London, when he took Mrs. Milnes in to dinner and she talked to him about Tennyson's wife—'a wise and tender woman such as ought to be entrusted with such a fragile affair as Tennyson's comfort and happiness.'[1] Annabel Milnes again reminded Hawthorne of 'the best-mannered American women.' On Friday, 11 July 1856, he went to breakfast at number 16 Upper Brook Street.

Milnes had named 'a little after ten' as the hour for breakfast. Hawthorne, who took the train up from Blackheath at nine, reached London too early and wandered over London Bridge, along Cheapside and into Guildhall. As a result he reached Upper Brook Street more than half an hour late, so that there was no time for his proper introduction to the fifteen people in the room. He recognised his compatriot George Ticknor, was presented to Lord Lansdowne ('an old gentleman in a blue coat and grey pantaloons —with a long, rather thin, homely visage, exceedingly shaggy eyebrows . . . and thin grey hair'), and assigned to take Mrs. Browning ('a small, delicate woman with ringlets of black hair . . . a pleasant, intelligent, sensitive face, and a low, agreeable voice') into the breakfast-room. The identity of the other guests slowly dawned on him—'a portly personage' opposite him at table was Macaulay, while 'an elderly lady with a very fine countenance, and altogether more agreeable to look at than most English dames of her age' was the mother of Florence Nightingale, whose sister 'Parthe' was also at the meal. Mrs. Browning seemed to be a vegetarian—'at least, she ate nothing but an egg.' Hawthorne, who had had cold beef and coffee before setting out for London, was not hungry: 'so I just ate some delicate chicken, and a very small cutlet, and a slice of dry toast, and thereupon surceased from my labors.' The conversation was not general, and Hawthorne turned first to Mrs. Browning (who talked eagerly of spiritualism, of Margaret Fuller and of Delia Bacon's Shakespeare theories) and then to Mrs. Nightingale who told him about London smoke. Mrs. Nightingale talked, too, of Lady Byron's 'beautiful verses,' and of her exemplary and unselfish

[1] *English Notebooks*, ed. cit., p. 377.

character, making her seem to Hawthorne 'an intolerably irre-
proachable person.' Robert Browning ('handsome, with dark
hair, a very little frosted . . . gently impulsive, talking as if his heart
were uppermost') had come with his wife. Another guest Hawthorne liked was the Reverend John Palfrey, the Unitarian clergyman from Boston who had owned and edited *The North American
Review*, and was now in London researching for his great five-volume
history of New England. Hawthorne was somewhat intrigued by
meeting Lord Lansdowne, who had his right hand wrapped in
a black silk handkerchief and thus offered his left hand to the
American to shake—

and, from some awkwardness in meeting it, when I expected the
right, I gave him only three of my fingers;—a thing I never did before to any person, and it is queer that I should have done it to a
Marquess.

Lord Lansdowne struck him as 'a kind old man,' and Hawthorne
received a shock when Henry Bright told him a few days later that
this ageing nobleman was in fact 'a most disreputable character'
and the original of Thackeray's Lord Steyne. Milnes had in his
time jotted down one or two of the scandalous club-room tales of
Lord Lansdowne's corrupt and corrupting tastes, for he was always
fascinated by the under-side of life, and was himself developing
interests which would have pained Hawthorne almost as much as
Bright's revelation of Lord Lansdowne's eccentricities, or the story
told him by a Cambridge man in 1855 of Charles Kingsley's sens-
uality and passion for making 'drawings such as no pure man would
have made or could have allowed himself to show or look at.'
Milnes' collection of erotic and sadistic literature, about which he was
always generous and jovial with many of his friends, seems not to have
been assembled till the late eighteen-fifties. He would have been
quite capable, on a less public occasion, of showing such books to
Hawthorne in the impish hope of creating an effect. As it was they
all looked quietly at some of Milnes' autographs—a page from
Swift's *Journal to Stella*, letters from Addison and Chatterton, the
signature of Oliver Cromwell. 'There seemed to be many curious
volumes in the library' Hawthorne commented, 'but I had not
time to look at them.'

I liked greatly the manners of almost all—yes, all, as far as I observed—all the people at this breakfast [was Hawthorne's conde-
scending verdict on this party]; and it was doubtless owing to their
being all people either of high rank, or remarkable intellect or both.

Other persons at this breakfast-party whom Hawthorne does not
mention, but who are listed in Mrs. Milnes' meticulous handwriting

(so clear a contrast to her husband's notorious 'hieroglyphics' or 'arrow-heads') were Lord Derby's son Lord Stanley, Lord Ripon's son, Lord Goderich, the Comte de Polignac, Arthur Russell and 'Mr. M. Butler.'

Mrs. Monckton Milnes kept a set of minute pocket-books in which she recorded the names of the guests present at each Upper Brook Street entertainment. In the first of these seven tiny volumes, Milnes has scrawled a quotation from the English journal of a sixteenth-century Venetian traveller, printed by the Camden Society: 'The English would sooner give five or six ducats to promote an entertainment for a person, than a groat to assist him in any distress.' It is this recognition of real values, this half-amused awareness that the London activities he relished were not an end in themselves, that makes Milnes, even at his most tiresome, a sympathetic and endearing figure, radiant against the lofty decor of that frigid social scene.

IV

In their first London season Milnes and his wife gave twelve large breakfast-parties. The company at these was mixed.

I am rather amused at your commentary on R's breakfasts [Richard's father wrote to Annabel], his having *too many* ladies—what a cynical uncivilized bear must you think me, for saying you don't go far enough—& that he should not have had one. It has always been my creed that women were not meant to be seen in a morning—never intended to be made society of, till well on in the afternoon.

Breakfast guests of the spring and summer of 1852 included Lady Ashburton, Mrs. Grote, Miss Williams Wynn and Mademoiselle Bunsen, but there were other occasions when Monckton Milnes presided alone over a company exclusively male. On these mornings Mrs. Milnes would drive out in the britzka her husband had given her (and which he would teasingly refer to as her 'open fly') to visit people on Richmond Hill, leaving the house free for Milnes and his friends. The most interesting of these masculine breakfast-parties were those at which Milnes entertained his fellow-members of 'that most select of all learned societies,' the Philobiblon.

The Philobiblon Society, founded in 1853 by Milnes and William Stirling, with the aid and advice of the Belgian Minister in London, Sylvain Van de Weyer, was named from the famous book of Richard de Bury. It had an existence of thirty-one years. Throughout this period, Monckton Milnes was its most active member, chief editor of its *Miscellanies*, and constantly re-elected as one of the two honorary secretaries who kept the Society up to the mark. Milnes' passion for collecting books was a dominant one. For long he had given it free rein. Four days after his marriage and on the way to Torquay, he had puzzled his wife by racing round the second-hand bookshops of Bristol and returning heavily laden with packages to their hotel. His father referred to the habit as 'ruining his family in books,' but not all of Milnes' vast library came from grand book auctions or expensive shops. 'I like your library,' Leigh Hunt told Milnes, 'it is the concentration of infinite bookstalls —it seems all made up of book-books.'[1] From the foundation of the Philobiblon Society in 1853 to its death in 1884 Milnes devoted close attention and a good deal of time to its entertainments and its *Miscellanies*. For this reason it is interesting to consider the Society here and to remember the lively and erudite group of persons who formed it nearly one hundred years ago.

'*The Philobiblon Society*' ran the first of the ten *Rules* governing the institution, '*is composed of persons interested in the history, collection, or peculiarities of Books. It consists of a Patron and thirty-five Members. Its officers are a President and two Joint Secretaries.*' These officers were chosen annually each March. Members were elected by ballot. Two black balls could exclude a candidate. The subscription was from one to three pounds per annum.

Milnes and Van de Weyer were anxious that the Society should assume an 'international character' and they consequently asked Henri, Duc d'Aumale, fifth son of Louis-Philippe, to become its first patron. The Duc d'Aumale was thirty-one, a leading member of the French Société des Bibliophiles and possessor of a splendid library, part of which he had with him at Twickenham, where he was then living in what Lord Houghton in after years described as 'sumptuous and studious exile.' The Duke became an enthusiastic Philobiblon, attending and giving breakfasts, contributing scholarly papers to the *Miscellanies* and even keeping up a vivid interest in its proceedings after his return to France in 1872. For some unrecorded reason, d'Aumale was shortly asked to cede the position of patron to Prince Albert, who proved a profound disappointment to the club, for his attitude to the Philobiblons was non-committal and positively neglectful. In the final volume of the *Miscellanies*, published in 1884, Lord Houghton squarely placed on record what he thought of the Prince Consort's behaviour:

He neither contributed to our miscellanies, nor joined in any of our assemblies. It would have been natural to so cultured a Prince in a German Court to have availed himself of such an opportunity of

[1] Commonplace-book 1850–1851.

investigating the most interesting libraries of the metropolis, especially such as those of Baron Heath and Mr. Huth, which had been little seen by the public.   It would besides have been within the rules of the strictest etiquette for His Royal Highness to have accepted the hospitalities of a French Prince connected by marriage with our Royal Family, of the Belgian Family Minister, of the Duke of Hamilton, of Lord Powys or of other of our colleagues with whom he had a personal acquaintance.   For myself I was not surprised at this abstention, for I had heard, either directly from Baron Stockmar, or indirectly from the Chevalier Bunsen, that soon after his marriage the Prince, at the suggestion of King Leopold, had made some advances towards a more informal intimacy with some leading men of letters, science and art . . . but that [he] had . . . found the social surroundings too strong for him, and that he had to content himself with the intimacy of the various important political personages with whom he was brought into contact at Windsor and Balmoral.

'He did very little for Art, or Science, or Literature (notwith-standing all the puff),' Milnes wrote to George Bunsen when the Prince Consort died in 1862.

After the Prince Consort's death, the Philobiblons remained without a royal patron, for the Prince of Wales showed no 'such especial care for books as books, as would have authorized our Society to occupy his time and attention.'   In 1882 the youthful Prince Leopold, Duke of Albany, the most cultivated child of Queen Victoria, was elected to the vacant position.   He died suddenly in March 1884 and with his death the remaining Philobiblons decided to put up the shutters, print a final *Miscellany* and declare the Society at an end.

But in 1853 and for the next twenty years the Philobiblon meetings were conducted with that eager rivalry and stimulating gusto peculiar to collectors.   Van de Weyer ceded his place as one of the two secretaries to William Stirling, who, together with Milnes and Matthew Higgins, made all the arrangements for the meetings and helped edit the *Miscellanies*.   The membership of the Society always comprised several elements—noblemen with important family libraries like the Duke of Hamilton, Lord Lansdowne, Lord Bath, Lord Ellesmere and Lord Powys; pure scholars like William Stirling, Edward Cheney and the Northamptonshire bibliographer Beriah Botfield; men of letters like Dean Milman and Monckton Milnes; painters like Sir Charles Eastlake; travellers like Richard Ford and Robert Curzon, and erudite publishers, chiefly repre-sented by John Murray and Thomas Longman.   The Society met regularly during the season, at Saturday breakfast-parties given once or twice a month; a few similar reunions were also held in the autumn and winter.   These breakfasts were offered to the other members by some selected Philobiblon who provided food, wine, and, most important of all, a series of bibliographical treasures for the inspection of his friends. The minutes of each meeting were recorded in a minute-book which was carried by the secretary to the breakfast in a black morocco bag with carrying-handles, straps and buckles, made by Leightons the Brewer Street booksellers. Leightons also printed and posted the invitation cards summoning members to the meals.

The work of Milnes and Stirling as secretaries was not entirely easy. When Sir John Simeon, a nephew of the famous evangelical leader Charles Simeon, was asked by Milnes to take on the secretaryship for a short time in 1870, he sent in a pertinent enquiry as to how the breakfasts were arranged: 'Is it a spontaneous effusion of grace on the part of a member or are you always forced to instigate the hospitality?' Here was the point. Lord Ellesmere had only to write to Milnes asking him to tell the steward at Bridgewater House how many Philobiblons would assemble on a certain day to see his Shakespeare documents. Similarly there was no sense of strain in meeting at the big Belgian Legation in Portland Place. But for Milnes in a smallish house in Upper Brook Street, and still more for Milman in the gloomy deanery of St. Paul's, with its dark plane-trees behind the heavy courtyard gates, Philobiblon hospitality involved careful planning. In January 1858 the Dean wrote nervously that he could only give 'a poor ordinary breakfast' and that he had no curiosities to show— 'I have never been rich enough to be a collector, and have been obliged to buy books for use not for rarity.' He suggested that members should treat the bibliographical aspect of the meal as 'a *pic-nic* as to the books which excite our admiration and envy,' bringing their own curiosities with them. This novel idea was accepted as 'a very reasonable one' by Stirling, who promised to 'furnish some bookish viand or condiment to the Dean's board.' Subsequently it became a precedent. Some members, usually the wealthiest ones, shirked giving breakfasts altogether, saying like Mr. Holford of Dorchester House that their dining-rooms or libraries were out of commission or being re-decorated, while in 1869 the collector Henry Huth actually resigned because he found it 'extremely inconvenient' to show his books to eighteen or twenty people at a time. 'The volumes get so disarranged and misplaced' [he wrote, and no one who owns books can fail to sympathise with him] 'that it takes me a long time to put them right again.' Mr. Huth even refused to give the Philobiblons a farewell meal.

As well as organising the breakfasts and carefully balancing the society's accounts, Milnes took chief charge of the editing of the

Philobiblon Miscellanies. These stout quarto volumes, printed on thick laid paper with very wide margins, appeared at irregular intervals. Fifteen *Miscellanies* were printed in all, as well as a few independent volumes produced at a Member's own expense, of which Milnes' 'Boswelliana,' an enlarged edition of the paper he had contributed to volume II of the *Miscellanies* (and containing stories too bawdy even for the restricted Philobiblon circulation), is a fair example. The contents of the *Miscellanies* were extremely varied. They ranged from 'Notes sur deux petites bibliothèques françaises du XVme siècle' (by the Duc d'Aumale), 'On the first Edition of the Adagia of Erasmus' (by William Stirling) and 'L'Historia di Casa Orsini, di Francesco Sansovino' (by Edward Cheney) to Milnes' 'Boswelliana' and 'Lady Harcourt's Journal,' John Murray's 'Unpublished Letters of Laurence Sterne,' Henry Bright's 'Unpublished Letters of S. T. Coleridge,' the letters of Sydney Smith to the Hollands, Charles Greville's 'A Visit to Paris in 1855,' and an alternative version of Keats's *Hyperion*. Octave Delepierre, a Belgian member of the Society, who printed an analysis of its transactions,[1] divided its papers into the four categories of *Bibliography, History, Biography* and *Variétés Littéraires*. The *Miscellanies* were in fact well edited and very comprehensive in their scope of subjects. What was abstruse was well balanced by what was easy or amusing, and they reflected the different characters and interests of the bibliophiles. Milnes and Stirling made stern editors, rejecting what seemed dull or nonsensical and exercising the editorial power in an almost alarming way. 'I have a nervous dread,' wrote one frightened member in 1855, 'of inflicting a mare's nest upon the Philobiblon.'

V

Like the Cambridge 'Apostles,' or Conversazione Society, to which Milnes had been elected in his youth, the Philobiblon Club was the expression of common interests shared by a small group of Milnes' closest friends. Its objects—the handling of rare volumes, the exploration of great libraries, the printing of literary curiosities—would have seemed mundane to the airy undergraduates of 1828, yet the Philobiblon was not only as select but in its leisurely way as earnest as the Apostles had ever been. Milnes had the entry to a great variety of London worlds, but the friends he really cared for in his middle and later years can be identified amongst the easy-

---

[1] Printed, in French, by Trübner & Co., Paternoster Row, in 1862. Delepierre's account of the sequence of royal patrons or presidents differs somewhat from Lord Houghton's in the 1884 *Miscellany*.

going, erudite book-lovers who assembled on Saturday mornings for a Philobiblon feast. Milnes' chief friend in the House, Charles Buller, had died in 1848; Stafford O'Brien he saw frequently but did not deeply like; Gladstone was gravely affable but very busy: Disraeli and Milnes did not get on. In the eighteen-fifties Milnes' closest friends were not political, and included Van de Weyer and William Stirling, while other Philobiblon members such as Edward Cheney or Robert Curzon were men he had known long and well, and whom he thoroughly enjoyed seeing. It was Milnes and Van de Weyer who first conceived the Philobiblon scheme.

His Excellency Sylvain Van de Weyer occupied a unique position in society, for during his thirty-five years at the head of the Belgian Legation in London he was on terms of unusual intimacy with the Court. As Count Walewski explained to the French Emperor in 1854 [1] Prince Albert's reserved manner made it almost impossible for any member of the diplomatic corps to become acquainted with him. Van de Weyer was an exception. The Prince relied on him almost as much as he relied on Stockmar, and Queen Victoria continued this friendship after the Prince's death. Described by a contemporary as 'one of the most agreeable men I ever knew,' Van de Weyer had made his way at the Court of St. James by 'the power of his personal charm.' He was a small man [2] with bad health, but according to Lady Holland he was 'very clever, good and popular,' and his intelligence and discretion were such that they had early won Palmerston's esteem. In his very young days (he was born in 1802) Van de Weyer had been exclusively interested in philosophy and in books—his father kept a lending library in Louvain and he himself was at one time librarian to the City of Brussels. The 1830 revolution had turned him, at the age of twenty-eight, into an active patriot and mordant pamphleteer; it was he who conducted in 1831 the delicate negotiations at the Conference of London which led to the exclusion of the Bourbon candidate from the throne of Belgium and the accession to it of Princess Charlotte's widower, Prince Leopold. The new King of the Belgians at once made Van de Weyer his envoy in England, a post which he retained (with a brief interlude as head of an unsuccessful government in Brussels in 1845) from 1831 to 1867. He died in London in 1874. Through his wife, a daughter of Joshua Bates, the wealthy American banker, senior partner in Barings and

---

[1] See Sir Theodore Martin's *Life of the Prince Consort* (1875–1880), vol. iii, pp. 123–124.

[2] 'M. Van de Weyer making his wife promise that she would not buy any cochin-china fowl larger than himself': Commonplace-book 1852–1854. At the time of his marriage old Lady Holland referred to him as a 'poor little man' (*Lady Holland to her Son*, ed. Lord Ilchester; John Murray 1946).

founder of the Boston Public Library, Van de Weyer knew the Ashburtons well and was often at the Grange. In London he lived in his father-in-law's great house in Portland Place, which had already served as an embassy on previous occasions. Madame Van de Weyer and her mother (who had been a Sturgis of Boston) gave advice to stray Americans in London society, and it was they who helped steer Mrs. Adams, wife of the new U.S. Minister, through the intricacies of English diplomatic life in 1861. 'Madam Bates and her daughter, Mrs. Van de Weyer, give us law, and their names are inscribed in high places in our household Gods. Altogether I feel pretty sick and tired of the whole thing,' wrote Henry Adams junior to his cousin Charles Francis Adams in May 1861.[1] The Van de Weyers also lived at New Lodge, Windsor, where Augustus Hare, who was taken to dine there in April 1860, much admired the quantity of books. Madame Van de Weyer, an 'immensely fat' woman, had lately been to a concert at Windsor where she and her husband had been jostled. 'Why, they take us for pages,' she said indignantly. 'No, my dear,' Monsieur Van de Weyer answered, 'they take me for a page, but they take you for a volume.'[2]

Some of Van de Weyer's friends compared him to Saint-Evremond, whilst others thought him more like Chamfort. The reason for the second comparison lay in the maxims, or *Pensées Diverses*, which he published.[3] These *pensées* have worn a little thin; perhaps they never can have seemed very startling: 'les belles âmes seules voient tout en beau' is a fair example, or 'il est plus facile de réussir que de se faire pardonner ses succés.' But if not noticeably original or remarkably sharp, Van de Weyer's maxims show a true experience of the world. Those treating of fashionable society are similar in tone to Milnes' own most private opinions on it:—'le Monde,' wrote Van de Weyer '. . . où sous de brillants dehors, tout est petit, mesquin et souvent ignoble.' 'The worst part of common society life,' Milnes had written in 1838, 'is its unimpressiveness if long continued.'

The atmosphere of general society is the great leveller [he noted on another day]. Sorrow is no longer grave there, nor madness

---

[1] *Letters of Henry Adams* (1858–1891), ed. W. C. Ford (Constable 1930).
[2] Augustus Hare's *The Story of My Life* (George Allen 1896) vol. ii.
[3] *Choix d'Opuscules: Philosophiques, Historiques, Politiques et Littéraires* of Sylvain Van de Weyer were published in four volumes, 1863–1876 (edited by Octave Delepierre: Trübner & Co., London) the last volume containing tributes to his memory and ending with Houghton's *In Memoriam* verses dated 23 May 1874 and signed 'H***,' while a long but undistinguished biographical study *Sylvain van de Weyer, Ministre d'État* by Theodore Just appeared during this subject's lifetime in Mucquardt's series *Les Fondateurs de la Monarchie Belge* (1871). A sketch of Van de Weyer also appears in Ch. de Chenédollé's *Cour de Bruxelles* (Brussels 1856).

terrible, nor Death a mystery—sorrow wears a ridiculous dress and insanity a merry one and death and life go hand-in-hand as if they were brothers.

Such had been Milnes' comments on the world as a young man, and he was no less clear-sighted in middle age. 'That grove of barren fig-trees commonly called London Society,' he remarked to someone in 1853 or '54. Van de Weyer, who had played an eminent part in his country's history, and Richard Monckton Milnes, who never did anything of the sort, had many things in common besides the love of books. Neither of them was readily deceived or englamoured by appearances. Neither of them judged life from the outside.

'The Art of Conversation is the happy counter-play of witty minds,' Milnes once sententiously declared. Van de Weyer's mind was reputedly most witty, but Milnes seems never to have recorded much that his Belgian friend said during the years of their long friendship, when they would be meeting regularly in London, or be spending days in each other's company at great houses like Nuneham and the Grange. Van de Weyer had contracted a loathing for old Rogers: 'Ne fiez-vous jamais à cet horrible homme,' he told Milnes, 'c'est l'homme le plus méchant qu'il ne fut jamais.' Milnes and Rogers had never, in any case, trusted or liked each other, and by the time Van de Weyer gave this warning in the early eighteen-fifties the old poet was in a garrulous and crotchety state of decline; he died in 1855. When Sylvain Van de Weyer himself died in the spring of 1874, Lord Houghton composed an *In Memoriam* of four verses, in which he expressed his conviction that the Belgian diplomat had:

> . . . left but few
> Who have played in Life's drama the vanward part,
> With so cool a head and so warm a heart.
>
> . . . . .
>
> So graced and so gracious—so genial and frank;
> With no taint of the pride of or riches or rank;
> While potent alike to rebuke or delight,
> His wit as the lightning was instant and bright.
>
> He is gone to his rest, and yet we weep,
> Who rather should envy his blissful sleep,
> None the less is the grief beneath which we bend
> O'er the Christian, the Scholar, the Statesman and
>   Friend.

The Philobiblons were so much moved by this death that they elected Van de Weyer's unwieldy widow an honorary member of the Club—the only woman ever to attain to this distinction.

The third person particularly involved in the birth of the Philo-biblon Society was William Stirling, known to posterity by his later name Sir William Stirling-Maxwell. Almost ten years Milnes' junior, Stirling had already made himself a literary reputation by his *Annals of the Artists of Spain*, published in 1848, and *The Cloister Life of the Emperor Charles V* which appeared in 1852 and went into a second edition at once. In 1852 also he entered the House of Commons as a moderate Tory member for Perth, though he was always more a scholar and a host than a politician. Stirling lived in considerable comfort in a roomy house in Park Street (just round the corner from the Milneses) where he kept a part of his very fine library and where he entertained on a scale that caused Prescott to call him 'that prince of good fellows.' Half his life was spent working day after day in the British Museum Library, half in going about in London, talking and cracking jokes. Stirling's special form of humour was the pun, now happily fallen into desuetude. When the carriage harness was damaged during an expedition with Milnes to Loch Katrine, Stirling exclaimed: 'So pleasant a day must leave some traces behind.' It was he who nick-named Dicky Milnes 'the Bird of Paradox.'

Possibly because he was himself an historian, Stirling was a shrewd judge of contemporary events.

I was in Paris at the moment the President strangled his Parliament in the night [he wrote to Milnes from Bowood, at Christmas-time 1851]. I agree with you for looking for no good from so bad a beginning—But Frenchmen in general I presume will disagree with us, & think wrong a very fit prelude to right. Obstruction to pro-gress, perhaps retrogression—& another social earthquake *seem* inevitable—& therefore perhaps will not happen—Madame de Flahault, who is here, thinks it all charming, & the general sentiment of the Society seems Presidential & Elysian. God is great! My business in Paris was not to assist at the State-blow, but to see & read the MS about Charles V's retirement, about which we went to Mignet last year. It is in the Archives of the Aff. Etrang. & I spent ten days or a fortnight on it, reading & noting. It is very full, very curious, & very subversive of much which I had previously written. . . . Your visit to Broadlands must have been interesting—just at the moment of Lord John's 'coup de colleague'—if Ld P's fall was so caused. Ld Lansdowne & Ld Seymour went to the Council yesterday at Windsor—but no news seems to ooze out . . . How good Carlyle's Life of Sterling is, & how bad Longfellow's Golden Legend!

It is likely that Milnes got to know Stirling well through their friend Caroline Norton. This impulsive woman was now carrying on into the era of the Great Exhibition and the Crimean War the legal battles and public rows with her husband which had first startled polite society in the reign of William IV. Mrs. Norton was what is often called her own worst enemy, and although much pitied she had in general estimate become a bore. 'Her society is saddening to me in itself,' wrote Henry Taylor in the winter of 1850, after he had taken her to see a play at which she had self-indulgently wept, 'so glorious a creature to look at even as she is—so transcendent formerly, and now so faded in beauty and foundered in life.'[1] In the midst of her success as a novelist, and at the small dinner-parties of clever talkers which she gave in her house in Chesterfield Street, Mrs. Norton never forgot her grievances, or let her friends do so for long. Through all these tempests Milnes remained constant, and she still sent him letters which started 'Dear Poet' just as she had done in the first years of the new reign, when he was considered an affected young man and she a tragic beauty, and when the benign Marguerite Blessington, whose death in 1849 her friends still mourned, had said that 'Monckton Milnes would be a delightful match for Mrs. Norton, if he could only be pathetic.' By the eighteen-fifties Caroline Norton had become altogether too 'pathetic,' and her public misery and somewhat fanatical activities over the rights of married women formed an odd contrast to the dignified, poetical, grief-laden life of her widowed sister Helen Dufferin, or the marvellous appearance of her other sister Lady Seymour. Lady Seymour, whose husband succeeded to the dukedom of Somerset in 1855, was as handsome as ever, and could still arouse feminine jealousy. 'She dresses so economically,' said a woman to Monckton Milnes of the new Duchess at some evening entertainment. 'She makes so much use of her skin.'

Stirling's fond, consistent attachment to Mrs. Norton, which began when she was forty-three and he not thirty, forms one of the most touching features of his admirable life. For twenty-seven years he looked after and helped her, having her to stay each autumn at Keir (the Scots house he inherited in 1847 and rebuilt between '49 and '51) and finally marrying her when she was sad, impoverished, elderly and ill in 1877, three months before she died. So good and humane a character would find a quick response in Milnes, whose intimacy with Stirling is much more explicable than some of the other close friendships of his life.

A far less sociable member of the Philobiblon circle was Edward Cheney, on whom Lord Houghton wrote an excellent short essay,

---

[1] Letter quoted in Miss Perkins' *Life of Mrs. Norton* (1909) and in Miss Alice Acland's more recent study (based on the Norton papers) *Caroline Norton* (Constable 1948).

printed in the last volume of the *Miscellanies* in 1884. Edward Cheney was primarily a book-collector and an Italian scholar. The only social sphere in which he moved with readiness or pleasure was the sphere of Holland House, for he was an old friend of Henry, fourth Lord Holland, and later the trusted counsellor of Lord Holland's widow, who did nothing without his advice, persuaded him to act as go-between for herself and her heir Lord Ilchester, and habitually made use of him with that good-mannered tenacity in which persons of her station then excelled. Cheney is an indistinct figure. We can only get blurred glimpses of him under the elm trees in the summer gardens of Holland House, or leaning towards Milnes at a Philobiblon breakfast to say: 'The library of a friend of mine consists of two classes of books—those which nobody can read and those which nobody ought to read,' a remark which Milnes evidently snatched and turned into a *bon mot* of his own, 'A library should be composed of books you would like to read, and of books you ought not.'[1]

Edward Cheney was one of two brothers, sons of a General who lived at Badger Hall in Shropshire. They had resided for many years in Rome, where Milnes had first met them in 1834 in the apartment of Lady Coventry (mother of Mary Augusta, Lady Holland) in the Barberini Palace. 'Very notable personages in the Anglo-Italian society of that time,' the brothers Cheney had both written romantic Radcliffean tales,[2] both collected books, both painted water-colours in the style of de Wint and both made frequent contributions to the *Quarterly Review*. Lord Houghton describes them as belonging to 'that generation of Englishmen who regarded Italy as a museum created and preserved for their pleasure and edification' and who were thus automatically on the side of Austria or any other suppressive power. Henry Cheney died in 1866, and Edward Cheney in 1884. They led 'peaceful and pleasant lives' in what Lord Houghton most charmingly terms a state of 'persistent and unbroken fraternity,' seeing very few people, yet neither 'selfish' nor 'morose,' a pair of bachelors whose 'very friendships were prejudices,' and whose outlook was made sharp and clear by a 'fastidiousness' which Milnes thought was 'their peculiar and not most amiable characteristic.'

One other Philobiblon should be noticed here, for he too was an old friend of Monckton Milnes and of almost exactly the same age.

---

[1] Commonplace-book 1852–1854.
[2] Edward Cheney's *Malvagna or The Evil Eye* was published by Bentley in 1838, while his brother's *Rossano, a Neapolitan Story* was printed in *Selections in Prose and Verse from the Papers of R. H. C[heney,]* privately issued by the Chiswick Press 1871. The Chiswick Press was the successor of Whittingham of Tooks Lane who printed the Philobiblon *Miscellanies*.

Robert Curzon, who lived at Parham, and succeeded his mother in the barony of Zouche of Harringworth in 1870 (himself dying in 1873) had written his extremely entertaining and popular work, *A Visit to the Monasteries of the Levant*, a few years before the founding of the Philobiblon Club. He contributed several papers to the *Miscellanies*, including his lengthy 'Account of the most celebrated libraries of Italy' which took up a good deal of space in the 1854 volume. Curzon, who had been most hospitable to Milnes in 1843 at Constantinople, where he was reluctantly serving as secretary to the exacting British Minister, Sir Stratford Canning, was one of the most delightful men of his time, and he wrote as gaily and as frankly as he spoke: 'his language,' writes the author of an anonymous memoir of Lord Zouche printed for the Philobiblon Club,

was the mirror of his mind. . . . The foundation of his character was sincerity, which, but for his natural good breeding and desire to avoid inflicting pain, might have sometimes given offence; but so checked and tempered, it laid the foundation of those few but steady and loving friendships of his often very chequered life. He was, indeed, a much loving and much beloved friend, as well as a companion, whose natural talent, varied experience, original conversation, and lively wit will live long in the memory of those who had the good fortune to be well acquainted with him.

After his own marriage, Milnes' friendship with Curzon was cemented by his wife's deep-rooted affection for Emily Curzon, a young friend and neighbour of the Crewes. Mrs. Curzon was a Wilmot-Horton, and her mother had as a girl been the subject of Byron's poem 'She walks in beauty, like the night.' Emily Curzon was devoted to her 'dearest Annabel' and would often come round from number 24 Arlington Street to walk with her in Hyde Park, or to sit with her discussing the all-absorbing topics of their children's talents and health. In 1866 she suddenly died, leaving her husband heartbroken. 'I send you a photograph and an inkstand that my dear Emily always used on her own table at Parham,' he wrote to Lady Houghton in October of that year. 'I hope you will keep these little remembrances of your friend, whose unexpected death has quite overwhelmed her unhappy husband.'

Such were some of the personal elements responsible for the foundation, and vivacious conduct, of the Philobiblon Club.

Chapter Four

1853 ___ 1854

I

Though she and her husband were doubtless unaware of it, the first seasons of Annabel Milnes' life as hostess in 16 Upper Brook Street formed the tail end of a social era. The process of change, steadily at work in London throughout the 'forties, was immensely accelerated by the outbreak and course of the War in the Crimea, which smashed English complacency and broke down certain social barriers, exposing the 'enlarged family party' of Lord Frederick Hamilton's recollection to unwelcome and drastic intrusion. Dr. Holland, the Bianchon of the mid-Victorian aristocracy—he attended Mrs. Monckton Milnes as he did every other delicate lady of fashion—has left us a most interesting analysis of these changes in a chapter of his *Recollections of Past Life*, which Longmans published in 1872. This work, the result of a lifetime of travel, professional activity and objective reflection, is a book that well repays perusal.

Few persons were better equipped to survey the contemporary scene than Henry Holland. Born in '88 on the verge of the first French Revolution, he had been Queen Caroline's physician in Italy, given evidence at her trial, attended Canning on his death-bed at Chiswick House, been consulted by Castlereagh not long before his suicide, known Melbourne intimately, been the doctor and friend of six Prime Ministers, of many ambassadors and of such European figures as Queen Hortense, Princess Lieven and Prince Louis Napoleon, as well as being acquainted with Abraham Lincoln and other great Americans. Holland was an extremely cultivated and civilised man, who occupied a position of privilege in London seldom accorded to other men of his profession at that time. He had been on the founding committee of the Athenæum Club, and had, for instance, been one of the twelve members (who included Milnes and Lord Lansdowne) selected to give Guizot a dinner of welcome at the club on his arrival here as ambassador in 1840. In 1853 Queen Victoria, whose physician-in-ordinary he had become, made him a baronet. From then until his death two decades later old Sir Henry Holland continued working and writing, putting into practice his own pet theories of the importance of using up 'small fractions of time' and of the inherent danger of 'premature admission of old age' which he thought led straight to senility and death.   He always walked briskly along the pavements, overtaking anyone who was ahead of him, and when he entered a square he crossed it diagonally to save time.   He examined London life with an experienced and also a scientific eye, constantly comparing past with present and not always to the detriment of the latter.   He did not romanticise Byronic London, readily admitting the 'absurd tyranny' of the old Almack's balls—'Even as a physician,' he wrote, 'I was often witness of the effects of this dominating passion, having seen more than one case, defying medicine, cured by a ticket for Almack's opportunely obtained.'   Unlike Monckton Milnes who preserved everything, Sir Henry Holland deliberately destroyed all his letters and private papers, leaving posterity his *Recollections* only.   The tone of these is unexcited, and we feel inclined to rely on his judgements of that past world every bit as much as his trusting patients would rely upon his professional skill.   'But Dr. Holland says' or 'Dr. Holland assures me' are recurrent phrases in Mrs. Milnes' letters.

The changes which Sir Henry detected in the 'fifties and 'sixties he defined as 'a miscellaneous intermingling of the different elements of society.'   Dinner-tables were far more crowded, evening assemblages stifled 'breath as well as conversation.'   He was oppressed by the sense of speed and multitude which we find also recorded in young Henry Adams' letters in 1863.   Adams termed it 'the rush and fuss of society.'

I had occasion to go last night to a reception over in Kensington [Adams wrote in June of that year].[1]   '. . . and as it was a soft moonlight night I walked part of the way.   Accustomed as I am to London, and after seeing three seasons in it, I could not help feeling impressed by the extraordinary scene.   I passed through Grosvenor Square and round Hyde Park to Apsley House, and the streets seemed alive with carriages in every direction.   Gentlemen in white cravats were scuttling about, like myself; cabs were rushing furiously in all quarters, hundreds of carriages were waiting, or setting down or taking up their people before great houses, as I passed from street to square, and from square to street.   There was a rush and roar all through the West End, that one can see only in London.

Sir Henry Holland, who thought the growth of clubs in the years 1830 to 1870 rather deleterious (since they encouraged gossip, 'ephemeral reading' and sleep in 'well-cushioned armchairs'),

---

[1] *Letters*, ed. cit. pp. 98–99.

declared that even pedestrians moved faster than in his youth, and that no one could escape the vortex created by 'the torrent of the world.' 'The loiterers in life are fewer,' he wrote, 'and the charm of a tranquil leisure is less appreciated and sought after.' Holland could remember the 'quiet coteries' of an earlier epoch, 'blending literature with general society, dispensing with cards of invitation and (what is essential to their well-being) having a lady for a hostess.' Richard Milnes, whose rate of living suited the times better than Sir Henry's or his own father's, had known one or two of these quiet coteries. He had now lived in London long enough to find with a shock that people he had known and loved, and accepted as part of the fabric of his life, could die. In November 1852 had occurred the death of his old friend Miss Mary Berry, who expired of 'exhaustion from sheer old age' in her ninetieth year.

II

Milnes' friendship with the Misses Mary and Agnes Berry dated from 1834—or that at least is the year of the first note from them which he preserved. At this period he had merely been perching in London on his way to Rome to join his family, but when he settled in Pall Mall he saw the Berrys often, either at their house in Curzon Street or at the summer villa they would hire at Petersham or Richmond. 'I find I cannot live without you—so pray come and eat a luncheon dinner with us on Tuesday next at 4 o'clock,' Miss Mary would write, or 'We have not seen you for an age . . . Come then and dine with "your dear Equals in your native land" on Friday next the 16th at real seven o'clock.' He had all his letters from them bound in a great album, which was playfully entitled *Berryana*, and contained a water-colour sketch of their Petersham abode. When the Berrys' papers were published in three bulky volumes, edited by Lord Clarendon's sister Lady Theresa Lewis (who had inherited the task from her husband Sir George Cornewall Lewis and herself died before the book appeared),[1] Milnes wrote an essay on the book which was more of a supplement or commentary than a review.[2] He began his article with an anecdote of the man who enquired 'Who are those Miss Berrys who have been running all over Europe ever since the time of Louis Quatorze?' reminding his readers that the sisters had 'been courted by Horace Walpole and . . . refused to be introduced to Dr. Johnson.' In the course of the essay Milnes examined the contrast

---

[1] *Extracts from the Journals and Correspondence of Miss Berry from 1783 to 1852 edited by Lady Theresa Lewis.* This bundle of a book appeared in 1865.
[2] Republished in *Monographs*, 1873.

between eighteenth and mid-nineteenth century psychology, in a manner perhaps less expert than that of Sir Henry Holland, but not therefore less instructive. Intended to enlighten mid-Victorians upon certain English eighteenth-century points of view, the essay is now in its turn useful to ourselves in our attempts to comprehend the mid-Victorians.

Lord Houghton wrote that Miss Mary Berry seemed hard to many people because she belonged to a generation which dismissed all manifestations of sentimentality as ridiculous. It was also a generation, he added, which found it much more difficult than his own to be resigned.

The *femme incomprise* of our time, as well as the unappreciated man of genius, have their metaphysical comforts, which the hard realists of the eighteenth century knew nothing about . . . When people were mystical in those days they gave themselves up to devotion; . . . when they were philanthropic they established foundling hospitals, or taught the deaf and dumb to communicate with the world; but they did not trouble themselves with the elevation of the lower orders of society or the salvation of the whole human race.

To people of that generation in England, good society was 'no mere pleasure or even grace of life; it assumed all the dimensions of a duty,' and he thought the Berrys' salon with its 'flavour of fashion' had moral and political importance besides its personal and superficial influences. The 'multitudinous shape' London society had assumed by 1870 (and here we are directly reminded of Henry Adams and Dr. Holland) made large reunions difficult, wrote Houghton, 'from the unfitness or inability of our houses to contain the whole of one's acquaintance,' with the result that people who in the Berrys' day would have formed part of general salon society had withdrawn 'into a very limited circle of relatives and friends.' The duties and responsibilities of Victorian public life were far more severe than at an earlier period, the external respect paid to grandeur was diminishing, and there was thus every inducement for

our wealthier, and nobler, and more fastidious countrymen to retain an exclusiveness of habits and an isolation of life which can be indulged in with impunity by Legitimists in Paris or Men-of-letters in Boston [but not here]. The great [wrote Lord Houghton] can no longer remain in an empyrean of their own.

In Lord Houghton's eyes, the greatest virtue of the vanished circle of the Berrys was its encouragement of conversation, an art so rare in England 'that it not only gives to those who exhibit it a peculiar and foreign manner, but easily subjects them [and here Lord Houghton was surely thinking of his own youth] to the imputation of frivolity or impertinence.' Count Pozzo di Borgo, the Russian Ambassador, was said by Milnes to have hustled a newly arrived foreigner into the corner of a room in some English country house, whispering 'Viens donc causer, je n'ai pas causé pendant quinze jours.'[1] The house in Curzon Street, with its lighted windows to 'beckon in the passing friend' formed a cheerful little enclave of eighteenth-century ways and talk in the hurly-burly of Victorian London. When their cousin Mr. Fergusson died, the sisters, 'with a trait of manners that recalled the old regime,' never wore rouge again. Milnes said that their salon, ruled simply by good nature and good sense, was so kindly and familiar as to be

liable to the invasion of the garrulous and the tiresome; but even the specimens of that inevitable species which were found there [seemed] inspired by the genius of the place with some sense of mercy or of shame.

Miss Agnes, the younger, had died not long before Miss Mary. Attending the latter's November funeral in the little graveyard at Petersham, Milnes was moved to write some stanzas which he sent off to *The Times*. Like much of his work, they have small claim to be called poetry, but because they are heartfelt and felicitous we may glance at some of them here:

> Two friends within one grave we place,
>   United in our tears,—
> Sisters, scarce parted for the space
>   Of more than eighty years;
> And she whose bier is borne to-day,
>   The one the last to go,
> Bears with her thoughts that force their way
>   Above the moment's woe.
>
>   ·   ·   ·   ·
>
> Within one undisturbed abode
>   Their presence seems to dwell,
> From which continual pleasures flowed,
>   And countless graces fell. . . .
>
>   ·   ·   ·   ·
>
> Our English grandeur on the shelf
>   Deposited its decent gloom,
> And every pride unloosed itself
>   Within that modest room;

[1] 'Mme de Staël surprised at the general shyness of Englishmen to talk—stopping in a stream of conversation to say "mais vous ne m'interrompez pas"': Milnes' commonplace-book for 1855–1856.

Where none were sad and few were dull,
  And each one said his best,
And beauty was most beautiful
  With vanity at rest.

⠀⠀⠀⠀·⠀⠀⠀·⠀⠀⠀·⠀⠀⠀·⠀⠀⠀·

As generations onward came,
  They loved from all to win
Revival of the sacred fláme
  That glowed their hearts within.
While others in Time's greedy mesh
  The faded garlands flung,
Their hearts went out and gathered fresh
  Affections from the young.

Farewell, dear ladies! in your loss
  We feel the past recede,
The gap our hands could almost cross
  Is now a gulf indeed:
Ye, and the days in which your claims
  And charms were early known,
Lose substance, and ye stand as names
  That history makes its own.

Farewell! the pleasant social page
  Is read, but ye remain
Examples of ennobled age,
  Long life without a stain;
A lesson to be scorned by none,
  Least by the wise and brave,
Delightful as the winter sun
  That gilds this open grave.

After the age of forty or so, Monckton Milnes almost entirely abandoned the writing of verse, save for occasional memorial poems —this, or the one on Van de Weyer already cited. By composing such verses Milnes was in a sense acting as the poet laureate of Victorian society, for he had a gift for expressing the feelings of others. Lady Eastlake, wife of the painter, joined in the general chorus of praise over the Berry stanzas. 'He has spoken,' she said to someone, 'the language of all our hearts.'

III

The office of Poet Laureate of England, thrown vacant by the death of Wordsworth in April 1850, and refused by Samuel Rogers on the score of age, had been given to Alfred Tennyson in November of that year. The popular favourites for the position had been old Leigh Hunt (who sent Tennyson a generous letter of congratulation) and Mrs. Browning, whose claims had been particularly pressed by Chorley in *The Athenæum* on the grounds that the reign of a female sovereign demanded a female laureate to do it justice. Tennyson's appointment was largely due to the public appreciation of *In Memoriam*, which had come out in the summer of 1850. The slow process of general recognition of Tennyson's genius, started in the late 'twenties at Cambridge by Arthur Hallam, Richard Monckton Milnes and other Apostles, had thus reached its culmination. The bearded, swart, short-sighted poet from Lincolnshire had become a national figure. Alfred Tennyson at first distinguished himself in his new office by publishing, under a pseudonym, some vulgar and abusive poems about Louis Napoleon and the Pope, in one of which he referred to the Catholic Church as 'that half-pagan harlot kept by France.' These jingoistic verses reflect the hysteria then rampant in England, when the fear of foreign invasion had almost completely corroded judgement and common sense. In 1852 Tennyson produced his fine *Ode* on the death of the Duke of Wellington, but on the whole the laureateship, with its official obligations, may be thought to have impaired rather than improved his quality as a poet. In his youth Alfred Tennyson had been wild and eccentric, a rebel against the tenor of his times. By accepting the laureateship he stepped down on the other side of the fence, and found himself involved in eulogising royal personages, putting into verse sentiments which no thinking man could sincerely have believed in, and celebrating battles and conquests often morally unjustifiable. Humour had never been 'dear old Alfred's' strongest suit. Shortly after his elevation to the laureateship he solemnly told Monckton Milnes: 'I look upon the office of Laureate as pledging me not to write against the Queen or her family.'[1]

Another important event in Tennyson's life took place in 1850, for in June of that year he married Emily Sellwood, to whom he had been engaged for twelve years. The view of this marriage which Mrs. Milnes gave to Hawthorne in 1856—that Emily Tennyson was 'a wise and tender woman such as ought to be entrusted with such a fragile affair as Tennyson's comfort and happiness'—was shared by most of Tennyson's friends, but there were exceptions, and one of these was Edward FitzGerald.

I used to tell Tennyson 30 years ago that he should be a Dragoon, or in some active employment that would keep his soul stirring, instead of revolving in itself in idleness and tobacco smoke [Fitz-

[1] Commonplace-book 1851–1852.

Gerald wrote to Milnes in April 1872].   And now he has sunk in
Coterie worship and (I tremble to say it) in the sympathy of his
most ladylike, gentle, wife—an old Housekeeper like Molière's
would have been far better for him *I* think . . . I mourn over him as
once a great man lost.

Milnes had suggested Fryston as a suitable place for the Tennysons' honeymoon (the gaunt house had already served others of his
friends in this capacity) and when they were house-hunting a few
months later he pressed them to settle in a wing of it, an offer which
they also, and most sensibly, declined.   Tennyson, who had stayed
there in 1835, had re-christened the house 'Freezetown'; moreover
Fryston had not been regularly inhabited since the death of Mrs.
Pemberton Milnes in 1847, and in some of the rooms the ceilings
had collapsed, while all the others were in a state of damp and dis-
repair.   After his marriage Tennyson's visits to London grew even
more infrequent, and when he was in town he seldom went out into
society: 'The Laureate cannot breakfast with anybody . . . I must
leave you to seek him in his lair,' wrote Spedding in an undated
note of the 'fifties.

I have given up dining out and am about to retire into utter
solitude in some country house [Tennyson himself informed Milnes
in a letter of August 1852], but if you feel aggrieved at sending one
invitation after another to me, unaccepted, I will come. . . .   Do not
bother yourself about giving me a bed, I can get one (and my own
way too in the matter of smoke) better at Spedding's.

Besides James Spedding, now thoroughly embarked upon his life-
work of editing Bacon and resident in Lincoln's Inn Fields, Milnes
may have kept in touch with Tennyson through Sir John Simeon.
A Liberal baronet, a Catholic and a scholar, Simeon was an ardent
member of the Philobiblon and in frequent correspondence with
Milnes over its affairs.   A neighbour in the Isle of Wight (which he
represented in Parliament) Simeon was the chosen friend of Tennyson's middle life; when he died at Freiburg in 1870, his widow wrote
to Milnes (who had proposed that the Laureate might produce a
memoir of her husband for the next *Miscellany*): 'I cannot say
whether it was more soothing or more intensifying to my grief to
hear him speak of my Darling as one whom he had loved better
than any man he had known since Arthur Hallam.'   Milnes
always remained on rather intimate, affectionate terms with Alfred
Tennyson, but as they both grew older they saw each other less and
less.

The bard was very agreeable and his wife and son delightful [Lord Houghton wrote to his wife of a summer's day spent at the Tennysons' house on Blackdown]. He has built himself a very handsome and commodious home in a most inaccessible site, with every comfort he can require, and every discomfort to all who approach him. What can be more poetical?

Milnes, whom Tennyson would fondly address as 'my old college comrade,' never shook off the quizzical, irreverent attitude which the Apostles had adopted towards Tennyson so many years ago.

If Alfred Tennyson could only make that long wail, like the winter wind, about Mariana in the Moated Grange, and could not get her to throw herself into the ditch, or could not bring her another man to help her ennui, he had much better have left her alone altogether [Carlyle remarked to Milnes soon after the publication of this poem].[1]

In 1848 Carlyle's affection for Milnes had been shaken by the publication of the Keats letters, of which Carlyle had greatly disapproved; but this mood of estrangement did not last. 'Carlyle has taken such a re-liking to you' (wrote Lady Ashburton in an undated letter from the Grange asking Milnes to get a set of Carlyle's works bound for her—'*very well* bound . . . but of somewhat *severe* exterior appearance, suitable to the character of the author'—to give to George Bunsen), 'not that he ever diverged into any other condition abt. you but he used to rail at yr. Dilettanteism —now however you have absolutely *mesmerized* him.' The truth remained that Carlyle was devoted to Milnes, and still capable of being surprised by him: 'I look on you as an intellectual marauder rushing about defending any villainy that may fall in your way,' he told him in 1852, and he was amused on some other occasion by Milnes' charmingly frank reply to a question as to 'why he put what he had to say into rhymes, "instead of just saying it."' 'Why you see a very little thought goes so much further in verse,' Milnes answered.[2] Friendships, like love affairs, pass through phases: the climax of Milnes' friendship with Carlyle had been reached in the eighteen-forties, and in the next decade they did not see so much of each other, perhaps because Carlyle was too hard at work. 'Vita brevis—Ars Una—Ah me!' Carlyle concluded a note asking Milnes to come and ride with him one March day in 1857; other notes refusing to breakfast or to dine are filled with references to his own and his wife's health ('We are so weak and low here,—sunk in the

---

[1] Commonplace-book, 1855–1856.
[2] Letter from Mrs. Carlyle to Miss M. Smith, 11 January 1857.

valley of the shadow of *bile*') or with the terrible, oppressive, sense of
claustrophobia which Carlyle's work on Frederick gave him, when
he felt that his condition of mind would be 'broken' and 'bankrupt'
'till once the Prussian horrors are got through, if they ever be.'
At times he would ask Milnes' serious help, as when he wrote to him
in May 1853 to try to persuade Gladstone 'to take off that extremely
scrubby little tax on Foreign Books' which would be 'a perceptible
benefit to the one or two serious students still extant in this country,'
and at others he would amuse himself by passing off on Milnes
some tiresome transatlantic visitor such as Miss Delia Bacon, the
first exponent of the Baconian theory of the authorship of Shakespeare's plays, who had come to London with a letter to Carlyle
in 1853 and whom he regarded as a proof that the 'Era of Moon-
calves' had arrived.   'The sight of your face will be illumination to
everybody in these premises' he wrote to Milnes in October 1855,
and again, in August 1860, from Thurso Castle where he was
staying with old Sir George Sinclair:

Are not you a shocking fellow, never to ask once this year whether I
was alive or dead, or whether the Devils had left me in a dog's
likeness or a man's:—for shame! However, you can do nothing to
provoke me utterly; and I must love R.M. actually more or less,
as I do no other, or hardly one, however he may behave.

In contrast to most of those which Milnes was constantly receiving, the Carlyles' invitations were almost deliberately homely,
providing the sort of change that Milnes enjoyed:

The Missus goes out generally in the best of the sunshine, that is,
about 2 o'clock, or perhaps you are not sure of her after 1.   Any day
between 2 and 3 (just going out for exercise at 3), you will find the
unfortunate literary man upstairs here.   Finally almost every
evening we are safe here,—tea at seven,—and nothing going on but
a little reading or the like.

They would ask Milnes to dine at the unfashionable hour of half-
past five or six o'clock, and if he drove unexpectedly up to the door
in Cheyne Row he was invariably welcome.   As a friend of long
standing, who had observed the Carlyle household from within for
close on thirty years, Milnes' views on that marriage, and in
particular on Jane's feelings about Lady Ashburton, should bear
some weight with posterity.   When Froude's books came out in the
early 'eighties, Lord Houghton wrote to Henry Bright that he himself thought the Carlyles 'were about as happy together as married
people of strong characters and temperaments usually are,' and to

one of his own daughters he wrote that Mrs. Carlyle had never been jealous 'in the vulgar sense of the word,' 'was really very fond of Lady Ashburton' and 'strongly enjoyed being at the Grange, though perhaps *froissée* by the indifferent formality and the fine ladies, whom Carlyle rather liked and admired.' He must have been quite aware of the neurotic elements in both the Carlyles' temperaments, but since he knew Lady Ashburton as intimately as he knew Mrs. Carlyle (and he was genuinely attached to each of them) Milnes was in a better position than Froude (who had only papers to go on) to judge the case, and to realise that the tension was not all on one side. Lady Ashburton affected the company of literary men. Those who clustered round her were contemptuously called her 'printers' by the other fine ladies, and this habit of friendship with people who were not only serious but in her eyes middle-class imposed an irking restraint upon Lady Ashburton: for though the public conversation at her table was always decorous, 'Lady Harriet' was as outspoken in *tête-à-tête* as her predecessors of the Regency or the great ladies who came after her in the 'eighties, and 'nineties and in the Edwardian era.

My Printers, as they call them—it has now become a sort of Order of the Garter—wouldn't one of them stand the sort of gross conversation that goes on in our class both with men and women [she pointed out to Milnes].[1] Fancy my saying to one of their wives what Lady Sidney said to me of Lady Melden—'she popped two chicks before she married'—or imagine my talking on such a subject at all to Venables as I talk to Byng.

'Poodle' Byng, the petted, middle-aged, curly-haired *homme de société*, acted as both confidante and butt for Lady Ashburton. 'I suppose one would die on the spot, if one knew all that is said of one behind one's back; it is bad enough to be told by Mr. Byng of the horrors that he tells me people say of me,' she once remarked to Mr. Byng's sharp embarrassment; and one day when he was speaking 'of his devotion to the sex' she cut him short with: 'The most dreadful thing against women is the character of men who praise them.' 'I should like the restoration of Polygamy very much,' Lady Ashburton announced another day. 'And for one wife to stay at home every evening, and receive, while I went out, or stayed, as I liked.' 'Wouldn't you like to be one of the *other* wives?' Milnes asked George Byng.[1]

---

[1] Commonplace-book 1855–1856.

IV

In 1845, before fame enveloped Tennyson, Carlyle had urged Milnes to try to obtain the grant of a Civil List Pension to the poet. Two years earlier Landor had turned to Milnes for aid in getting a similar pension for Southey's widow: 'Pray, my dear Milnes, exert your great and noble faculties on behalf of a man whose principles and pursuits were the same as yours.' Tennyson's candidature had been successful, that of Mrs. Southey had not; but the point to stress is the assumption of serious persons like Carlyle and Landor that Milnes, neither rich nor politically powerful, was nevertheless in a position to bring decisive influence to bear. In 1848 Jane Carlyle told Emerson of Milnes' remarkable generosity with his money 'rare among people of fashion,' and of his willing aid to 'young people of merit.' Mrs. Carlyle was thinking perhaps of Coventry Patmore, whose marriage and indeed survival had been made possible by Monckton Milnes: 'There is only one thing which makes me discontented' wrote Patmore to him in 1851, giving an account of his small but firm prosperity, 'and that is, that I do not think you well know how happy and really well-off I am, mainly through your goodness.' Florence Nightingale, who adored Milnes' 'genius of friendship in philanthropy,' remembered that he had once said to her: 'If there is any good in me, it is that I would lay out my life in good service to others.' Miss Nightingale most admired his work for Juvenile Reformatories and other schemes well within the scope of her own sympathies. Although these activities were admirable, and sometimes useful as well, it was Milnes' imaginative attitude to unlucky writers that was unusual in his age. He would not have appreciated a letter he received from Lord Stanley in November 1866: 'As a rule, authors in these days ought not to want pensions. The public pays those that are good for anything—and those that are not deserve no payments.'

All public men (and Monckton Milnes was now irretrievably inside this category) receive begging letters—asking for money, for advice, for aid, for pensions and for jobs. Literary figures fare even worse, for these are the recipients of innumerable packages of manuscript—novels, plays, poems and above all short stories—sent them, with covering notes, by aspirants to their profession. The Houghton Papers contain a remarkable quantity of both kinds of missives, for Milnes was a political as well as a literary man. Far stranger, the boxes yield up a nearly equal number of fervent letters of thanks. Milnes, so lackadaisical in many ways, so fickle a correspondent to distant friends, took impressive trouble to help people he did not even know, and in this direction he acted always with astounding energy. His Yorkshire blood gave great force to a personality that had at one time seemed in danger of becoming merely febrile. It made him unexpectedly reliable.

To-day the job-hunting letters written by our Victorian ancestors seem blatant and even gross. The spectacle of Charles Kingsley intriguing for a vacant Canonry at Westminster in 1856 (when, writing to Milnes for a word to Palmerston, he reminded him of 'the work which my wife's family have done for the Whigs these fifty years')[1] is distasteful, and to know that Kingsley's behaviour was typical of that epoch makes it seem little better. Yet, in common justice, we must not overlook the realities of life in mid-Victorian England. The whole edifice of public affairs rested upon a scaffolding of Patronage which seemed neither odd nor wrong to the majority of those whose lives were passed within it. Acquaintance-ship (and, still more useful, family connection) with some public man was the only way of gaining a foothold, and, often enough, of earning an honest livelihood. While not entirely disregarded, merit was in some ways a secondary consideration.

Dear Milnes [Carlyle excitedly wrote in March of 1854], I wish you would tell me something definite about that grand Proposal of manning the Civil Service by persons chosen according to their merit? . . . Certainly there never was in my time such a 'reform' set on foot as this same might be; a thing worth all other 'reforms' put together.

The foreign, civil and colonial services, commissions in the armed forces, livings and preferments in the Church of England were all controlled in terms of private contacts. The results were often excellent, but the principle was only slightly more defensible than the open forms of bribery habitual to the bourgeois governments of contemporary France.

Monckton Milnes did his ordinary share of pushing forward his friends and relatives—the career of Sir Charles MacCarthy in Ceylon, or of his own verbose cousin George Mathew, a consul in the United States, being fair examples. 'I am likely to see the Duke of Newcastle soon, and will not forget your suggestion. I have already spoken of you to him more than once,' is a characteristic phrase from a letter to the former; while of Mathew he wrote crossly in 1853: 'George Mathew is here, moving heaven and earth to get promotion. If all my thirty cousins had given me the

---

[1] Letter of 11 June 1856 quoted in full in Una Pope-Hennessy's *Canon Charles Kingsley: A Biography* (Chatto & Windus 1948). Kingsley was not awarded this Canonry.

trouble he has, I should have left Parliament long ago.' Of more interest to us is the very wide variety of literary persons whose first thought in any difficulty was to write to Monckton Milnes for help. These ranged from James Anthony Froude, who asked Milnes to intercede for him with Lord Palmerston for the Professorship of Modern History at Oxford in 1857, to Camilla Toulmin[1] who pathetically begged him to support her application for a Civil List Pension; from sad, pale-seeming youths like shadows, cherishing hopes that never flowered (a John Baldwin Fosbroke, for instance, who bombarded Milnes with German mythological poems and long idolatrous letters from Saffron Walden) to smug popular writers like Miss Agnes Strickland, who wrote in her own inimitably unctuous vein on behalf of her old friend, the poet and journalist Alaric Watts. 'I hope that to a brother poet, and patron of literature and the fine arts I shall not plead in vain,' read the letter headed 'Reydon Hall, near Wangford, Suffolk' and with the proud words 'The Historian of the Queens of England' scrawled beneath the signature: 'I should be so very happy if I could interest so accomplished and influential a person as yourself in his favour; for then I think he would have every hope of obtaining the appointment.' The appointment was that of Librarian at the London Library, an institution Milnes had helped to found and continued to work for till the year of his death. Watts was a ghost from the minor literary salons of the eighteen-twenties, when he had been kind to the youthful Strickland sisters at their cousin's house in Bedford Square, and had been celebrated in the famous fatuous couplet:

> Alaric A, Weaver of 'New Years Gifts,' ingenious Watts,
> Of 'Souvenirs,' 'Albums' and 'Forget-me-nots.'

In the year before this London Library application, Watts had published the first edition of his practical compendium *Men of the Time*, a kind of international 'Who's Who' of 'Eminent Living Characters.'[2] This edition had caused a sensation by reason of the inordinate length of Watts' account of his own importance and career, and by a surprising passage on Bishop Wilberforce, described as 'a sceptic as it regards religious revelation, he is, nevertheless, an out-and-out believer in spirit movements.' Milnes, who was

[1] Camilla Toulmin, afterwards Mrs. Newton Crosland (1812–1895) was the author of various novels but is memorable for her charming reminiscences, *Landmarks of a Literary Life* (Sampson Low 1893), one of the most interesting and unaffected books of its kind, containing a brilliant eye-witness account of life at Gore House.

[2] *Men of the Time. Biographical Sketches of Eminent Living Characters* (David Bogue, Fleet Street 1856) contains a supplement of *Women of the Time*.

written down in *Men of the Time* as a Wordsworthian poet, a Moderate Conservative, and a 'warm advocate of liberty of conscience' had a copy of it bound for his library, writing on the title-page 'First edition, with singular character of the. Bishop of Oxford.' The page on Wilberforce, which seems moderately funny to us now, must have delighted Monckton Milnes and his friends, for it is savagely thumbed and brown with reference. Looking at this stout little volume one gets a sudden vision of Milnes laughing as he holds it out to some lady after a breakfast-party, on a sunny day in the London season when the nearby park is sparkling with fine carriages, and morning is just turning into afternoon. There was a delicious leisure (or, as Gladstone called it, a sense of dissipation) about Milnes' morning entertainments: 'I like breakfasts,' Ruskin wrote accepting an invitation to one in Upper Brook Street in the early 'sixties: 'It is nice to begin the day idly—as if one never expected any end to it. I should like always to breakfast on lotus—and make tea of Lethe—very hot.'

One person whom Milnes had never managed to persuade to breakfast with him during her short visits to the capital was Charlotte Brontë; but with Mrs. Gaskell's connivance he did apparently succeed in getting the Reverend Arthur Nicholls' stipend so increased that he was able to be married to Miss Brontë. Monckton Milnes had been an early enthusiast for the Brontës' work. In 1847 he had read their poems aloud to the Nightingales; later he had pumped the whole tale of Bramwell's decline out of Mrs. Gaskell, noting this, and a few striking phrases from Charlotte's writings—'a woman with cairngorm eyes' for instance—down in his commonplace-book, together with a comment of hers on *Jane Eyre:* 'a mermaid of a book, all the third volume is a tail.' In the case of the Brontës, Milnes' interest, first aroused by that 'affinity to genius' which Froude so much admired, was augmented by the fact that they were Yorkshire people. Unable to accept an invitation from Thackeray to meet Miss Brontë on her first journey to London in 1849, Milnes had gone up and introduced himself to her at a lecture of Thackeray's two years later. There, a shy little person in a bonnet lined with pink silk, she had had to endure the ordeal of being stared at through the lorgnettes of the fine people who crowded Willis's Rooms, and who later formed an 'avenue of eager and admiring faces' down which she had to pass to leave the lecture hall. Although he had not got her to Pall Mall, Milnes was determined that Miss Brontë should come to stay at Fryston. In this he was equally unsuccessful. In January 1852 W. E. Forster wrote to him from his house near Leeds that both he and Miss Martineau knew that 'there is no use in our trying to get her away from her father . . . she will not, I expect can not, leave him.' Undaunted, Milnes proceeded to ask both father and daughter to stay : again he drew a blank.

Were I in the habit of going from home [wrote the Reverend Patrick Brontë], there are few persons, to whom I would give the preference over yourself,—such not being the case, you will permit me to retain my customary rule, unbroken, and kindly accept my excuse. My daughter . . . begs me to express the pleasure she felt, at meeting you in London,—as well as her gratitude for the present attention.

According to Wemyss Reid, the comparative poverty and 'loneliness amid her fame' of Charlotte Brontë had touched Milnes keenly. He had put up to Mrs. Gaskell the familiar solution of a state pension. Mrs. Gaskell replied that she thought her friend would not accept a pension, but that one hundred pounds a year given to Mr. Nicholls

as acknowledgement of his merits as a good and faithful clergyman, would give her ten times the pleasure that £200 a year would do if bestowed upon her in her capacity as a writer . . . Her father's only reason for his violent and virulent opposition is Mr. Nicholls' utter want of money or friends to help him to any professional advancement.

What Milnes did for Mr. Nicholls is not clear, but since it made possible his union with Miss Brontë this was one intervention we should perhaps regret.

In seeking to achieve a truly balanced picture of Milnes' life we should envisage him as constantly engaged in a series of well-meaning and even arduous actions in aid of literature. They were as integral to his daily life as his attendance at the House or his parties in Upper Brook Street. They were also, in some cases, of lasting use.

V

It had always been Prince Albert's intention that the Great Exhibition of 1851 should serve as prototype for other similar displays in after years. The first of these, held at Dublin in 1853, was opened by the Queen at the end of August. This second royal visit of the reign was made the occasion for gay festivities in Dublin ; many English persons not connected with the Court flocked over to Kingston in the same week as the Queen, Prince Albert and the little princes, taking the opportunity offered by the Exhibition of

Irish Industries to pass a week or two in the great country houses of the Anglo-Irish aristocracy. One of these persons was Richard Monckton Milnes, who embarked at Bangor on the Welsh coast, leaving his wife, who was not well, in her cousin's care at Chester. Milnes thought the Dublin Exhibition superior to that at the Crystal Palace, since it was 'all comprehensible at one glance' and, being smaller, was less indistinct and confused. He stayed in Phœnix Park, as the guest of his friend Sir John Young, the new Chief Secretary appointed by Lord Aberdeen in 1852, later known as an unsuccessful Lord High Commissioner in the Ionian Islands, and a Governor-General of Canada, raised to the peerage as Lord Lisgard. The crossing was notoriously stormy, and the Molesworths, who were also expected in Phœnix Park, affronted the Youngs by prudently going to Cornwall instead; while some of the other guests remained prostrate in their Dublin hotel rooms and could not be persuaded to move, so that Milnes found at the Youngs' only Sir John, his wife, his wife's mother, and this lady's second husband, the squinting Marquess of Headfort. A day or two after his arrival he moved over to Viceregal Lodge at the invitation of the Viceroy, Lord St. Germans, and his accomplished wife.[1] Here he found a houseful of guests awaiting the Queen, including a fortunate child, 'the little Cornwallis heiress,' whose income, at the age of nine, was already twenty-five thousand a year. 'More worldly parents,' wrote Milnes, 'would, I suppose, have been contrasting her with what our Amy might have been, but I didn't.' Milnes, we may remember, had violent views upon the Irish question, and had been shocked by the widespread blarney with which Queen Victoria was welcomed to Dublin on her initial visit in 1847 after the famine. He had called it 'utterly unworthy of a free, not to say ill-used, nation.' This time he accompanied the Youngs to Kingston to welcome the royal party, returning in the same train as the Queen and following her round the Exhibition, where the little princes trotted about hand in hand. A million people watched Victoria enter Dublin, without noisy demonstration but with what Milnes termed 'eager satisfaction and earnest interest.' 'The magical little Queen' had had the luck generally attributed to her of bringing good weather, for before her arrival

[1] Lady Jemima Cornwallis, who had married the future Lord St. Germans in 1824, is an example of the high standard of erudition attained by some (though by no means all) of the 'fine ladies' of her day. *Fragments of Writings on Various Subjects* by Jemima, Countess of St Germans was printed and privately distributed to her friends in 1858 after her death. The notes she made on books read 1848–1853 are illuminating—*Dombey*: 'The story is trash'; *Vanity Fair*: 'Very clever, very true . . . not desirable for young people'; Balzac: 'If a true picture of Paris life shows how corrupted it is,' etc. Such were the literary judgements of the fine people.

the city of Dublin had been swathed in mist and rain. 'H.M. looked rather cross than otherwise,' Milnes told his wife, 'except when she was speaking to Mr. Dargan, the author of the Exhibition, when she broke into one of those benignant smiles, that gain so much from the preceding sullenness.'[1] In the Queen's journal she records her special pleasure at the simple manners of a Mr. Dargan, a public benefactor who had paid for the whole Exhibition building and refused a baronetcy she wished to bestow upon him.

'Encumbered with proffered hospitality,' Milnes soon left the 'regal puppet-shows' of Dublin for a round of country visits. Sending his wife the drawing of a collapsible garden chair which he had purchased for her at the Exhibition, he addressed his next letter to her from the Duke of Leinster's, at Carton, Maynooth. This 'kind, hospitable house,' reached between the 'gleaming hillsides' and through the 'verdurous lanes' of Wicklow, stood near enough to the college of Maynooth for Milnes to drive over to see that institution once more. In spite of the vociferous hostility of his Pontefract constituents, he had supported Peel's Maynooth Grant in 1845, and now he wanted to see how the money devoted to extending the college had been spent. He found the place much altered for the better: 'the students looking so much cleaner & more academic than they did, & the new buildings' (he added, in evident ignorance of the fact that Pugin had withdrawn his designs) 'in Pugin's best & simplest style.'[2] Building seemed, indeed, to be going on all over Ireland, though not much of it was for objects as elevated as those of Maynooth. At Kilruddery, near Bray, Milnes discovered that his host and hostess, Lord and Lady Meath, were making huge alterations to their house, which, lying on low ground not far from the windy heights of Bray Head, was surrounded by groves of ancient ilexes and 'yews planted before the flood,' with two big straight ponds which made 'the place look damp . . . but are characteristic and handsome.' Regardless of conditions in the country, only slightly improved since the famine-years, the Meaths were 'spending largely' in 'beautifying' their house—though not all of their embellishments can properly have deserved the name: 'They have put up 1000£'s worth of coloured glass—historical & genealogical, not good enough as works of art & too good for transparencies.' At Muckross Abbey, Killarney, Milnes saw yet another

---

[1] The limitations under which an official Victorian biographer laboured are, incidentally, exemplified by my predecessor, Sir Thomas Wemyss Reid's, transcript of this letter in his first volume, where 'rather cross' becomes 'rather tired' and 'sullen' becomes 'sombre.'

[2] The sum of £30,000 originally settled as the Government contribution to the building having been suddenly reduced to £18,000 Pugin declared that he could not continue as architect to the College. See Ferrey's *Recollections of A. N. Pugin* (1861), and M. Trappes-Lomax: *Pugin, A Medieval Victorian* (Sheed & Ward 1933).

example of that encrusted and romantic style of architecture which the Irish land-owners, inspired like those of England and Scotland with the grandiose, feudal ideas of Pugin and of Barry, were imposing on that haunted countryside. At Muckross, where he had the Blantyres and the Kildares as fellow-guests, Milnes stayed in the new house which his friends the Herberts had begun to build just before the famine came, and which in consequence remained half-finished and half-furnished, though comfortable. They had carefully chosen the most beautiful site for their house, but it was at the same time the most exposed one, and Mrs. Herbert's 'sadly poor health' prevented her enjoying the splendours of Killarney—the colouring and the changing lights and shades which Milnes adored. 'It is only Italian beauty that you can have the full satisfaction of, without moving from your sofa or your carriage,' he wrote to Annabel in a note scribbled one sunny afternoon while the phaeton waited at the door to pick up Mrs. Herbert with her drawing-board and himself with his book. 'She likes to sit in the sun like a lizard,' he explained, 'and shivers at the faintest shade.'

From Killarney, Milnes journeyed by the wayward Irish railroads (which reminded him of German ones) towards Parsonstown to see the giant telescope and to visit the Rosses at Birr. The third Earl of Rosse, 'a philosopher, a patriot and a philanthropist,' had cast his telescope—fifty-eight feet long and seven in diameter—and the great specula which it contained, with purely local labour in the eighteen-forties. He had now been making his important observations from it for nearly nine years. To Milnes' disappointment the nights were not dark enough for observation during his stay at Birr Castle, and he had to content himself with walking down the interior of the telescope and looking at the craters on the moon. Lord Rosse tried to console him by saying that there were only forty nights a year suitable for observation, and that these sometimes fell three or four consecutively—'I once had six, which was very tiring.' His astronomer host gave him much miscellaneous information of a scientific and medical kind, snatches of which Milnes aimlessly jotted in his day-book—'Influenza is a mild form of typhus,' or 'Malachite is nothing more than the petrified stalactite of flint and copper.' Lady Rosse, an amiable Yorkshirewoman, begged him to return to Parsonstown 'some more advantageous lunation.' After a short stay at Bessborough, where he was oppressed by memories of his 'good old friend' the fourth Earl, now dead, and displeased by the 'finery and folly' of the new Lady Bessborough, Milnes returned to Phœnix Park and crossed the Irish Sea to find his wife waiting for him with her maid at an hotel in Bangor.

It was now October 1853, one of the final months of the long, happy peace forged at the Congress of Vienna. In this pacific climate, Monckton Milnes and other men of his generation had grown up, and had in due course stepped forward to fill the ranks, thinned by age and death, of the famous men who flourished in the period of the Prince Regent and the Napoleonic Wars. In the winter of 1853, the British public, muzzy with war-fever, raised their outcry against the Court, and particularly against Prince Albert, whom they supposed to be standing between themselves and the carnage they desired. Milnes wrote to his wife at this time that the Queen though 'not actually hooted' had been 'received coldly enough' at the opening of Parliament: 'The last popular legend is "that the young man with whom the Queen has been keeping company all this time is not Prince Albert at all, but the younger brother of the Emperor of Roossia."' 'That incompetent Claren-don,' he had written from Parsonstown, 'seems to be sliding us into a war without honour.' In February 1854, with bands playing and drummer-boys strutting, the Coldstream Guards (shortly to be followed by the Grenadiers and the Scots Fusiliers) marched through delirious crowds in Trafalgar Square on the way to the coast. Reflective persons did not share the passion of the London mob: 'This morning we went to see the Guards inspected by Albert in front of the Barracks,' Annabel Milnes told her sister. 'It was a mournful sight, thinking how soon they are to depart—so many perhaps never to return! Among the officers too, so many leaving Mothers & Sisters behind! Harry Greville must be in the very thick of it.'

Before March was over, just as the greenish snowdrops were sprinkling the broad shadowy grass-rides of the Fryston woods, and as nurse Oliver was wheeling Amy Milnes (wearing her round white hat with a pale blue ostrich feather over her golden curls) in her novel child-carriage, the 'perambulator,' through the sharp sunlight of Kensington Gardens, England and France declared themselves at war with Russia. 'People still cling to the notion,' wrote Amy's mother, 'of its not being a *long* or *general* war.'

Chapter Five

1854   1856

I

'If there is a war, how are you going to get to Düsseldorf?' Mrs.
Milnes had written to Henriett Crewe, whose failing eyesight made
her wish to consult an eminent oculist in that Rhenish town.   This
artless enquiry suggests the kind of misconception and hazy uncertainty then prevalent regarding the size and probable *locale* of a
war known to posterity by the limited, ominous title: *The War in
the Crimea.*   In Lord Aberdeen's coalition Cabinet the war party,
led impulsively by Palmerston, were bent on extending the scope of
the war as far as possible, and on involving in it as many of the
Great Powers of Europe as might be.   A war designed to protect
Turkey against the Emperor of Russia became magnified in their
minds into a crusade against Russian influence everywhere.   The
peace-loving members of the Cabinet, headed by Lord Aberdeen—
whose fine pacific speeches Mr. Pemberton Milnes dismissed as
'womanly'—and by William Gladstone, found themselves slowly
manœuvred into war through a set of divers forces which, combined,
proved irresistible: the determination of the French Emperor, the
headstrong policy of Palmerston, the jingoism of the English public
and (possibly most potent of all) the deliberate prevarications of
the English ambassador to the Porte, who carried out the Ministry's
instructions to the letter only.   Unable to recall Lord Stratford de
Redcliffe, since this would involve Palmerston's resignation, the
break-up of the Cabinet and the consequent dissolving of the last
mist-like hopes of peace, Aberdeen faced a dilemma that was in-
soluble, and ended, as end it must, in an ultimatum and in war.

These grave events, in which his old friend Gladstone and his
patron Palmerston were playing leading parts, were naturally unaffected by any little verbal contributions in the House of Commons
from Richard Monckton Milnes.   He was clear-sighted enough to
dislike the Crimean War, its motives, its management, its course and
its results: 'There does not seem to have been a single branch of the
service which has been sufficient for the purpose,' he wrote to Delane
in November 1854, 'neither the force, nor the arming, nor the

71

provisioning, nor the doctoring, nor the housing; but all this may be incidental to any war undertaken by a nation of shopkeepers, while the miserable casualties consequent on Lord Lucan's & Sir J. Cathcart's inconsiderate courage & on Lord Raglan's neglect of material precautions, demonstrate that what we most want is Men. I remember Thiers talking of the chances of any contest in which England might come to be engaged, & saying "what are the odds that you will produce a single *General*, when all our revolutionary & imperial wars did not bring out half a dozen."' 'We are going to close a discreditable war by an inglorious peace: we shall have 10 p.c. income tax & o p.c. benefit to mankind,' he wrote early in 1856. In his comments on the Crimean War we find again Milnes' special value to posterity, as a witness undeceived by the illusions of his contemporaries. Sufficiently sharp to judge events without preconceptions, warm, compassionate and volatile in his attitude to life, Milnes was at the same time intimately acquainted with all that was going on in governing circles, and assimilated as much political and London gossip (much of it surprisingly accurate) as the most practised wordling. Writing to his wife almost daily when separated from her he would send frequent snippets of information about the war, though he pretended to be dubious of her interest in it: 'I am glad Omar Pasha had a fine day yesterday for crossing the Danube,' he wrote from Drayton in October '53, 'but you probably thought more of Amicia's going out upon Liquorice.'

It is not untrue to say that the chief effect of the Crimean War in English politics was to assure the triumph and long supremacy of Palmerston. 'Lady P. writes "Every event in which P. is concerned ends in his standing higher than before"—There's a nice deluded wyfee for you,' Milnes wrote after the ten-day resignation of Lord Palmerston from Aberdeen's cabinet in December 1853: 'all is forgiven & forgotten, & they are both in capital spirits,' he wrote later, from Broadlands. The scandals of the first Crimean winter, followed by Roebuck's notice of a motion for a committee of enquiry into the conduct of the war, and the immediate and cowardly resignation of Lord John Russell, lofted Lord Palmerston into the Premiership; there was great rejoicing at Broadlands and at Cambridge House:—'The Première is as happy as Amy with a new toy: she really may rejoice in thinking how fairly & honestly he has won the prize,' Milnes reported after a visit to Lady Palmerston. 'Lady P. told me to-day that the Duchess of Cambridge was quite pleased with Mr. Layard's not being in the Government: that is what the aristocracy call "public opinion,"' he wrote more sensibly a few days afterwards. As John Morley remarks, tenure of the supreme power by Lord Palmerston, so long distrusted by the Court, and already more than seventy years old, might normally have been expected to last a twelvemonth: in fact, with one short interval, he reigned Prime Minister for the next ten years. During this period his followers looked to him to give them places, and many were well rewarded for their past support. The developments of 1855 thus held for Monckton Milnes a double interest— the interest of a distasteful war on the one hand, and the revival of hope for his own career set once more throbbing in his head. But in February 1855 'after a large amount of palaver about his difficulties &c. &c.' Palmerston asked Milnes to 'join him' at the Treasury. 'This euphemism of course had no success, and though he pressed it much, was civilly declined,' Milnes told his father. The offer of a junior Lordship of the Treasury to a man of Milnes' experience and position was no compliment; its acceptance would have made him feel, as well as look, absurd. And so, Milnes' thoughts began to wander in a fresh direction. He had once asked Peel to make his father a baronet. Could he not drop hints to Lord or Lady Palmerston that Robert Pemberton Milnes should be a peer?

Needless to say old Mr. Milnes disagreed with his son on the subject of the war. 'No nation has flourished without it,' he wrote. '. . . It has shown we have become as women in forty years. Don't believe it engenders bad passions—it appealing to the noblest.' He added that, statistically, the rate of births in England exceeded the rate of deaths in battle ten times over, and that the country was saving annually the sum the war was costing. 'War goes on famously,' he wrote in another missive, '. . . and I would have it go on—wars are serviceable, as thunderstorms are—there would be no breathing at Crewe Hall between Manchester & the Potteries, but for them.' He compared the war feeling in 1854 with that in 1815, when (so he declared) no one had felt 'nervous' about the outcome of the battle of Waterloo; and he enjoyed brooding over 'a pet project' for defeating Russia by setting fire 'to the Steppe.' But he showed good sense by his lack of confidence in 'Lord Fitzroy Somerset,' better known as Lord Raglan: 'he, the kindest, calmest, most gentlemanly of men, but in my estimate no more fitted to fight against Suwarrow, than I am.' When the appalling mismanagement of the war gradually dawned on England, Mr. Milnes changed his tone about Lord Fitzroy: 'Mr. Milnes says the only promotion he would give Ld Raglan would be that of Admiral Byng!' his daughter-in-law reported.

The first summer of the war, when the Allied troops were encamped at Varna, on the pestilence-infested seaboard of Bulgaria, was balmy and enjoyable in England: 'of the old-fashioned nature of August,' Mrs. Milnes wrote to her sister from a little hired house, Rock Cottage, which she had taken at Tunbridge Wells. There was a glorious harvest, the days were cloudless, the nights so dry and starlit that she stayed out driving in her carriage till nine o'clock; the only catastrophe of these months was a fire when her father-in-law was staying at the cottage, caused by his bed-curtains catching alight whilst he was reading in bed. In the autumn she and her husband went north to stay with William Stirling at Keir. There, in perfect autumn weather, with the yellow leaves along the walks still thick upon the branches, 'a soft fruity bloom on the hills,' and sudden sunlifts lighting the distant mountains, they heard the first news of the battle of the Alma, presented by the communiqués as an outstanding victory for Allied arms. 'War continues—Battles of Balaklava—Sebastopol—Allies victorious but great losses,' Mrs. Milnes further noted in her pocket-book. And as the autumn changed to winter, the mood of the country changed from excitement at Allied victories to anxiety, followed by fury, at English losses and defeats. The reports of Russell, *The Times* correspondent, contradicting the anodyne despatches of Lord Raglan, and describing the verminous conditions of the hospitals and boats in which young Englishmen were rotting alive, staggered the public: and neither the idealistic vision of those romantic artists sent out to draw battle-scenes for the *Illustrated London News*, nor the private letters from officers in the Crimea, praising the cheerful way in which 'the men' endured amputation, septicæmia and death, placated desperate families at home. At this phase of the war any fragment of authentic information from the battle-front became of passionate interest. The newspapers were filled with letters 'from a Dragoon,' 'from a Connaught Ranger,' 'from a gallant hussar,' 'from a corporal in the Crimea': whole columns were headed 'The Blue-Jackets at Therapia' or 'A Sussex letter from the East.' Persons in railway-carriage compartments pulled letters from a nephew before Sebastopol out of their breast pockets and handed them to strangers. Acquaintances at country-house tea-parties volunteered to one another evidence that *The Times* was, or, as the case might be, was not exaggerating Crimean conditions: 'A Miss Goodenough told me her brother wrote exactly in the sense of the Times & said the men did not die at all of disease as is put in the papers, but of sheer exhaustion & misery,' wrote Richard Milnes from his cousins' house at Thornes.

The implications of the Crimean War, during which the whole system of aristocratic government in England was for the first time in history exposed to nation-wide criticism, were more evident to a foreigner like Hawthorne (who noted that the war 'has given this country a vast impulse towards democracy') than to Englishmen themselves. While the aristocracy were responsible for the miserable chaos which reigned in the Crimea—where, as a modern writer on the subject has astutely noted, the French army was commanded by officers, the English army by gentlemen—the territorial families of England lost a proportion of their young men from disease and wounds. 'Poor Ld. F. Gower,' wrote Milnes, of the Duke of Sutherland's son who died a lingering death on one of the hospital ships, 'a sad transition indeed from the green velvet of Stafford House, to the wretched transport where he lay dying for 20 days, without any one, who even knew his name, near him.' In some ways the psychological effects of the war were even greater than its political ones: for though it is tempting for us to over-stress the sense of security of early Victorian England—any bundle of family letters shows that 'early Victorians' were almost as harassed by money or servant troubles as ourselves—the war of 1854–1856 brought back the phenomenon of sudden and promiscuous death into a country unfamiliar with it for forty years. In Richard Milnes' youth and early middle age sudden death seemed as unlikely as it is unnatural: the death of Arthur Hallam in 1833, of Charles Buller in 1848, or of Lord Jocelyn who expired of the cholera on Lady Palmerston's sofa in twelve hours, were events to wonder at as well as mourn. But the war in the Crimea brought the fear of bereavement into many English homes, whether in Manchester or in Carlton House Terrace, in the Five Towns or in Berkeley Square. This war altered the psychological climate of England, perhaps for ever.

II

There was one conspicuous feature of the Crimean War which proved at first bewildering to ordinary English people. This was the sudden fact of the French alliance. The rise of Louis Napoleon and his restoration of the Empire had been the signal for widespread panic in this country; the panic had manifested itself in numerous ways, but most noticeably in the development of the volunteer movement in which Monckton Milnes, like other men of his class and station, had tried to take an active part. In 1852 Englishmen had been openly discussing the chances of a French invasion, and now, but two years later, they found themselves closely allied to their potential enemy and fighting shoulder to shoulder with the successor of Napoleon the First. Nor did the French find the alliance easy to stomach. Shrewd observers noticed that during France's rapturous welcome of the English royal family when Queen Victoria paid her state visit to the Emperor and Empress in August 1855 the Parisians yelled 'vive la Reine!' but never 'vive l'Angleterre!'[1]

Although much balderdash about Anglo-French amity was printed in the newspapers, the second summer of the Crimean War witnessed a step forward in the everyday relations of English and French people, for with the *Exposition Universelle* of 1855, and the royal visit a new habit of cross-channel travel set in, and a new phenomenon, the English middle-class tourist on excursion, appeared in France. The Exposition, in some ways finer than its prototypes, the Great Exhibition of '51 or the Dublin Exhibition of '53, had architectural stalls upholstered in red velvet and was dominated by a seven-foot reproduction of the Parthenon Minerva in ivory, with a gold tunic, bronze helmet, and sapphire eyes. To accommodate the swarms of English and provincial visitors who came to gape at the Minerva, new noisy restaurants and cheap hotels sprang up. Cards with the words '*English Spoken Here*' were fixed for the first time in Paris shop-windows. English residents in Paris considered that this invasion of the ignorant middle-classes was leading to the vulgarisation of Parisian café life. Earlier in the century English visitors to Paris had all been educated persons of the upper class, who spoke French fluently, stayed, as Milnes had always done, at the Meurice or at the Bristol, and dined, when they ate in public, at superb fastidious restaurants like the Café de Paris with its thick carpets, wood-fires and lamps, where the word '*addition*' was unknown, and where the kitchens were so far away you did not believe that they existed at all. At the Café de Paris, or at the older establishments with sanded floors like Vèry's or the Café Anglais, you had to be known to the proprietor to get a table; across the river in the Quartier Latin were the students' and artists' places of rendezvous where no foreigner ever went, or wished to go. The Paris of Milnes' youth was still a city of winding medieval streets, few bridges and some great eighteenth-century squares. Modern Paris, the creation of Haussmann and Napoleon III, had only been conceived when the Crimean War began. 'Il détruit comme Attila pour construire comme Aladdin,' remarked Guizot to Milnes when discussing the Emperor's architectural projects, in Paris in 1855— for Milnes of course went over to see the Universal Exhibition and

---

[1] See, for an admirable account of this and other events in Second Empire Paris: *An Englishman in Paris: (Notes and Recollections)* published anonymously by Chapman and Hall in two volumes in 1892. The book went through four editions in two months.

to attend the ball at Versailles for Queen Victoria and watch the great military review. But before this visit he had taken his wife to Paris for Easter 1854. Arriving there in mid-April, a few days after the declaration of the war with Russia, they spent a happy fortnight investigating the changed atmosphere of the French capital under Napoleon the Third.

> I shall be glad [wrote Mr. Pemberton Milnes to them at the Hôtel Meurice] to hear from you the impressions of the new Paris Anglo-mania, & of their Czar & Czarina—The time of your going was ill-chosen for a better acquaintance with Their Majesties. Events of such magnitude on hand & Chiefs to entertain, they cd give little thought to obscurer guests.

Paris was warm that April. The chestnuts and the lilacs were in bloom, the carriages in the streets were already open. Driving in the Champs Elysées the day after their arrival, the Milneses encountered the Emperor and his suite; in the first carriage Napoleon III and the young Empress, married just fourteen months, in the second the Duke of Cambridge, cousin of the Queen and youngest of the generals commanding the expeditionary force. This glimpse of the gleaming cortège of the imperial couple gave Milnes food for reflection upon human destiny. He had known the Emperor in London in the old days, when the young exile had seemed to many people merely a seedy and absurd hanger-on of Lady Blessington and Count d'Orsay, and to some (such as Disraeli who had met Louis Napoleon at Milnes' own breakfast table) a madman. Milnes had also known the Empress in her less exalted days, for when he had been in Madrid in '47 he had been taken to the house of her mother, Prosper Mérimée's friend Madame de Montijo, and there he had been struck by the beauty of Eugenia. Milnes and his wife were not long in Paris before they received a summons to a small, 'brilliant and formal' party at the Tuileries, where they were presented to the Empress and conversed with both of 'them.' On leaving the palace that night they drove off to spend the remainder of the evening at the house of the arch-enemy of the regime, Adolphe Thiers. Next day two shiny pale-blue invitation cards stamped with eagles and emanating from the office of the Grand Chambellan, the Duc de Bassano, were delivered at the Hôtel Meurice, bidding Mr. and Mrs. Monckton Milnes to attend a ball at the Tuileries. Milnes eagerly accepted, but his wife declared herself 'headachy' and would not go.

Apart from these imperial civilities, the Milneses spent their time gaily and freely in Paris—going to the theatre to see *La Vie en Rose* and *Le Pendu*, driving out to St Germain, dining with Thackeray at the Café de Paris, eating ices at Tortoni's, and visiting Richard Milnes' old friends. Mrs. Milnes enjoyed herself thoroughly, finding the red wine and coffee a welcome change from the porter and cocoa which English doctors at that time forced young mothers to consume in quantity. She was taken to the Lamartines in the Rue de l'Université, and thought him very agreeable and 'not so melo-dramatic' as she had expected; she also dined with Richard at the Embassy, and with Duvergier de Hauranne, and attended soirées at such houses as those of the Imperialist deputy Comte Hervé de Kergorlay and the Marquis and Marquise de Boissy. She met the Guizot family, Prosper Mérimée (much to the fore under the new regime), and Alfred de Vigny. Vigny (who was one of the few Parisian friends of Richard not 'frondeur'—i.e. opposed to the Empire) came to the hotel one morning after luncheon and stayed more than an hour defending the coup d'état. After two weeks in Paris the weather, which turned cold and dark, drove the Milneses back to London. Their last evening was spent at Monsieur Guizot's, in the company of Montalembert, more Catholic and reactionary than ever, whom Milnes had known now more than twenty years, and of Monsieur de Villemain, perpetual secretary of the Académie Française.

On Milnes' second war-time visit to Paris he went alone. His wife, who was expecting a child, remained in Cheshire, while Milnes set off in July 1855 to see the Paris Exhibition, to spend a month at Vichy doing the cure, and to return to Paris for the closing days of Queen Victoria's stay in that capital.

Richard Milnes' taste in pictures and in *objets d'art* was of his time. At the Exposition Universelle he immensely admired the gold and ivory Minerva, which his French friends ridiculed, and the tiles of Minton. Great preparations were already under way for the reception of the English royalty; Milnes heard that all the furniture at St. Cloud was being altered to bear the English arms, and the words *Victoria Regina*. He was told that the fête given at Versailles was to be 'incredible—it will all make the little woman think it is a poor matter to be a constitutional Queen.' The problem of the hour was whether the Emperor should go himself to welcome the Queen at Boulogne (as in fact he did), or send a deputy: Lord Cowley, the British Ambassador, declared he ought to go himself, while the new Minister for Foreign Affairs, Comte Walewski, thought it sufficient to send Prince Napoleon. 'I dine with the Walewskis on Monday,' Milnes wrote to his wife, '& by that time this awful question will perhaps be arranged.' He also dined, and slept the night, at the house outside Paris of Walewski's predecessor, Drouyn de Lhuys, who had fallen from grace two months before.

The fallen Minister was, as usual in such cases, much more communicative & interesting than if he had been in power: he evidently thinks that the continuance of the war will be the ruin of the Emperor & the cause of much evil to France.

Milnes found Guizot in a similar state of mind, and both he and Madame de Lieven were delighted to find how closely Milnes' pacific views agreed with theirs. The alliance, which had now lasted more than a year, had bred the customary discontents between the allies; Milnes was amazed to find the French accusing the British of conducting the war with 'unnecessary cruelty,' and to be informed that British sailors were burning 'helpless villages' and slaughtering women and children on the shores of the Baltic. The Emperor and the Empress had left Paris for the sea, so Milnes pretended he felt safe since he could not be 'exposed to be corrupted by any of the Court civilities' which had 'completely subdued' Lady Ashburton. Paris was sweltering, and after a few days there he and his manservant took the train for Vichy, a resort to which Milnes had never been.

Milnes' first experience of Spa life had been at Marienbad in 1850; he now found Vichy 'handier, pleasanter and sociabler' than any of the German watering-places, and from 1855 on he made almost annual visits to this town in which, thirty years later, he died. His sister had kept urging him to try the waters at Harrogate in which she had great faith: 'I believe it is an excellent place,' he remarked, 'but we shall never go to it—it is so near one's home.' His weeks at Vichy made a breathing-space in Milnes' busy life. He found time to read a new book a day and to write letters, as well as to drink hot water and to gossip with English acquaintances like 'Poodle' Byng and Albany Fonblanque who had also come to Vichy to try to neutralise the bad effects of heavy mid-Victorian London food. In spite of close weather broken but not cooled by constant thunderstorms, Milnes took such a fancy to Vichy that he imagined his family returning there year after year—'Amicia can flirt with the Zouave officers & you keep up your French, while I am keeping off the gout in coming years,' he wrote to his wife. Mrs. Milnes had been reading Tennyson's new poem *Maud* aloud to her friends the Tolletts, a family who lived at Betley Hall near Crewe.

I have not got 'Maud' [her husband replied in a letter from Vichy], & only heard it that morning in his own fine under-song, but it did not make on me the impression of *raising* Tennyson: I don't indeed know why we should expect a great writer to be always rising, but somehow it is so. I did not read the 'Idyll,' which Alfred's own friends think the prime of the volume. I am afraid that if I ever *really* become a public man, we shall have to give up our present *independent* &, I may say, contemplative London life & not have time for talk of books & men, as we have now!

At Vichy Milnes heard detailed reports of what a fiasco or as he termed it 'a melancholy failure,' the Queen's entry into Paris on the eighteenth of August had been. The length of the journey from Osborne to Boulogne had been misjudged, the yacht *Victoria and Albert* had arrived late, and by the time the royal party reached Paris it was twilight: they could see nobody and nobody could see them.

It would have been better if she had come *later* [Milnes told his wife], for then the Boulevards would have been lit up . . . There must have been above a *million* of people thoroughly disappointed: the gay dresses & the beautiful flowers all invisible: the French say 'elle est entrée comme une chauve-souris'; it will take much to change this bad impression.

But the Parisians soon forgave the flitter-mouse entry, and the royal visit passed off in a blaze of popular enthusiasm. It was a shimmering Cinderella treat for Queen Victoria, who succumbed to the Emperor's practised charm and adored every moment of this magic holiday. 'The Queen looks very happy, but no amount of pleasure can make her pretty,' Milnes, who had hurried up from Vichy for Paris, reported to his wife. Monckton Milnes had always loved spectacles—the carnivals at Rome, the Eglinton Tournament, the Queen's entry into Dublin—and this series of Parisian fêtes for the Queen of England was the finest which had been staged in Europe in his adult lifetime. He attended the great ball at Versailles (where Windsor Castle was represented in *feux d'artifice*), went to several of the dinners, and to the military review, where he caused comment by 'riding with the staff' dressed in his Yorkshire militia uniform. 'It is to be hoped that our Richard will have the legitimate *entrée* into the kingdom of Heaven,' remarked Vernon Smith on this occasion, 'but if not, he will certainly hustle St. Peter and get a good place in spite of him.' Though much amused by the proceedings, Milnes was not dazzled, and when he wrote that the fête at Versailles was 'as grand as a festival could be, with no women of distinguished appearance & no men, except two novel-writers, one had ever heard of before,' he had laid his finger upon the essential weakness of the imperial court in these early days, when the Tuileries receptions were still boycotted by the great families of France, and the leading statesmen put up a dour opposition to the new reign. Nor was he over-impressed by the military display put on for the Queen's benefit.   He suspected that it must have made Victoria 'think there were still French soldiers enough left to continue the war as long as she pleased.'

In March 1856, Milnes made a third journey to Paris, to watch the celebration of the signature of peace and of the coincident christening of the Prince Imperial.   On this occasion he stayed a short time only, and though he saw his usual friends—Tocqueville, Guizot, Mignet, Montalembert, George Sand and the Breton Rio (the latter old, ruined and crippled, but still 'the liveliest creature I have seen in France')—talked to some of the Crimean generals and called on Rosa Bonheur in her studio, most of each day was spent inspecting juvenile prisons and comparing the French and English systems for the correction of young criminals.   He did not again visit France till the summer of '57, when he joined the Galways at the fashionable new resort of Trouville on the Channel coast: 'a curious-looking place, like a sea-place on the stage, all the houses run up for the occasion & let at fabulous prices.'   They went expeditions in small carriages along the coast to Honfleur, and Harriette Galway bathed in 'trousers & a bloomer petticoat to her knees.'   From Trouville he went on to the old abbey of Val Richer near Lisieux, which Guizot had bought and rebuilt, and in which he had settled to spend the remaining years of his life, writing in peaceful retirement in the midst of his de Witt grandchildren.   Milnes liked the thickly wooded country round Lisieux, and he enjoyed talking to Guizot who was 'in great force & full of political & literary gossip.'   The small de Witts, of whom there were four under nine years old in the house, seemed to Milnes more talkative and precocious than English children of like age.   They came to eat dessert in the dining-room at the end of meals, and one of them stoutly remarked to him: 'Je n'aime pas le lait, mais j'aime le rhum.'   'If Amicia dines at your luncheon, let her learn to cut up her own meat,' Milnes wrote to his wife from Val Richer.

III

Although Milnes loved to tease his wife about her doting attitude to 'the sweet Amice,' and though he accused his aunts of making 'a cult' of the child, his own parental affections were unfolding as Amy grew.   'Amicia,' he wrote to MacCarthy in February 1856, 'is getting companionable and amusing; a large, light-hearted, cherubic-looking child, excitable and intelligent, wilful and yet sensible.'   He began to take her for walks, wrote her short letters in block capitals, and arranged for her to be taught his '*Lady Moon, Lady Moon*' and the fables of La Fontaine.   He was forever

comparing with her the children he saw in his friends' country
houses; in one house he would find a prodigy 'just Amy's age, who
said all the rivers of Russia after dinner & got seven figs' and in
another he was shown an infant under two who, when asked 'Es-tu
sage?' replied 'Oui, comme une image' in a faultless French accent.
Amicia's imagination developed very early. Her father was
worried to discover that she invented songs and stories for herself:

I told Miss M. about Amy's song [he wrote from Miss Martineau's
house at Ambleside], & she said some of the most fanciful children
she had ever known had become the most truthful men & women—
which is consoling, but she spoke strongly on the importance of
making her understand that she *thought* these things & did not see or
hear them.

In appearance Amicia was a pretty Pre-Raphaelite child, with long
gold curls and most engaging ways; her grandfather declared that
he 'never before saw anything at once so hilarious & so graceful.'
It was an age in which small children were still becomingly dressed:
'in her distinguée new Pelisse & feathered Chapeau she really
looks like a juvenile Lady Aylesbury,' wrote her great-aunt Caroline
in 1854. Mrs. Monckton Milnes' letters are filled with descriptions
of the little girl—learning to spell with an ivory alphabet on the
drawing-room carpet in Upper Brook Street, riding about the
Bawtry paddock on her pony, taking her favourite doll 'Roberty'
to salute the Emperor and Empress as they passed in procession
on their visit to London in 1855, or being held aloft on the stalwart
shoulder of Tom the young footman above the swirling crowds of
Euston Square railway station. Her parents did their best to
give Amy a reasonable as well as a happy childhood, and there
were many secret comments on the foolish, spoiling way in which
Lord and Lady Galway were bringing up their little son Georgie,
who was allowed to run wild all day in the Serlby gardens, cheek
his French governess and over-eat until he gave himself diarrhoea.
The Milneses were naturally anxious themselves to have a son, but
Mrs. Milnes was not strong. In spite of the attentions of Dr.
Holland, and of Dr. Locock the celebrated accoucheur whom the
Emperor was said to have told that the Prince Imperial must be
born on the birthday of the Roi de Rome ('Il le *faut*, monsieur
le médecin' Milnes heard that he had said), a boy was born dead.
But in December 1855, when the orange fogs of Victorian London
were shrouding the streets, and you needed candles to read by at
mid-day, Mrs. Milnes gave birth to a second daughter. Had it
been a son, Lady Ashburton had promised to stand godparent;
as it was, the child was christened Florence in honour of the heroine

of the hour whom Milnes had tried so hard to marry six years
before. After her final refusal to accept Richard Monckton Milnes
in 1849,[1] Florence Nightingale had gone to the East to forget him.
In the autumn of 1854 he heard suddenly that she was going to the
East again.

IV

'The D. of Newcastle writes to Richee that *Florence* has organised
a band of Nurses & is going directly to look after the wounded &
sick': Annabel Milnes sent this astonishing piece of news to Henriett
Crewe in October 1854. Monckton Milnes had long sympathised
with Miss Nightingale's efforts to be of use in her generation, but
he had not thought her position as head of the new charitable
nursing-home for sick governesses in Harley Street 'very suitable.'
He still went sometimes to stay with the Nightingale parents and
their other daughter Parthe at Lea Hurst; he found they talked
quite easily of Florence, but were puzzled by her: 'we are a duck's
nest that has hatched a wild swan,' her sister had said to him
in December 1853. No one then needed friends or sympathisers
more than Florence Nightingale, for her high aims exposed her both
to criticism and to ridicule.

I hear you are going to the East [Milnes wrote to her in a farewell
note]. I am happy it is so, for the good you will do there, and the
hope that you may find some satisfaction in it yourself. I cannot
forget how you went to the East once before, and here I am writing
quietly to you about what you are going to do now. You can
undertake *that*, when you could not undertake me. God bless you,
dear Friend, wherever you go.[2]

Milnes played an influential part in the organisation of the Nightingale Fund to send supplies to the hospitals at Scutari, and when he

[1] An instructive side-light on Miss Nightingale's weakness for Milnes is provided
in her 'private notes' for March 1851, now first published in Mrs. Woodham-
Smith's biography, *Florence Nightingale 1820–1910* (Constable 1950). From these
it is clear that although she had consistently refused Milnes' offers of marriage
over a period of nine years, she was displeased to find that he regarded her refusal
as final. Meeting him unexpectedly at Lady Palmerston's that Spring, Miss
Nightingale was hurt to see that he treated her as an ordinary friend: 'The
noise of this room is like a cotton-mill,' she said lightly to her, and when she saw
him again on 16 March she found that 'he would hardly speak . . . I was miserable'
(she continues) ' . . . I wanted to find him longing to keep open another decision.
. . . He did not show indifference but avoidance.' This incident occurred two
months before Milnes' engagement to Miss Crewe.
[2] Letter quoted anonymously in Sir Edward Cook's *The Life of Florence Nightingale* (Macmillan 1913), vol. i, and, as from Milnes, by Mrs. Woodham-Smith,
op. cit. p. 147.

wrote *A Monument for Scutari*[1] in the autumn of 1855 he devoted a stanza to Florence Nightingale's work.

A Monument for Scutari created a sensation when it was published in *The Times* in the September that marked the close of the Crimean fighting. The argument of the poem was that Scutari, till then a subject for romantic verse, had changed its character and would forever symbolise the horrors and the suffering of the war:

> Now other passion rules the soul;
> And Scutari's familiar name
> Arouses thoughts beyond controul,
> A tangled web of pride and shame;
> No more shall that fair word recall
> The Moslem and his Asian rest,
> But the dear brothers of us all
> Rent from their mother's bleeding breast.
>
> Calmly our warriors moulder there,
> Uncoffined, in the sandy soil,
> Once festered in the sultry glare,
> Or wasted in the wintry toil.
> No verdure on those graves is seen,
> No shade obstructs the garish day;
> The tender dews to keep them green
> Are wept, alas! too far away.

There were eleven stanzas, all equally sentimental but equally popular: 'Nothing could be more welcome than the beautiful lines with which you embellish our otherwise dreary columns,' wrote John Delane, the brilliant and powerful editor of *The Times* with whom Milnes and other Members of Parliament took care to stand well:

They will shine with the more lustre from among the gloomy record of 'battle murder & sudden death' which is now our staple commodity . . . Actually, as I write the news comes of our second failure at the Redan & the French success at the Malakhoff. We shall lose as much character by the victories of our allies as by the resistance of our enemies.

Milnes was always liable to spasms of conceit, followed by periods of self-analysis and gloom; the tendency towards self-satisfaction had perhaps been increased by the companionship of an adoring wife. He asked Mrs. Milnes to send copies of *Scutari* to all their friends and some of their acquaintances, amongst these latter being

---

[1] *A Monument for Scutari* was written in the same metre, and began with the same verse, as Milnes' *The Greek at Constantinople* published in his *Palm Leaves* (1844).

Lady John Russell, who was living at Pembroke Lodge in Richmond Park. Lady John seems to have sent an insipid or inadequate note of thanks.

I wouldnt have sent my lines to that fool Lady John, if I thought she would have dared to call them 'pretty' [Milnes wrote pettishly]. it has put me out of humour for the whole day: a pretty husband she has got & a pretty mess he has made of it: I wish you would write this to her.

When the French victories and English defeats had been resolved into a peace which glorified France, spared Russia and humiliated England, Milnes published a somewhat pretentious sonnet (containing the strikingly unmelodious line 'O blessed Peace! if peace were peace indeed!') to the newspapers. Once more he scored a distinct success:

Oh blessed Peace if Peace were Peace indeed [wrote Parthe Nightingale excitedly from her parents' house]. Your sonnet is so beautiful that we cannot hold our tongues. It expressed what we are all feeling—deeply & sadly. F's last letter says she looks 'upon progress & civilisation as at an end in the East.'

Simpler, and more moving, are Milnes' lines *Crimean Invalid Soldiers Reaping at Aldershot*, of which the first of three verses runs:

> Reap ye the ripe, ripe corn,
> Ye have reap'd the green and the young,
> The fruits that were scarcely born,—
> The fibres that just were strung.

For some weeks the returning soldiers, many thousands of them lacking an arm or a leg, were much in evidence in England; but like all victims and reminders of war they were soon forgotten. Public attention was diverted by fresh events, most notable amongst these being the outburst of the Indian Mutiny.

V

In the first week of February 1856, Richard Monckton Milnes' own attention was sharply diverted from the final stages of the Crimean War by a matter for personal excitement which turned overnight into one for personal chagrin instead. This matter was the chance of a family peerage.

Milnes had prudently refused the minor post at the Treasury which Lord Palmerston had offered him when he had become Prime Minister the year before.

I sometimes fancy [he told his wife in a despondent letter], that the Destinies know very well that public life is not the thing for me & thus, in all little but effective ways, check any progress I might make in it : I begin to think they are right.

He recalled that Sydney Smith had once remarked to him : 'How few men are on the right rail !'—'and when,' Milnes added, 'you have continual collisions, you should perhaps infer that you are on the wrong one.' Recognising that he could never now play a significant part in the House of Commons—he was, according to Disraeli, 'the only man of whom it can be said that, beginning badly, every time he spoke worse'—Milnes' ambitions were now concentrated upon a seat in the House of Lords, which he affected to regard as 'the token of a half-success in life—a second-class in politics.' He told Disraeli about this time that he 'would sooner be an Under-Secretary of State than a Peer,' and when the latter reminded him unkindly as well as untruthfully that 'had he stuck to his party, he certainly might have been U.S. and probably something much higher,' Milnes (Disraeli's note alleges)

began to blubber, and say that he had always had a singular affection for me, and looked unutterable love in the highest style of comedy. I put him right [Disraeli continues] by some gossip, and after telling me two or three good stories, he went out of the room splitting with laughter.

In the same note, his memorandum on the genesis of certain characters in his novel *Tancred*,[1] Disraeli quotes Lady Palmerston as 'always' saying that 'the younger Milnes was too ridiculous to make a Peer, and that it could only have been managed by inheritance.' It was indeed a fact that, since Milnes' father was alive, the only decorous way in which a peerage could be introduced into the family was by giving one to the old man. Mr. Milnes senior was a determined Tory, while the party in power, the party which his son vociferously supported, was Whig; but a little detail of this sort bore no weight with Richard Milnes, who afterwards declared that if any 'real principle' had been involved he would have taken care that the offer had never been made. He had often hinted at, lately perhaps even demanded a peerage for his father : and so it came at length to pass, one winter's day early in 1856, that the Premier took Milnes aside in the House of Commons and told

[1] Disraeli's memorandum, already quoted in my *Years of Promise* pp. 99–100 was printed in part by Monypenny & Buckle in the third volume of *The Life of Benjamin Disraeli, Earl of Beaconsfield* (John Murray 1914). The authorities at Hughenden Manor have kindly supplied me with a complete transcript of the original note (*Disraeli Papers*, Box XVII, packet 12).

him that having 'kept in mind for many years' the 'desire for a peerage' which he had expressed he was 'now able to oblige' him. Lord Palmerston had already despatched a letter to the West Riding, informing Robert Pemberton Milnes of Her Majesty's intention to raise him to the House of Lords. Richard Monckton Milnes returned in ecstasy to Upper Brook Street; but at Fryston Hall a different and more thoughtful mood prevailed. On receiving Lord Palmerston's missive old Mr. Milnes sat quietly down at his desk in the Fryston library. Without consulting any member of his family, without a moment's hesitation, and by return of post, he sent the Prime Minister a note in which he courteously but quite deliberately declined to become a peer.

'There never was such blank astonishment!' Disraeli gleefully recorded: '. . . Dicky was in despair.' And indeed Monckton Milnes' consternation was tremendous, his disappointment resentful and severe. 'I find myself singularly dull in my appreciation of the conduct of other men—as in this instance of my Father,' he wrote: for to him the old man's scruples seemed preposterous. Disraeli, who could be spiteful as well as vulgar, attributed Mr. Milnes' refusal to a wish to 'mortify' his son; 'besides worrying his son,' he adds, 'old Milnes liked to be mentioned as a man who had refused a peerage.' Mr. Milnes had in fact no such motive or ambition: in refusing the honour he was merely behaving in a manner entirely consistent with his character and with his earlier career. In his extreme youth he had refused the office of Chancellor of the Exchequer, replying to his wife's expostulations with the simple words: 'With my temperament I should be dead in a year.' After this episode he had retired from public life, making one brief and brilliant re-appearance during the Corn Law agitation of 1846, as a supporter of Disraeli. When he received Lord Palmerston's letter offering the peerage, he had assumed that the Prime Minister had wanted his support in the Upper House; but this support he was not prepared to give. Being an old-fashioned man, he had supposed that the Prime Minister's confidential letter was in fact written in confidence. He declared that he had intended never to mention the subject to any living soul, least of all to his son. When he found that Palmerston had spoken to Richard before having received his own reply, Mr. Milnes was shocked. When Richard wrote and said that the proffered honour was a consolation prize for his own services and not a compliment to his father's merits, Mr. Milnes was indignant and also intolerably amused and sceptical. In a letter of glacial fury Richard Milnes told his father that the refusal was 'a blow at confidence': 'I feel the just disappointment which any man has a right to do when he sees his interests sacrificed to an untrue position and an unreal embarrassment.' Furthermore Monckton Milnes cherished the quaint conviction that a peerage in his family would influence his wealthy brother-in-law, Lord Crewe, to make the Milnes children his heirs. He felt from every point of view defrauded. Lord Palmerston was persuaded to send the old man another, and even more explicit letter.

Every hour's subsequent thought confirms me in the conclusion that mine was a right decision [Mr. Milnes answered]. I could not have entered the House of Lords, with that erectness which befits an English Gentleman—Anyhow my position there would have been equivocal.

'Dear Richd,' he wrote in answer to his son's letter:

In Paley's chapter on Happiness, he uses the very word you do—It is indispensable to it, to have, '*Occupation*.' But you use the word in a sense the opposite to that in which he or any moralist would. You write of '*Occupation*' as opposed to '*Usefulness* & *Honor*'—they would say, that both are comprehended in it. It would have been candider, had you defined that by 'Usefulness' you mean 'Office,' & by 'Honor' you mean a Peerage. As to the latter, you should have foreborne the expression, on recollecting that you had it not, because I deem'd it to be *dis*honorable—because in regard to myself, I considered it as being the same, as that of a slave in Cuba, who had serv'd under one Master, on being bought to serve under another master.

Many years before, in the little travel journal he had compiled in Italy in 1831, Mr. Milnes had made a profession of his faith in the country gentlemen of England—'an Order which no other sovereign but ours of England has, and which Kings and Princes have no conception of.' At this time he also recorded his earnest hope that no grandson of his should change this status for that of a newly ennobled peer.

For a few weeks the Milnes family were in a state of turmoil and suspense that bordered in some cases on hysteria. One of the Torquay aunts declared that the 'peerage question' had nearly 'been the death of her,' and even Harriette Galway remonstrated with her father far beyond her wont. Two persons in the family alone remained sane upon the subject—Lord Galway, who warmly supported his father-in-law's intransigent stand, and to whose 'foolish influence' Richard attributed half the trouble, and Annabel Milnes, who attached no importance whatever to names and titles, and was only 'disturbed' because this 'annoyance' had 'worried poor Richard considerably.' Richard and Harriette forced their father to come up to London, to attend a Levée, to see Lord

Palmerston and to consult Disraeli, to whom Richard, in his desperate quandary, had appealed. Nothing came of these 'negotiations': bullied by his family, Mr. Milnes endeavoured to come to terms with Palmerston, and to enter the House of Lords independent of party. But, irritated at being snubbed and contradicted, the Prime Minister had soon tired of the whole subject. He let the matter drop, spoke to Richard Monckton Milnes in a 'tone of evident annoyance' and treated him for some weeks with a marked coldness. When Palmerston's Ministry fell in February 1858 over the Orsini Conspiracy, a concerted effort was made by the family to get Derby's Tory Government to revive the offer to Mr. Milnes, who, though virtually dying, was then ready to take the title of 'Lord De Rhodes' or of 'Lord Austerfield.' 'The family,' writes Disraeli, 'including Lady Galway, who had every claim on the party, made strong appeal to me to put the matter right. . . But it was out of the question.' Disraeli adds that 'young Milnes' engaged that the borough of Pontefract as far as Fryston 'should be secured to the Tories.'

When contrasting the behaviour of father and son during this incident it is essential to see the thing in its correct perspective. 'In this lord-loving country, one ought not to decline anything that helps to make other people listen to one,' Monckton Milnes wrote to a friend on another occasion. Snobbery still odiously dominates much of the life of England, but whereas to-day the wish to become a peer would seem to most people a ludicrous and antiquarian ambition, it was not in 1855 held by any one at all to be either pathetic or absurd. Writing in 1890, Milnes' first biographer related this episode and Monckton Milnes' reactions to it with no suggestion of any call for an apologia; for at that period members of the nobility still wielded great power in England and could, had they so wished, have done great good. That deference to rank which gives us claustrophobia when reading Victorian recollections was so inherent in the air they breathed that few of our ancestors even questioned it. Milnes himself was a rare example of an intelligent man who was not deceived by the fine airs of the 'fine people': 'we never,' he had written in 1848, 'calculate among the democratic influences, as we should do, the effect of the stupidity and helplessness of our present aristocracy.' Yet even he was not averse to joining their ranks, and to benefiting by their privileges. In one of his letters to his father on the subject of the peerage he accused him of 'checking' the 'social advancement of (his) family' —a phrase which would mean little in modern England, but which in the epoch when it was written meant a very great deal. Some years before her death in 1847, Richard Milnes' own mother had

told him that he might have difficulty in finding a wife since
'no girl now-a-days likes to marry without the prospect of a title.'
Mrs. Pemberton Milnes was no snob.   She was a realist.

Milnes felt the peerage episode to be not merely a check, but in
some sense a checkmate:

I am strongly tempted to give up political life altogether & enjoy
home & art & literature & travel—What say you? [he told his
wife].   After this check-mate, is it not ridiculous to continue the
game?

His friends in London were laughing at his predicament behind his
back; to his face they merrily asked him whether he and his 'governor' were on speaking terms.   It is not an agreeable sensation to
know that your father has made you look, publicly, a fool.

Chapter Six

1857   1858

I

The Premier's coldness did not long endure. At the beginning of January 1857 Milnes and his wife were once more down at Broadlands, where Mrs. Milnes was as usual charmed by Lady Palmerston's old-fashioned manners. She was, in addition, astounded by the energy of the Prime Minister, then nearly seventy-three but quite equal to tramping all day through the rain with a gun, playing billiards with the young men half the night, or rushing up to London for an afternoon of work, returning to Broadlands to dine. The railway had made Lord Palmerston's family house easy of access from London and he and his wife entertained there regularly when Parliament was not in session. Broadlands, close to the abbey town of Romsey, from which it was divided by a long lichened wall, was a white pillared house, placid and modestly elegant, standing back from the swirling river that hurried between banks planted with low cedars and lofty chestnut trees.

The Milneses spent four days at Broadlands, attending service in the great Romanesque abbey of Romsey on Sunday morning, and on Monday driving a short distance along the Salisbury road to visit the Nightingale family at Embley, their pretentious neo-Jacobean mansion in orange brick commanding a long view over the Hampshire fields from its gravelled terrace, and having behind it a steep umbrageous garden, famous for the azaleas, camellia-trees and towering rhododendrons that give you the mysterious feeling of entering some Antillean forest. It was at Embley, in 1849, that Monckton Milnes had proposed to Florence Nightingale for the last time. She was not in the house this January, but the Milneses passed an agreeable day with her parents and her sister Parthe, and drove back in the early twilight to Broadlands, through the cold Hampshire countryside with its frozen water-meadows and thatched cottage roofs congealed with frost. Here they found the house-party returned from an afternoon in Southampton. Amongst the dozen or so people staying at Broadlands on this occasion were two friends of Milnes' Italian youth—Augustus Craven, the diplomat, whom he had known at Naples in 1832 and had described as the 'only fine man' he 'ever liked,' and his wife, a daughter of the Comte de la Ferronayes, and later celebrated as the author of the saccharine *Récit d'une Sœur*. Also at Broadlands, with two of her three young sons in tow, was one of the cleverest women of that age in England—Milnes' friend and warm admirer Lady William Russell.

Born in 1792, brought up on the Continent where her parents had been trapped by Bonaparte's edict after the peace of Amiens, Lady William Russell had been given an education unrivalled among the Englishwomen of her day. She spoke French, German and Italian faultlessly, read Latin and Greek, and had studied Sanskrit and Hebrew with success. As she grew up, Miss Rawdon's beauty, wit, scholarship and powers of conversation made their mark first in London and then in Paris. The Emperor Alexander declared her to be 'the most charming woman in London,' while even such difficult judges as Lord Byron and Madame de Staël joined in the general pæan of praise. The daughter of Captain Rawdon, a younger son of Lord Moira, she married in 1817 the brother of the Duke of Bedford, a general who became a diplomat and was sent *en poste* to Stuttgart and then as ambassador to Berlin. After her husband's death in 1846 she continued to travel, devoting herself to the upbringing of her three sons Hastings, Arthur and Odo Russell, each of whom she tended to dominate. In the year 1850 Lady William settled into a corner house in Audley Square. Here, until her death at the age of eighty-one twenty-five years later, she kept one of the last and choicest salons of Victorian London. Prominent amongst its habitués was Richard Monckton Milnes.

The house at number 2 Audley Square was neither large nor grand.[1] The front door was opened by an aged Italian man-servant who, though doddering, knew whom to admit and whom to refuse. He conducted you up to the first floor, where heavy folding doors opened into a dark, high drawing-room lined with bookcases and hung with gilt-framed family portraits. This room was 'somewhat scantily furnished' by mid-Victorian standards, being 'absolutely deficient in all the modern prettinesses of china and lace.' It had simple tables and many easy chairs, was lit by few and shaded lamps, and on cold or foggy winter evenings when the square echoed only to the rattle of a passing cab, a huge fire blazed in the hearth. The room was alive with books and cats. Books were scattered over the tables, were heaped on the chairs, stood on the floor in piles: yet Lady William was said to know

---

[1] This account of Lady William Russell (1792–1874) and her house is taken from the short *Memoir* of her written by Mrs. Harvey of Ickwellbury, privately printed by the Chiswick Press in 1876. Lady William is said to have been the 'Aurora' of Byron's *Beppo* (stanzas 83 and 84) 'whose bloom could after dancing dare the dawn.'

exactly where each volume was. The cats were equally ubiquitous: the biggest tabby lay comfortably on the hearth-rug, but kittens had been found picking their way along the mantelpiece, and one evening a guest suffocated a litter of them by sitting down suddenly in an easy chair. 'Come and eat Catsmeat in the Catacombs, unless a Cataclysm swallows up Lady Catesby,' the owner of the house, who was addicted to assonance and alliteration (as well as to all other verbal whimsicalities), wrote to Milnes. In this room Lady William Russell practised the genial art of conversation as she had learned it from the friends and contemporaries of Germaine de Staël in the best Parisian salons as a girl. Her conversational gift was an exceptional one, for she could listen as well as talk. She could deftly describe events in a way so 'sparkling' that her hearers felt that they were themselves witnessing the scenes of which she spoke.

Unfortunately Lady William kept no journal, and her letters are the only relics of her remarkable abilities that have survived. These letters were scrabbled down on apple-green writing-paper in thick, expressive black ink, and are scored with frantic underlinings and wild triple exclamation-marks. Those to Milnes date from the late 'fifties, the 'sixties and the early 'seventies; he seems not to have known her well before this time. They contain many French phrases and comical non-sequiturs. 'Le plus aimable des Beaux Esprits,' she called him, 'brightest of brilliant men,' 'Paragon Paradox,' 'Phœnix of friends.' 'On ne peut pas se passer de vous,' she scrawled in one note: and 'tell me you are sorry I am breaking up.' Though a cripple for the last years of her life (she had fallen, smashing her thigh, in Rome) Lady William never let her spirits flag: 'What universal joy any and every marriage gives in *this* Country,' she wrote in a long, fantastic letter about Julian Fane's lightning engagement,[1] 'It is quite Bacchanalian!' Lady William extended her affection for Milnes to include his wife—whom she referred to as 'la voix flûtée'—and his children, 'Pre-Raphaelite snowdrops and muguet.' Even before her accident, she stayed in no English houses but Broadlands and Woburn; when Monckton Milnes lured her to Fryston in September 1859 the prospect of entertaining this accomplished and imperious cosmopolitan alarmed his wife. The visit went off well, however. As Lady William, carrying a big posy of lavender, stepped into the carriage for

---

[1] Julian Fane (1827–1870), diplomatist, poet and translator of Heine, was one of Milnes' younger friends. In September 1866 he married Lady Adine Cowper, a daughter of the sixth Earl Cowper and (according to Lady William Russell) speechlessly shy. Lady Adine, who was twenty-three at the time of her marriage, died in her twenty-fifth year, a shock from which her husband, who survived her by only eighteen months, did not recover.

Knottingley station she assured her hostess that she had seen 'nothing so pleasant,' as Fryston, 'since the best days of Holland House.'

Lady William's eldest son succeeded his uncle as eighth Duke of Bedford; her youngest son became a successful diplomat and was made Lord Ampthill. The middle son, Arthur, did nothing very notable at all. Monckton Milnes, who liked youthful companions, had a fancy for Arthur—'your protégé, Arthur,' Lady William called him—and took him travelling in France in the summer of 1858, when they visited Tocqueville at his Norman château, and the exiled Victor Hugo in Guernsey. On this *giro* Arthur Russell proved somewhat disappointing: 'hardly the man to take a little tour with in which one desired to "*se distraire*,"' Milnes told his wife. 'He has all the repose of the Vere de Veres & a good deal of physical apathy besides.' There is nothing so disconcerting to lively middle-age as the quiet and over-serious young.

II

In the first week of March 1857, Palmerston's Ministry was defeated by a majority of sixteen on the issue of the Chinese war. In the General Election which followed (and which became a plebiscite for Palmerston, returned with a personal following of three-hundred and seventy members) it was at first suggested to Richard Monckton Milnes that he should stand for Manchester instead of Pontefract. The chances of success were uncertain, and he did not wish to take risks. It was a terrible March of sleet and snow; Milnes fought the election with a fever and a sore throat, while his wife canvassed the icy countryside in her carriage, the victim of piercing headaches from the cold. The voting at Pontefract was conducted along traditional lines, with huge drink bills at the local pubs and all that 'knocking-about' of the candidate by which old Mr. Milnes (who unexpectedly voted for his son) was 'excessively entertained,' and which the candidate himself would have given worlds to avoid.

Spare and feeble, with hardly twenty months to live, Mr. Milnes still continued to write his daughter-in-law long descriptive daily letters—of his re-reading of the odes of Horace, of comments on Goldsmith and on Johnson in the Hebrides, or telling her he had sent off hampers of geese and fowls, trout, sweetbreads or whatever fruit might be in season. His life was always a shade less reclusive than he planned it to be ('I intending not to have one biped to eat with me this spring and summer') and he secretly relished visits

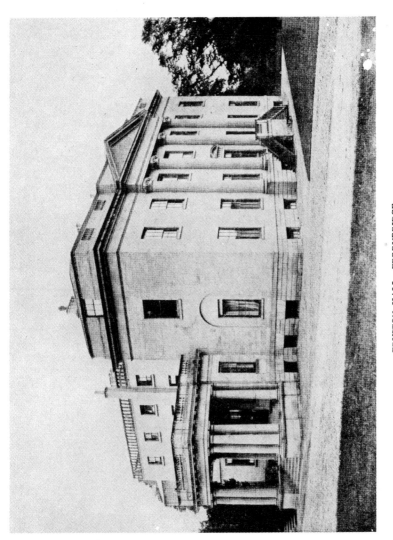

FRYSTON HALL, FERRYBRIDGE

from his own old friends.   He also still enjoyed his dabs at Richard, which he was as unable as ever to resist:

It was at that house at Boulogne [he wrote in a letter rummaging amongst memories of earlier days] that I had a letter from Cambridge, which I hoped was to inform me that Richd had got into the first class at Trinity—It was to inform me R. had just left Cambridge in a balloon.

'With all Richard's fancy for books, I have a notion I read as much as he does,' he wrote in another letter; and he would complain that Richard did not send him enough news, computing that a letter required only a quarter of an hour to compose, or 'one sixty-fourth' of the period which Mr. Milnes regarded as a normal working day. 'This is an age of the most intense selfishness,' he declared to his daughter-in-law. He was quick to point out that Richard's absence from the House during a vote on the Scots Education Bill, a measure on which the Government had been defeated in 1854, had made 'all his concern for "*Juveniles*" look very much a sham.' It did not make matters better that Richard had, on this occasion, absented himself from St. Stephen's in order to attend the French Embassy's fancy-dress ball. 'Am glad you sat through a debate,' old Mr. Milnes told Annabel in 1857, '. . . your husband seldom does.'

In the opening weeks of the new Parliament of 1857 the debates were in truth extremely dull and politics seemed stagnant. The Season, on the other hand, was of an intense brilliance, for the engagement of the Princess Royal to Prince William of Prussia was made the excuse for a series of entertainments so lustrous and frequent that they utterly exhausted Von Moltke and the Prince's German suite.   The Milneses attended several of these functions, gave some breakfasts and dinner-parties, and went to the theatre. Charles Kean's magnificent productions of Shakespeare were then in full swing at the Princess's Theatre, and though the grandeur of the decor was thought to extinguish rather than to enhance the acting, they were a great popular success.   In April Mrs. Milnes went to see Kean in *Richard II*, and throughout the summer she and her husband went to the various exhibitions—of water-colours, of the Royal Academy, of the Duke of Devonshire's jewels at Hancocks —being held in London at that time.   On 23 June, Sir John Simeon escorted her to the first Pre-Raphaelite exhibition, organised by Ford Madox Brown in Russell Place, where she gained ideas for her own assiduous amateur painting, now taking on a distinctly Pre-Raphaelite tinge.   As they drove back along the hot streets crowded with cabs and pedestrians, the carriage-horses slipped and

fell, injuring themselves so badly that they could not be used for a
week.   This happened to be the very day on which the country was
proudly celebrating the centenary of the Battle of Plassy, un-
perturbed by rumours of a small revolt in Bengal.

It was on Sunday the twenty-eighth, the hottest day for twenty
years, that the Milneses first heard 'terrible news from India'; but
it was some weeks before the governing classes, the newspapers and
the public grasped the full extent of those Indian disasters which had
started with a mutiny of some sepoys at Meerut on the tenth of May.
By August the whole of England stood aghast before the horrors of
the sack of Delhi and the Cawnpore massacre, and waited in grim
anxiety for news of the relief of the Residency at Lucknow.   Once
the facts of the situation in India were realised, the Government
(goaded by the Queen and the newly-titled 'Prince Consort')
despatched regiment after regiment to the East, while the newspapers vied in imaginary accounts of the massacres and in criticism
of the Governor-General, Lord Canning, and of the East India
Company's administration.   Each mail and telegraph brought
news of fresh disasters.   The reconquest of the rebel territory
moved at a snail's pace.   Delhi, sacked by the sepoys in May, was
not re-occupied until September.   As ships with widows, orphans
and other refugees reached England from Calcutta, grotesque
stories began to circulate.   Some ladies were rumoured to have
landed without arms, many without breasts, and several were reported to be so badly mutilated that they would have to spend the
remainder of their lives in masks.   None of these tales was authenti-
cated.   All were believed.   England became even more frenzied
and bloodthirsty than it had been in the early days of the Crimean
War:

Altogether [wrote Queen Victoria to her Uncle in September][1] the
whole is so much more distressing than the Crimea—where there
was *glory* and honourable warfare, and where the poor women and
children were safe . . . There is not a family hardly who is not in
sorrow and anxiety about their children, and in all ranks—India
being *the* place where every one was anxious to place a son.

III

Mr. Milnes wrote from Fryston:

Also tell R. to keep me inform'd of all he hears further, respecting
India.   There has been no event of late which has so impress'd me,
& I conjecture that great events are to arise out of it.   I will not

[1] *The Letters of Queen Victoria, First Series*, edited by A. C. Benson and Lord
Esher (John Murray 1907) vol. iii, p. 313.

believe [he added sagely], that that vast region is to remain permanently, or even for long, the property of a Merchant Company —this has, for years, been one of my reveries.

Mr. Milnes did in fact live to see the transfer of authority from the Company to the Crown, the most important result of the Mutiny, take place in August 1858.

Less historically-minded than his father, Richard Monckton Milnes viewed the Indian news in terms of personalities and blood-curdling anecdotes. He collected horrid specimens of these last for his current commonplace-book—noting down the instances of Miss Jennings (raped before her parents' eyes), of Mrs. Macdonald (murdered in front of her husband who was strapped to a tree), of 'Captain . . .' (castrated and blinded at Meerut), and of an anonymous lady dragged from her phaeton, covered with straw and set ablaze.

I have no very near relatives to regret in these late calamities [Milnes wrote almost wistfully to Sir Charles MacCarthy], but I have an image of a very pretty girl some four years ago singing and dancing in a large family connected with me, and who has died at Cawnpore, with two little children.

But if not actually connected with any of the victims of the Mutiny, Milnes was kept well posted about what was going on in India by correspondents such as Sir James Colvile, Chief Justice of Bengal, and Sir Charles MacCarthy, Colonial Secretary at Kandy. Neither a regular nor even a conscientious correspondent, Milnes had kept up intermittent contact with these two exiled friends of his earliest youth, and had cheerfully endured their numerous letters in return. His tolerance was suddenly paying dividends, for he was now equipped with first-hand information on the Mutiny with which to entertain guests at his own breakfast-table (the American George Ticknor, who thought the mutiny had taken place at Bombay, found India the all-absorbing topic one July morning at 16 Upper Brook Street) or in the country-houses which he visited.

The practice of relying on private letters to supplement newspaper information, widespread in the Crimean years, was again general during the Mutiny. At Bowood Milnes was shown a letter to Lord Lansdowne's daughter-in-law from Lady Canning, 'evidently inclined to diminish the horrors, and make the best of the thing, which I have no doubt is the tone that infuriates the Calcutta people': an oddly unfair comment on that moving series of journal-letters which poor Lady Canning sat courageously writing in the suffocating heat of Government House, Calcutta, or the cooler, danker drawing-room of the Governor-General's country residence at Barrackpore, and which form the finest section of Augustus Hare's *Story of Two Noble Lives*. Milnes was slightly acquainted with Lady Canning; he gave a letter for her, as well as for Sir James Colvile [1] and Sir Arthur Buller, to a young military protégé of his own, named A. W. Twyford, who reached Bengal on a crowded troopship in March 1858. This young officer, who declared that he felt for Milnes the gratitude of a son, was attached to the 7th Hussars on reaching Calcutta, and immediately sent up-country. He deserves to be remembered for the extraordinary vivacity of his letters which, headlong in style, give a far more convincing picture of the later stages of the Mutiny than those of Milnes' more knowledgeable official friends, for Twyford's letters form an excellent example of that peculiarly English gift for letter-writing, sincere, and instinct with life itself. He was evidently an intelligent, sentimental, altogether typical young man of his epoch: he shed tears over the 'miserable little ditch' in which Wheeler had held out in Cawnpore, he picked up a young lady's embroidered collar on the site of the massacre, he examined the pathetic inscriptions on the walls of the hospital, made a pilgrimage to the well into which the murdered women and children had been hurled, and sat with satisfaction below the gallows which General Havelock had erected for emergencies nearby. Wounded by an 'ugly sword-cut' above the elbow in a fight in which he captured and 'strung up' six sepoys, Twyford admitted to Milnes that a 'fearful desire for blood for blood' rose in him as he contemplated the ruins of Cawnpore and the streets of Lucknow which stank of putrefying bodies and animal decay. Throughout the European communities of India and Ceylon terror over the Mutiny had now in the natural course of human nature given way to extravagant demands for vengeance: 'I am afraid we shall have a counter-chapter of horrors of our own enactment, or perpetration,' Sir Charles MacCarthy wrote to Richard Milnes from Ceylon. 'The cry for blood, which is, I fancy, louder even here than in England, sickens me.'

---

[1] Sir James Colvile (1810–1880), a Fifeshire Scot and grandson of the first Lord Auckland, was one of Milnes' most intimate friends at Trinity and had travelled with him in the Pyrenees in '29. Called to the bar in 1835, his Indian connection led to his appointment as Advocate-General in Calcutta and then as Chief Justice of the Supreme Court in Bengal. These Indian dignities did not improve him: from a teasing jocular youth he turned, in the steaming commercial world of the Victorian empire, into a pompous elderly man, boring Milnes by writing long sententious comments on 'stale' English news. When he returned to England with his very young wife in 1859 he was stand-offish with his old friend: 'It is rather odd,' wrote Milnes, 'that a man should ask you to write to him in India for some 16 years, and never come near you when he is in England.'

While receiving the letters of Colvile, Twyford and Sir Charles MacCarthy, Milnes was himself laboriously composing for the *Quarterly* an article entitled 'The Siege of Lucknow.' 'It will be purely personal, without politics or criticism of public events,' he told MacCarthy. In collecting facts for his article, which took the form of a survey of the many 'personal narratives' of the siege which had begun to flood the London booksellers, Milnes received some aid from the widowed Lady Havelock, an hysterical lady whom he had once met at Heidelberg. In tone this article is emotional and bombastic. In execution it is neither brilliant nor neat. Altogether it compared badly with another paper in the same issue of the *Quarterly*, 'Fictions of Bohemia,' a lucid exposition of the *Vie de Bohème* as idealised by Murger and by Champfleury. This article was also written by Richard Monckton Milnes, who was invariably better at literary criticism than at commentaries on current public events. The fact that a single number of the *Quarterly* contained two anonymous articles by his son proved irresistible to Mr. Milnes' sense of the comic: 'The Press writes favorably of "Bohemia,"' he scribbled gleefully from Fryston, 'it makes no mention of "Lucknow"—May it be, that Lucknow is known to have been by you?—the other, not known?'

Save for providing an exciting new topic for conversation for a few weeks, the Indian Mutiny had but a transitory effect on the daily life of the English upper classes. By the close of 1857 it was already becoming a subject for jest: 'Mrs. Dudley Carleton,' wrote Milnes from Erle Stoke, where he was spending Christmas, 'is so idle and apathetic that one feels a short residence at Lucknow under the late circumstances would have been a very good thing for her.'

Life in the country houses, so much more deeply rooted, so much more indestructible and real than the fashionable kaleidoscope of life in the metropolis, went on as smoothly and as happily as ever. Moving from house to house, Milnes sent his wife daily letters of gossip or of instruction; would she send to Chappells for copies of Tennyson's *Swallow, swallow* and *The Brook* which he proposed to sing in the evenings; would she hire a suitable pianoforte for the season; would she see that Tom was measured for a smart new dress livery with 'bright blue inexpressibles.' Mrs. Milnes remained peacefully in London, for she was again expecting a child.

In October 1857 Monckton Milnes was at Ashridge, a large house in a park with vistas down long grassy glades filled with deer, belonging to Lady Marion Alford, the accomplished amateur painter and writer, a considerable patron of artists and a daughter of Milnes' old friend Lord Northampton. At Ashridge that autumn a party of forty were assembled to receive the Princess Mary of Cambridge, by far the largest of the royal persons of that era, and irreverently called by old Mr. Milnes (who had sat near her at a theatre and said that he had not been able to sleep after it) 'that mountain of a girl.' To entertain this amiable but out-size royalty Lady Marion had commissioned Stafford O'Brien, now called Augustus Stafford, to write and produce an *extravaganza*, *Hearts and Tarts*. Princess Mary played the Queen of Hearts, the Duke of Manchester the King, while Lord Clarendon, then Foreign Secretary, acted as stage manager. The younger guests formed the chorus. Milnes, who was only a spectator, thought the whole thing went off well, and sent his wife the elegantly printed programme of the entertainment. There is something both gay and terribly nostalgic about such mementos of those high Victorian gatherings, in which people seem to have enjoyed themselves with a gusto and simplicity unknown to-day. According to this programme the chief chorus, by the Queen of Hearts and her ladies, was sung to the old tune *Nelly Bly:*

> Parasols
> Parasols
> On a sunny day,
> > Are so small
> > As not at all
> To intercept a ray.
> Ah! what with lace and fringe of such a size
> > They perhaps,
> > Act as traps
> To catch the summer flies.

We can almost hear the finale, chanted by the whole company to the lilting strains of the *Olga Waltz*:

> So pull out the plums that are pleasing,
> Forget all the stuff that is teasing,
> And pardon us now we are ceasing,
> For ours is humble pie.

But life is never what it seems, and has a way of ending suddenly. Augustus Stafford, much beloved for his Irish glitter, his high spirits, graceful manners, and that talent for improvising amusements which made him far too welcome to the languid owners of great houses, had been Milnes' bosom friend at Cambridge, and the object of the most intense affection of his youth. They had remained on terms of intermittent friendship ever since, though, watching Stafford's career, Milnes recognised in him an instability or flimsiness of character not apparent at Cambridge: 'Mr. Manager Stafford is in great force, with not only a Princess in his "troupe," but the President of the Council, a live Duke, & any number of inferior peers, & above all, Miss Treherne as Prima Donna,' he wrote from Ashridge that October. Within a month Augustus Stafford lay dead in an hotel bedroom in Dublin, the victim of heart disease and an overdose of laudanum.

IV

Stafford was not the only intimate friend whom Milnes had lost in the year of the Mutiny. On 4 May, in the season of *les marroniers en fleur*, Harriet, Lady Ashburton had died of dropsy in Paris, while being dressed by her maid. She had been ill for some months at a villa in Nice. Unbelievable rumours that her condition was really dangerous had percolated through to her London friends. Lord Ashburton, who rightly thought the Riviera a 'nerves-exciting climate' had sent optimistic bulletins on her health to Richard Milnes, begging him to write any piece of gossip 'true or untrue' which would provide his wife with 'food for rumination, better than aches and qualms.' Lady Ashburton had shown a stoical composure during her illness, and when at last told that she had dropsy she tried to joke about it in her old off-hand manner: 'You see I have been crying,' she said to someone, 'but tears must be good for—for—for the dropsy.' Her death occurred when least expected, and at a moment when her husband, relying on the positive assurances of the best physicians, had come over to London for a few days to arrange for her return to Bath House.

On the day that the news of Lady Ashburton's death reached London, Milnes hastened down to Chelsea to bring it to her greatest admirer, Thomas Carlyle. Carlyle was out. Mrs. Carlyle, who was in, broke down, and implored Milnes to wait, as she dreaded herself to tell her husband of this death.

God bless you for your kindness [she wrote to Milnes early next morning], I shall not forget your waiting there, that weary long time, to spare me the pain of telling him. It was indeed a cruel moment you so spared me. I am ashamed you should have seen me so wanting in composure and courage . . . You have heard that Lord Ashburton arrived two hours late? And that she died of a fainting fit?

Mrs. Carlyle had a good deal to reproach herself with concerning Lady Ashburton: it was only in the previous summer that the famous railway-carriage incident had occurred, when Lady Ashburton, already ill, had hired a royal saloon carriage with a sofa in it for a journey to Edinburgh, and had put the Carlyles in the next compartment with her doctor and her maid, speaking to them through the open communicating door. Mrs. Carlyle's morbid imagination had magnified this trivial incident into an affront, and she had written her husband some cruelly satirical letters on the subject of his fine friend. Carlyle himself had found Lady Ashburton 'in a worse humour than usual' and 'capable of being driven to extremities by your setting up a peat from its flat posture,'[1] when staying alone with her at Loch Luichart that September. But now the great lady who had deliberately fascinated the one and unknowingly tormented the other had for ever vanished from the earth: no longer need Jane Carlyle glare with aversion at the yellow stones of Bath House, no longer lock herself into her bedroom at the Grange to weep. All that was left of this magnanimous, witty, sharp-tongued and haughty woman were the inchoate recollections of her friends—fragmentary memories of her generosity, of her quick and funny jokes, of the fantastic turns she would give to some ordinary conversation, of her practice of that lost form of humour called 'quizzing' by people of her day.

When the successful Orator, Actor, Journalist, and Pamphleteer must be content . . . with the fame and the work of their own short day . . . how are the social celebrities of any time to live even here beyond the shifting scene, in which they have played their part?

wrote Milnes in the essay on Lady Ashburton which he included in his *Monographs, Personal and Social*, published in 1873. For Milnes was the only one of Lady Ashburton's circle who deliberately set out to pay homage to her memory, and to try to transmit to posterity some notion of her originality. Other of her friends like Henry Taylor said that Milnes' article (of which Carlyle had read the proofs) gave no faithful impression of the strange quality of Lady Ashburton's talk; but Milnes had at least noted many of her verbal sallies, and at the end of his essay he had printed a careful selection from these.

Carlyle's reaction to this death was one of profound and irreparable sorrow: 'How well I still remember the evening Richard Milnes brought down the news,' he wrote in his old age; 'the moonlit streets, and dirge-like tone of everything.' 'I have indeed lost such a friend as I never had, or am again in the least likelihood to have, in this *stranger* world,' he told his brother, and in his journal he wrote sadly 'Her work—call it her grand and noble endurance of want of work—is all done'; for Carlyle had always admired the

---

[1] J. A. Froude: Thomas Carlyle *A History of his Life in London* 1834–1881, vol. II.

manner in which Lady Ashburton struggled against the twin handicaps of great position and great wealth. He and Milnes were amongst those who went down to the Grange for her funeral. They stood there in the churchyard at Alresford on a sunny morning in May, watching as the richly-plated coffin was carried down the steps of the Baring vault and lodged on a cold stone shelf.

Around the vault [wrote Milnes], stood an assembly of men foremost in the political and literary history of their time, who felt that there ended for all of them much of the charm of English society, and for many the enjoyment of a noble friendship.

To Milnes, as to Carlyle, Lady Ashburton had proved herself a noble friend. 'Whatever else she was,' old Mr. Milnes wrote from Fryston to his daughter-in-law, 'Ly Ashburton had such regard, & whatever *affection* her nature was susceptible of, for Richd, you will lament her unexpected death.'

Staying at the Grange after Christmas of the same year, haunted by memories of Harriet Ashburton in every room, Milnes found 'just as much mirth and laughter' there as ever, though the widower stalked about alone 'with a grave sad smile that is very pathetic.' Lord Ashburton, however, was by nature a dependant and uxorious man, and in November of the new year, 1858, he married, in the drawing-room of Bath House, Miss Louisa Stewart-Mackenzie of Seaforth. This youngish woman, whom Milnes once said he had almost married himself, was not generally considered an ideal choice. Lady Palmerston wrote to Milnes that to her the marriage seemed 'a great pity. I believe he saw her in Scotland,' she added. 'She is still handsome and I always wondered why nobody married her before. She is in all ways I believe a contrast to his first wife.' Even those who, like George Bunsen, were already friends of 'Loo' Mackenzie, feared that the match would bring Lord Ashburton 'many slightly insipid new connections.' In fact his second marriage brought him some happiness for the remaining six years of his life. The new Lady Ashburton produced a child, unhappily a daughter, and entertained as lavishly if not as eclectically as her predecessor. Carlyle, who had naturally enough disliked the remarriage at first, gradually became much attached to Louisa Ashburton, who treated Mrs. Carlyle, in Froude's specially Victorian phrase, 'as a sister.' Milnes also liked the second wife, and we may fancy that Mrs. Milnes, who had always been a little out of sympathy with 'Lady Harriet,' found the new less intellectual, less exacting atmosphere of the Grange more to her taste.

Although it is not wise to generalise about the Victorians, it is safe to suggest that their official attitude to death differed essentially

from ours. It was far more direct: for while reticent on those
sexual subjects which it is now usual to discuss with freedom,
English people who lived a century ago thought and spoke far more
of death than is habitual or considered acceptable to-day. Quantities of sermons were preached upon the subject, and though few
people imitated Annabel Milnes' brother Lord Crewe, who went to
three sermons every Sunday if he could, sermons were well attended.
Not far from the gates of each country house the village church
stood in its shady churchyard, a perpetual reminder of mortality.
'There I was at the very spot where I proposed his health when he
came of age,' wrote Monckton Milnes in 1858 from Stafford's
family house, Blatherwycke Park: 'and there was he in the churchyard hard by—so men may come and men may go.' Death was a
constant theme of Victorian poets, while novelists lingered over the
details of death-bed scenes. Physical mementos of the dead such
as braids of hair made into brooches, rings or bracelets did not
arouse the revulsion which we instinctively feel when we come
across them in some dusty bureau drawer. Contemporary letters,
from those of Queen Victoria downwards, show an almost Elizabethan satisfaction in the contemplation of corpses which were
often exposed for several days, and were thought beautiful. In a
poem addressed to his wife before their marriage Charles Kingsley
referred to the grave as 'our churchyard nest.'

Milnes, who did not romanticise the act of dying, and who
deeply resented the laws of change and dissolution by which our
lives are ruled, wrote some lines on the year 1857 at the Grange.
Entitled *From The Grange, December 31, 1857* these verses, though in
no sense of the word poetry, have an interest all their own:

> Go by! you sorrowful Year!
> With a stifled sigh and a secret tear
> For those we have lost in your dark career,—
> Harriet Ashburton, Francis Ellesmere,[1]
> And others still more near and dear;—
> Go by! you sorrowful Year!

> Away! you terrible Year!
> Take Madeleine Smith 'for better for worse';
> Give Robson and Redpath the care of your purse;
> Choose, as your ferryman over the Styx,
> Captain Rogers who kill'd the lad by his kicks.

[1] The poet and statesman Francis Egerton, 1st Earl of Ellesmere (b. 1800)
had died at Bridgewater House on 18 February 1857. References in the second
verse are to notorious criminal cases of that year.

Begone! you pitiless Year!
You, that are branded with the shame
Of India's broken faith and name,
You, that have heaped that hideous store
Of noble death in the well of Cawnpore;
You, for whom British heroes died
Batter'd, and burnt, and crucified:
But the sword of Justice, sharp and sheer;
Has fallen at last—you merciless Year!

Make way!—let the stage be clear
For another and happier Year,

　　·　　·　　·　　·　　·

Welcome, Lord of the unborn Fate,
Eighteen hundred and fifty-eight!

For Richard Milnes the year 1858 opened auspiciously, for on 9 January his wife gave birth to a son. The child was christened Robert after his paternal grandfather (as well as in memory of two medieval Crewes who had borne that name), Offley after his mother's clergyman cousin, and Ashburton after his godfather. Two years before, Milnes had privately asked Lady Ashburton to stand godmother to his first son; and though she humorously protested that she did not see why she should be thought more capable of helping a boy than a girl, 'Lady Harriet' had readily consented. Her husband now performed this duty sadly in her stead, attending the large christening breakfast given at 16 Upper Brook Street in the middle of March. The Galways and other near relations were also guests, as well as young Arthur Russell, Venables, and Mrs. Thomas Blackburne, whom Milnes used to say he 'regarded as a mother-in-law.' The child's grandfather remained in Yorkshire; at seventy-three, old Mr. Milnes was entering a decline, and his physical powers were waning. He declared that he was now so thin that a carrion crow could not have lived on him for a week, and as the months of 1858 went by his languor grew. He would lie with his feet up on a sofa in the newly-painted drawing-room at Fryston, but by the end of the summer he was practically bedridden, and stayed mostly in his own room, cared for alternately by his daughter, his daughter-in-law and his sisters. Each night he would say philosophically that he did not expect to be alive in the morning, and at length, in November weather so clear and brisk that Mrs. Milnes could take the baby 'Robin' and Amice driving in the pony trap, he had another of his recurrent crises, rallied so much that Doctor Oxley gave Richard permission to return to London, and then tranquilly expired at breakfast time on the morning of November 9, ten months to the day after his grandson's birth. Robert Pemberton Milnes was buried in the family tomb in the quiet little churchyard of Ferry Fryston. His son put up a brass tablet to his memory near the pulpit in Ferry Fryston church.

'I thought much of all your own suffering when I heard of your Father's death,' wrote Lady Marion Alford from Ashridge, in one of the many kind condoling letters Richard Milnes received.

Every year some heavy stone seems thrown into one's heart—the waters rise and overflow and then all is calm again on the surface, and the lights and shadows of each day and the least breath of change ripples and illuminates the surface, and this is all we see of each other—but only each heart knows its own bitterness and the heavy weight it drags about.

Although Richard's relations with his father had never been easy—and were not improved by Mr. Milnes' whimsical carping attitude to his son's career, or by the peerage incident of '56—he had been very genuinely fond of him and was saddened by this new death. On the whole Richard Milnes seems never to have recognised his father's unique qualities—and in particular his talent for getting his personality across in his letters which, piously taped and labelled by his daughter-in-law, make far livelier reading than his son's. In 1861 Harriette Galway suggested to her brother that the box containing their father's papers should be handed to some friend like Venables to sift for publication. Richard replied that he did not 'well see what Venables or any other comparative stranger' could do with them:

There is nothing literary in the tin-box except those verses which he wrote towards the end—curious flickerings & flames of genius but without any care of diction or connexion of thought. They would hardly look sane, if printed as they stand.

He added that he hoped to print 'judicious extractions' from his father's letters one day himself, but this he never achieved. The sense of grievance he had always felt towards Mr. Milnes, to whose early influence he liked to attribute his own failure in public life, persisted:

The whole subject [he told Lady Galway], is more & more painful to me, when I think what he & I might have been & done together in the world, had he done all he could & made me do the same.

This theory that his father had failed him, and had unduly interfered in his life, no doubt inspired the careful education and training which he successfully gave to his own son.

Meanwhile, in 1858, the birth of his son and the death of his father shifted the emphasis of Richard Monckton Milnes' existence, bringing him new responsibilities and urgent obligations.   He now found himself the owner of Fryston Hall, and thrust into the inconceivably unsuitable rôle of landowner and Yorkshire squire.

Chapter Seven

1858   *1861*

I

Among the many letters which Richard Monckton Milnes received at the time of his father's death were several congratulating him upon his long-delayed inheritance of Fryston. 'You will now start from a fresh point in the estimation of the world,' wrote the Whig statesman, Charles Pelham Villiers. 'Regarded through proprietary glasses your merits will (not be magnified but) duly appreciated.'

The fact that he was now a man of property instead of an only son with expectations may have modified the world's view of Monckton Milnes, though it cannot have radically altered his contemporaries' settled opinion on this stout and talkative dilettante. When he inherited, Milnes was in his fiftieth year: his thick and long brown hair was flecked with grey, his face was heavier and somewhat whiskered. Hardly yet the 'good-natured old fellow,' the 'Baron Tattle of Scandal' of Swinburne's letters, Milnes no longer looked in any way youthful. By his father's death he had come into six small family estates, the chief of which were Fryston, near Ferrybridge, and Bawtry, in Nottinghamshire, 'a fair gentleman's fortune' of thirty-five thousand pounds, and 'a considerable amount of debt.' Although even after his marriage to Miss Crewe Milnes had only had limited sums of money to spend, he had to endure constant criticism of his expenditure from his father, who never failed to point out that had he not 'imposed a stern restraint' upon himself, Richard 'never by possibility could have own'd & occupied Fryston.' In 1854 Mr. Milnes had let Bawtry Hall, the house he had inherited at his stepmother's death in 1835, and in which he had lived with his wife for many years, to a Roman Catholic family named Gandolfi who set aside a room for an oratory in it, and (according to Mr. Milnes, who watched their activities with a benevolent curiosity) had filled the house with 'handsome furniture with crosses on it.' Bawtry thus 'alienated,' Mr. Milnes turned his attention to making Fryston, deserted since his wife's death in 1847, once more habitable. He took the whole roof off and put it on again, renovated the east, or garden, front of the house, and spent several thousand pounds on re-decoration. Fryston was thus in a comfortable state of repair when Richard Milnes came into possession of it.

His son's complete ignorance of country matters had always been an unremitting source of anxiety to the old squire, and to his faithful steward Nicholas Lee. Lee, who died not long before his master, passed 'many bad nights' worrying over this situation: 'He talked to me yesterday of Mr. Richard,' her father-in-law wrote to Annabel Milnes (whom he used to call his '*man* of business') 'saying it prey'd heavy on him—& he was sure he wd come to a standstill— & that he does not know half he should, about servants &c. &c.' Domestics formed one aspect of Fryston life which old Mr. Milnes himself found very tedious:

I rather think I may go to London, to look out for some servants, tho' I should have preferr'd storming that trench on the Alma [he wrote during the Crimean War]. I wish the whole generation of London Butlers & Valets was extinguish'd, & to be attended only by women-slaves from Circassia.

He was quite happy at Fryston with a cook, a kitchen-maid and a 'whipper-snapper' page-boy from Bawtry village ('did you ever see a humming-bee walking? that is just his pace,' he wrote of this round-shouldered youth), but this meant that if people came over from Pontefract there was no one but the kitchen-maid to hold the horses' heads; he did not mind this himself, he said, 'but it might not do to have Lady Aylesbury.' He knew that his daughter-in-law was perfectly capable of running a house well, and engaging and, more important, keeping, good servants; but it annoyed Mr. Milnes to find that his son could not even supervise the treatment of the greys that drew the Milnes' brougham, and were stabled in the mews adjacent to Upper Berkeley Street. Then, Richard never shot, pleading an astigmatism, and his father, who forbade the gamekeeper at Fryston to have a gun, relying on his own friends to shoot over his land, wondered how Richard, who had no friends who shot, would stock the table after his death. But many of Mr. Milnes' doubts were serious and legitimate—his son knew nothing of the turnip crop, or what to do in a year when there was an excess of apples. He had no idea of the proper number of sheep to have on the land at different seasons so as to make best use of it, and would be forced to rely on the advice of obstinate farmers, or the rather sketchy knowledge of Nicholas Lee's two sons, Tom, who was honest but stupid, and Joe, who was quick-witted but frequented the dram-shops. In his last years his father kept sending Richard somewhat pathetic pieces of advice for later reference—always buy cattle in March and sell cattle in July, always ignore gardeners' arguments for crowding fruit-trees, never let the grapes be watered too much—for though this doubles their size it makes them 'tasteless as water-melons.' Richard had developed a sort of generalised, landscape-gardener's interest in the appearance of the portions of the Fryston estate near the Hall—asking his father to have the beeches in the Upper Park disbranched to form an avenue, suggesting that any trees felled should be replaced by deodars and the other newly fashionable oriental species. Mr. Milnes had a profound distrust of eastern trees: he suspected that in England the deodar might easily attain the giant size of trees in tropical jungles, and dwarf or elbow out the elms and oaks. On the one hand he had always criticised Richard for his lack of interest in the estate, and on the other he snubbed or rejected most of the suggestions he made. It would have surprised, and might have pleased, Mr. Milnes to know that in the seventeen years between his own death and the destruction of the main parts of the Hall by fire in 1875, his son, by his enterprising and imaginative hospitalities, had made of Fryston a famous centre for literary, and even cosmopolitan, life—a house 'whose name will live in the records of English society, as well as English literature.'[1] Life at Fryston, and the appearance of the house, have already been described in my earlier volume. It will however be relevant to glance again at them here.

Though it amused him, towards the end of his life, to concoct plans for the reconstruction of Fryston Hall, old Mr. Milnes only renovated the east front, and took the measures needed for the safety of the roof. The rest of the house remained as his own father, Richard Slater Milnes, who bought Fryston in 1784, had left it—a large rambling country house of dark corridors and staircases, to the front of which a conventional eighteenth-century façade, with pillared portico and white stone slabs, had been added. The front portion of the house, which contained the big drawing-room, the dining-room and the long library, was more modern, having been built by Richard Slater Milnes, and it was entirely gutted by fire in 1876, while Lord Houghton and his son were in Dublin, and there were only frightened servants and inept Pontefract firemen to fight against the blaze. In the county Fryston Hall was noted for its vast fruit and vegetable gardens, for its glass-houses, and its venerable trees: no one thought of it as an alluring house, or as a place one would choose to live in oneself, and in old Mr. Milnes' day there were very few flowers. He liked roses and, above all, the blue convolvulus; his daughter-in-law planted lavender beds,

[1] See the article 'Lord Houghton at Fryston Hall' published in *The World's* series 'Celebrities at Home,' 20 June 1877. The writer was Lady Burton, but the paper was re-cast by Edmund Yates.

borders of stocks, nasturtiums and sweet-pea. As we have seen, Annabel Milnes was not at first sight enamoured of Fryston; but she managed to make this bleak Yorkshire house 'pretty and enjoyable,' and, with her husband's full approval, to mitigate the sense of roughness and austerity which still made Northern country houses a contrast to those in the South. Even the excessive drinking then customary in Yorkshire (where, Mrs. Milnes used to say, they 'needed a Father Mathew') did not soften the stark outlines of life in the great houses of the North, where relations between master and servant were more patriarchal than in the South, and the manners of the servants themselves homely and outspoken. Lord Galway, who was never happy off a horse, was typical of the Yorkshire and Nottinghamshire squires; his brother-in-law, who hated any kind of exercise, was not.

The big drawing-room at Fryston had last been done up during the early years of the Napoleonic Wars. Except for a cursory coat of whitewash to the ceiling, it had been untouched since those days. In 1854 the wallpaper was 'torn and bemired,' the ceilings stained with the brown insidious marks of damp, the plaster was rotting and the gilding round the great mirrors had gone dull and black. Locks and door-handles throughout this part of the house also needed to be regilt. Mr. Milnes said that he did not mind things being old and shabby, provided they looked clean, and this the Fryston rooms no longer did. Employing a decorator from Leeds, and quickly spending over two thousand pounds, he set about having the rooms re-done. While acceding to his son's and his daughter-in-law's request that the walls might be painted, not papered, and while nominally consulting them at many points, Mr. Milnes took an entirely independent line about the colour-scheme of the re-decoration. He chose colours on a theory popular in his own Regency youth, but which must have seemed annoyingly out of date to the Upper Brook Street household: 'I have no green on them,' he wrote happily of the drawing-room walls, giving as his reason the fact that he had once

sat next at dinner—it was at Lord Carleton's—to Tommy Hope, Anastasius, he who wrote a book upon furniture & decoration & was regarded as the Corypheus of Art & Taste.[1] All our talk was on·it, & it was his main injunction to avoid having green. He said it was the color of Nature's freshness & Nature disdain'd imitation.

---

[1] Thomas Hope (1770?–1831), author and collector, patron of Canova, Chantrey, George Dawe, Flaxman and Thorwaldsen, and owner of Deepdene, was a writer on furniture and decoration who, though at first ridiculed, had considerable influence on the English taste of his day. *Anastasius or Memoirs of a Greek written at the close of the Eighteenth Century* appeared anonymously in 1819, when it was at first attributed to Byron.

She showed it, by having her green turn brown by candlelight. It was the color of all others to have where apartments were in accompanyment with out-door scenery—as summer houses, & villas on the Thames—these intended only for enjoyment in the day—Thus, on these walls, which are for the night, there is no tinge of green. They are of violet & pale yellow.

The chairs in the drawing-room were re-covered in bright 'French chintz,' though Mr. Milnes was forced to allow Harriette Galway to instal some 'Jenny Lind chairs,' a form of furniture he specially disliked. He took the opportunity to re-hang the pictures, incidentally solving one of the perennial Fryston problems—what to do with the vast full-length portraits of George III and his Queen given by these royal personages to Sir Robert Milnes, the Governor-General of Canada, which occupied the whole of one dining-room wall. These huge canvases were now 'stuck' in an upper passage: 'the Queen in front as you mount the stairs. She is finely painted by Sir T. Lawrence, but is slightly faded. The King, I don't like—he looks half tipsy, & I put him in the darker part, where he is indistinctly seen.' Like most owners of English houses, Mr. Milnes was vague about the actual painters of the pictures he owned, attributing this pair of Allan Ramsays to Sir Thomas Lawrence, and calling his beautiful sentimental Wright of Derby, *Edwin,* 'our Gainsborough.'

With Fryston so recently furbished-up Richard Milnes and his wife at first had little to alter in their new domain. During the summer of 1859 they began to entertain at Fryston, filling the house with London guests and a few country neighbours, and often sitting down as many as twelve or sixteen to dinner. Milnes was an early riser, and he had usually been up some hours before the guests assembled at small round tables in the breakfast-room for a meal which he and they regarded as his especial province. He would seat himself in some vacant chair at one of the tables, or wander from group to group with a book in his hand, talking and joking away as briskly as at his breakfast-parties in London. These breakfast-room discussions were one of the peculiar features of a stay at Fryston. Another was the lack of billiards, for Milnes stood out against this game in a period when almost every country house in England contained a billiard-table in a converted room or new annexe. A third peculiarity of Fryston was the absence of 'circulating library books.' This drove people staying in the house to the thorough investigation of the Fryston library. The books were carefully organised and housed everywhere—the library itself was filled, there were books in bedrooms, in passages, on staircases and in cupboards. Robert Lowe, later Lord Sherbrooke, compared Fryston to 'one of those amorphous animals which have their brains all over their bodies,' and though the analogy is too strained to be effective it does suggest the atmosphere of the house. This library was as orderly and universal as it was ubiquitous. Comprising English, French, German, and Italian books of four centuries, as well as good editions of the Greek and Latin classics, it was a justly celebrated collection. In itself this library was by far the most significant contribution which Monckton Milnes made to his newly inherited Yorkshire house. His wife would have liked to add furniture other than book-cases to Fryston: 'Don't talk of furnishing Fryston,' Milnes, who was staying with the Rothschilds at Mentmore, wrote to her in the month following his father's death—'how can one *furnish*, without damask or Dresden, or Sèvres, or porphyry, or marble, or three clocks all going in one room, or *anything?*'

II

As an entity the Fryston library no longer exists. Many books were lost, or charred, or spoiled by water in the fire of 1876. Others have been dispersed, while the remainder are now distributed among Lord Houghton's descendants. But even in this imperfect state the collection has a personal character and a high quality that are impressive.

In scope, Milnes' library was representative of European literature in the widest sense. Round a core of the great as well as the curious classics of the past, Milnes built up a collection of contemporary poetry, fiction, biography, history, memoirs and works of criticism in four languages. Aside from his big collection of seventeenth and eighteenth century autographs, Milnes formed the admirable practice of binding holograph letters, or fragments of manuscript verse, into the relevant books of his contemporaries. Thus we find a few lines in John Keats' handwriting bound into Milnes' *Life, Letters and Literary Remains* of that poet; some of Landor's letters bound into the first editions of his various works; a copy of Prosper Mérimée's anonymous memoir of Stendhal,[1] with a wittily disin-

[1] Milnes bought one of the twenty-five copies of the original edition of this extremely important anonymous pamphlet by Mérimée, which Firmin-Didot had printed privately in 1850. The '*H.B.*' in which Mérimée describes Stendhal's private opinions—his contempt for Christianity, his belief that most of the remarkable men of history have been sexual inverts—has only lately been reprinted, under Mérimée's name, (*Les Maîtres*, Jacques Haumont, Paris 1935). 'Cher Mr. Milnes,' Prosper Mérimée wrote from the British Museum one May evening, without date. '. . . Je n'ai jamais rien écrit sur Beyle que la préface de l'édition complète de ses œuvres. Il y a des gens mal-intentionnés à mon égard qui m'attribuent une brochure, non pas in-4°, mais in-8°. Elle est immorale, et cela doit vous prouver qu'elle n'est pas de moi.' Milnes knew him well enough to understand what he meant.

genuous note from the author denying that he had ever written this short book; there are the earliest editions of Shelley, a presentation copy (though not to Milnes) from Goethe, a piece of Voltaire's dressing-gown folded into a fine edition of *La Pucelle*; there is Richard Burton's passport to Mecca and the visitors' book from Burns' cottage at Alloway. There are also a great number of 'association copies,' and fine bindings from celebrated royal and other libraries. Pamphlets on cognate subjects were bound together to form volumes for which Milnes invented the titles—Mrs. Norton's spate of passionate appeals for married women's rights, for example, being labelled *The Wrongs of Women*. The modern books were all rebound for Milnes by Leightons of Brewer Street, mostly in half-calf and boards with his gilt wheat-sheaf crest stamped on the side. Some of the bindings were more ambitious however—a part of the vast collection of books on the history of the French Revolution, one of Milnes' favourite subjects, was bound in red, white and blue leather, while those on the United States were stamped with gilded stars and stripes. All his friends testify to the fact that Milnes was an omnivorous reader, even by the exacting standards of those days. The remnants of the Fryston library bear witness to a culture that would have been exceptional even in a less sociable or more reclusive man.

Naturally enough, the library reflected Milnes' particular interests, and there were many thousand more books on some subjects than on others. English poetry of his own century was one of these. The French Revolution was another. A third, as we might expect in that age of doctrinal dispute and religious doubt, was theology. Magic and witchcraft were a fourth, and crime, both its execution and its punishment, formed a fifth. A sixth was Milnes' important collection of French and Italian *erotica*, some examples of which were almost as choice as anything owned by Monsieur de la Popelinière or the other amateurs of the Régence. There was also a series of books on school punishments, and all the available printed works, as well as some fragmentary manuscript ones, of a man to whom Milnes would refer as the 'odiously famous' Marquis de Sade.

'He is *the* Sadique collector of European fame,' wrote Swinburne to Rossetti in an enthusiastic letter of July 1869, which Monsieur Lafourcade first published in 1927.[1]

His erotic collection of books, engravings etc. is unrivalled upon earth—unequalled I should imagine in heaven. Nothing low, nothing that is not good and genuine in the way of art and literature

---

[1] Lafourcade's *Jeunesse de Swinburne* (Oxford Press 1927) vol. 1.

is admitted.   There is every edition of every work of our dear and honoured Marquis.

Milnes' position as the first serious English amateur of the writings of Sade, and the alleged influence on Swinburne of the sadic collections at Fryston, have been given considerable publicity in the last thirty years, till most people who know Lord Houghton's name know it only in this context.   To Milnes the works of Sade were interesting curiosities: he is unlikely to have recognised in him, as Sainte-Beuve was then doing, 'one of the greatest inspirers of the moderns.'   *Justine* and *Juliette* found their natural place amongst the *erotica* at Fryston, for Milnes' collection is only interesting for having been so comprehensive and complete.   The collection itself has long since disappeared: but by means of bills from Paris book-sellers, notes from Brussels, and the detailed letters of Milnes' Parisian adviser Frederick Hankey, it is not difficult to form some notion of the character of this all-too-celebrated section of his library.   Examined critically, these lists of Milnes' erotic books show that his collection chiefly consisted of superlative copies of all the best-known works of this nature of the French eighteenth century.   An examination of examples of these books themselves leads one to suspect that the patience with which he collected them, and the ingenuity expended in trying to get them into England, were seldom commensurate with the innate interest of the volumes acquired.

The conversational freedom which is one of the distinguishing marks of our present epoch makes it extremely hard to reconstruct the attitude towards sexual matters and 'loose books' prevalent among English people living a hundred years ago.   In some circles the very idea of a novel in French was anathema.   In 1860 Sir Walter Trevelyan obliged the young Swinburne to leave the house after having lent Lady Trevelyan a volume of the *Comédie Humaine*: 'he was a rash man who in those days recommended a French book to an English lady,' writes Gosse in reference to this incident. 'Even if she made no objection, her male relations were sure to take umbrage.   Sir Walter Trevelyan threw the book on the fire with a very rough remark.'[1]   In one of Milnes' later commonplace-books he records an incident told him by a friend of having met, in the Burlington Arcade, at an unusually early hour, a young man whom they both knew.   Asked what he was doing, he explained that he was hurrying to a bookshop—'I have just brought a charming girl within one French novel of being seduced and now I am off to Bentleys to choose the finisher.'   'Have you read Mlle de Maupin

[1] Gosse's *Swinburne* (Macmillan 1917) pp. 71-72.

which the Parisian ladies rave about?' wrote another friend of
Milnes in a postscript to a salacious letter describing the habits of
an hermaphrodite, 'It was recommended to me by quite a young
woman—It is beautiful French, but a perfectly bawdy book, I
cannot conceive how the censorship has allowed it to appear.'[1]   In
a society which judged Gautier indecent and Balzac corrupting, it
is easy to see why the *chefs-d'œuvre* of Nerciat and of Restif de la
Bretonne, with their *gravures libres* and frank descriptions seemed
more forbidden and enticing than they can ever be to us to-day.

Swinburne's emphasis upon the quality of the component volumes of this library was evidently justified, for Milnes owned
exemplaires of many famous illustrated books then considered
suspect—*La Pucelle* with Fragonard's engravings, the illustrated
Religieuse of Diderot, and *Les Liaisons Dangereuses* of Choderlos de
Laclos.   One book for which he had searched in Paris, and which
was finally bought for him in 1859 and sent to London with the
pages gummed together in case of discovery at the customs, was the
big edition of the alleged Caracci illustrations to Aretino's sonnets.
This large quarto, *L'Arétin d'Augustin Carrache ou Recueil de Postures
Erotiques . . . avec texte explicatif des sujets*, contains a number of
engravings after water-colours supposed to be by Agostino Caracci
and to have been discovered in Italy during Napoleon's first
Italian campaign, and representing classical personages making
love in ways as inconvenient as they are gymnastic.   Milnes also
obtained with some difficulty a good copy of Louvet de Couvray's
four-volume serial, *Les Amours du Chevalier de Faublas*, and of La Riche
de la Popelinière's *Tableaux de Mœurs*.   Other books in his possession included Nerciat's *Monrose*, *L'Etourdie* and *Félicia*, *L'Anti-justine*
and the other works of Restif, *Le Jou-jou des Demoiselles* of Jouffreau
de Lazarin, *L'Histoire des Flagellants*, *Venus en Rut*, Lalmond's *Pot-
Pourri de Loth*, the French translation of Cleland published in 1751
as *La Fille de Joie*, *La Saladière*, an unidentifiable volume entitled
Les Yeux, le Nez et les Tetons, *Le Soupé de Julie*, the *Bibliothèque des
Amants*, *La Victime de l'amour*, *La Nouvelle Sapho*, Mirabeau's *Libertin
de Qualité*, *Les Travaux d'Hercule* and *Le Petit-fils d'Hercule*, and books
of elegant erotic verse such as *Le Petit-Neveu de Grècourt* printed in
1782, and its companion volume *Le Petit-Neveu de Boccace*.   These,
with innumerable other works of an equally resolute impropriety,
went to make up the erotic library of Richard Monckton Milnes.

Of rather more interest than the actual contents of this library
were the methods by which it was assembled.   An avid buyer of
books, Milnes did not in this instance have to rely upon his own

---

[1] Undated letter from Colonel Studholme Hodgson. *Mademoiselle de Maupin*
had been first published in 1835.

annual visits to France to enrich his erotic collections, nor was he without the constant advice and aid of an expert in this line. This expert was an Englishman, and he lived in Paris.

III

It is common knowledge that when, towards the end of his life, Edmond de Goncourt began to publish extracts from the journals which he and his brother Jules had kept since the year 1851, he suppressed many scandalous passages. After his death his friends decided to suppress the rest of the manuscript, and in spite of his instructions for their posthumous publication in twenty years' time, the journals now lie locked away in the Bibliothèque Nationale, accessible only to the ten members of the Académie Goncourt. In some cases Goncourt had published conversations but omitted the speakers' names; and this was so in one strange passage which aroused a horrified attention when it was published, and which many people have since been inclined to attribute to the excessive credulity or sensationalism of the Goncourts. This famous passage describes a visit paid by one of the Goncourts and their friend Saint-Victor to a young English disciple of de Sade, whose conversation seemed to them so evil and disgusting that they could scarcely believe their ears. In *The Romantic Agony* Professor Praz [1] has skilfully shown that this description was largely responsible for the stock figure of the English sadist to be found in the French and Italian novels and novelettes of the fin-de-siècle. Goncourt himself used this young man as the basis for his character of the sadistic 'Honourable George Selwyn' in *La Faustin*; he recurs in d'Annunzio's *Il Piacere* in the person of the Marquis of Mount Edgecumbe; in Toulet's *Monsieur du Par*; in Barbey d'Aurevilly's *A un dîner d'athées*; in Pheladan's *La Vertu Suprême* and in *Le Vice Errant*, published in 1902. Professor Praz sees this recurrent figure as gradually 'distorted by legends,' 'After all,' he writes, 'in the whole series of descriptions of English sadists which we have quoted, there are to be found only three persons who actually existed—the real George Selwyn of the eighteenth century, the anonymous gentleman whose acquaintance the Goncourts made in 1862, and Swinburne, whom Maupassant met in 1868.' On the evidence of his own letters and of those from Richard Burton to Monckton Milnes, as well as by references in Milnes' common-place-books and in the unpublished journal of the Cervantic

---

[1] Praz's *The Romantic Agony*, trans. A. Davidson (Oxford University Press) pp. 417–429.

scholar Henry Spencer Ashbee [1] we can now beyond any shade of doubt identify 'the anonymous gentleman whose acquaintance the Goncourts made in 1862' with Milnes' Parisian acquaintance and cicerone, a certain Mr. Frederick Hankey who was resident at number 2 Rue Laffitte, in the 'fifties, 'sixties, and 'seventies of the last century. Time, and the prudence or perhaps revulsion of his relatives, have long obliterated any memories of young Fred Hankey; but so singular an individual should never be forgot. As Milnes' chief adviser and agent for the purchase of erotica in the great Paris sale-rooms, Fred Hankey was in actual fact the inspirer and architect of the erotic library at Fryston.

'Lundi 7 avril,' begins the relevant entry for the year 1862 in the Goncourt diaries. [2] 'Aujourd'hui j'ai visité un fou, un monstre, un de ces hommes qui confinent à l'abîme. Par lui, comme par une voile déchirée, j'ai entrevu un fonds abominable, un côté effrayant d'une aristocratie d'argent blasée, de l'aristoratie anglaise apportant la férocité dans l'amour, et dont le libertinage ne jouit que par la souffrance de la femme.' With this dramatic opening Goncourt goes on to record how his friend Saint-Victor had been introduced to a young English gentleman at the Bal de l'Opéra. The stranger had at once remarked in a casual tone that Paris was less fun than London, for in London there was a house kept by a Mrs. Jenkins to which you could go for the purpose of whipping girls—'les petites, oh! pas très fort, mais les grandes tout à fait fort. On pouvait aussi,' he explained thoughtfully, 'leur enfoncer des épingles,' and he showed the length of these pins by the end of his finger. He went on to say that he had once hired a window from which to see a murderess hanged; he and a friend had planned to take two women with them 'pour leur *faire des choses*' during the hanging—but unhappily at the last moment the Queen had pardoned the murderess. Aghast at this novel form of small talk, and knowing the Goncourts' curiosity over anything new or strange, Saint-Victor took one of them to call on the Englishman in his apartment in the first week of April.

Goncourt judged their young host to be about thirty years old. He was rather bald, his temples swollen like an orange, his eyes blue, clear and piercing, his skin so delicate that you could see the veins; the whole head horribly similar to that of some emaciated and ecstatic young priest attending on a bishop in an old painting. He was elegant, but moved stiffly, with the mechanical and feverish

[1] Henry Spencer Ashbee, 1834–1900, bibliographer, formed the finest Cervantic library outside Spain, and bequeathed this, together with his collection of erotic and other curious books, to the British Museum.
[2] Edmond et Jules de Goncourt: Journal—*Mémoires de la vie littéraire*, vol. ii (1862–1865), édition définitive (Flammarion and Fasquelle, Paris), p. 24.

gestures of someone with incipient disease of the spine.   Well-bred
and exquisitely polite, he was at once noticeable for an especial
sweetness or gentleness of manner.

As at the Bal de l'Opéra, the young man started at once upon his
obsession.   Going to a large piece of furniture he opened it and took
out a volume on flagellation, displaying the phalluses, death's-heads
and instruments of torture stamped upon the inside of the binding.
He had had some trouble over these stamps, he told them; the
binder, who worked for one of the best *relieurs* in Paris, had at first
refused to execute his designs; but by lending the man books he had
managed to corrupt his mind, give him the taste for pursuing small
girls, ruin his marriage and get the stamps made.   He next held out
an unbound volume, saying that the human skin for binding it was
still being tanned—a lengthy process taking six months.   It was not
an interesting skin, he added, as it had not been stripped from a
living victim—'heureusement, j'ai mon ami le docteur Bartsh[1] . . .
vous savez, celui qui voyage dans l'intérieur de l'Afrique . . . eh bien,
dans les massacres . . . il m'a promis de me faire prendre une peau
comme ça . . . sur une négresse vivante.'   'Caro Milnes,' wrote
Richard Burton on 31 May 1863 in a merry letter from the kingdom
of Dahomey, 'I have been here 3 days and am grievously disappointed.   Not a man killed, nor a fellow tortured.   The canoe
floating in blood is a myth of myths.   Poor Hankey must still wait
for his peau de femme.'

As he spoke the young man kept staring with maniacal fixity at
his finger-nails, holding his hands stretched out before him.   'Il
parle, il parle continûment,' wrote Goncourt, 'et sa voix un peu
chantante et s'arrêtant et repartant aussitôt qu'elle s'arrête, vous
entre, comme une vrille, dans les oreilles ses cannibalesques paroles.'
'Moi, j'ai les goûts cruels,' the young man told them, 'mais je
m'arrête aux hommes et aux animaux.'   'Hankey's love of cruel
enjoyment & his strong sense of the wickedness of killing animals for
food,' we find in Milnes' commonplace-book for the years 1857–
1860.

Before considering Hankey's influence on Milnes, and his
position as inspirer of the erotic library, it is instructive to compare
the Goncourts' description of this psychopathic being with another
record, hitherto unpublished.[2]   The Goncourt entry is dated 7
April 1862; in the manuscript journal of the scholar, traveller and
amateur of erotic books, Henry Spencer Ashbee, occurs the following
entry, dated 8 April 1875:

[1] Evidently a misreading for Burton.
[2] For permission to quote from this journal I am indebted to the grandson
of H. S. Ashbee.

Spent the afternoon & evening with Mr. F. Hankey among his unique volumes [Ashbee wrote carefully in his journal]. His collection is small, but each vol is a gem either of rarity or choice binding. Hankey himself is a remarkable man, quite a study, he appears to me like a second de Sade *without the intellect.* He has given himself up body & soul to the erotic mania, thinks of nothing else, lives for nothing else. Nothing is bawdy enough for him, whether in expression, thought or design. Besides his books, all of which are erotic, this is a sine quâ non with him, he has two of the most charming erotic statues which exist, & is further surrounded with . . . every other obscene object possible to be procured. Hankey himself I should take to be about 50 years old, lean, tall, with yellow hair, a white skin, & soft blue eyes, a good forehead, & yet his expression is entirely devoid of energy or determination. In his youth he must have been good-looking, but effeminate, much as the Marquis de Sade is pictured to have been.

Ashbee concludes with a description of the situation and discomfort of the apartments in which Hankey and his mistress lived in the Rue Laffitte, 'in the best part of Paris,' looking out on the boulevard and facing the Café Anglais and the Opéra Comique, and the remark that Hankey's 'debaucheries are beginning to tell on him, & he complains much of his health, he is not I think destined to make old bones.' Ashbee saw Hankey again in London three years later, when he dined with him and his French mistress in a friend's rooms in the Albany; Lord Houghton came in afterwards, and Ashbee then met him for the first time. Hankey was still flourishing in March of '82, when Ashbee, the painter Félicien Rops, and Octave Uzanne passed 'a very pleasant evening' looking at the 'treasures' in the Rue Laffitte. After this we lose track of Fred Hankey, who presumably died towards the end of the century, perhaps, like his prototype, in a Parisian lunatic asylum.[1]

The only son of a General with a distinguished record for administration in Malta, by his second wife, a beautiful Greek from Corfu, Fred Hankey seems to have been born about 1828. His father Sir Frederick had two brothers, one of whom settled at Fetcham Park near Leatherhead and had several children, among them Milnes' acquaintance Thomson Hankey, a well-known economist, politician and director of the Bank of England.[2] The General put his only

[1] Frederick Hankey appears to have died intestate. His father, Sir Frederick, whose will was proved in August 1855, had left him 4,000 pounds with instructions to his executors to sue his son if he did not surrender certain securities then in his keeping. Sir Frederick's second daughter by his first marriage, Emma Hankey, who died at Boulogne in 1864, left her 'dear' half-brother one hundred pounds. These bequests suggest that he was not in good odour with his immediate family.

[2] Thomson Hankey, 1805–1893, politician and senior partner in his father's West Indian mercantile firm; a director of the Bank of England 1835; Governor 1851–1852; liberal M.P. for Peterborough 1853–1868 and 1874–1880; published works on questions of political economy.

son into the Guards, but he seems soon to have resigned his commission and moved to Paris, where he was already attending book
sales in 1847. He appears to have been reasonably well off,
banking with Mallet Frères, paying large sums for rare erotic books
and for expensive bindings, and devoting all his time and money to
his monomania: his pastimes included the organisation of complicated 'représentations' and 'tableaux vivants' at the house of a
Monsieur Guillaume. He made periodical visits to London to
attend to his affairs and to frequent such establishments as that
which he had described to Saint-Victor, his particular haunt being
the house of Mrs. James, whose servant knew his tastes. Hankey's
mistress always travelled with him, and for this reason he was unable to accept an invitation to Fryston. From his letters to Milnes
one may judge that they first met at some date in the late 'fifties;
this, as well as the fact that Fred Hankey was some twenty years
younger than Milnes, would account for the formal tone of his early
letters—'Dear Mr. Milnes' in October 1857, changing gradually to
'My dear Milnes . . . tout à vous Fred Hankey,' twelve months later.
Though Milnes sent Hankey an inscribed volume of his own
poetry, and went to look at his books whenever he was in Paris,
their relationship was mainly business-like: Hankey notifying Milnes
of some rare volume that he thought might be of interest—'it is not
a very objectionable Book', he would write, 'as it is erotique but very
convenable & artistique,' or 'it is not *my sort* of loose book.' Although
Milnes sometimes dealt direct with Paris booksellers—'Milord,' runs
one note, 'j'ai l'honneur de vous adresser le *Roman des Pyrénées* et le
Roman de Bade, qui me viennent de Bruxelles. A la lecture vous
saurez vite pourquoi'—it is quite clear that had it not been for
Frederick Hankey's assiduity, the Fryston erotica would never have
been assembled at all.

One recurrent problem, which it taxed all Hankey's ingenuity to
solve, was how to transmit certain volumes to Monckton Milnes in
London. The English customs were extremely strict, and any
books of an erotic or salacious nature, whether illustrated by
Fragonard or by Félicien Rops, were equally liable to be seized.
Octavo volumes and daguerreotypes (though these last were very
fragile) could be slipped into an overcoat pocket—some were sent
thus, for instance, by Hankey's cousin Arthur's valet. Others were
sealed up in the bag of a sympathetic Queen's Messenger returning
from Constantinople with despatches for Lord Palmerston. Others
again were sent in the British Embassy bag, addressed to a friend of
Hankey's in the Foreign Office. But the courier whom Hankey most
preferred was Mr. Harris, the manager of Covent Garden, who lived
in Pelham Place, and was always going backwards and forwards

to France on musical business. 'He is not only most devoted to me,' wrote Hankey, 'but a very good hand at passing quarto volumes as he has done *several* times for me in the *bend* of his *back*.' It was Mr. Harris who transported two fine Louis Quinze statuettes in Sèvres *pâte tendre*—le Maître d'Ecole and la Maîtresse d'Ecole—and dumped them at Upper Brook Street, and it was perhaps he who brought over a 'sapphic group' by Pradier which Swinburne especially admired. Hankey himself had two figures by Flaubert's Provençal friend Pradier; he arranged them 'on a meuble for Books in my salon . . . with a looking-glass behind them.' Reading the letters of 'Monsieur Henkai' as some of the Paris bookshops called him, it is not easy to share the Goncourts' moral indignation at his way of life: for there is much that is pathetic as well as absurd in this victim of sexual obsession concocting descriptions of the 'priaps' on some title-page or seriously writing 'It has a rather nice *gravure libre* representing the two principal personages in a curious position on a chair.' Milnes, with his wealth of interests and his zest for every kind of life, took such things very much in his stride and was not all morbid; beside Hankey he seems more than usually bluff, inquisitive and sane. This pallid, elegant young sadist, with his maniac's manner and his dedicated face, is more an object for compassion. Condemned by some hereditary strain, or by the thwarting circumstances of his childhood—the General, described by Henry Fox as 'narrow-minded and hard-hearted,' had made himself hated in Malta and may well have been a detestable parent—Fred Hankey was in a sense the captive of his own imagination, serving his sentence out in the apartment of the Rue Laffitte near the Place de l'Opéra in rooms untidily littered with sapphic figurines, with bawdy books, with obscene objects, as well as with whips, rods and all the inescapable paraphernalia of his frenetic and unassuageable desires.

IV

'Fred Hankey wrote to me to-day "I have just written de nouveau (sic) to the person who is to get the Betuliad printed at Bruxelles (sic etiam) saying I *must* have a rendezvous *immediately*,"' Richard Burton told Milnes in a note dated February 1860 from Boulogne. '. . . The italics are the author's own—you recognize the style I imagine.' It seems likely that Milnes had brought Hankey and Burton together in London in the previous year. Himself an expert on the erotic literature and practices of the Arab world, Richard Burton would have had some interests in common with Fred Hankey; but though he readily volunteered to bring him a human skin from the legendary kingdom of Dahomey, his letters show that this splendid and full-blooded traveller, one of the most ardent spirits of that or any other English century, regarded the decadent youth of the Rue Laffitte with mild amusement. Burton's letters to Milnes from Fernando Po, or from his subsequent consular posts at Santa Cruz, Damascus and Dieppe, contain offhand enquiries—'What of Hankey?' he would write, or still more casually, 'What of poor old Hankey?'

Captain Richard Burton had returned from his three-year expedition to find the source of the Nile in the late spring of 1859. In August of that year he paid the first of several visits to Fryston, where he stayed a week in the company of Spedding, Venables, the painter Samuel Laurence (who was at work on a chalk head of Mrs. Monckton Milnes), and Mr. and Mrs. Mansfield Parkyns. Parkyns had been Milnes' boisterous companion up the Nile in 1843; but sixteen years, and marriage to an English lady, had much subdued this headstrong youth, who, settling down to a routine country life in Nottinghamshire, had abandoned pugilism and Abyssinian exploration for the hobby of carving oak choir-stalls. He also became the contented father of eight little girls. At one moment Mansfield Parkyns, who had led a wild life in Abyssinia, and had published an account of this, had seemed a small-scale version of Richard Burton: no doubt the reason for which Milnes asked them together to Fryston. But where Parkyns was an original, Burton had genius: nothing quelled his magnificent ambitions, and his runaway match with Isabel Arundell in 1861 brought him an enthusiastic and devoted ally in his unorthodox career.

In 1859, Captain Burton was nearing forty years of age. A swarthy, fierce-looking man, both cheeks scarred by a spear hurled through his face near Berbera in 1854, his thick dark hair growing low on his forehead, his cruel mouth shielded by long drooping moustachios, Burton was immensely tall, but owing to the great muscular development of chest and shoulders seemed well-proportioned. He had perfect manners, an hypnotic charm, as Swinburne was quick to recognise, and all the proud and ruthless allure of a hero:

> A wider soul than the world was wide,
> Whose praise made love of him one with pride . . .
> Who rode life's lists as a god might ride.

All this, combined with what Milnes termed his 'wonderful endurance of physical hardships,' his 'sensitiveness of character and

delicacy of perception,'] his 'varied knowledge and literary acquir-
ments' and a thoroughly good sense of humour, made Burton
irresistible to those who knew him, and now exerts a compelling
power over those who embark upon the rewarding task of reading
Isabel Burton's monumental *Life* of her husband, an untidy,
crowded book which appeared with many appendices and a
curiously touching cover, in 1893.[1] Although still in his 'thirties,
Burton had already led a spectacular life, which had begun with a
commission in the Indian Army during the Sikh war, and had
included his celebrated solitary pilgrimage to Mecca in disguise in
1853 and his three-year expedition to Lake Tanganyika from 1856
to '59. He had published a number of books, though his real
popularity did not come until later: Milnes, who reviewed Burton's
book on Mormonism in an article on that subject for the *Quarterly* in
1861, was of considerable assistance in his career, and helped to get
him posted to places to which he wished to go. Mrs. Burton, who
was as much attached to Milnes as was her husband (and, unlike
him, felt it important to cherish influential English contacts), was
quite aware of what they both owed to this friend: 'I don't like
Swinburne for neglecting *you*,' she wrote to him in 1874, from
Trieste. 'He, Richd and I and many others I know, would have
remained very much in the background if you had not taken us by
the hand and pulled us into notice. . . .'

Whenever they were in England, which was rarely, the Burtons
would go to Fryston, which Isabel Burton described in an article for
The World in 1877. Like Milnes' other friends, Burton would
sometimes make cynical jokes about him behind his back—'Some
good luck must be coming my way,' he is once reported to have said,
'Houghton has been so damned civil'; and from a letter of Swinburne's to Burton of January 1867 [2] we may glean something of their
attitude to Milnes:

I am still the centre of such moral chaos [wrote Swinburne] that
our excellent Houghton maintains a discreet and consistent neutrality. . . . I have not set eyes on his revered form for months. Your
impending opulence, and my immediate infamy, will too evidently
cut us from the shelter of his bosom.

Burton was an outspoken man, who did not bother to conceal his
feelings:

[1] Lady Burton's lengthy and combative biography was published by Chapman
and Hall in 1893; the cover, presumably of her own design, is embossed with a
picture of a dog mourning over Burton's gravestone on one side, and of herself as
a widow on the other.
[2] Letter from Holmwood dated January 11, 1867, published as No. xxi of the
Gosse and Wise selection of Swinburne's letters (Heinemann 1918).

My dear Houghton [he wrote from Turin in September 1869] Swinburne and I have been busily devoting your venerable head to the infernal gods. There are a dozen good hotels in Vichy—why did you send us to the only cabaret? to the Hôtel de France . . . where we were cheated robbed and had to pay 'at least as much as in the best of the best . . . I was delighted to leave the hideous hole [he continued, in scathing reference to Lord Houghton's favourite watering-place] with its jaundices, gouts and diabetes. Out of Paris the French are perfect savages—the Casino of Vichy would disgrace Constantinople. Separation of the sexes complete.

'The prospect of a book which can produce horripilation is refreshing. I cannot believe in it till the operation really takes place,' Burton had written to Milnes before his first visit to Fryston in August 1859. Whether he was or was not disappointed by this aspect of the Fryston library we cannot tell, but his intimacy with Milnes was certainly increased by his summer week in the West Riding; during the following winter he and Milnes spent many bachelor evenings together in London, sometimes with Burton's crony Colonel Studholme Hodgson, an elderly libertine who enjoyed describing his conquests and seductions, as a third.[1] In 1861 Burton was appointed consul at Fernando Po (a pestilential island to which he could not take his wife) and during his four years on the West Coast he made many gallant expeditions into the hinterland, which provided him with material for *Wanderings in West Africa, Abeokuta and the Cameroons, Gorilla Land or The Cataracts of the Congo*, and three other books. Although he professed to believe that 'the pleasure of correspondence decreases according to the ratio of the distance of the two correspondents,' Burton would write Milnes boisterous letters. Headed 'Kanna,' 'Brass River' or 'The Gaboon' these would make a welcome appearance amongst the piles of constituents' complaints, pleas for money, place or pension, and lawyers' letters which lay waiting for Milnes on the Fryston breakfast-table. 'Caro Amico—Did you ever hear of the Brass R.? I am almost ashamed to write to you from such a place,' one letter begins; while in May 1863 he sits down to describe his experiences in the land of Dahomey, notorious at that time for the bloodthirsty habits of its king, alleged to keep a canoe floating in human blood and an amazonian army of five thousand virgins. Avowing himself 'grievously disappointed' at his first sight of this place, he went on, in a highly characteristic vein:

The victims are between 100 and 200 a year instead of thousands. At Benin . . . they crucified a fellow in honour of my coming—here

[1] Studholme John Hodgson, d. 1890, general, had entered the army in 1819, served in Ceylon, India and Burma, and later commanded the forces in Ceylon and the Straits Settlements.

nothing! And this is the Bloodstained Land of Dahome!! The 'monster' as your papers call the King is a jolly looking party about 45 with a pleasant face, a frank smile and a shake of the fist like a British shopkeeper. He made me Captain of his Corps of Amazons. About these individuals a fearful amount of bosh has been talked and written. I was looking forward with prodigious curiosity to see 5,000 African adult virgins never yet having met with a single specimen. I found that most of them were women taken in adultery and given to the King as food for powder instead of being killed. They were mostly elderly and all of them hideous . . . I took up a few presents of cloth, several boxes of liqueurs which he seems from his blear eyes to like considerably—malt whiskey being the decided favourite—and (keep this quiet) three very dégagé coloured prints of white women in a state of Eve-ical toilette. This charmed him and he inquired whether such articles are to be pro-cured alive. I told (Heaven forgive me) a fearful fib and said that in my country the women are of a farouche chastity. . . . Disgusted with the tameness of this place . . . I shall go up the Niger and attempt Timbuctoo in a canoe. Really it will be a curious spectacle for the immortal Gods to look down upon, a chap starting in a hollowed log of wood for some thousand miles up a river with an infinitesimal prospect of returning!

In 1862 Burton wrote to his wife that he had christened a 'tall cone' in the Cameroons range 'Mount Milnes.'

It is not difficult to understand Milnes' immediate and enduring interest in Captain Richard Burton. It is even less so to imagine the electrical effect of this noble, savage personality upon Milnes' latest protégé, Algernon Swinburne—an emotional youth lately removed from Oxford, a small, delicate boy of nineteen who gave promise of becoming a great poet, and whose most marked trait was the masochistic one of hero-worship. The two first met at Milnes' house in Upper Brook Street on 5 June 1861. To Swinburne it was like meeting the spirit of the greatest of the Elizabethan heroes, re-incarnated in the body of this swarthy adventurer seeming so curiously out of place at Milnes' round breakfast-table that morning in Mayfair.

Chapter Eight

1861   1866 (I)

I

The way in which Richard Monckton Milnes, aged fifty, and Algernon Swinburne, aged twenty-three, first met each other is uncertain. Edmund Gosse suggests Signora Fronduti, an acquaintance who read Italian to Swinburne in 1853, as the medium of this successful introduction, though he thinks it also possible that it was Pauline Lady Trevelyan, the short-lived friend of Ruskin, 'a woman of singular and unique charm,' living in Northumberland who first brought Swinburne into Milnes' orbit; while Lafourcade points out that both Milnes and Swinburne had been elected 'non-artistic' members of the Hogarth Club in 1858. It seems more likely that Milnes' interest was aroused by hearing of Swinburne through J. B. Payne, the manager of the publishing firm of the late Edward Moxon, which was still issuing reprints of Milnes' edition of *The Poetical Works of John Keats*[1] and which produced Swinburne's first volume, *Rosamond and the Queen Mother* early in 1861, after he had, for some reason now unknown, withdrawn the poems from his first choice as publisher, Pickering. Swinburne's life at this early period is not well-documented, and there has in the past been also some confusion as to the date at which his important friendship with Monckton Milnes began. In the spring of 1861[2]

[1] Milnes' edition of Keats' poems, with an introductory memoir by himself condensing the information in his *Life, Letters and Literary Remains of John Keats* (1848) first appeared in 1854 (an edition without a memoir having been published in the same format in 1851), was reprinted in 1858, and, with a different typographical set-up, in 1861. In 1862 the work was republished by Routledge, Warne and Routledge in a handsome volume illustrated by George Scharf.

[2] I follow G. Lafourcade (*Swinburne: A Literary Biography*, G. Bell & Sons 1932, p. 92n) rather than Gosse (*The Life of Algernon Charles Swinburne*, Macmillan 1917, pp. 74–75), in assuming that Swinburne did not take lodgings in Grafton Street, Fitzroy Square until 1861. Gosse was misled by the apparent date '60' on the long letter from Swinburne to Milnes of October 15, 1861 which he and Wise published as No. III in their edition of *The Letters of Algernon Charles Swinburne* (Heinemann 1918, two volumes); but internal evidence proves that this letter can only have been written after Swinburne's visit to Fryston in August 1861. This misunderstanding also led Gosse to give May 1860 instead of May 1861 as the date of Swinburne's first formal note to Milnes (simply headed 'May 4th') : while there is no mention of Swinburne's being at Upper Brook Street in 1860, we find that he breakfasted there on 5 June 1861 (four weeks after his first call), and was at Fryston in mid-August of that year, whence he went to stay with the Trevelyans at Wallington while the Milneses proceeded for a few days to Studley Royal, where Lady de Grey gave Milnes an invitation for Swinburne which he duly passed to the poet, who thanked him for it in the letter of 15 October.

Algernon Swinburne, oblivious of the London season, had settled in
Bloomsbury lodgings, near Burne-Jones and the British Museum.
It was there that he received a summons to call on Milnes at 16
Upper Brook Street on the fifth of May. Swinburne replied in
three lines that he 'would be happy to come tomorrow.' This
short note in his schoolboyish handwriting forms the preface to one
of the most sparkling of all the series of letters that constitute
the Houghton Papers.

Fifty-seven letters, or fragments of letters, from Swinburne to
Milnes have been preserved: an early gap in this correspondence
makes clear that there must once have been more. These letters,
last examined by Gosse, who printed some of them, and tactfully defined the tone of others as 'high facetious familiarity,' deal partly
with Swinburne's own poetry, with the contributions which Milnes
arranged for him to make to *The Spectator* (at that time, under
Hutton's editorship, the most eminent of our weeklies) and with the
writings of the Marquis de Sade, which Swinburne read under
Milnes' auspices though against his advice. These letters scintillate
with examples of Swinburne's special brand of burlesque humour
which it has long been the convention to suppress as 'puerile' and
'obscene.' Blithely begun in 1861, this set of letters spans a period
of twenty years, though the most interesting belong to the decade of
the 'sixties, when Milnes was of real value to Swinburne and before
the poet's regard for him had dwindled, as in the 'seventies it did.
The last letter in the bundle has an almost symbolic significance:

I see there is a letter from you lying here for Swinburne [wrote
Theodore Watts to Lord Houghton, from The Pines, Putney Hill,
probably in 1882]. I thought it might, perhaps, be an invitation
which required answering. . . . Swinburne enjoyed the little
luncheon the other day. But what a joke it was Lord Lytton
(whom he didn't in the least know) being there!

But in 1861, before either celebrity or Watts had come his way,
Swinburne found in Richard Monckton Milnes a benevolent and
very painstaking friend.

The strange young gentleman whom the Milnes' butler ushered
up the staircase of the Upper Brook Street house that spring
evening of 1861 looked, at first go, preposterous. His head was
crowned with frantic scarlet hair, his little face was white and
pointed, his eyes were green and fringed with dark brown lashes.
In stature he was even shorter than Monckton Milnes himself. He
had a girlish figure, bottle shoulders and a dainty skipping walk: a
wraith-like darting creature, comparable to the marshland *fourolle*

of the Amiens folk-tales, and forming a definite contrast to his plump, red-faced, gouty host, whom George Smythe had called 'Sancho Panza' and 'Bozzy to the life' and whose features—'a countenance cut out of an orange' with a mouth that 'was one long slit'—must have seemed coarse beside Swinburne's pallid, well-bred face. Nor did the contrast stop at physical appearances. Milnes was a travelled cosmopolitan with a spacious arc of acquaintances across the map of Europe: Swinburne had been little abroad, had met few people, hated the Mediterranean, and had lately fled in disgrace from the third of three discontented years spent cooped-up in Oxford University, a place which he found depressing, amid companions whom he had despised. His genius went still unrecognised—in 1862, he said that *The Queen Mother and Rosamond* had sold seven copies—and his only real friends were the 'poet-painters,' a circle with which, as it happened, Monckton Milnes was not then familiar. Swinburne's evenings in London were spent either with his hero Rossetti, who was on the point of marrying Lizzie Siddall, or with Burne-Jones, also to be married that June. His family life formed no acceptable alternative to his lonely, somewhat baffled existence, for though his parents were affectionate, solicitous and well-disposed, he found their atmosphere oppressive:

They doctor me with tonics & champagne [he wrote to Lord Houghton during a sojourn at their house at Henley-on-Thames in August 1867], & I thrive so well that having no one to speak to & nothing to do beyond the family wall I shall end by writing something which will make the author 'du hideux roman de J——' turn enviously in his grave. One always writes des horreurs when one is en famille.

II

From the outset Milnes' attitude to Swinburne was helpful and avuncular. His influence was a constructive one, 'for' (in the words of M. Lafourcade) 'he would have no more Border Ballads or translations from Boccaccio, and the result was that Swinburne wrote *Faustine*'[1]; Milnes also arranged for him to publish signed poems and unsigned reviews in *The Spectator*. Milnes was the first man of letters to recognise the immense potential importance of Swinburne's work, but it is quite apparent that he never really grasped its purport. In an article on *Atalanta in Calydon* which he concocted for *The Edinburgh* in 1865 (and of which Swinburne wrote that 'nothing yet said or written about the book has given me

[1] Lafourcade: *Swinburne, A Literary Biography* (1932), p. 97.

nearly as much pleasure')[1] Milnes praised the poet's gifts, but attacked him for his 'anti-theism,' warned him against his 'insolence of originality' and his 'obscurity,' and declared that there was 'even serious difficulty of comprehension' in many passages. For though, as Froude has remarked in his *Life of Thomas Carlyle*, Milnes had 'open eyes for genius, and reverence for it, truer and deeper than most of his contemporaries' he did not always understand its achievements. For example, Milnes was one of the only Englishmen of his day to recognise the overpowering brilliance of Alexis de Tocqueville; but the article which he published in an 1861 *Quarterly*, after this friend's death, clearly reveals that he had no conception whatever of Tocqueville's position as an historian, and no understanding of his political theory. Milnes' own most vital gift was a flair for detecting genius or originality. He had a sense for quality in human beings of any calibre, and he allowed this sense to guide him even into regions in which he felt intellectually bewildered, morally disapproving or simply at a loss. His unerring instinct led him to realise that the astonishing, voluble, red-haired boy who called on him in May 1861 was potentially one of the greatest poets England had produced; but whereas Coventry Patmore, whom Milnes had befriended in 1846, wrote verse which Milnes could admire without effort, Swinburne was at times too revolutionary, too modern, too 'obscure.' In this context an astute comment by Henry Adams is apposite: that although Milnes was 'regarded as an eccentric,' he was really only a man with 'ideas a little in advance of his time.' 'His manner,' adds Adams, 'was eccentric but not his mind, as any one could see who read a page of his poetry.'[2] There is indeed a considerable difference between *The Beating of my own Heart* or *Strangers Yet* and the first series of Swinburne's *Poems and Ballads* which appeared in 1866. Yet, blindly, by instinct, Milnes helped create the conditions in which *Poems and Ballads* were composed. By giving Swinburne needed self-confidence, by introducing him to books and people he did not know, by freeing his mind and by sympathizing with the sadistic inspiration of his verse, Milnes cleared the way for the great upsurge of lyrical poetry which produced *Laus Veneris*, the *Hymn to Proserpine*, *Ilicet*, *A Match*, the *Ballad of Burdens*, *Les Noyades*, *Faustine*, and *The Triumph of Time*, poems which, together with several critical essays and *A Year's Letters*, mark 1862 as 'the crucial year of Swinburne's early life.'[3] It is also possible that Milnes, realising

[1] Swinburne to Lord Houghton, 'Friday,' August 1865 Gosse and Wise, letter XVI.
[2] *The Education of Henry Adams*, ed. H. C. Lodge (Boston 1918).
[3] Lafourcade, *op. cit.*, p. 96.

'with his great experience, that the curb of a classical form was exactly what Swinburne's genius required at the moment in order to produce a work which would be acceptable to the public,'[1] suggested to him that he should write the Greek tragedy that became *Atalanta*.

In the spring of 1861, when he first made Milnes' acquaintance, Algernon Swinburne had just succeeded in getting his father's agreement to his taking up writing as a career.   It must have been a hard tussle, for after his failure at Oxford he was for some time faced with the fear of having to enter some profession:

What *is* one to do? [he had written to his friend Lady Trevelyan from Mentone, in January 1861].[2]   I can't go to the bar: and much good I shd do if I did.   You know there is really no profession one can take up and go on working.   Item—poetry is quite enough work for any one man.   Item—who is there that is anything *besides* a poet at this day except Hugo?

That spring he met a living proof of his theory in the busy, sociable person of Richard Monckton Milnes.   It is instructive to think how incredulous and irreverent Swinburne would have been had he learned that his idol, Walter Savage Landor, had once sincerely hailed the young Milnes as 'the greatest poet now living in England.' Those days were long ago.

In May 1861 Swinburne was newly returned to England from a first view of the Mediterranean.   It is likely that his ready hatred for this region surprised Richard Monckton Milnes, who had often expressed his own youthful passion for it in verse, comparing

> The bland outbreathings of the midland sea,
> The aloe-fringed and myrtle-shadowed shore,

with the 'cold ground' of his native country.

Whatever you or anyone may say [wrote Swinburne to him, in a letter of March 1868],[3] I maintain that the Nizza-Mentone province is unpleasant, angular, arid, sharp-edged, stony, *frowzy*—neither grand nor sweet—& landscape must be one or the other, if it is not to be (as Shelley says) 'damnable—and damned.'

But the more singular the impression Swinburne created the more fascinated Milnes would have been.   A month later, on 5 June

---

[1] Lafourcade, *op. cit.*, p. 113.
[2] Gosse and Wise, Letter IV.
[3] Unpublished letter to Lord Houghton, headed Arts Club, Hanover Square, March 28, no year.

1861, Swinburne was one of the eight guests at a bachelor breakfast-party given by Milnes, whose wife had taken the children down to stay at Tunbridge Wells. The other guests were Coventry Patmore, Aubrey de Vere, Arthur Russell, three gentlemen named Stigant, Cartwright and Mansfield respectively—and Captain Richard Burton, who had come back from a swift tour of North America earlier in the year and was now due to take up his new appointment as Consul at Fernando Po. This was Burton's first encounter with Swinburne, who seems to have fallen immediately under his spell. We may suppose, though we do not know for certain, that they saw each other again during that summer in London, but it is established that Swinburne was at Fryston in August when Richard Burton and his bride visited there for four days. From the entries in Mrs. Milnes' pocket diaries it is not clear whether Swinburne arrived with the Burtons on August 12, or was already in the house. When they left on August 16, Swinburne remained there, going over to luncheon at Temple Newsam on the 23rd in a carriage party consisting of his host and hostess, the painter Holman Hunt, Francis Turner Palgrave, a friend of Mrs. Milnes' named Minnie Clive, and that downright Parisian Englishwoman Madame Mohl. These details are worth recording because of the melodramatic light in which Milnes' introduction of Burton to Swinburne has been placed by the imaginative biographers of the poet.

The most recent English writer on Algernon Swinburne has used the phrase 'a piece of calculated corruption' to describe Milnes' part in initiating the passionate friendship of Burton and the young poet.[1] Like other Swinburne students he supposes the first meeting to have taken place at Fryston, a house which Monsieur Lafourcade, in his otherwise penetrating study *La Jeunesse de Swinburne*, dramatises as 'l'auberge des rencontres étranges,' a sinister Yorkshire mansion filled with sadic literature and presided over by a 'feline' and malicious host. Although Monsieur Lafourcade somewhat modifies this Latin view of Monckton Milnes' character in his excellent *Swinburne: A Literary Biography*, published here in 1932, in which he chides 'ill-advised reviewers' of his earlier book for calling Milnes a 'villainous tempter,' his first interpretation of Milnes' character has persisted with all the deathless vitality of ill repute. In that useful work, *The Romantic Agony*, Professor Mario Praz goes farther. Embroidering on Monsieur Lafourcade's theme, he writes of Monckton Milnes as a man of 'Mephistophelean malice,' a sinister Virgil 'guiding Swinburne through the Inferno of his

---

[1] Humphrey Hare: *Swinburne: A Biographical Approach* (H. F. & G. Witherby 1949).

library,' a man of the world crouching spider-like at Fryston to watch the counter-play of his guests' characters with evil pleasure, and using his friends 'as instruments in order to put together some strange cruel comedy.'[1] These writers, and their followers, have succeeded in lending Milnes a baleful attraction to which, alas for his biographer, he has no real claim. In at least two recent works of American scholarship we find the tag 'unedifying' attached to Monckton Milnes and his interest in erotica.[2] To prudish and illiberal persons his name has become a bogey, to the prurient a decoy.

Truth alone is interesting in biography. I have neither the wish nor the ambition to 'whitewash' Monckton Milnes. It is however only just to point out that this apocryphal version of his character does not stand up to any commonsense investigation, and is not supported by contemporary evidence.[3] Some of the people who knew Milnes did not like him at all—finding him, as Disraeli found him, vain, envious, trivial and conceited, or as Lady John Russell did, gross, and, in the words of the first secretary at the American Legation, 'smutty.'[4] None of them thought of this bluff, good talker as Mephistophelean or regarded the somewhat haphazard parties at Fryston Hall as incidents in 'some strange cruel comedy.' 'Oh how wide is the diapason of my mind! From what a height to what a depth!' Milnes had once written elegantly in an early commonplace-book. He was flattering himself. Incapable of passionate love, lacking poetic or political genius, Milnes was also incapable of real evil. He collected erotic books; he shared with

[1] Praz, *op. cit.*, pp. 215–216.

[2] See Professor Hyder E. Rollins' *The Keats Circle* (Harvard University Press 1949) and the equally impressive monument of American scholarship, Dr. Gordon N. Ray's *Letters & Private Papers of W. M. Thackeray* (Oxford 1945).

[3] In this context an unpublished letter from Robert Buchanan to Lord Houghton, written after a visit to Fryston in November 1868, during which he had borrowed one hundred pounds from his host, is relevant. 'I far too thoroughly disagree with you in matters of taste to feel with you on literary questions or to be influenced by your dictum,' wrote Buchanan; 'I think it has been a dictum for evil in Swinburne's case. You will not misconceive me! I regard you with admiration and even affection, and shall be grieved if you felt hurt by my words ; but I cannot in honesty conceal my feeling that many of your views would be fatal were they not counteracted in your case by a heart so infinitely more noble than themselves. . . Regret nothing that you did for David Gray! God will remember that.' Buchanan (1841–1901), a Scots poet and novelist of notoriously combative temperament, who attacked and satirised the Pre-Raphaelites and in particular Swinburne with great ferocity, wrote to Houghton in a later letter, dated April 1871, of the 'vile set' which Swinburne had 'got among' : 'slaves who flatter and pollute him' wrote Buchanan of the Pre-Raphaelite Brotherhood, 'mean crawlers on the skirts of literature.'

[4] 'Houghton as usual told some smutty stories but I shan't repeat them,' Moran wrote in his journal for 22 February 1864, of Mrs. Adams' first reception at the Legation (*The Journal of Benjamin Moran* (1857–1865), ed. Wallace & Gillespie, University of Chicago Press, 1949).

Thackeray, with Burton, with Swinburne, the specially English interest in flagellation; but his attitude to these things was an extraverted, sensual attitude. In the calm words of the *Dictionary of National Biography*, Milnes was a man with 'many fine tastes and some coarse ones.'

The story of Lord Houghton's genially pointing out the choicest corner of the erotic library to his guests before setting out with Lady Houghton for Ferry Fryston church on Sunday morning has an authentic ring about it. There was the same casual, beneficent atmosphere about the two actions of Monckton Milnes for which he has chiefly been condemned—his introduction of Swinburne to Burton in the summer of 1861 and to the writings of the Marquis de Sade the year after. Milnes later became much concerned at the effects of both these introductions—for he found that Burton made Swinburne drink and he feared that Sade was becoming an obsession. The necessity to Swinburne's work of the twin stimuli of alcohol and a sadistic fancy seems never to have dawned upon Milnes' kindly mind.

III

Before considering Milnes' effect on Swinburne in any detail, it is helpful to establish the tempo and duration of this friendship which, starting in May 1861, quickly became intimate and continued so for the next six years. Officially, the friendship never ended: but in the early 'seventies Swinburne's warm personal regard for Lord Houghton had evaporated, and was replaced by a peevish disdain. 'Thank something,' he wrote in January 1877,[1] 'there are spirits of another sort—and I have met with my share of them as well as of Houghtons and Rossettis (D.G.).'

I have never shrunk from attack or from blame deserved or undeserved [he wrote to John Morley in May 1874, on learning that Houghton was to review his *Mary Stuart* for the *Fortnightly*], but I must confess that I do shrink from the rancid unction of that man's adulation or patronage or criticism.[2]

Swinburne's choice of words was at times more venomous than the feelings he intended to express. It is probable that he felt nothing more than impatient indifference towards his old friend, to whom he was still writing occasional amiable letters, and whose 'faithful

[1] Letter quoted in Lafourcade's *Swinburne: A Literary Biography*, p. 250.
[2] Swinburne to Morley, 23 May 1874, printed as No LXXXIII in Gosse and Wise. 'I was on the whole agreeably surprised on reading Lord Houghton's notice of *Bothwell*' he wrote to Morley on 20 July 1874. '. . . I found it more thorough and careful (in a sort) than I expected.'

labour,' and 'strenuous devotion' to the memory of Keats he publicly defended in *The Athenæum* in 1877, when he acclaimed Lord Houghton as the one man who had done for Keats 'and for us all the one service most truly and most thoroughly worth doing and worth thanks.'[1] The revolutionary influence of Mazzini on Swinburne's mind and work, which lasted from 1866 to 1871, and made him abandon Pre-Raphaelite æstheticism for the production of the great political lyrics published as *Songs Before Sunrise*, led the poet to dismiss as trivial and unidealistic most of the interests and friends of his youth. It is not entirely surprising that Lord Houghton should have been an early victim of this holocaust, nor was there any special ingratitude in what Lady Burton called Swinburne's 'neglect.' In discarding Monckton Milnes after digesting all that he had to offer—his knowledge of Keats, of Blake, of Sade, his advice over work, his help over publication— Swinburne was merely exercising that practice and prerogative of genius, the habit of getting through a person as though he were a meal. There was also a secondary factor; Lord Houghton scolded Swinburne for his excesses. 'I am at a loss to guess what has called down such an avalanche of advice,' Swinburne wrote to him in 1865,[2] evidently in answer to some reproachful letter.

I have probably no vocation & doubtless no ambition for the service of Bacchus: in proof of which if you like I will undertake to repeat the conversation of Wednesday evening throughout with the accuracy of a reporter, as it happens to be fixed in my memory. I don't doubt your ability to do likewise, any more than the friendliness of your feeling towards me, of which I have proofs in plenty.

This Wednesday evening had been an occasion which Houghton had planned hopefully, but which had turned out wrong—the occasion of Swinburne's presentation to the Poet Laureate, up in London on one of his short and solemn visits.

I had been spending the soberest of evenings here [Swinburne wrote in the same letter, from his rooms in Dorset Street], before starting to pick you up at 11 o'clock, which I understood was the order of the day. You as we returned seemed considerably infuriated with my unpunctuality—which I did not attribute to any influence of Bacchus on yourself. I am not aware of having retorted by any *discourtesy* . . . (and) the rest of the evening had been spent, after the few words of civility that passed between Mr. Tennyson and me, in discussing Blake & Flaxman in the next room with Palgrave & Lewes.

[1] Letter to the Editor of *The Athenæum*, January 1877.
[2] Undated letter of December 1865, published as No. XVIII by Gosse and Wise.

Lord Houghton even went to the length of consulting about their son's health and habits with Admiral Swinburne and with Lady Jane:

I fully appreciate the kind feeling which has made you write to me on the subject of the sad state in which you found my poor Son [wrote Swinburne's mother in July 1873],[1]—the case is a most grievous one and seems to me hopeless. We have done our utmost to make our home a happy one for him. . . . Since his Father's death I have not been able to persuade him to come to me—I have tried in every way to make him do so. In one letter to me he told me that nothing would induce him to come here again,—that he hates the place—& that, can I not be satisfied with seeing him in London? . . . I quite agree with what you say about Medical supervision, but I have no power to enforce it & persuasion I fear would be useless. It is a heavy grief.

Swinburne, who regarded all such concern as maddening inter- ference, must have suspected Lord Houghton of some form of collusion or intrigue, and reacted violently. His final verdict on his old friend is not, however, very bitter: 'He was a good-natured old fellow,' Swinburne wrote ten years after Lord Houghton's death,[2] 'but when made into a peer his title might have been "Baron Tattle, of Scandal."' As we shall see, Swinburne used certain outward characteristics of Monckton Milnes when com- posing his unattractive portrait of the cynical old Mr. Linley in *Lesbia Brandon*.

Apart from the affectionate and excited letters which Swinburne wrote to Milnes during the first years of their acquaintance, the only existing data on the course of it are supplied by entries in Mrs. Monckton Milnes' pocket diaries and carefully kept dinner-books. These only show how often Swinburne ate a meal in Upper Brook Street or stayed at Fryston. For the rest we may surmise un- recorded calls, dinners at London clubs, evenings spent with Burton when he was in England, or at the rooms of Meredith or Rossetti, to whom Swinburne had introduced Monckton Milnes. The invitation to breakfast on 5 June 1861 was followed by Swin- burne's first visit to Fryston that August, which lasted about a fortnight. In February 1862 we find that Swinburne breakfasted at Upper Brook Street in the company of Browning, Palgrave, the sculptor Woolner and other artists, and again at a more ambitious entertainment centering round Prince Frederick of Schleswig- Holstein. In November and December 1862 he made a prolonged

---

[1] Lady Jane Swinburne to Lord Houghton, Henley-on-Thames, 23 July 1873.
[2] Letter of September 1896 to Clement K. Shorter (published as No. CLI by Gosse and Wise).

stay, apparently of five or six weeks' duration, at Fryston, and he was there once more in April 1863 when Thackeray brought his daughters to the house for Easter. In May, June and July 1863 Swinburne went to five breakfast-parties. At one of these his friend Ruskin was present, and a few days later Mr. and Mrs. Milnes and Swinburne made an expedition to see the Turner sketches at Denmark Hill; on the 19th of June Matthew Arnold met 'a sort of pseudo-Shelley called Swinburne' at a large dinner-party at Monckton Milnes',[1] and in mid-July Swinburne brought Whistler to luncheon. In March 1864 he was with Milnes in Paris; he breakfasted twice at Upper Brook Street in July, and was at Fryston from the 6th to the 22nd of August. In 1865 he breakfasted, lunched and dined on five occasions, and was once more at Fryston in August, apparently his final visit there. By 1867 the poet's health was breaking down: 'Swinburne accepted but never came— "more suo" as Amy will translate to you,' Lord Houghton wrote to his wife after a specially successful dinner-party at which Gladstone had figured on 2 July of that year. The next morning Houghton received a note from Swinburne excusing himself on the grounds of a severe bilious attack. Ten days later, Swinburne did dine at Upper Brooke Street, and, two days after that, on the 13th of July, he came to breakfast, with disastrous result.

Dearest A— [ran Lord Houghton's daily bulletin to his wife on July 13 1867], We were sitting after breakfast, when Swinburne fell down in a fit: Tweed was out, but I got Dr. Williams in a few minutes & there is no immediate danger. I have telegraphed to his family, & I suppose someone will come up & look after him: he was looking wretchedly ill before. Dey is quite in his element looking after him. Jowett seemed much affected.

On receiving Lord Houghton's telegram Admiral Swinburne hastened up to London with his family doctor, removed his son to his lodgings, and finally took him down to his own house at Henley-on-Thames, Holmwood.

I gladly avail myself of this occasion to express my grateful sense of the kindness you have shewn to my Son for many years [the Admiral wrote to Houghton]. I purpose to show him your Lordship's letter, I think it may strengthen his resolves.

Swinburne himself wrote five days after his attack, in tearing spirits:

I am prescribed 'light literature' of all things! [he wrote], as if I ever indulged in heavy! I am sure Alison has a vague idea of hours

---

[1] Letter from Arnold to his mother, of June 1863, printed in G. W. E. Russell's *Letters of Matthew Arnold*, 1848–1888 (Macmillan 1895).

spent in hard study of philosophy & history—tho' I assure him that the most abstract authors I read are Flaubert & Trollope. . . . Nothing could be more attentive than your people were to me until I was able to move. I was quite sorry for the trouble given to you and them.[1]

Mrs. Milnes' records of Swinburne's appearances are almost exasperatingly tenuous. Her letters to her sister describe the visits of the Palmerstons or of the Orleans princes to Fryston, but those written during Swinburne's sojourns concern only her children and make no mention of him at all. It seems possible from the tone of the diary entries that Mrs. Milnes did not altogether relish Swinburne's company: and he also had a disturbing habit of staying on. 'All our guests departed except Sir J. Metcalfe and Mr. Swinburne,' we read, or 'Mr. Swinburne remained.' On one occasion (perhaps when he was working at Blake) he even out-stayed his hosts, a fact recorded by his hostess in the charming sentence: 'Left Mr. Swinburne at Fryston with Aunties.'

But though neither Lord Houghton nor his wife has left us the fuller records of Swinburne at Fryston that we should relish, two of his fellow-guests have done so—the young American attaché, Henry Adams, who met Swinburne there in December 1862, and Anne Thackeray, who as a little girl was fascinated by him in April of the following year. Both accounts are illuminating.

IV

The year 1862 was a dark spot in Henry Adams' life, [we read in his autobiography][2] and the education it gave was one that he gladly forgot. As far as he was aware, he made no friends; he could hardly make enemies; yet towards the close of the year he was flattered by an invitation, from Monckton Milnes to Fryston, and it was one of many acts of charity towards the young that gave Milnes immortality. Milnes made it his business to be kind. Other people criticised him for his manner of doing it, but never imitated him. Naturally, a dispirited, disheartened private secretary was exceedingly grateful, and never forgot the kindness; but it was chiefly as education that this first country visit had value.

With these simple but oblique sentences Henry Adams clears the way for his well-known description of Algernon Swinburne at Fryston; for though primarily interested in ideas rather than in people, Adams had a superlative talent for re-creating a personality or reviving an atmosphere, as this and other compelling passages of his autobiography show.

[1] Letter dated Holmwood, Henley-on-Thames, July 18 (1867).
[2] *The Education of Henry Adams*, ed. cit., p. 138.

THE HONOURABLE MRS. MONCKTON MILNES IN 1860

In May 1861, at the age of twenty-three, young Henry Adams had come to England as secretary to his father, the new Minister. In the intervening months between this arrival and his first country-house visit in December 1862, Adams had remained in London, receiving a succession of shocks, the earliest and worst of which had been the discovery that the supposedly friendly Whig Government had recognised the belligerency of the Confederacy a few days before President Lincoln's new envoy reached Liverpool. In spite of an earnest anxiety to make friends, the young American found London life crowded and not intimate: 'the London season,' Milnes used to say to him, 'is a season for making acquaintances and losing friends.' Over the American Civil War, which had burst out in April 1861, Richard Monckton Milnes was, as usual, in a minority. He warmly supported the cause of the Union, while almost everyone else in London society hoped, and hoped openly, that the reactionary Southerners would win. Young Adams could thus set out for Fryston without fear of meeting there hostility or ridicule.

Commonly, country visits are much alike [Adams continues], but Monckton Milnes was never like anybody, and his country parties served his purpose of mixing strange elements. Fryston was one of a class of houses that no one sought for its natural beauties, and the winter mists of Yorkshire were rather more evident for the absence of the hostess on account of them, so that the singular guests whom Milnes collected to enliven his December had nothing to do but astonish each other, if anything could astonish such men.

Adams writes that he found only four men in the house—his host, who was 'the oldest, and perhaps the sanest in spite of his superficial eccentricities, for Yorkshire sanity was true to a standard of its own, if not to other conventions'; 'a quiet, well-mannered, singularly agreeable gentleman of the literary class,' William Stirling of Keir; a grave and charming man of thirty, with his arm in a sling, who turned out to be Laurence Oliphant, just back from Japan where he had been wounded in a fanatic's attack on the British Legation; and finally a little person whom Adams took at first to be a boy.

The fourth [he writes], was a boy, or had the look of one, though in fact a year older than Adams himself. He resembled in action . . . a tropical bird, high-crested, long-beaked, quick-moving, with rapid utterance and screams of humor, quite unlike any English lark or nightingale. One could hardly call him a crimson macaw among owls, and yet no ordinary contrast availed. Milnes introduced him as Mr. Algernon Swinburne. The name suggested nothing. Milnes was always unearthing new coins and trying to give them currency. . . . When Milnes lingered a moment in Adams's room to add that Swinburne had written some poetry, not yet published, of really extraordinary merit, Adams only wondered what more Milnes would discover, and whether by any chance he could discover merit in a private secretary.   He was capable of it.

Adams' account of the dinner that evening, to which he says that the five men sat down 'with the usual club manners of lady-less dinner-tables, easy and formal at the same time,' suggests Milnes' abilities as a host.   The conversation was opened by Oliphant's describing his late adventure in Japan;

from him the talk drifted off into other channels, until Milnes thought it time to bring Swinburne out.   Then, at last, if never before, Adams acquired education.   What he had sought so long, he found; but he was none the wiser, only the more astonished. . . .
For the rest of the evening Swinburne figured alone; the end of dinner made the monologue only freer, for in 1862, even when ladies were not in the house, smoking was forbidden, and guests usually smoked in the stables or the kitchen; but Monckton Milnes was a licensed libertine who let his guests smoke in Adams' bedroom . . . and there after dinner all sat—or lay—till far into the night, listening to the rush of Swinburne's talk.   In a long experience, before or after, no one ever approached it; yet one had heard accounts of the best talking of the time, and read accounts of talkers in all time, among the rest, of Voltaire, who seemed to approach nearest the pattern.

The shy young American quickly recognised that Swinburne 'was altogether new to the three types of men-of-the-world before him' and that they found him 'quite original, wildly eccentric, astonishingly gifted, and convulsively droll.'   What more he was 'even Milnes hardly dared say.'   Adams was more and more bewildered: 'The idea that one has actually met a real genius dawns slowly on a Boston mind, but it made entry at last.'
    Swinburne held the field till far into the night—reciting Sophocles and Shakespeare, 'forward or backward, from end to beginning'; quoting Dante, Villon, Victor Hugo, declaiming his own unpublished ballads, *Faustine, The Four Boards of the Coffin Lid*, and the *Ballad of Burdens* 'as though they were books of the Iliad.'   Young Adams was very much aware of his own inadequacy to cope with this amazing youth: 'Adams could no more interest Swinburne,' he wrote ruefully, 'than he could interest Encke's comet.   To Swinburne he could be no more than a worm.'   At one point in the evening Swinburne 'tested him' with his favourite questions—what did he think of the two greatest living poets, Victor Hugo and Landor? When Adams admitted that they bored him, nothing more was needed, for 'one who could feel neither Hugo nor Landor was

lost.' As he lighted William Stirling downstairs to retrieve a copy of Swinburne's *Rosamond* from the library table Adams kept trying to assess the young poet in his own mind; he was greatly helped by Stirling's own 'explosions of wonder,' which reached a climax at the foot of the Fryston staircase with the ejaculation: 'He's a cross between the devil and the Duke of Argyll!' Realising that Stirling was as surprised as himself, Adams felt comforted.

Then [he writes], came the sad reaction, not from Swinburne whose genius was never in doubt, but from the Boston mind which, in its uttermost flights, was never *moyenâgeux*. One felt the horror of Longfellow and Emerson, the doubts of Lowell and the humor of Holmes, at the wild Walpurgis-night of Swinburne's talk. What could a shy young private secretary do about it?

The end soon came to this 'wonderful visit to Fryston.' Adams, who kept up his acquaintance with Laurence Oliphant, declares that he only saw Swinburne once again in his life, when he sat next him at a dinner of the Authors' Fund and found him 'famous then, but no nearer.' Writing in 1905 of people he had known half a century earlier, it is not odd that Adams should have forgotten a third occasion on which he met Swinburne, for they were both guests at a breakfast-party Milnes gave in July 1864, when the poet was still known only to what Edward Lear called 'small circles.'[1] But it is, to say the least of it, interesting to find how Henry Adams' memory misled him about the outward circumstances of the 'wonderful visit to Fryston.' Precise entries in Mrs. Milnes' diaries prove that far from having 'fled south,' leaving her husband to entertain a bachelor party that December, she was herself in the house, together with two of her husband's aunts and all of their three children at the time of the visit of Swinburne, Stirling and Henry Adams. 'Drove with R. and Mr. Adams round the woods,' she records on 5 December 1862; on December 8 little Florence Milnes had a birthday party, and 'Mr. Stirling left'; on the 13th 'Mr. Swinburne left'; and for the remainder of the year the Milneses were either together at Fryston or severally elsewhere.

On this occasion Swinburne and Oliphant seem to have lingered on from a November house-party, which had included William Rossetti, Hamilton Aidé,[2] and a sensational-looking Hindoo barrister

[1] 'Bye the bye', wrote Lear to his friend Chichester Fortescue, in October 1861, 'there is a new spadmodic [*sic*] poet, by name Swinburne, who seems to amaze small circles' (*Letters of Edward Lear*, ed. Lady Strachey, T. Fisher Unwin 1907, p. 198).
[2] Charles Hamilton Aidé (1826–1906), the son of an Armenian merchant, was born in Paris and educated at Bonn. A composer, novelist and amateur artist, he devoted his life to music, art and literature, and entertained widely in London.

Mr. Coomara Swami, who wore a turban and came from Ceylon.
The Yorkshire air did not agree with Mr. Swami: 'Hindoo gentle-
man so poorly that he determined to leave Fryston,' Mrs.
Milnes notes sadly on 2 December, and: 'he left at one' the next day. To
enthusiasts for that uproarious mid-Victorian satire, Laurence
Oliphant's *Piccadilly*, the presence of Mr. Coomara Swami at
Fryston that winter has a distinct incidental interest. When
Piccadilly first appeared in *Blackwood's Magazine* for 1865,[1] it was
recognised that Dickiefield, the comfortable country house in which
the opening scenes of the entangled plot are laid, and where Lord
Frank Vanecourt first meets the determined Hindoo, Juggonath
Chundango, was a picture of Fryston Hall, and that the 'warm-
hearted and eccentric' host, Lord Dickiefield, was a representation
of Lord Houghton. 'We shall be certain to meet a choice assort-
ment of pagan and theological curiosities in that most agreeable of
country-houses,' the Irish Lord Grandon tells Vanecourt; but even
they are not prepared for the company they find at Dickiefield,
where they arrive one evening when most of the guests are upstairs
dressing for dinner, so that

When Grandon and I entered the drawing-room, we found only the
deserted apparatus of the afternoon tea, a Bishop and a black man.
. . . The Bishop had a beard and apron, his companion a turban,
and such very large shoes, that it was evident his feet were unused
to the confinement. . . . Neither of them was the least embarrassed
when we were shown in; Grandon and I both were slightly.
'What a comfort that the snow is gone,' said I to the Bishop.

Also staying in the house are the chief characters of the book, Lady
Broadhem, who is intriguing to marry the rich Chundango to her
daughter Lady Ursula, and when this plan fails, attempts to marry
him herself; Lady Broadhem's son and second daughter; and 'a
petroleum aristocrat from the oil regions of America' Mr. Wog. By
no stretch of the imagination could the young vulgarian, Wog, be
interpreted as a travesty of the young Henry Adams; but it is
entirely plausible to assume that the appearance, and perhaps the
behaviour, of Mr. Coomara Swami at Fryston suggested to Oliphant
the presence at Dickiefield of Juggonath Chundango.

Florence Milnes' seventh-birthday party was enlivened by the
presence of Swinburne, who was always happy with children,
sharing a 'love and tenderness' for them with the 'three demi-gods
of my adoration in boyhood and youth and manhood alike'—
Landor, Mazzini and Victor Hugo.

---

[1] *Piccadilly* was published in book form by Blackwood in 1870, with illustrations by Doyle. An annotated copy from the Fryston library confirms the
identification of Houghton ('Dickie Milnes') with Dickiefield. The book was
republished in *Constable's Miscellany* in 1928.

I hope Florey has not forgotten her conditional engagement to me in ten years' time *if* I am rich enough to give her a trousseau of rubies [he wrote from the Trevelyans' house at Wallington a few days after this birthday],[1] I told Ly Trevelyan of the affecting ceremony, & she expressed herself 'only too thankful to hear that I have a chance of being saved by a virtuous attachment.'

Florey's sister Amicia seems also to have caught his fancy, for we find him using her archaic Christian name, and its family diminutive, 'Amy,' for the heroine of the novel which he was writing in 1862, and which he finally published as *Love's Cross Currents: A Year's Letters* in his own old age.[2] It is not improbable that his description of Amicia Cheyne in childhood was in fact a sketch of Amy Milnes, still a child of singular beauty. Little Amy Cheyne is described as

one of the few girls who have no ugly time . . . the most perfect child of eight that can be imagined. There was a strange grave beauty and faultless grace about her, more noticeable than the more usual points of childish prettiness: pureness of feature, ample brilliant hair, perfect little lips, serious and rounded in shape, and wonderful unripe beauty of chin and throat.

It is also not unlikely that the bleak, dank aspect of Fryston in December is to be recognised in Swinburne's description of Captain Harewood's gloomy house, Plessey, where Amicia Cheyne's half-brother Redgie is brought up, a place

muffled in woods, with a grim sad beauty of its own, but seemingly knee-deep in sere leaves all the year round, wet and weedy and dark and deep down, kept hold of somehow by autumn in the midst of spring; only the upper half of it clear out of the clutch of winter even in the hottest of August weather, with a bitter flavour of frost and rain in it all through summer.[3]

'It's very cold here, but no one knows it but myself,' wrote Madame Mohl from Fryston on just such an August day as Swinburne must have had in mind.[4] 'I wonder everyone don't live in London all the year round, the trees are of a better green, all trees a hundred or even fifty miles north of London are of a blue-green.' Mary Mohl was an old friend of Monckton Milnes, who

[1] Postscript to unpublished letter to Milnes, headed 'Wallington, Newcastle-on-Tyne, Dec. 27th' and clearly belonging to 1862.

[2] This accomplished novel deriving from Balzac and Choderlos de Laclos was published, on Watts' insistence, in 1905 (Chatto and Windus), though with some modifications.

[3] *Loves' Cross Currents*, ed. cit., p. 21.

[4] Madame Mohl to Lady William Russell, 21 August 1864, printed in M. C. M. Simpson's *Letters and Recollections of Julius and Mary Mohl* (Kegan Paul 1887).

seems to have gone first to her house in the Rue du Bac during the
revolution of 1848,[1] and who always asked her to Fryston during her
rare visits to this country.   Madame Mohl was twice at Fryston at
the same time as Algernon Swinburne—in August 1861, and in
August 1864.   In 1861 she thought Milnes 'the model of a master
of a house—thinking of everybody'; and admired the

incomparable drollery which would come out in spite of himself.
A lady asked 'who was the bishop's wife'—so like a country cousin's
question.   He replied with the utmost gravity, 'She is the daughter
of the King of the Cannibal Islands.'   He is for ever breaking out
in such rich explosions.

But though she was interested by Swinburne, and even went to call
on him when she heard he was ill in London, she has, alas, left us no
account of his behaviour in Yorkshire.   On the 1861 visit she particularly liked Holman Hunt, in spite of his unpunctuality, and
after August 1864 she wrote to Lord Houghton to say that she
thought her fellow-guests the Burtons

se sont distribués les Rôles he acts a ferocious musselman to her
lovely oppressed and impassioned slave and I suspect they chuckle
over our simplicity instead of fighting in their secret apartment and
if she told you that he had beat her I believe it unhesitatingly.

Of Swinburne she says nothing; and for a last glimpse of the
young poet at Fryston we must turn to the reminiscences of Thackeray's eldest daughter, who was there with her father and sister in
April 1863, as a girl of fifteen.
    Although Lady Ritchie's short account[2] is not accurate as to date
(she told Gosse that the visit was in the summer of '62, instead of at
Easter '63) it is amusing as once more showing the explosive
impact Swinburne made on startled Fryston guests.   Anne Thackeray recalled that 'the Houghtons stimulated the curiosity of their
guests by describing the young poet, who was to arrive later,' and
that she was in the garden when he came and 'saw him advance up
the sloping lawn, swinging his hat in his hand, and letting the sunshine flood the bush of his red-gold hair.'   To the girl he looked
'like Apollo or a fairy prince' and immediately attracted Thackeray
by his conversation, and the two sisters by his 'playfulness.'   On
Sunday evening, after dinner, when asked to read some of his

---

[1] Mary Mohl (1793–1883) was originally a Miss Clarke, a young English
devotee of Madame Récamier and Chateaubriand, and later an adorer of Miss
Florence Nightingale.   She married Professor Julius Mohl in 1847, and gave some
of the most amusing intellectual receptions of Paris for nearly forty years.   She
sent Milnes many trenchant, breathless and unpunctuated letters.
[2] Gosse *Life*, pp. 95–96.

poems aloud he made what Gosse primly calls an 'injudicious choice': 'he is believed,' writes Gosse, 'to have recited *The Leper*; it is certain that he read *Les Noyades*.' The Archbishop of York, who was present, 'made so shocked a face that Thackeray smiled and whispered to Lord Houghton, while the two young ladies, who had never heard such sentiments expressed before, giggled aloud in their excitement.' Swinburne was naturally offended by these giggles, and had to be 'soothed' by Mrs. Milnes, who remarked 'Well, Mr. Swinburne, if you *will* read such extraordinary things, you must expect us to laugh'; though it is hard to see what can have been mollifying in this comment. Swinburne resumed *Les Noyades*, which

was then proceeding on its amazing course, and the Archbishop was looking more and more horrified, when suddenly the butler like 'an avenging angel' threw open the door and announced 'Prayers! my Lord!'

Lady Ritchie added that she was so captivated by Swinburne's 'kind and cordial ways' that when the time came for her to leave Fryston with her father, while the poet stayed behind, she burst out crying. She also thought that Milnes must have shown some of Swinburne's manuscript poems to her father, who, dying in December of that same year, never saw the bulk of them in print.

V

It is probable that in these early years Milnes had a good number of Swinburne's manuscript poems through his hands, but most of these seem to have been returned since only seven of the poet's holographs now remain amongst the Houghton Papers. Two of these, written out on the deep blue foolscap which Swinburne often used, are fair copies of the two first poems—*A Ballad of Life* and *A Ballad of Death*—of *Poems and Ballads*, published in 1866. Both show slight variant readings when compared with the final versions. There is also a draft of the three last stanzas of the *Ballad of Burdens*, and a draft of the three opening ones of the poem published in 1866 as *Ilicet*:

> The end is come of joy and sorrow;
> Peace for to-day, peace for to-morrow,
>   But never a time to laugh or weep.

This latter scrap, headed *Salve*, and scrawled on the back of a letter from William Rossetti, of 2 November 1861, asking Swinburne to arrange for him to see Milnes' collections of Blake, is clearly the earliest draft of this beautiful poem.   Later Swinburne sent Milnes a copy of his *W. S. Landor at Florence* (published by Wise and Gosse in the *Posthumous Poems* of 1917), and there are also two unknown, and so far as I am aware, unprinted, works—a love-song beginning:

> Say, is it day, is it dusk, in thy bower,
>   Thou whom I long for, who longest for me?
> O be it night, be it light, 'tis love's hour,
>   Love's that is fettered as love's that is free.

and a long poem in French, of one hundred and eighteen couplets, entitled *Charenton en 1810*.   Both these have seemed to me to be worth printing and they will be found *in toto* in an appendix to this book.[1]

Completed on 27 October 1861, *Charenton* is of some interest, since it epitomises Swinburne's attitude to Sade before he had read any of his works.   A friend of Meredith's who was shocked by Swinburne's talk at Chatham Place in December 1861, described him as 'strongly sensual; although almost a boy he upholds the Marquis de Sade as the acme and apostle of perfection, without (as he says) having read a word of his works.'[2]   It seems evident that Swinburne, who confided to Milnes how much he had enjoyed being birched at Eton, and whose temperament was an exceptionally masochistic one, had early come to reverence de Sade as a genius who alone understood the universal triumph of evil and pain. A pastiche of Victor Hugo's *La Judée*, this poem on the old man in the mental hospital at Charenton conveys what Swinburne had hoped Sade might have been:

> En ce temps-là c'était un vieillard calme et fort:
> Il avait le front grave et l'œil serein: la Mort
> Avait peur à l'aspect du satyre sublime;
> Et la Douleur qui ronge et mord comme une lime
> Se tordait sous son pied comme un chien écrasé.
>
> .   .   .   .   .
>
> Il touchait au bon temps, au siècle antique, aux dieux;
> A le voir, on sentait un frisson aux cheveux.
>
> .   .   .   .   .
>
> Il souriait.   Cet homme avait des dieux à lui.
> Il vit tout, mais jamais il ne fut ébloui.
> Un appétit grouillait dans son âme profonde
> Plus grand que Bonaparte et plus grand que le monde.

---

[1] See Appendix, p. 256.
[2] *The Letters and Memoirs of Sir W. Hardman*, edited by E. M. Ellis, 1923.

After a long elaborate description, with allusions to many of the
most notorious characters, real or mythical, of the antique world,
Swinburne imagines Sade's impact on a young man at Charenton:

> Or, un soir, un jeune homme âgé de vingt-quatre ans
> Vit ce front blême et fier, chargé de cheveux blancs,
> Ces yeux noirs, cette bouche impérieuse et fine ;
> Il frissonna.
>   L'enfant lisait ce jour *Justine* ;
> Il levait ses regards, comme on fait en priant,
> De la page proscrite au vieillard souriant.

The narcissistic introduction of this innocent youth is typical of
Swinburne's humour, for he himself was twenty-four at the time.
The only difference between himself and the 'enfant' of the poem
was that Swinburne had not yet read *Justine*.

We find *Charenton* included amongst the imaginary works of the
imaginary French decadent poet Félicien Cossu, about whom
Swinburne composed a serio-comical article for *The Spectator* in 1862.
The Editor's refusal to print the first of these farcical essays, that on
'Ernest Clouet,' led to Swinburne's final breach with the paper.
It is not odd that Hutton refused, for amongst the principal works
of the 'Breton poet,' Cossu, Swinburne had listed : *A quinze ans je ne
suis plus vierge, Une Nuit de Sodome, Spasme d'Amour, Au Peuple Anglais*
('*Anglais, vous avez fait d'abominables choses*'), *Cœur Eunuque* and
Charenton. He must have sent the manuscript of *Charenton* to Milnes
at Fryston with other papers in 1862 : for in August of that year
Swinburne mentions it in writing to him about *Justine*. A well-
known and much-quoted letter of a few months earlier refers to
Monckton Milnes' promise to show him 'the mystic pages of the
martyred marquis de Sade; ever since which, the vision of that
illustrious and ill-requited benefactor of humanity has hovered by .
night before my eyes.'[1]   Swinburne's obsessional, almost idolatrous,
attitude towards Sade put Milnes in a quandary; for while on the
one hand naturally wishing to satisfy the young man's burning
curiosity, he felt on the other that the perusal of the actual works
might at that moment do him harm.   When he received *Charenton*
he kept it, calling it a 'physiological extravaganza' and begging
Swinburne to 'clear his head of the subject.'   Swinburne's long
reply to this letter may now be made available, since it contains
some of the sanest criticism of Sade's work yet written.   Swinburne's
initial revulsion was that of an artist, whose sense of style was
naturally offended by the weary numerological compilations of the

---

[1] Letter of 15 October 1861, incorrectly dated 1860 by Gosse and Wise, who
print it as Letter II of their edition.

Marquis de Sade. He later came to recognise them as 'a valuable study to rational curiosity';[1] but his first reaction was an æsthetic one.

> You retain my Charenton [he wrote to Milnes on 18 August 1862], & desire me to clear my head of the subject. I am in a very fair way to do so; for I have just read 'Justine ou les Malheurs de la Vertu.' As you seemed anxious to know its effect on me I mean to give you a candid record, avoiding paradox or affectation. I would give anything to have, by way of study, six or seven other opinions as genuine & frank as mine shall be.

There follows a brilliant analysis, exhaustive though hastily thrown down, and largely written in the form of an apostrophe to Sade.

> I drop my apostrophe to M. de Sade [writes Swinburne towards the end of the letter], having relieved my mind for good & all of its final judgement on a matter of some curiosity & interest to me. I should like to know (if you forgive me for writing such a farrago on the chance of its finding you désœuvré for half an hour) whether you agree or not. . . . I am very glad *not* to have waited (as you advised) some 29 years on the chance of being alive then to read Justine. You see that whether it drives curates or curates' pupils to madness & death or not . . . it has done decidedly little damage to my brain or nerves : . . . . If you keep *Charenton* 'as a physiological extravaganza' perhaps you will keep this prose rhapsody with it by way of comment & remark, giving as it does a sincere & deliberate opinion on the life's labour of Stylites de Sade.

Swinburne's reactions to Sade are remarkable for their clarity. He begins by explaining that he

> quite expected to add another to the gifted author's list of victims; I really thought I must have died or split open & choked with laughing. I never laughed so much in my life : I couldn't have stopped to save the said life. I went from text to illustrations & back again, till I literally doubled up & fell down with laughter—I regret to add that all the friends to whom I have lent or shown the book were affected in just the same way. One scene between M. de Verneuil and Mme d'Esterval I never thought to survive. I read it out & the auditors rolled & roared. Then Rossetti read out the dissection of the interesting Rosalie & her infant, & the rest of that refreshing episode : & I wonder to this minute that we did not raise the whole house by our screams of laughter. But on reflection I found the impression left on me to be precisely the same as that of Landor's heroine on her first view of the sea. 'Is this the mighty

---

[1] Letter to unspecified correspondent, quoted by Lafourcade in *La Jeunesse de Swinburne*, p. 265. This phrase makes it clear that Sade's importance as the first methodical recorder of sexual aberrations did not escape Swinburne.

Satyr? *is this all?*' I did think—I did hope that this one illusion might have turned out a reality. Weep with me over a shattered idol!

That Swinburne should have been vastly amused by Sade's arithmetical style and throng of virtuous victims was predictable, for his sense of the ridiculous was especially acute. That he should have been disgusted was also to be expected, since even at its most lurid his own imagination was always fastidious and more than a little Pre-Raphaelite—'*This*, I call real delicate torment,' he wrote, describing to Milnes a birching in a scented fir-wood near Eton, and another occasion on which his tutor let him 'saturate' his face with eau-de-cologne before being punished. But it seems oddly inconsistent that having seen through Sade to such a degree, Swinburne could return with an almost childish obstinacy to his original illusions about 'the martyred marquis.'

I only regret that in justly attacking my anti-theism you have wilfully misrepresented its source [he wrote tersely to Lord Houghton of the latter's *Quarterly* article on *Atalanta*]; I should have bowed to the sentence if instead of 'Byron with a difference' you had said 'de Sade with a difference.' The poet, thinker & man of the world from whom the theology of my poem is derived was a greater than Byron. *He*, indeed, fatalist or not, saw to the bottom of gods & men.[1]

This was in 1865, when the initial impact of Sade's work had perhaps been forgotten, and when the idea, as against the actuality, of Sade had re-asserted a lingering ascendancy over Swinburne's mind. The apostrophe to Sade which he sent to Milnes in the letter of August 1862 is of a very different tone:

As it is, your book misses aim [he tells the 'shattered idol']; with half your materials another man would have built a better palace of sin—a fairer house to sweep and garnish for the advent of the seven devils. You have gathered up and arranged in rows all manner of abominations & your work is *fade* after all—flat, flaccid, impotent, misshapen, hung awry. It might be bound up with Télémaque or Paul et Virginie. . . . You take yourself for a great pagan physiologist & philosopher—you are a Christian ascetic bent on earning the salvation of the soul through the mortification of the flesh. You are one of the family of St. Simeon Stylites. . . . It matters little that you have forgotten your own genealogy or that you operate rather on the flesh of others than on your own. Your one knack is to take common things, usual affections, natural pleasures. & make them walk on their heads; by the simple process of *reversing* anyone may write as good a Justine as you.

[1] Letter of August 1865, published by Gosse and Wise as No. XVI. They oddly misread the word 'anti-theism' in this letter as 'Charenton'.

He has found only one merit in Sade:

why did you never tell me what a good lyrical poet the man was?
[he asks Monckton Milnes]. There is a song in the 8th part of
'Aline et Valcour' which seems to me about the most exquisite
piece of simple finished language & musical effect in all 18th
century French literature.

It seemed to him very like the poetry of Blake in England, and 'as
unlike any contemporary work—mediæval rather in grace &
quietness of beauty.' Milnes need not really have worried: with
the inborn purity of genius Swinburne had come through the fire
unscathed. He had emerged from it carrying a 'sweet and perfect'
lyric in his hand.

Disappointed though he was by Sade's style, Swinburne quickly
realised that he had here found an ideal new medium for his own
form of humour. Henceforth his letters echo with comical references to *Justine*; addressing Milnes as 'Monsieur Rodin' he sends
long absurd petitions signed 'Zulina de Cardoville.' 'Il est
dommage que ce cher et digne marquis n'ait pas imaginé des
supplices de mer,' he wrote in December 1862, describing the
lashing waves of the North Sea in a passage which Milnes copied
into his commonplace-book, and which Swinburne himself used in
the storm scene of *Lesbia Brandon*. Some of these high-spirited letters,
which he would complain that Milnes had failed to answer, were
also composed in a mock schoolboy style, and signed 'Frank Fane'
or 'Redgie,' imaginary characters who re-appear in *The Whipping-
ham Papers*.

Please, Sir, don't hit very hard this time [he wrote in 1865 to Lord
Houghton, who had proposed to review *Atalanta*]. . . . I do think
it's no end of a chown for a fellow to be swished for his verses when
he showed them up in time for school & there were no false quantities
in them I'm sure. . . . As to quantities & metre & rule of rhythm &
rhyme, I defy castigation. The headmaster has sent me up for
good on that score. Mr. Tennyson tells me in a note that he
'envies me' my gift that way. After this approval I will not
submit myself to the birch on that account. The moral & religious
question I give up at once. . . . I *did* shirk Chapel. I *did* take to
profane swearing instead of singing in the choir. I am fully
prepared for a jolly good swishing in consequence. I can't complain if you take my name out of the list for Confirmation & insert
it in the flogging-bill. Only don't say with my old friend of the
Spectator that it isn't Greek—because it *is*. I recognise in that
attack the avenging hand of outraged virtue mindful how nearly
that paper was induced, through a shameless trick (I was in the
fourth form, then, you know), to admit into its chaste pages a

flaming eulogy of M. le marquis de Sade. . . . I will tell Payne [1] (pretty name for an usher) to send you the material for flagellation at once . . . I have been well flogged some four or five times already for the same fault. Tennyson & Jowett, the Athenæum & the Spectator, have each had their innings. Twice I have been swished in private & twice in public before the whole school—for 'irreverence.'

Though a high proportion of these letters of Swinburne to Richard Monckton Milnes can be classified as *jeux d'esprit*, and were for this reason withheld from publication by Gosse and Wise (who timidly printed six),[2] others of them deal with such serious subjects as the poetry of Walt Whitman (whom Milnes was one of the first Englishmen to admire), or the novels, then suspect in this country, of Gustave Flaubert. Swinburne's youth and intelligence, Milnes' habit of watching out for what was good and little known, meant that they had in common several enthusiasms which their contemporaries did not yet share. Chief amongst these, and of far more importance and gravity than their jokes about Sade, was their interest in the works of William Blake. William Rossetti, who was helping Mrs. Alexander Gilchrist complete the big book on Blake which her young husband had left unfinished at his death in 1861, wrote to Swinburne in November of 1862 that he had decided that he 'really *must* make an effort' to see Milnes' Blake collection. This was indeed a remarkable one, as the frequent references to it in Mrs. Gilchrist's text and Rossetti's *catalogue raisonné* show. The eighteen lots of Blake's works sold at Sotheby's by Milnes' son in 1903 included not only editions of his books, and pulls of his wood-cuts and engravings in the finest possible state, but two large portfolios of original water-colour drawings—twelve of them for Milton's *L'Allegro* and *Il Penseroso*, and twenty-one illustrating the Book of Job; nor does this represent the full wealth of Milnes' collection, for the late Lord Crewe retained certain works of Blake's which are still in the possession of his family.

In his interest in Blake, as in his love for Keats, Milnes was essentially a pioneer. In Swinburne he found a passionate and excited pupil. 'I spent days in the print-room of the British Museum scribbling in pencil the analysis of Blake's 'prophetic books,' and hours at Lord Houghton's in the same labour with pen and ink—to produce a book which was received with general contumely, ridicule and neglect,' Swinburne told an acquaintance

---

[1] J. B. Payne, his publisher.
[2] *Letters from Algernon Charles Swinburne to Richard Monckton Milnes (Afterwards Lord Houghton) and other correspondents*, ed. Thomas J. Wise—London; Printed for Private Circulation, 1915.

in 1881.[1] This book, *William Blake, A Critical Essay*, has in fact,
since come to be regarded as an illuminating piece of interpre-
tative criticism. Originating as an article on the Gilchrist-Rossetti
life, the manuscript was dilatorily expanded over five years until it
became a full-sized volume, containing analyses of the Prophetic
Books, and published by Hotten in 1868. *William Blake, A Critical
Essay* was accorded the same suspicious and philistine reception by
the English public as Milnes' own *Life, Letters and Literary Remains
of John Keats* twenty years earlier; though the prior appearance
of Gilchrist's biography and catalogue (completed and published
in 1863) meant that in 1868 Blake's work was more widely known
than that of Keats in 1848. 'You will receive in a day or two, a
copy of my 'Blake,' which but for you could not have been
what it now is, a tolerably adequate and complete monograph,'
Swinburne wrote modestly to Lord Houghton in an undated letter
of December 1867. 'I . . . shall be curious to hear what you think
of it.' Though Swinburne might choose to forget in later life that
he owed any thanks at all to Lord Houghton, he had not always
been of this persuasion.

If I begin to indulge in the deleterious virtue of gratitude there will
be no end to my letter [he wrote to him from Italy in March 1864].
Happily, when most overburdened with direct, or indirect, benefits,
I remember the precept of a great & good man: 'La reconnaissance,
ma chère Justine, est une chimère vraiment méprisable. Toutes
les formes de la vertu sont pour le véritable philosophe des exécra-
tions dignes de la potence ou de la roue; mais celle-ci—! Et en
parlant ainsi ce libertin'—&c &c ad libitum.[2]

The benefits for which he was expressing thanks concerned his
second and last Italian journey, the course of which had been much
eased by letters of introduction from Lord Houghton, who had also
made possible the real object of it—an audience with 'the most
ancient of the demi-gods,' Milnes' aged friend and Swinburne's
literary deity, Walter Savage Landor.

I cannot thank you enough for procuring me this great pleasure &
exquisite satisfaction [wrote Swinburne]; —I am seriously more
obliged for this than for anything that could have been done for me.
I have got the one thing I wanted with all my heart.[2]

VI

It was now thirty years since, as a boy just down from Cambridge
travelling with his parents about Italy, Richard Monckton Milnes

[1] Letter to R. H. Horne, 16 November 1881, printed by Wise in 1920.
[2] Letter to Lord Houghton from Florence, 31 March 1864, published as No
VIII by Gosse and Wise, who misread the day of the month as '4 March,' and
silently suppressed as unprintable a description of a Titian *Venus*.

had made a little summer *giro* to see the Pisan illuminations in the company of his new acquaintances, the Comte and Comtesse Adolphe de Circourt. Driving with them in an open carriage at nightfall he had caught a chill, developed malaria, and been for some weeks convalescent in the stimulating but not peaceful atmosphere of Walter Savage Landor's hospitable villa at Fiesole. While there Milnes had gained confidence from Landor's volcanic, exaggerated praise for his mild verses, and had met Charles Armitage Brown, the friend of Keats. 'My love knows no more of forgetfulness than children do of death,' Milnes had once written in a notebook; and he did indeed keep up with all these early friends, seeing Anastasie de Circourt in her Paris salon, where she lay in pain for ten years upon her sofa, having been badly burned during Queen Victoria's state visit to Paris in 1855[1]; entertaining the Count when he came to England; and calling on Landor at his house in Bath. But in 1864 Madame de Circourt was lately dead; Armitage Brown was dead; Richard's father and mother were dead; and Landor, once more resident at Florence, was dying of old age and discontent in his ninetieth year.

After his own father's death in '58, Milnes had asked Landor to compose a Latin epitaph upon him to be placed in Ferry Fryston church. This the old man had amicably declined to attempt, on the grounds that, like most English surnames, 'Milnes' could not be Latinised—'It may,' he wrote to Browning, 'be Mil*nis* or Milnetis'—and because he thought it 'an absurdity to place a Latin epitaph in a country church, where only the parson, and *perhaps* the squire can ever read it.'

English names, titles, and occupations, are intractable to Latinity [he told Milnes]. In a country church the parishioners should be able to read the merits of the deceast. Even in cathedrals not one in ten thousand can read a Latin epitaph. What a figure do English names make in that language! . . . You alone can do justice to your father, do it.[2]

When Milnes was made a peer, Landor wrote again: 'I did not congratulate you on your elevation to the peerage—it elevates others. . . . At the close of the present January I enter my 90th year. God grant that I may not live into the middle of it'; he died a few

[1] Having given her servants leave to go to see the celebrations in honour of Queen Victoria's state visit to Paris in August 1855, Madame de Circourt, alone in her house, had accidentally set her dress alight. The burns, from which she never properly recovered, made her an invalid for the rest of her life, and she would conduct the conversation in her salon from a sofa.

[2] W. S. Landor to R.M.M., undated. A Latin epitaph on 'Robertus Milnes' does however occur in Landor's *Heroic Idylls* (1863).

months later, in September '64, after publishing his final volume of poetry, *Heroic Idylls,* dedicated to Edward Twisleton. 'My school of poetry is now shut up,' he wrote in a letter to Browning, which was passed on to Monckton Milnes,[1]

and there is an impenetrable door between it and the present now open and flourishing. Some gentlemen ride in the Park to show their horses. I kept within my own old grounds and wisht for nothing but exercise in them. Parr said I ought to have written in Latin my dialogue of the Ciceros. He did not know that whatever satisfied me in my English I tried in Latin.

He added that he was sending Browning his 'last and slender volume.' 'Milnes,' he ended, 'and, I hope, you too, will like a few morsels on my small desserte-plate.'

When he declared that an impenetrable door separated his own poetry from that of 'the present now open and flourishing,' Landor was thinking of his immediate juniors, men like Tennyson who were already middle-aged. He did not realise the passionate admiration he was inspiring amongst the very young, or that a new generation was growing up who would understand his work better than his own contemporaries had ever done. Algernon Swinburne had first read Landor's works at the age of twelve, when they had given him 'inexplicable pleasure & a sort of blind relief.'

My first recollection of them [Swinburne wrote to Milnes], is the Song of the Hours in the Iphigenia. Apart from their executive perfection, all those Greek poems of his always fitted on to my own way of feeling & thought infinitely more than even Tennyson's modern versions. . . . Not that I am disloyal to Tennyson, into whose church we were all in my time born & baptized as far back as we can remember at all; but he is not a Greek nor a heathen; & I imagine does not want to be; & I greatly fear believes it possible to be something better; an absurdity which should be left to the Brownings & other blatant creatures begotten on the slime of the modern chaos.

To meet, or rather to throw himself on his knees before, Landor was at this moment Swinburne's most dear ambition: 'it is better than a publisher to me,' he told Milnes after the interview, which took place at the end of March 1864: 'what more can a "rimailleur inédit" possibly say?'[2]

Realising that Landor's great age made it unlikely that Swinburne would ever see him if he did not see him now, Milnes had furnished the young poet with a warm letter of introduction, and, after

---

[1] W. S. Landor to Robert Browning, undated. (Houghton Papers.)
[2] Letter of 31 March 1864, already cited.

meeting him in Paris where he himself was spending a few days *en route* to Hyéres, he packed him off to Florence. Swinburne stopped one night at Genoa, where he called upon Milnes' connection, Charlotte Williams Wynn, who was kind to him and 'put me in the way of doing what was to be done in the way of pictures—the one good office I supremely appreciate in an unknown city.' From Genoa he hurried on to Florence, hunted up Landor's apartment with great difficulty, rushed in to pay his homage—and found his 'demi god' 'too much weakened & confused to realise the fact of the introduction without distress.' 'In a grievous state of disappointment & depression' Swinburne crept away. He felt that he had come too late.

'Taking heart of grace,' Swinburne next day dropped a letter of apology on Landor, explained about Milnes' introduction, and received an invitation to return. This interview, or rather this act of worship, was everything that Swinburne could desire:

If both or either of us die to-morrow, at least to-day he has told me that my presence here has made him happy [he wrote to Milnes in ecstasy]; he said more than that—things for which of course I take no credit to myself but which are not the less pleasant to hear from such a man.

Swinburne thought that his own grandfather had been 'on the whole *mieux conservé*; but he had written no Hellenics,' and when Landor mentioned his age, Swinburne fervently 'reminded him of his equals & precursors, Sophocles & Titian.' He told Milnes he could not see why Landor should not reach the age of Sophocles:

if he has people about him to care for him as he should be cared for. I should like to throw up all other things on earth & devote myself to playing valet to him for the rest of his days. I would black his boots if he wore any—*moi*.

Faced at last with a tangible deity, Swinburne worked himself into a state of tremendous emotional excitement.

He has given me the shock of adoration which one feels at thirteen towards great men. I am not sure that any other emotion is so durable & persistently delicious as that of worship when your god is indubitable & incarnate before your eyes. . . . If I let myself loose [he told Milnes in a renewed jet of gratitude], I shall go on giving you indirect thanks for bringing me acquaintance with Landor, till time & paper fail me & patience fails you.

On his side, Landor was 'much gratified' by Swinburne's visit, but also very much exhausted by it: in a short note of thanks sent to him next day he told him that he would be 'unable ever to converse with' him again. 'Eyes and intellect,' the old man wrote, 'fail me.' Mentioning this interview in his biography of Landor, John Forster points out how long had been Milnes' own friendship with that poet:

The very last of Landor's letters from Italy to Southey was brought over in 1835 by Mr. Milnes, whom it introduced to the Laureate; and one of the last received in Italy by Landor, also a letter of introduction for a young poet, was taken over to him by Mr. Swinburne from Lord Houghton after nearly thirty years. Their friendship during the interval had been uninterrupted.[1]

In the article which he wrote for the *Edinburgh* on Forster's biography (and which later he reprinted in his volume of *Monographs: Personal and Social* in 1873) Lord Houghton expressed his lifelong admiration of the *Imaginary Conversations* and wished that he could increase the

degree of knowledge and use of Landor's writings; I say advisedly the use, because, though often surprised that they are not more the objects of literary dilectation and amusement, I still more regret the neglect of their obvious utility as examples of English composition. Abounding in strong even passionate diction [Landor's style] is never vague or convulsive; magniloquent as declamation can demand, it is never pompous or turgid; humourous throughout, it avoids contortion and abhors caricature. In strange contradiction to the temper of the writer, its chief characteristic is self-command.[2]

It is in fact the fumy violence of Landor's temper, as reflected in his letters, and demonstrated in the myriad rows of his long life, that make his personality so vivid to us; he stands out not only as a poet but as a man, and we feel we know what he was like. As the dead smoothly recede from us upon the waves of time, like gliding ships drawn levelly to sea, it is the sharpest outlines that are clearest seen. The stern and irate temperament of Landor seems more actual to us than that of Wordsworth or of Robert Southey. Those angry traits which make men most difficult to live with in their lifetime become helpful to posterity once they are dead. We welcome the turbulence and rage that rendered intercourse with Landor hardly tolerable. For us these qualities facilitate a distinct vision of this fine old poet across the shadowy wastes of more than eighty years.

[1] *Walter Savage Landor: a Biography*, by John Forster (Chapman and Hall 1869), vol. II, p. 261.
[2] *Edinburgh Review* no. 265, July 1869; reprinted in *Monographs: Personal and Social* (John Murray 1873).

VII

I have in hand a scheme of mixed verse and prose—a sort of étude à la Balzac plus the poetry—which I flatter myself will be more offensive and objectionable to Britannia than anything I have yet done [wrote Swinburne to Burton in January 1867]. You see I have now a character to keep up.

The work in question was the novel of *Lesbia Brandon* which, still unpublished to-day, exists only in a manuscript version formerly in the possession of Wise, and in an incomplete set of corrected galley-proofs, now in the British Museum. It is luckily not needful here to disentangle the far-fetched, tortured plot of *Lesbia Brandon*, a book in which much excellent prose and some good verse is devoted to a theme of pure melodrama; in which passages of perceptive literary criticism, and many pages of brilliant conversation— reminiscent of Wilde at his best—are juxtaposed to accounts of schoolboy birchings which, occurring with an obsessional regularity, taint the whole novel with an emetic quality very far removed from the virile, universal genius of Swinburne's model, the author of the *Comédie Humaine*. But *Lesbia Brandon* is of relevance to any study of Monckton Milnes since (as Monsieur Lafourcade was the first to signal) it contains a character founded to some degree upon his. This character, Mr. Henry Linley, is the elderly, cynical, sadistic uncle of Lord Wariston, whose wife's brother, little Bertie Seyton, is the much-flogged hero of the book, the victim of a cruel tutor, of a strangulated sensual love for his sister, and, finally, of a hopeless passion for the sickly sapphic poetess who gives her name to this very improbable specimen of Pre-Raphaelite literature.

As we should expect the novel of *Lesbia Brandon* is in many ways autobiographical. It contains a loving self-portrait of Swinburne and a heroine who has been recognised as a cross between Christina Rossetti and 'Boo' Faulkner, the mysterious girl to whom Swinburne dedicated his *Triumph of Time*. The book fails because it is written with divers aims—to shock the public, to form a vehicle for some of Swinburne's songs, to provide an *étude de mœurs* of English country-house life, and to hammer home some of its author's favourite æsthetic theories. The philosophical basis of the book is the identity of pleasure and pain: 'Torture and rapture, hatred and love, lie surely as close together, are perhaps at root as inextricable and indissoluble, in essence as simply one and identical, as evil and good.' In accordance perhaps with this theory, the chief characters are of ambiguous sex: Bertie who 'ought to have been a pretty and

rather boyish girl' is first presented to Lesbia in a girl's attire,[1]
while Miss Brandon herself, who broke down when her governess
was married, declares that she is not 'marriageable,' and finally
commits a 'sad and slow suicide with time and care,' killing herself
'off by inches, with the help of eau de cologne and doses of opium'
in a lamplit room with curtains drawn, has an appropriate first
name.

Mr. Linley, 'a slight smooth-faced man, with thin hair and good
features, though somewhat too like a shaven satyr with the ears
rounded; fair-skinned, with large reverted lips and repellent eyes,'
does not resemble Milnes physically; nor does the melodramatic
description of him as 'a thing foul and dangerous,' who had perse-
cuted his dead wife and son, in any way tally with what we know,
or Swinburne could have thought, of Monckton Milnes. As the
spokesman of views intended to shock Swinburne's readers most, it
was inevitable that Linley should make so satanic an entry; but
later on in the book we come to a more convincing description of
him in which Swinburne most evidently had his old friend in mind:

He was a scholar and collector [we read], fond of books, coins,
prints and bric-à-brac of a secret kind, kept under locks and behind
curtains; he had lived much in Paris, and when decrying the
English would hint at close relations with French public men.
Some two years after this, in 1852, he used to assert that he had
watched the birth, baptism, vaccination, schooling and adolescence
of the second empire; giving the dates.   'If you like to believe him,'
said Lady Midhurst, who professed a faith in the house of Orleans,
'it was he who suggested the massacre to M. Beauharnais, and he
was on the boulevards by the side of Leroy. . . .   For my part,' Lady
Midhurst wound up, 'I believe him (not the emperor) capable of
half he says; that is, he has the heart for it, if not the head.   As for
the correspondence with MM. Fielin et Cie I should like well to see

---

[1] Further evidence of the autobiographical nature of many incidents of *Lesbia
Brandon* is provided by the unpublished letters to Milnes. In the novel, Lady
Wariston dresses Bertie as a girl for a charade, and adds false hair, saying she will
present him to Miss Brandon as a 'rising young poetess'; 'Ah heaven, to run back
four years!' we read in an undated letter to Milnes, 'would you believe that at
that time I did quite well (that is I was a *credible* being I don't say *attractive!*) in
female attire . . . It is a lamentable truth that Lady Trevelyan had then a dark
project of passing me off upon Madame Sand as the typical *miss anglaise émancipée*
& holding the most ultra views; we made no end of a history about it, & infinite
adventures for the British Mademoiselle de Maupin.' He also describes the
cruelty of the sea in a passage very like that in which Bertie saves a boy from
drowning; and he told Milnes on another occasion (recorded in the latter's
commonplace-book) how his tutor had once flogged him when wet from bathing,
an experience which Bertie Seyton likewise undergoes. The many Eton stories
he told Milnes clearly show that Swinburne's inborn masochism was immeasur-
ably encouraged by his experiences under a practised and sadistic tutor at that
school.

his autographs!' She called him among friends Talleyrand-Bridoison; he called her in private Madame de Faublas.[1]

Much of Mr. Linley's conversation, too, has an authentic Milnesian ring:

'I am for plastic art against drastic morals' [for example, and his explanation of the purpose of 'good looks' in the young]: 'To give pleasure while they last to others; as a singing-bird does, or a flower. You don't ask a rosebud to turn into an apple; and a deer doesn't enjoy venison.' Here the philosopher, who had an innocent relish for sweet scraps worthy of his notice as his one harmless taste, absorbed certain prepared fruits with amorous suction.

In the best episode of the book, the after-dinner conversation at Ensdon ('a green moist place,' surrounded by fishponds), when the ladies have left the table and Bertie has been sent out with them since Lord Wariston is 'aware that (Mr. Linley's) talk across the wine did not pay to the possible innocence of boys that delicate respect enjoined by the Roman moralist,' we seem to hear Milnes speaking; and in the shocked silence of the country neighbours, followed by the protests of Sir John Fieldfare, we may fancy that we are witnessing some scene at Fryston Hall:

'It wasn't the face,' proceeded Mr. Linley, his own more suggestive of a niche or corner in some improper basrelief; 'and the shoulders were bad . . .' Mr. Linley, who as he said really could not talk English after a certain point had been reached in the debate, plunged into a French anecdote illustrative of legs; beyond which no story-teller could pass.

Again, in Linley's repartee to Lady Midhurst's question 'Did you ever write moral essays, Mr. Linley?' we can hear Milnes speak: '"I thought of it once," he said simply and gently, "but a friend suggested the addition of a syllable to the adjective, and of course, I refrained"'; while in Lady Midhurst's acid comment that 'his notion of talk was monologue *plus* a listener,' we recognise the complaining voices of many of Milnes' contemporaries and friends, who found him a selfish talker as he aged.

Begun in 1864, the manuscript of *Lesbia Brandon* must originally have been less self-consciously scandalous, closer in intention to *Love's Cross Currents*, and more exact in portraiture, than it became after the 1866 outcry against *Poems and Ballads*, when the exacerbated Swinburne determined to make the book as scabrous as he could. Abandoned, probably under Mazzini's influence, in

[1] Proofs of *Lesbia Brandon*, folios 69–70 (Brit. Mus. cat. no. Ashley 5265).

1867, the book was at last put into proof-form in 1878; but the printers of Chatto and Windus so confused the manuscript with those of two other of Swinburne's works, that he became impatient and finally gave up all idea of publication. To-day it would be interesting to see this extravagant work in print, for in spite of its distortions, its absurd dénouement and the angry, childish wish to horrify which pervades the whole, *Lesbia Brandon* does represent a serious attempt to introduce into mid-Victorian literature themes, characters and situations which no other writer then living in this country dared to touch. Moreover, the novel of *Lesbia Brandon* is also of a certain historical and biographical interest for the partial character-sketches of Swinburne himself and of his early friends which it contains; though to accept the mischievous Mr. Linley—'an idle Iago turned out to grass,' now able 'to bring forth only the cold grey sins of the intellect'—as a photographic likeness of Lord Houghton would be as foolish as to contend, on the basis of this novel, that Christina Rossetti tried to kill herself with slow doses of opium and eau de cologne.

Chapter Nine

1861   *1866 (II)*

I

The emphasis placed in the last chapter upon Milnes' friendship for Algernon Swinburne may be justified by our general interest in that poet, as well as by the fact of new material found amongst the Houghton Papers; but we must not forget that what may seem to us an absorbing subject was to Milnes merely incidental to his own packed life. Swinburne's poetry, his four visits to Fryston, his jokes on Sade, his difficulties with family and publishers, his epileptiform fits and tendency to drink, were side-issues to Richard Monckton Milnes, whose existence became even fuller, his social, literary and philanthropic activities more numerous, as he approached his sixtieth year.

Even . . . when increasing age might have been expected to have a sedative influence [writes Herbert Spencer],[1] he was ever moving hither and thither, to be present at gatherings, grave and gay, of various natures.

After the winters of 1862 and 1863, when he was seriously ill for several weeks, Milnes' enjoyment of life was always hampered by bouts of ill-health; his hands and legs would be crippled by painful gout, and he suffered from bad colds in the head. These ailments, probably due to his own excessive indulgence in wine as well as in food—'Look at life through the purple veil of the grape!' had been his youthful aspiration in 1836; he was now cheerfully putting it into practice—did not curtail his 'locomotiveness,' but rather increased it; for, sometimes alone, sometimes accompanied by his wife, who, now never well herself, was subject to melancholia and neurotic headaches, Lord Houghton journeyed from spa to spa across the Continent. In his youth he had travelled abroad because his parents had not the money to live in Yorkshire; now in late middle age he began to do so again because he had not the health. Large portions of the years 1864, '65, '67 and '68 were passed in France, in Italy and in Germany. In 1867 he lived for some months in Paris as one of the jurors of the great International Exhibition; in April

[1] Herbert Spencer's *Autobiography*, vol. ii, p. 96.

1869 he visited the Queen of Holland at The Hague; and in September of that year he committed the irresistible folly of trundling off to Egypt to take part in the marine festivities which marked the imperial opening of the Suez Canal, returning, ill and weary, by way of Rome to be in time for the first session of the Vatican Council of 1870.

To observant English people, the first two years of the new decade of the 'sixties seemed hopeful enough. Having annexed Nice and Savoy in February 1860, Napoleon III had issued his November Decrees liberalising the constitution of the Empire that same year; Garibaldi had freed Sicily; a delightful 'dissolution' of the United States of America seemed likely to result from the Civil War which had flared up there in April '61. But in December 1861, without warning, the Prince Consort died. Since the close of the Crimean War, the Prince had been a wise, consistent power for peace in European politics. His death, and the Queen's stubborn retreat from public life, marked virtually the beginning of a new reign, for the Prince's ascendancy over his wife had been so firm as to make him monarch in all but name. In the autumn of the following year, Bismarck became Prussian Minister-President and Minister for Foreign Affairs at Berlin; and for the remainder of the decade this giant personality made havoc of the old European balance of power, and destroyed for ever the Europe constructed at the Congress of Vienna. It was that Europe, civilised, friendly, modified but not radically altered by the various liberal Revolutions and autocratic reactions since 1815, that had formed the framework to the lives of all Lord Houghton's contemporaries. The power of England suffered with the rest. Palmerston died in 1865, but already two years before this 'the day of success for Palmerstonian policy had virtually passed. No longer would haughty words, orders to the fleet, and patronage of smaller continental states give England a pivotal position in international affairs.'[1] In 1864 came Bismarck's war on Denmark; in 1866 the war on Austria; in 1870 the Franco-Prussian war, the siege of Paris, and the abdication of Napoleon III. The pillaging of Europe had begun.

Lord Houghton, who believed history to be 'the summary of biographies,' and who approached every public event from a personal and anecdotal angle, naturally discussed these developments in conversation and in letters. Houghton was never profound, but because his comments are passing and immediate, like reflections in a flashing mirror, they give one some sense of these past events, and of how things must have seemed to contemporaries,

[1] Bell's *Lord Palmerston* (Longman 1936), vol. ii, p. 337.

which the more solemn and exhaustive disquisitions of Gladstone or John Morley fail to bring. Pro-Prussian over the Austrian war—'I have been ostracised in society for my Prussian velléités and I am the only public man who has dared to have Bernstorff to dinner,' he told George Bunsen in 1866—Lord Houghton was equally so at the beginning of the war of 1870, which he termed 'the most un-justifiable war in history,' and 'this atrocious invasion of Germany by the French.' But he was soon amazed, and then appalled, by Prussian behaviour inside France. Advising young Frederic Harrison to send the French ambassador, the Duc de Broglie, an article on 'Bismarckism' which he had published in a *Fortnightly* in 1870, Lord Houghton told him the 'wonderful story' of the occu-pation, by a Prussian princeling and his staff, of the Château de Broglie:

He said it was the strangest anachronism you could conceive [Houghton wrote of the Duc's account of this incident]—an invasion of Teutonic knights with all the apparatus of modern culture—they showing 'de certains égards' for M. le Duc, and being utterly implacable towards everyone else—delighted to find Madame de Staël's autograph in his books and carrying them off without scruple—a Middle Age militarism absorbing a Nineteenth Century civilisation.[1]

While working at the Houghton Papers I have at times been puzzled to determine just where the basic difference between our-selves and the educated Victorians lies. Save in their frank attitude towards death, their earnest love of theology and sermons, and their distaste for the open discussion of sexual problems, they do not seem so unlike us as we have often been led to assume. But in Lord Houghton's use of the single noun 'anachronism' to describe a brutal military occupation of a European power we come up against the difference so suddenly that we seem to bang our heads. It is a difference not of character but of circumstance, and we realise what a wide world of damnable experience separates our own lives, conditioned by two annihilating wars and forever threatened by a third, from the progressive Europe of the last cen-tury, when a barbarian conquest was not an everyday occurrence,

---

[1] Frederic Harrison's *Autobiographic Memoirs* (Macmillan 1911), vol. ii, p. 13. An author and positivist, Harrison (who was born in 1832 and died in 1923), was a devotee of his 'dear and inimitable Lord Houghton.' 'I doubt if in all the twenty-five years since we lost him, any one has replaced the unique position held by Monckton Milnes,' he wrote in 1911, recalling Milnes' '*bonhomie*, his vast knowledge of men and things all over Europe and America during more than fifty years, his hearty kindness and love of any kind of ability or gift, his lavish hospitality, his wit, his inexhaustible store of anecdotes and epigrams.'

a perennial threat, but something so historical as to merit the word 'anachronism'—something unknown in Europe since the Dark Ages that had followed the collapse of Rome.

Because the Victorians' optimism and their faith in progress are too remote from our own philosophy for us to understand, we call them hypocritical or fatuous. We feel that our grandfathers were living in a fool's paradise. In one sense this was true; but we cannot criticise that generation for being unaware of what was going on beneath the surface of its daily life.

What did Wellington or his contemporaries know of the retiring officer, Clausewitz, who, in the peace that followed Waterloo, hammered out the concepts of war that made Germany the dominant military power of 1870? What did Queen Victoria know of the burly, bearded Jew who sat cogitating on Primrose Hill while she was holding decorous Drawing-rooms at Buckingham Palace? And yet it was Karl Marx and not Queen Victoria and her Empire builders who was planning the new world.[1]

Clausewitz had died in 1831, but, assiduous *niebelungen*, his theories of war had continued working underground, forging the military machine that destroyed France forty years later, sweeping before it the weaker, because political, concepts of the Napoleonic empire. The theories of Marx have taken longer to germinate; but, rooted in the East, they have transformed Russia from the mysterious tyrant-ruled empire of Lord Houghton's day—unpopular in Europe for such reasons as Alexander II's bloody suppression of the Polish revolt of 1863, as well as for its expansionist aims and unpredictable bouts of diplomatic intervention in Austrian and Italian affairs—into a mortal danger to the western world.

As I have suggested, Milnes had none of the prescience of Tocqueville, who foresaw that Russia would be the greatest threat to twentieth-century Europe. Milnes took events as they came along, confining himself to the part of chorus, while at the same time doing his best to alleviate industrial conditions in his own country, and to make England a juster country for the poor. He could not be expected to realise the subterranean historical processes relentlessly at work; or that, all the time that he was improving the Fryston property for his descendants, or addressing artisans' institutes in Sheffield or in Leeds, wintering with his wife at Interlaken or spending a hot spring month at Hyères, teaching his son the Latin declensions or beginning to prepare his girls for the day when they would 'come out,' there were already sown in Europe the seeds of mondial wars and gigantic revolutions which would, in

[1] From *Durham Company* by Una Pope-Hennessy (Chatto & Windus 1941).

his son's lifetime, unrecognisably alter the conditions of Christian civilisation all over the West. Milnes was not given to peering into the future; the views he formulated, which were usually contrary to those of most of his friends, were based on facts and not on theories. In 1861 he developed and expounded some very decided and very sane opinions on the needlessness of the transatlantic civil war.

II

Ever since he had first become a 'social power' in London, Richard Monckton Milnes had made a point of befriending Americans in this country, both visitors and members of the United States Legation. He was one of the few men of that time to stand out against the universal ridicule with which they were then treated in London society, and even though most Americans disliked the breakfast-party system, they came willingly to eat at Upper Brook Street. 'One of the best fellows in London,' Motley wrote of him in 1858.[1] 'If he would only shove his entertainments to the other edge of the daylight and give us cups that inebriate instead of cheering, I should have no fault to find with him.' When the Civil War broke out, the fashionable world of London, and most English politicians, Whig or Tory, backed the Confederacy, hoping to see the Union split apart, and a reactionary regime established in the South. The people of England and especially the people of the industrial areas, were for the North; and thus an element of class conflict coloured the attitude of the English audience to this tragic civil war.

Monckton Milnes was one of very few men in the House of Commons, still more of the landed gentry, to support the North, which he did so loudly and warmly that for the first time in his life he found himself a public hero, with a popularity up and down the country which he had never experienced before. He loathed 'the abominable selfishness of the South in breaking up a great country.' He was also automatically against slavery and Confederate reaction. His sympathy with the inhabitants of Leeds, Sheffield and other northern cities led him to understand and share their political views. There may also have been the fact that his dead friend Tocqueville's book, *Democracy in America*, had become the bible of the Union, and the basis for many people's faith in a Northern victory. 'Milnes

---

[1] J. L. Motley to his wife, 27 June 1858, published in *The Correspondence of John Lothrop Motley, D.C.L.*, ed. G. W. Curtis (John Murray, two vols., 1889). Motley, who later became Minister to the Court of St. James's for a short period (1869–1870) was often in England, and frequently visited Milnes at Fryston or came to 'roost on his mahogany tree' in Upper Brook Street.

himself is one of the warmest Americans in the world,' Henry
Adams wrote to his brother in July 1863, on a day when the fall of
Vicksburg had enraged English partisans of the South.

You can't imagine how spiteful and vicious they all were [Adams
continued]. Sunday evening I was asked round to Monckton
Milnes' to meet a few people. Milnes . . . received me with a hug
before the astonished company, crowing like a fighting cock. But
the rest of the company were very cold. . . . I went with Mr. Milnes
to the Cosmopolitan Club afterwards, where the people all looked
at me as though I were objectionable. . . . The emergency has produced here a mere access of spite, preparatory (if we suffer no
reverse) to a revolution in tone. It is now conceded at once that all
idea of intervention is at an end.[1]

Enthusiasm for the cause of the South had at first made many
Englishmen favour armed intervention in the Civil War. In May
1861 Palmerston's Cabinet had granted recognition to the Confederate envoy, and this fact, taken in conjunction with the coldness
of Ministers towards the United States Legation, had persuaded the
members of this mission that Russell and the Premier really wanted
war. In November 1861 they nearly got it, when Captain
Wilkes, commanding the United States warship *San Jacinto* stopped
a British mail steamer in the Bahama Channel and removed from it
Messrs. Mason and Slidell, deputed to come to London by the
'Rebel' leaders of the South. Writing to MacCarthy in January
1862 of the belligerent tone of a letter he had just received from
Hawthorne—'he says, that "he could not have conceived anything
so delightful as civil war" and deeply regrets that his youth was spent
in a quiet time'—Milnes told him that he had, of course, met Mrs.
Slidell. This lady had declared to him that Wilkes had told her

that he was so disgusted with the Northern cause that if it had not
been for his dressing-box, with all his silver things in it, being on
board the *San Jacinto*, he could cut the concern altogether and go
to England with them in the *Trent*.

Whatever the truth of this anecdote, Wilkes did not desert. His
action in arresting Mason and Slidell so enraged England that, had
it not been for the moribund Prince Consort's skilful personal
intervention, it would surely have provoked an Anglo-American
war. 'I am satisfied that the act will do more for the Southerners
than ten victories, for it touches John Bull's honor, and the honor
of his flag,' Secretary Moran of the United States Legation noted in
his London journal. The United States Minister, Mr. C. F.

[1] Henry Adams to his brother, London, 23 July 1863. (*A Cycle of Adams Letters 1861–1865*, ed. Worthington Chancey Ford, Constable 1921, vol. ii).

Adams, was out of London and had left Benjamin Moran in charge: 'I telegraphed the news at once to Mr. Adams, and fear it has not added to his enjoyment of rural retirement,' Moran noted. 'It is odd that he never goes out of town that something serious don't arise to call him home.'[1] The Adams's 'rural retirement' consisted in their first, and last, visit to Yorkshire, where they were peaceably staying, in the company of Froudes, Gaskells and Forsters, at Fryston Hall.

'Telegram delivered to Mr. Adams while he was inspecting Pomfret Castle announcing *the North* had captured Southerners off Eng. ship,' Mrs. Milnes jotted down in her pocket-book for November 27; 'the Adams's returned to London' for November 28. The drive to see the ruins of Pontefract Castle, site of the murder of Richard II, was an agreeable, stock ingredient of a first stay at Fryston, but on this occasion, so Mrs. Milnes told her sister, there was a storm—'not ominous we trust of political tempests!' 'This terrible threat of War in the *far West* is hanging over England!' she wrote to Henriett. 'May God in his mercy avert such a calamity! . . . *Richee* and *all England* are feeling anxious about this American dispute.' She had been able to show Fryston to the wife of what Richard called 'the Minister for the Dis-United States'— 'Mrs. Adams had not been in Engd before & appeared much struck with all the organisation of a British Country House, full of Guests.' Back in London, Mrs. Adams 'assured' Moran, who detested her for her social ambition and her loudness of style, that she had been 'miserable' at Fryston after the telegram had arrived:

She felt that they were provoked at what had occurred, friendly as they were, and she couldn't enjoy herself knowing how uncomfortable her presence must necessarily make them after such news. In future she will not go on such visits, for it seems something painful is sure to occur while Mr. Adams is away on such pleasure.

Henry Adams did not share his mother's superstitions about country visiting, for as we have seen he was himself at Fryston the next year; but even this intelligent young man was not immune from the insidious anxiety-complex of all Americans in mid-Victorian London. The *Trent* crisis made their situation here infinitely more vexatious, for where, before, by modifying their accents and by warily threading their way through the minefields of polite society, they could with caution avoid open ridicule, they were now met with unconcealed hostility, and cut with cold contempt. It was in this brittle, icy atmosphere that Henry Adams first learned his heartfelt respect for Richard Monckton Milnes,

[1] Moran's *Journals*, ed. cit.

'one of the warmest Americans in the world.' All the same, though he tried to be just about America, and amiable to transatlantic friends, Milnes was not especially smitten with the American way of life:

For my part, I see no gleam of good in anything American [he wrote to a friend during the Civil War]; the lower civilisation, as represented by the South, is so much braver & cunninger & daringer than the cultivated shopkeepers of the North—it is just as if the younger sons of the Irish & Scotch nobility were turned loose against the bourgeoisie of Leeds.

He added that the old liberal feeling against slavery was dying out in this country: 'I shan't be surprised to see the slave-trade going briskly before you & I retire,' he wrote: 'It is quite curious to see how the old Clarksonian feeling has weakened in Engd. among all the genteel classes.'

III

The *Trent* war scare was not the only ominous event of that freezing December 1861, when the cold throughout England was of immemorial intensity and the river Ayre a sheet of ice on which the people of Ferrybridge and Ferry Fryston could disport. On the night of 14 December, the Prince Consort, taken ill with typhoid fever only a few days before, died. Writing to her sister of this 'stunning blow' Mrs. Milnes declared that there had been no such 'national sorrow' since the death of Princess Charlotte in 1817, a distant calamity which Richard's elder aunts could well recall. Richard, who was in Cambridge when the Prince died, and thought it 'the greatest public sorrow I have ever seen—quite different from anything else,' hastened to London to pick up any intimate bits of news. He found Lord Palmerston so affected that his family feared a paralytic stroke. 'It is impossible to think of the Queen alone—I never saw her come into a room without Prince Albert,' remarked Lady Palmerston to Milnes. From Colonel Bruce, who had been at the death-bed, he had a first-hand report of the Queen's behaviour, of how she had thrown herself upon the body crying out 'no, no it is impossible,' and presently, assembling the Prince's attendants, had thanked them calmly for all they had done and spoken 'of herself and her duties in a queenly kind of way.' Milnes, who had never had much admiration for the Queen, shrewdly annotated this account: 'The truth is she is an emotional but not an affectionate woman; & the great way she will feel his loss is in that which will affect her position & her daily comfort.'

In the months immediately following the Prince's death, the Queen set herself to the dedicated task of implementing what she knew to have been his wishes concerning their children. In July 1862, Princess Alice, who had caught the public's fancy as her father's careful nurse during his short illness of the previous December, was mournfully married at Osborne to Prince Louis of Hesse; while the Queen determined to carry on the plan already formed before her husband's death for the union of the young Prince of Wales with Alexandra, the eldest daughter of the 'protocol Prince,' the former Duke Christian of Glucksburg whose succession to the throne of Denmark when his cousin King Frederick should die had been ratified by the Treaty of London in 1852. In her behaviour over 'Bertie's' marriage, Queen Victoria displayed more than her usual egotism. Since she herself was miserable, she made the whole occasion as depressing as she could.

The Prince of Wales and Princess Alexandra had first met in the Cathedral of Speier in 1861—a stage-managed, casual-seeming meeting which had resulted from the good report on the two Danish sisters sent to her parents at Windsor by the Crown Princess of Prussia, who had been to look them over earlier in that year. After his father's death, the Prince was despatched by his mother to the Middle East, but in September 1862, she herself proceeded to Belgium to interview Princess Alexandra and her family at the palace of Laeken. Queen Victoria liked the girl, but was irritated by her family, especially by her mother Princess Christian, who was deaf. When the Prince of Wales had proposed and been accepted, the Queen commanded that the princess be brought to Osborne and left there with her alone. The marriage was finally fixed for 10 March, 1862. On 7 March Princess Alexandra landed at Gravesend in pouring rain. Met by the Prince, she travelled to London in a small railway coach, was escorted by Royal Horse Guards across the city in a poor little procession of six carriages, and left for Windsor from Paddington railway station. At Ostend and at Gravesend the British sailors had been by the Queen's orders expressly forbidden to cheer. The same command had gone out to the Eton boys who lined the roads to Windsor. Even the Queen's most loyal subjects felt that a better show should have been put up; and the fact that the Princess's first morning at Windsor was passed in a visit to Prince Albert's illuminated mausoleum was not encouraging. The Queen had also insisted that the wedding should be solemnised at St George's Chapel at Windsor, instead of in Westminster Abbey.

Tempted by the fine March weather, and by the chance for 'sweet Amice' to see her future King and Queen, Mrs. Milnes had brought her eldest child to London for these poor festivities. By the time they arrived, sunshine had given way to cold and rain. Standing in the Ashburtons' windows at Bath House, they watched the procession of the Prince and Princess down Piccadilly on their way to Paddington.

The rain kept off till the poor *little Dane* got near Windsor when the Eton boys were drenched and saw nothing but the shut carriage trot by! [wrote Mrs. Milnes]. . . . Georgy [Monckton] told me however they were ordered not to cheer, the poor Queen feeling it would be more than she could bear. As a pageant the Procession was nothing! As one of the Papers said probably no other nation *could* have spent so much & made so little effect; but still it was very striking that crowd of well-behaved, happy looking people, something 'which passeth show,' & certainly Alexandra played *her* part admirably, bowing, smiling . . . as if she never had enjoyed anything so much!

On the wedding day itself Monckton Milnes and his sister started at eight for Windsor, where they had places in St. George's Chapel and saw 'the poor Queen & her two widowed friends, looking down on it all in her sadness!' from the Royal Closet above the chapel. Though at Windsor the weather was bright, London was draped in fog, so that Mrs. Milnes and Amy stayed indoors all day, waiting for the return of the wedding guests. At half-past six, after an early dinner, they set off in the brougham to see the illuminations, Milnes on the box attempting to direct proceedings. 'Then indeed were Amice's ecstasies at their height,' but the great difficulty proved to be how to get home, and after being jammed in the streets for seven hours an exhausted little family returned to Upper Brook Street, Amy sleeping heavily, and her mother rejoicing 'to think these carnivals don't come often.' Lady Galway, and many others, had had worse luck and had not managed to see any of the illuminations at all. Writing to his wife, who withdrew next day to Fryston, of how 'upset' he had been at 'uselessly' tiring them out, and saying that his bad management of the expedition made him 'begin to think that Pam is quite right & that I was never meant to be a statesman,' Milnes told her that the Archbishop of York's carriage had been held up in Bedford Street for five hours; boys tossing squibs in through the window had set the crinoline of the Archbishop's wife on fire. After the fog and the exacting tour of the illuminations, Fryston seemed refreshing. The three children were happy with their rabbits, two new ponies, and the busy preparation of odd-

ments for the annual church bazaar. Florence and Robin ran
about the garden in the March weather, spouting Tennyson's
refrain:

> O joy to the people and joy to the throne,
> Come to us, love us and make us your own;
> For Saxon or Dane or Norman we,
> Teuton or Celt, or whatever we be,
> We are each all Dane in our welcome of thee.
> Alexandra!

IV

The marriage of the Prince of Wales was of more than historical
interest to Richard Monckton Milnes, since it was now on every
side agreed that Lord Palmerston could not decently avoid placing
Milnes' name among those of eminent commoners to be raised to the
peerage on this occasion, or—as Mr. Brookfield (who was staying at
Crewe that January) put it—that Monckton Milnes was certain to
be one of 'the rockets that go off at the Prince of Wales's marriage.'
As we have seen Milnes himself was unashamedly anxious to get a
peerage. His wife was less so, and said she should feel 'very shy'
of changing her name and that she was content to continue with
that she had taken twelve years ago. From January 1863 on there
was a tiresome, rather public uncertainty about the question;
letters of congratulation began to flutter in, but there was still
nothing official to congratulate about. Milnes, who affected to
regard a barony as 'a token of a half-success in life—a second-class
in politics,' tried his hardest to find out what was in preparation, and
at one moment learned that the Queen had determined to create
no political peers on the marriage, since this might identify the
Prince with one or other Party in the public mind: 'with my usual
fairness,' wrote Milnes, 'I see something in this.' At length,
towards the end of July, Palmerston sent for Monckton Milnes and
offered him a peerage: in the first week of August he was gazetted
Baron Houghton of Great Houghton, an old house of the Rhodes
family 'through whom Milnes was able to trace his descent from
one of the companions of the Conqueror.' He was one of only two
new peers created, and congratulations now poured into Upper
Brook Street and Fryston, for Milnes' many friends were happy to
think that he had at last obtained what he had so long and so
overtly desired. 'Speaking of it or not, it is a thing we are all glad
of, and wish well to,' wrote Carlyle kindly. Some of the tributes

were in verse, and included Planché's popular lines about the pronunciation of the new peerage—should it be Howton, Horton or
Huffton?—beginning:

> The Alphabet rejoiced to hear
> That Monckton Milnes was made a peer;
> For in this present world of letters,
> But few, if any, are his betters.

and a curious little Lewis Carroll rhyme from old Mrs. Procter:

> He enters from the common air
>   Into that temple dim;
> He learns among those ermined peers
>   The diplomatic hymn.
> His peers? Alas! when will they learn
>   To grow up peers to him?

Outside the colossal circle of Milnes' friends, the news of his
peerage was received without delight. He himself was aware of
what was likely to be said in many quarters and nervous of the press
reactions, which, in the case of *The Times*, he attempted to influence
by a confidential letter to Delane.

As the depository of so many great secrets, you probably know a
small one [he wrote to Delane on 26 July from Fryston] that I have
accepted a Peerage. . . . I am very desirous that I should not be
thought to owe it to any undue subservience to Lord Palmerston.
For it is not the fact. I certainly made myself somewhat prominent
in my indignation at his treatment by Ld John . . . but since he
has been Premier, I have opposed him openly whenever I had a
conscientious difference of opinion. . . . I do wish it to be known
that there is nothing unworthy, either in the offer or the acceptance.
. . . I cannot close this letter without expressing to you my strong
sense of kindness you have shown me while in the H. of C., & your
benevolent appreciation of my abilities. A little more of the same
treatment in high quarters, would, with my temperament, have
enabled me both to do & to be more than I have done or been.
But, after all, the fact of a man's being misunderstood and under-
rated is the consequence of some intellectual or moral defect in
himself: it may be the fault of the play that the actor is hissed—
but he should not have undertaken to play the part.

In spite of this sensible letter *The Times* printed a somewhat acidulated paragraph, concluding that if Milnes 'cannot be said to deserve
it as Wellington or Brougham deserved it, he deserves it far better

than most of the country gentlemen who have been ennobled by virtue of territorial influence,' while the *Daily Telegraph* more agreeably called him

one of the most generally popular men in England. He was one of the heroes of Young England in Disraeli's novel of 'Coningsby' [this newspaper inaccurately stated]; few who now see him trotting along Birdcage Walk on his fat, iron-gray roan cob, would believe that he was ever one of the exquisites of the White Waistcoat party. But it is not his politics that have earned Lord Houghton his enviable position—nor his poetry—. . . nor his wealth, which is sufficient—nor his taste in art and literature, which is far above the average; but it is the combination of all these with the most extraordinary geniality. Monckton Milnes had—perhaps, if the gout will let him, may have still—a kind word for everyone, and a taste for everything.

Having applied for the Chiltern Hundreds, and been thwarted by his doctor in a sudden plan to make a journey to see MacCarthy in Ceylon, Milnes or, as we must henceforth call him, Lord Houghton arranged to take his wife and his eldest child to Carlsbad and Bonn for a couple of months that summer. This, the first of now constant and lengthy journeys in search of health, was, of course, planned to take place when the 'season' was ended, for no amount of pain in hands or legs could make Houghton forego the crowded pleasures of London at that fashionable time of year.

It has been a dull & agreeable season and Session [he wrote to MacCarthy in June 1863]. The great obstacles to social comfort are T.R.H. the Prince and Princess of Wales. They crowd the streets to look at her, they go to exclusive parties, making the uninvited sick with envy & wounded pride—they take away any notable you happen to have asked to dinner two days before the party was to have come off—& they are clearly about to bring the level of London life down to that of two most goodnatured & quite ignorant children.

The Queen's determination that the Prince should be excluded from any serious knowledge of politics was partly dictated by the Prince Consort's views on his son, partly by the fact that she foresaw that 'Bertie' would naturally side with his bride's country over the looming question of the ownership of the Schleswig-Holstein duchies, soon the cause of the six-week war of 1864, in which Queen Victoria sided with Prussia. The Queen's decision condemned the Prince of Wales, forbidden to see important State Papers or to shoulder any responsibility, to adapt himself to a purely social rôle: from 1863 until his accession his life became a stereotyped round—Marlborough House and the London season,

Ascot, Goodwood, Cowes, Homburg, Scotland, Sandringham. Its effect on the Prince himself, a man of good political intelligence, is well known: its effect on London society Lord Houghton was one of the first persons to observe. He quickly perceived, and resented, that lowering of the general conversational and intellectual standards inevitable to the admission of modern royalty into the society of more normally educated persons. Since youth, Houghton had cherished a strong dislike for the false sentiments and pompous artificial values which infected not only members of the Royal Household but anyone who came within the periphery of Windsor or Buck House. Even his own family was not entirely immune, for Mrs. Milnes used the phrase 'this little page of English history' to describe a garden party at which she and Amy had watched 'the P. of W. and his Alexandra' play a game of croquet ('which is in fact the old one of "Pall Mall"') on the sunny lawns of Chiswick House.

V

On the day on which the new peerage was gazetted Lord and Lady Houghton, accompanied by the Honourable Amicia Milnes, her ladyship's maid Dawkins, and William the under-butler at Fryston (who had never been abroad before and muddled up the luggage) were methodically proceeding from Brussels to Namur, on their way to Bohemia. The ordeal of this 'immense' railway journey in blazing heat was alleviated by pleasant evening arrivals in Namur, Treves and Frankfurt. Strolling beneath the oleander trees in the secluded courtyard of the convent of the Sœurs de Notre Dame at Namur, which had an English abbess, Lord Houghton declared that when he was ruined he would come and live in that quiet town; his wife thought that under the same circumstances she would prefer Treves. The last two days of the journey were spent more comfortably in the old-fashioned *voiturier* method of travel, for no railway had yet penetrated the rocky, afforested valley in which Carlsbad lies. After travelling across Europe for nine days it was a relief to settle down in airy rooms in an hotel high up on the hillside above Carlsbad; Amy, who at eleven had never been out of England, was enchanted with everything she saw, and spent the days exploring the mossy paths that curled away uphill in the shade of beeches and birch trees, or collecting fir cones and picking the pale hare-bells that quivered amid the heath, or peering into the china-shops of the little town.

Although the Carlsbad waters had been of local fame since the Renaissance, it was only in the mid-nineteenth century that the town acquired an international vogue, and that speculators had built concert-halls and big hotels. Sir Joseph Paxton, who was there that summer, told the Houghtons that he would like to improve the drainage, and compared the new spa adversely with Matlock in his native Derbyshire; but on the whole visitors were delighted with the place in spite of the smelly rivulet which ran down the main street. While Amy trotted about the woodland paths, 'Papa' drank eight glasses of hot water a day, and 'Mother' took iron and steel baths under the direction of Dr. Hofleyer, who made her seriously ill within a week and had to be 'given his congé.' Lord Houghton was soon in his element at Carlsbad, for ever since his first experience of spa life at Marienbad in 1850 he had adored the gossiping, leisurely existence led in such places, with its endless opportunities for making new acquaintances among the ailing great. To him by far the most interesting personage at Carlsbad that August was the Grand Duchess Helena, widow of the Grand Duke Michael, sister-in-law of Nicholas II, and aunt of Alexander, the reigning Emperor of Russia.

The old Grand Duchess Helena, 'very clever' according to Lady Houghton, and very curious 'about English habits and politics' was doing a semi-state cure at Carlsbad, protected from the outer world by 'an agreeable Courtier-like man . . . Chamberlain or something of the sort,' Baron de Rosen and a nice Russian demoiselle d'honneur. She had begun by holding 'royal sort of audiences at first,' but soon, perhaps under Lord Houghton's mellowing influence, she started to give small dinner-parties at three in the afternoon, and shortly after that announced that she was 'at home' (to those who had been presented) every evening after eight. Lady Houghton made limited use of this permission, but Houghton himself was always dropping in on the Grand Duchess, talking over recent Russian history with her, and recording her remarks in his note-book.

L'Impératrice Catherine [the Grand Duchess observed one evening], n'était pas comme les autres femmes. Elle faisait tout ce que les hommes font, et ce qui aurait ruiné une autre femme, sans en souffrir ou physiquement ou moralement.

She explained to him why there could be 'une vraie aristocratie' in Russia, and talked of her brother-in-law's melancholia during the Crimean War, which he told her he knew had turned 'tous les honnêtes gens de l'Europe' against him. Seeing the Emperor Nicholas looking very ill in the week before his death, the Grand Duchess had remonstrated with him for not taking more care of his health: 'Je suis un cheval de poste,' replied the Emperor, 'je cours jusqu'à ce que je crève.' Together with these imperial anecdotes, Milnes collected the latest stories of Cavour and Garibaldi, Prussian nicknames for Bismarck, Paxton's tales of bridge-building, and other scraps of information which might later be of conversational use. The hot water and the gossip did him good; his pains disappeared; the family set out for home. But, by the time they had reached Dresden, Lord Houghton felt the first agonising twinges in his hands and feet. For the remaining twenty-two years of his life gout, the scourge and heritage of the English gentry, held him firmly in its burning grip. On the way back to England they had promised to go and see George Bunsen, who lived at Bonn, and who entertained his old friend almost too well.

My wife declares that the good living you gave me on the Rhine destroyed all the advantages of Carlsbad [Lord Houghton wrote to him in the spring of '64]. Somehow or other I have never been able to walk five miles since I was there, and think the waters over-drenched my blood.

IV

Since 1831 Hans Christian von Bunsen, his wife and several of their ten children had formed a constant Prussian element in the life of Richard Monckton Milnes. Originally introduced to them by a letter from his Trinity tutor, Milnes had, at twenty, bounded eagerly into the pietistic circle of this German Protestant scholar who was then functioning as Minister of the King of Prussia at the Vatican. He had received a kindly but very temperate welcome. For the Chevalier Bunsen Milnes soon felt respect; for the Chevalier's wife, a simple, saintly Welsh gentlewoman from Llanover, who would enliven earnest evenings at the Palazzo Caffarelli by singing her native airs, he felt admiration. In 1839 Bunsen had been transferred to Berne, and in 1841 he was promoted to the prize post of the Prussian corps diplomatique—Minister to the Court of St. James. In London the Bunsens settled in one of the great houses in Carlton Terrace, where for more than a decade they exercised a brilliant, formal hospitality, as well as entertaining at more intimate meals English and foreign men of letters.

Milnes was a frequent guest at Carlton House Terrace. Returning from the House of Commons of an evening, he would find on his table the pasteboard visiting-card of 'Le Chevalier Bunsen, Envoyé Extraordinaire et Ministre Plénipotentiaire de sa Majesté le Roi de Prusse,' with some hasty pencilled message scrawled upon it:—'Will you breakfast with us tomorrow at ten *precisely* to meet George Borrow (the Gipsy man)?' After the Chevalier's resignation in 1854, Milnes would go to see him at his beautiful villa at Heidelberg, a town the Bunsens had selected for retirement because of its fine library and stimulating university milieu. Here Milnes would walk with the learned old man beside the Neckar, through the fields of grape-vines, or stand watching as he played bowls with his coat off on long summer afternoons. Spending four or five days at Heidelberg, Milnes would then move on to Burg-Rheindorf, a little château encircled by poplar trees close to Bonn, with views of the Drachenfels from its windows. At Rheindorf lived George, the Bunsen son whom Milnes preferred and who had, in Berlin in 1845, been captivated by the Englishman's 'tenderness' and charm. The Chevalier Bunsen had died in 1860; and so it was to Bonn, and not to Heidelberg, that Lord Houghton took his wife and daughter in 1863. George's mother was then at Burg-Rheindorf, mourning the death of a favourite daughter Theodora von Ungern Sternberg, who had died, very suddenly, two years after her father, in the spring of 1862. Two other Bunsen daughters were also at Rheindorf, as well as a bevy of children with whom Amicia Milnes could play.

As a boy of twenty, studying German literature at the University of Bonn, Monckton Milnes had been much attracted by the displays of 'intense domestic feeling' to be witnessed at each parting or reunion of some little German family on the Rhine boats. The large and loving Bunsen family were themselves ideal examples of such true domestic emotions, and they had not recovered from the two recent intrusions of death. In 1863 George Bunsen was still suffering physically and mentally from the experience of his father's death-bed; whilst his mother, writing to Charlotte Williams Wynn of the third anniversary of the Chevalier's end, strikingly defined her existence since that event as 'not so much *living* as *waiting*, moored to that point of time.'[1] Moreover, one of George Bunsen's little children was wasting away with an incurable illness, an ordeal for her parents in which Milnes greatly sympathised. He would write (unusually often for him) to ask for news.

George Bunsen, a generation Milnes's junior, was amongst his most faithful and devoted friends, and a very frequent correspondent, sending letter after letter to Upper Brook Street in his even, characterless script. In spite of his mother's nationality, George Bunsen's use of the English language remained excessively Germanic. Asking Milnes, whom he addressed as a 'pattern of true human virtue,' to stand sponsor to his son Carl Christian

[1] Letter of December 1863 published in Augustus Hare's *The Life and Letters of Frances Baroness Bunsen* (Daldy, Isbister & Co. 1897). Baroness Bunsen occupied these years in the construction of her very interesting *Memoir* of her husband's life, published in two volumes in 1868.

Richard, he explained that when the boy grew up and enquired
'after the origin of his name' he would 'hear many a tale that is
both heart-refreshing and mind-upbrightening.' Fryston, where
he stayed in 1861 at the same time as the Orleans princes, and
again with all his family in August 1864, he termed 'a good climate
for human beings to live in.' In other ways, too, George Bunsen
was charmingly German, regarding Amicia as a fairy-tale figure,
and admiring the way in which her long hair flowed 'in golden
streamlets' through her father's hands. After getting a particularly
warm letter from Milnes two days before Christmas of one year he
wrote:

It is so charming a letter that I will rather cover it with Goldschaum
& place it in a prominent place among the sweetmeats on our
Christmas-Tree, to vye [*sic*] with Pfeffernüsse & Mandeln &
Rosinan; [adding, next day], The letter *is* gilt & fastened & now I
can write about it with a better conscience.

A Parliamentary deputy and a man of liberal tenets, George
Bunsen had far more in common with Monckton Milnes than had
his father, and took a real interest in his many philanthropic
activities. In reference to one of Milnes' agitations over a pet
reform the old Chevalier had written in 1844:

I am sorry to see you indulge in so subjective, esoteric, sentimental,
materialistic, yankee, subversive, impossible schemes as intramural
executions! Depend upon it, *we* shall never do such things! A good
old German execution is a most beneficial & solemn act as it ought
to be, & deservedly popular. . . . I scarcely ever loved John Bull
better but [*sic*] when I saw him behold Good's execution (who had
murdered his wife): evidently with that feeling of divine justice,
entrusted with awful privilege to man. There *may* have been pick-
pockets & wenches among the crowd: but there was a very good
specimen of true, unsophisticated John Bull, & I hope all were
edified as I was! It was like seeing Richard III. Dr. Lieber is a
man we shall never look up to for our legislations. Let him pro-
pose intramural whipping of boys, with birches grown *intra muros* if
desired!

George Bunsen, on the other hand, often wrote expressly to congratulate Milnes on his success in drawing public attention to the
need for Juvenile Reformatories, or on one of the other humanitarian
campaigns which took up so much of his public life. He shared
Milnes' literary interests, sending him new German books and the
latest editions of Goethe, and helping him about a German translation of his *Monographs*; it is also likely that it was Bunsen who got
the popular composer, Chevalier Neukomm, to do a setting for
Milnes' *I Wandered by the Brookside*. The younger Bunsen was an

intimate friend of Lord Ashburton's first wife, and an acquaintance of his second; like many another German intellectual he was very fond of Miss Charlotte Williams Wynn and her sister Mrs. Lindsay; he knew Thomas Carlyle, and had other literary connections with England, a country he was always visiting, for a sister and a brother had married into English families and settled here.

During the 'sixties and 'seventies George Bunsen wrote much to Lord Houghton on the topic of European political prospects. As far back as February 1856, he had predicted that Prussia would go to war: and had asked Milnes why he did not come to Bonn

before the war that must come visits us? Although I can well understand the curiosity of Englishmen & Frenchmen to visit Inkermann & the ci-devant Malakoff—yet for a Cosmopolitan & a Poet the scenes of a coming war must be still more remarkable. To stand on an eminence & to look on the carnage of Six Eagles that is to be:— who would not prefer that to the mournful impression of fresh & not even over-grown graves?

While some members of his family, including his mother, admired Bismarck, George Bunsen regarded him with suspicion—'Bismarck is destroying us,' he told Houghton after the Congress of Princes at Frankfurt in 1863. Two years later he wrote of Prussia as

swayed by a man I greatly dislike. His power is as yet on the increase. He has understood 'riding'—as his own prediction was in Octr 1862—riding the King in a manner which no Prussian statesman would have deemed possible. This is far more wonderful than his having gained for Prussia a dominant position in a particular corner of European politics.

Yet, a lifelong opponent of Bismarck, who sued him for libel in 1881, Bunsen could not exorcise and did not dissemble a certain satisfaction at the immense prestige and strength which Prussia had achieved under Bismarck's rule:

Surely you will agree with me [he wrote to Lord Houghton] in thinking (je ne suis pas payé pour louer Bismarck as you know) that for a man who had to *invent a German policy*, the first since who shall I say? Frederick Barbarossa? or Henry III? he has done well, on the whole, before & at & since the Congress of Berlin.

For George Bunsen was a Prussian, after all.

Settling down at the Star Hotel, which was cold at night, although in Bonn itself it was still warm enough to eat out of doors, the Houghtons passed each day of their visit either at Burg-Rheindorf, or driving with members of the Bunsen family into the surrounding country to look at the scenery or to call on some such notability as

Baron Stockmar, now living permanently out of England. In George Bunsen Lady Houghton had early found one of her most imaginative admirers. In the short reminiscences of his friendship with Lord Houghton which he prepared for my predecessor, Sir Thomas Wemyss Reid, Bunsen included a tribute to Annabel Houghton which merits re-printing for the light it casts upon this calm and most ethereal figure, whose attraction was of an elusive personal quality not always to be sensed in the affectionate but unexciting family letters which are all that she had left behind:

Never was it my good fortune [wrote Bunsen] to enjoy the confidence of a gentlewoman of more perfect equipoise, or of a nobler woman than the late Lady Houghton. In dealing with her husband's paradoxes and humorous leaps in the dark, she transferred into daily practice the inimitable apophthegm that 'tout comprendre c'est tout pardonner.' For behind every jest of her ever youthful, often frolicsome, lord she distinguished—and she inwardly prayed that everybody would duly distinguish—the meditative mood, the continuity of thought and of mental elevation, and the well-tutored wisdom of experience not lightly bought. She was glad, also, when others would perceive in her husband, through a charming veil of apparently half-conscious *bohème*, a powerful good sense, that gave solidity to his judgement on human affairs, and rendered his intuition of character all but infallible.

From Bonn, the Milnes family moved on through Ghent to Ostend and so to England and home. It was perhaps Amy who had benefited most from the expedition to Bohemia; but no sooner did the child reach London than she developed face-ache, and was hurried off to Mr. Crampton, the dentist who provided her father's famously ill-fitting dentures, to have 'a double tooth drawn.' 'Very brave and good' at Mr. Crampton's, Amy began coughing in the afternoon. Her parents returned from a theatre that evening to find her covered in mustard plaster, and that the maids had summoned Mr. Tweed, the doctor who lived next door, and was called on in such emergencies as the children's sudden illnesses, or Mr. Swinburne's epileptic fit. Amy's illness, though alarming, was not, however, serious, and she was soon up and about again.

V

'This is a beautiful coast but it is haunted by odious winds—the "Mistral" to-day—the "Bise" to-morrow,' Lord Houghton wrote to George Bunsen on 1 April 1864, from Cannes. He told Bunsen that this first experience of the newly fashionable French Riviera was 'only an excursion' to 'see some friends who are invalids in body, and poor Lord Brougham, with whom I am staying, whose mind is gradually declining.' On his way through Paris, Houghton had stopped to investigate the condition of Sir Charles MacCarthy, now Governor of Ceylon and struck down by a fatal illness at the peak of his career: 'I have played Providence to some three or four remarkable men,' Houghton wrote, again to George Bunsen, after Charles MacCarthy's death at Spa the following August, '& Nemesis has just come in when they were in their prime of work & satisfaction & carried them into the Infinite.' He found Mac-Carthy, that March, in 'a frightful state of debility' and gone back to the appearance of his youth when they had first met with Nicholas Wiseman in the high-walled garden of the Collegio Inglese at Rome. With the intention of diverting his dying friend, Houghton produced Algernon Swinburne, who happened to be in Paris at that time. This meeting was more than any invalid could stand, for Swinburne's recitations 'so excited MacC. that he had quite a bad night: he thought them wonderful & they quite haunted him.' Having interviewed MacCarthy's French doctor, with whom he was not impressed, Lord Houghton journeyed south to visit the second invalid on his list, the Milnes' relative and near neighbour Tom Bland of Kippax, who lay yearning for the smoke-laden atmosphere of the West Riding amid the shady palm trees of an hotel terrace at Hyères.

'Quite blistered' by a walk along the sea-shore where he had seen 'once again the rich sapphire of the Mediterranean with its bright white setting of foam against the rocks,' Lord Houghton sat writing to his wife in a room with the blinds drawn, a precaution 'against the effects of the sun on the skin to which I am so subject.' The dream-like beauty of Hyères and the islands of Porquerolles, beloved of Robert Louis Stevenson, left Houghton comparatively unmoved, for as he aged he was becoming less sensitive to natural scenery, and more eager for human company than ever. Hyères, he told Annabel, was 'much larger & more frequented' than he had expected. It even had possibilities which the Blands had mos tiresomely failed to exploit.

They complain a great deal of the dullness of this place, but they don't seem to have looked out for acquaintances [wrote their indefatigable cousin]. Queen Christina of Spain has been here the whole winter & must have had some pleasant people about her if they had only known how to look after them.

Tom Bland, a straightforward Yorkshire squire, did not take kindly to his exile, and in consequence was peevish with his wife: 'He is rather rough with Emily,' wrote Houghton, 'treating her in a paternal rather than a conjugal fashion.' Socially unenterprising, personally irritable, Bland was not an ideal companion, particularly in the rain which began to patter down that Easter Sunday upon the tumbled roofs of the *vieille ville* and the tiled verandahs of the new villas that looked out across the marshes to the sea. After an interesting day at Toulon, where he inspected the 'great iron ship' *La Gloire* and observed how much more cheery the French convicts seemed than their English equivalents in the hulks at Portland, Lord Houghton could stand it no more, and hastened across the Esterels and along the coast to Cannes. On arrival there he went to an hotel but soon discovered 'that Ld Brougham seems to wish me to go to his house, so I do so.' At the moment of issuing this invitation Lord Brougham, who was eighty-six, had appeared 'very old and benign,' but a few days' residence at the Château Eleanore Louise made it disappointingly clear that Houghton's host was senile: 'Poor Ld Brougham himself is seemingly unconscious of what goes on.' The only symptom of mental activity that Brougham gave while his guest was at the château was to send a sharp rejoinder to a note from Theresa Longworth, the plaintiff in the notorious Yelverton case which was coming up before the House of Lords that July.[1] Miss Longworth, who 'left her card The Hon. Mrs. Yelverton,' appealed to Lord Brougham to take up her cause with the same energy with which he had in old days defended Queen Caroline. She wrote that she had come to Cannes on purpose to see him, but Brougham refused to let her call, since as he was to be one of her judges in the House of Lords he would not permit himself to prejudge the issue. In fact, when the case did come up, Lord Brougham declared in 'Mrs. Yelverton's' favour, but this did not alter the majority verdict on her appeal. Though no longer mentally vigorous, Lord Brougham was in a characteristically scandalous frame of mind, mumbling out after dinner the sort of scurrilous reminiscences about eminent statesmen which we are always eager to hear: 'There was little doubt at the time of Pitt's pederastic inclinations,' he remarked one evening, 'especially for Canning: in Cobbett's Register on the debate respecting his debts, he put the epigraph "Praised & lamented by the *Men* he loved."'[2] Lord Houghton, who had been told many years earlier of Canning's alleged tendency to make unrestrained advances to young men even

---

[1] Maria Theresa Longworth (1832?–1881), authoress, had thought herself legally married to William Charles Yelverton, afterwards 4th Viscount Avonmore, at a ceremony in a Catholic chapel at Rostrevor in 1857. Her husband quickly married another lady the following year, and Miss Longworth began her long legal process which ended with her final defeat in the House of Lords judgement of 1864, upholding the husband's declaration that the marriage had never been valid in law.

[2] Commonplace-book 1861–1864.

inside the House of Commons, noted this story down with interest
as well as one of a similar nature about Mr. Windham and his
five male lovers, contributed by another guest in the house. Lord
Houghton's thirst for gossip, and better still, for scandal was
notorious. It was also unquenchable. He did not trouble to
check stories he was told, and any anecdote sufficiently odd, unlikely or outrageous found its place in the leather-backed notebooks
without which he never travelled. The malicious dotage of Lord
Brougham was an ideal source for 'Baron Tattle, of Scandal'
(as Swinburne called his old friend). Houghton left the Château
Eleanore Louise with a stock of new and sometimes scabrous tales *salacious*
about the great figures of the past.

Apart from his enfeebled host, who still managed to hold a small
weekly reception culminating in a dance, Lord Houghton found
little company at Cannes he liked. Prosper Mérimée and Victor
Cousin had left just before his arrival, and the only Frenchman
there of any interest was Odilon Barrot, the old liberal leader of the
'Dynastic Left,' who had played a great part in the 1848 Revolution,
as well as in that of 1830 when he had been one of the Commissioners
appointed to take Charles X to Cherbourg and to hand over to him
the Crown Jewels. With Barrot Houghton discussed the new
'liberalising' measures introduced by the French Emperor, and
learned that in the old man's view these did not amount to much,
for the Emperor had merely 'taken some power from the Ministers
to give more to the Préfets, i.e. he has shortened the handle to give
more weight to the blow.' It may have been Barrot who told him
of a Préfet at whose house Napoleon III had stopped and who was
found bottling the water in which the Emperor had bathed and
distributing it to his friends; and that another Préfet was alleged to
have folded up the sheets in which the Emperor and Empress had
slept and laid them away 'to be given to each of his daughters for
their bridal night.' To the French their government was, as it has
always been under any regime, a subject for witticisms. Their
quick jokes made a welcome contrast to the more sombre political
humour of the Whig and Tory clubs along Pall Mall.

'From what I see of this place it would only be agreeable for
people who have all their resources about them & have not to look
for them elsewhere,' Lord Houghton wrote to his wife, who later
made this discovery for herself when condemned by the doctors to
spend the whole winter of 1867 to 1868 in the Hôtel Beau-Site at
Cannes, alone with Amicia, some English books and a box of water-
colours.

The two subjects of conversation are lungs & anemones [wrote her
husband]—whether the former are really injured & whether one

lady has found some variety of the latter which the other has not
got. They go out on regular anemone hunts under the olive-
groves & are tremendously proud of a double-orange or a treble-
pink. The scent of the air in the drives is very peculiar. You
have a gust of lavender, or a puff of jonquil, or a mild incense of
fir-cones. The fields of roses are however not out & the year is so
backward that even the nightingales do not gush out as usual.

For those accustomed to think of the French Riviera as it is
to-day—an essentially summer resort, pandering to every pleasure,
a region of vulgar hotels, villas on inaccessible promontories,
extortionate restaurants, sensational jewel robberies and expanses
of human bodies baking on the shingle in the August sun—it is hard
to imagine the appearance and the atmosphere of this coast one
hundred years ago. Lord Brougham had discovered Cannes
and La Napoule during the cholera epidemic of 1839 when, held
there by an enforced quarantine on his way into Italy, he first
realised the beauty of these fishing-villages. These wayside places
had since then become, for foreigners, objectives in themselves. In
these early days the English and Russian personages who converged
in moneyed cavalcades upon these little ports came not for pleasure
but for health; they came in the autumn, stayed the winter, and left
in the spring. At the first sign of summer heats they flitted to the spas
of Germany and Czechoslovakia. The modern cult of the sun was
something of which they had no conception, for they thought (who
knows how wisely?) that exposure to the sun not only destroyed the
complexion but fevered the blood and addled the brains. In the
'forties and 'fifties these intruders bought land behind the fishing
ports, built palaces and villas, and designed carefully planned sun-
proof gardens filled with cypresses, umbrella pines, acacia-trees and
what Lord Houghton termed 'astonished palms.' The French
soon followed suit; new hotels sprouted on the hillsides, people
brought down their carriages from Paris, and the fashionables of the
Second Empire indulged in the novel pleasures of the sea-side.
This changed attitude to the sea was visible elsewhere along the
French coasts—at Trouville, which Lord Houghton had seen with
some surprise in 1857, at Pau and Biarritz, where he took his wife
and their elder daughter to hob-nob with the little Prince Imperial
in the autumn of 1866. But it was most noticeable of all at Nice
and Cannes.

'Cannes,' wrote the historian of maritime Provence [1] 'est une ville
ou l'on ne sent pas le besoin du travail.' The English residents, an
industry in themselves, were automatically the victims of the local
inhabitants, who had to make enough during the 'season' to keep

[1] Charles Lenthéric *La Provence Maritime* (Plon, Paris, 1880).

them in comfort and idleness for the rest of the year. In a sense the visitors deserved such treatment, for, quite incurious about their surroundings, quite unaware of what country lay behind Grasse, or westward of the Esterels, they formed a self-absorbed, self-sufficient foreign community, encamped in conditions of great luxury upon one rim of France. Lady Houghton, who had the sensibilities of an artist, enjoyed driving out to the hill village of Auribeau, or gazing at the panorama of the Esterel mountains from the Duchess of Buccleuch's terrace at the Château de Garibondi, a turreted, tomato-coloured mansion shrouded in orange trees and giant cactus plants, with splendid vistas to the sea from its balustraded terrace; but most people were content to drive out to leave cards on their acquaintances, to attend receptions and dinner-parties, to discuss how to get a good chef without being cheated, to scan the local newspaper for the names of new arrivals, or to do a little languid shopping for kickshaws and Paris hats in Nice or Cannes. And when all else failed there was the eternal topic of the many drawbacks to life on the Riviera—chief amongst them, as Lord Houghton had immediately recognised, the 'almost continual wind.'

My conclusion about wintering abroad is that—except in very extreme cases—the comforts of a good English house & good English food more than counterbalance the advantages of a hot sun & a harsh wind, which require the almost simultaneous protection of a greatcoat & a parasol,

wrote an old friend of Lord Houghton's who now habitually spent the cold months of the year at Nice. Matthew Higgins, a giant Irishman known in his lifetime for his brilliant letters to *The Times* and other newspapers signed 'Jacob Omnium,' was the next person whom Houghton visited after leaving the Château Eleanore Louise at Cannes. Driving along the Corniche road to Nice, which had only become French territory four years before, he spent a day with the Higgins family before he took ship for Genoa *en route* to Turin where he was hoping to catch a sight of Count Cavour and at least to glance at the new united Italy.

Higgins gave me a grand lionising the day I was at Nice [he wrote], & I think quite decided me in favour of it, as a residence, if one came abroad for the winter. The dearness & the cheating are the main objection.

Higgins, who was more than six and a half feet in height, was of the same age as Lord Houghton, and interested like him in philanthropic as well as literary undertakings. As a young man he had frequented the Blessington salon, where Count d'Orsay had drawn his profile; always popular in London society, he was also a man of serious tastes, a member of the Philobiblon and an intimate friend of the scholarly Stirling of Keir. His letters to Lord Houghton give the strong impression of a man of firm and sane values: 'Your friend Swinburne's book has been withdrawn from circulation,' he wrote in 1866, 'as too warm for our chilly clime—notwithstanding which Smith has had the pluck to publish a poem of his in the last Cornhill.' The demonstrative passion of Caroline Norton for his friend Stirling caused Higgins a good deal of amusement; for a relationship which Mrs. Norton declared had begun with her sincere anxiety to help William Stirling, 'a poor wounded bird' then suffering from a hopeless passion for her sister Helen Dufferin, had now become a rather public affair. 'Mrs. Norton has, I see, published some verses on a chestnut tree at Keir—the property of Sir W. S. Maxwell, Bt,' wrote Higgins in one letter; and in another, from Marienbad where he was taking the waters in August 1862:

I want to know something of Stirling of Keir—whether he is at home—& sees company in Scotland this year—'Il suffit à un homme de rencontrer une femme qui ne l'aime point, ou qui l'aime trop—pour que toute sa vie en soit derangée.'—I am afraid that S. has met the latter & that . . . he is spending the summer in his yacht on the Baltic—beyond the reach of the post office—& messengers from Chesterfield Street.

Higgins' letters give one the distinct feeling that here was a funny, sensible man one would have liked to know.

For some reason, perhaps connected with the illness from which he died in 1868, Matthew Higgins, his wife and children lived each winter at Nice. His letters from that place provide us with an authentic picture of the routine of a mid-Victorian Riviera winter:

My dear Houghton [he writes in one of them, dated 2 January 1865], I wish I could comply with your request to write to you a letter from hence that would be worth reading: but, ex nihilo nihil fit, and our life here is so purely leguminous that it is impossible to do.—There are scarcely any English here whose names you would recognise if I were to enumerate them to you. . . . The winter seems set in dry & bright & cold—snow-covered Alps in the background —and ripe oranges & full blown roses immediately around us. Russians abound in consequence of the presence of the Empress, who leads a very retired life. Twice a week she drives up here and strolls about our garden; and her Grande Maîtresse—Countess Pratasoff—invites us to tea in return every Friday. The Roth-schilds of Naples give solemn heavy feeds once a week, good of their kind—and on New Year's Eve gave a very pretty ball—and that is about all that has been doing here as yet. The Duchess of Manchester came here for a few days to see her sister . . . Lady Milbanke was also here for a short time . . . Mr. Joseph Hawley & his wife are occupying Villa Gastrel No. 1 & No. 3 is still unlet. Mrs. Seymour Bathurst & her daughter are occupying Villa Solferino next to ours—& the Thomson Hankeys are staying with them.

One can see that, however much lionised, Lord Houghton would find little to hold his errant attention for long at the Higginses' Villa Hélène at Nice.

VI

'My dearest Annabel, I cannot tell you how pleasant your husband has been!' wrote Miss Charlotte Williams Wynn from the Casa Pallavicini at Genoa where she had been wintering.

We could do little for him, but he is so willing to make the best of every thing and every body, and he enjoys *seeing* as no one now does. . . . Today he is off to Turin, where he seems to have many notable people to see.

Writing himself from Genoa to ask his wife to have the panels of the dining-room doors outlined in gold, and to leave cards on Lady Selina Bidwell, Lord Houghton explained that though he liked that city he intended pushing on to Turin. There he found much that allured him: 'This place is new to me, & not easily got at again, & the personages amusing, so I have settled to stay here till the end of the week.' The Prefetto of Turin gave a dinner for him, and though the King of Italy was 'in the country with his mistress and her family,' and did not 'come to town' during Lord Houghton's visit, he found many other interesting people to see, and was able to gauge the strength of the fury which Garibaldi's triumphal progress through London was then giving at Turin:

Everybody here from the King downwards is angry at the reception of Garibaldi . . . it is the same sort of thing as if Bright was to receive an ovation in Paris & our Govt. was told it was a compliment to them.

Houghton thought the English minister, Mr. Elliott, competent, and his wife, who had been an Antrobus, 'a cheery little woman.' After a sufficient stay in Turin, and armed with a pretty Genoese chandelier ('all arbutus leaves & fruit') for the embellishment of Fryston, Lord Houghton set out for Paris and for home. He reached England in time to attend the Shakespeare Tercentenary celebrations on 23 April 1864. For this festival he stayed with his acquaintance Lord Leigh, at Stoneleigh near Stratford-on-Avon, driving over to watch the ceremonies at the Birthplace with quizzical detachment, since he was firmly convinced that William Shakespeare could not have been the author of any of the Plays.

After his usual bout of country-house visiting, alternating with his own hospitalities at Fryston, Lord Houghton once more set out for France, once more alone, that August. On this occasion Vichy was his objective: but on the way thither he stopped in Paris to see his old enthusiasm of earlier, more revolutionary days, George Sand. 'I paid a visit to & dined with Mdme Sand in the country yesterday, & got back in time to see the Empr. & Prince Humbert at the Opera,' he told his wife. Lord Houghton clearly felt that this meal had been successful, for he could not refrain from repeating one joke that he had made. Madame Sand had been

charming in her grand simplicity: she asked about you & I said you were very aimable, with a good deal of humour & 'autant de justesse d'esprit que le bon Dieu a accordé aux femmes' on which she sd. 'Je vous remercie.'

After this passage of wit they went on to discuss the state of French literature and of French politics: 'She says they've no books, & no men in France now & I said it was much the same with us.' It is not likely that Houghton further enlivened the dinner by telling his hostess a malapropism over which he had chuckled the year before: 'Englishman to a French littérateur:—"Si vous dites que Rousseau est votre plus grand écrivain, assurément Madame Sand est votre plus grande écrevisse."'[1]

'Epris de Madame Sand' during the stirring days of '48, Milnes had since maintained a vivid interest in that lady, and always collected any stories about her that he could. In 1865 he recorded a complete conversation about her which had been repeated to him by his friend Duvergier de Hauranne:

Monsieur Planet [it runs] insisting to Duvergier de Hauranne 'que Madame Sand était la plus chaste des femmes.' 'Mais j'ai cru qu'elle a eu une trentaine d'amants, commençant avec Mérimée?' 'Ah! pour Mérimée, elle l'a chassé la deuxième nuit à cause de ses polissonneries... Elle a l'adultère en horreur.' 'C'est possible, mais son avocat et amant Monsieur Michel était un homme marié.' 'C'est vrai, mais avant de l'admettre à sa couche, elle l'a fait jurer d'abandonner complètement sa femme.' 'N'a-t-elle pas couché avec lui pendant qu'il la défendait dans son procès avec son mari?' '... Ce n'était que la nuit après la défense.' Planet saying he had

[1] Commonplace-book 1861–1864.

often travelled with her dressed 'à l'étudiant' & slept in the same room & nothing had ever passed between them—'mais c'est vous non pas elle qui faisait le chaste alors.' Mérimée telling Duvergier that she had never any pleasure of an erotic nature & that the picture in Lélia of the woman who is debauched by curiosity & desire witnout satisfaction is a true representation of herself.[1]

The narrator of these anecdotes, Duvergier de Hauranne, was one of Milnes' more recent friends in France. Rather paradoxically, the French statesmen and political thinkers Milnes had known best in his youth had been reactionaries—Alexis de Tocqueville, Montalembert, Guizot, Lenormand, Adolphe de Circourt—though their views had never accorded with his own fluid liberal creed. He had also known Thiers, though never intimately. Now in later life he was becoming closely connected with a group of Frenchmen who had helped instigate the '48 Revolution, and who staunchly opposed the Second Empire—men such as Odilon Barrot, Duvergier de Hauranne, and Rémusat. Milnes' own sympathies were as variable as ever. From distaste at Napoleon III's methods of gaining power he had, by the mid-fifties, veered round to enthusiasm for the Emperor; by 1870 he disliked him again. His admiration for the theatrical regime at the Tuileries provided many occasions for disagreement and argument between Houghton and his new French friends, none of whom, we may safely suppose, took his political opinions very seriously.

Je viens de passer quatre jours à Mortefontaine avec Barrot [wrote Duvergier to him in June 1860], & en nous promenant dans les allées où nous nous promenions ensemble l'an dernier, nous avons plus d'une fois pensé à nos querelles de cette époque.

'Rémusat que j'ai vu hier soir m'a parlé de votre enthousiasme,' he wrote in another letter, and again:

Nous nous querellerons probablement au sujet de votre admiration pour le grand homme (l'homme extraordinaire, dit Lord Derby) qui nous gouverne et vous me trouverez peu flatté de vivre sous son règne (l'ère d'Auguste, dit Lord Palmerston) mais ça ne nous empêchera pas d'être bons amis.

Milnes' imperial proclivities naturally made Duvergier assume that he would be on the 'wrong' or Southern side in the American Civil War: for, publicly known as a pronounced liberal in England, Milnes and his politics were considered unpredictably ambiguous by the more logical French. On another occasion Duvergier wrote

---

[1] Commonplace-book for 1865.

in a tone of raillery to commiserate with Lord Houghton on having
missed the Emperor and Empress at Vichy; he felt sure that in the
imperial circle his English friend would have found 'd'excellens
originaux des deux sexes, et vous auriez pu juger par vous-même
du haut degré d'intelligence et de vertu qui distingue cette noble
cour.' He went on to regale Lord Houghton with the latest
scandalous stories of the Courts of Love held by the Empress at
Fontainebleau. Two of the questions asked at these masquerades
were alleged to be: 'Dans quelles circonstances est-il permis à une
femme de tromper son mari?' and 'Lui est-il jamais permis de
tromper son amant?' 'Je ne connais pas les réponses,' Duvergier
added, 'mais la nuance entre les deux questions est délicate.'
Whatever the moral eccentricities at the elegant, creeper-covered
châlets in which the Imperial party merrily lodged at Vichy, the
management of the large hotels patronised by English persons kept
up a firm Victorian tone: describing the 'disagreeable adventure'
of an English acquaintance who had come to Vichy in August 1864,
Lord Houghton explained to his wife:

She came here alone & from her very 'prononcée' look was taken
for a 'femme légère': the women of the Hotel got frightened & as
much as told her to change her quarters, but there was luckily some
one in the Hotel who knew her & on telling them that she was the
wife of an M.P. & the niece of a Ld Chancellor—the people made
the humblest apologies. It seems she has divorced her husband as
far as a woman can do & gets into this trouble in consequence.

There was perhaps some justice in Richard Burton's condemnation
of Vichy (whither he went with Swinburne on Houghton's recom-
mendation in 1869) as a 'hideous hole,' the haunt of 'French
Grundy and bourgeois society.'

The heyday of Duvergier de Hauranne, a man some five or six
years older than Lord Houghton, had been the revolution of 1848,
when he had organised the Charter banquets which had helped to
effect the overthrow of Louis-Philippe. He now spent a good deal
of his time at his country place, the Château de Herry near La
Charité-sur-Loire, leaving politics to his promising elder son,
Emmanuel, whom he had brought to London in 1858 to introduce
him to Milnes and other useful English friends. It was to the
Château de Herry—at that moment, according to its owner, 'maison
déserte et peu animée'—that Lord Houghton proceeded on his way
back to England from Vichy that autumn. Harriette Galway, who
had been with her husband and son at Plombières, and was apparently in the grip of a malady inducing moments of lassitude
followed by periods of great activity, met her brother at Lyons, and,

after visiting the French educationalist Monsieur Arlès-Dufour, they travelled together to La Charité where the Duvergier de Hauranne family genially awaited them. At Monsieur Arlés-Dufour's Lady Galway had formed the unwelcome habit of appearing in her brother's bedroom at seven in the morning; and in contrast to, probably as a result of, this excessive energy she had had attacks of giddiness when walking and had been 'obliged to sit down in a shop for fear of falling in the street.' Lord Houghton thought that 'a French country-house would amuse her,' for having made a conventional English marriage and early taken on the duties of châtelaine of Serlby, Harriette had missed her brother's considerable experience of French château life, often so infinitely more pleasant than its English equivalent. The Duvergier de Haurannes begged their English friends to return to Herry whenever they wished to do so; from 1864 until the death of M. Duvergier *père*, which occurred only a few months before his own, Lord Houghton would often stop at this hospitable house, with its cosy family life, on his way to or from the *bains de Vichy*. As in the instance of the Bunsens, and of many of Lord Houghton's other Continental friends, he exerted his charm upon every member of the family: Emmanuel Duvergier de Hauranne, as well as his poor young brother Ernest, an adventurous boy who had journeyed in the wildest areas of Canada and the western States, but died young of tuberculosis at Cannes, felt a warm and earnest affection for Lord Houghton, whose gift for winning friends wherever he went well compensated for his restlessness and lack of political equilibrium.

The journey home of Lord Houghton and of Lady Galway was marred by one of those nasty little incidents from which no traveller need think himself immune. This was an altercation about seats on the train from Paris to Amiens: it would have been easily forgotten had not one of the parties to it composed a note of protest to the Editor of the London newspaper *The Standard*. Headed *John Bull Abroad* and published over the initials D.F.C., this displeasing letter began by stating that 'during an autumn excursion of six weeks on the Continent,' the writer had 'endeavoured to discover the reason why certain English travellers, of the upper class especially, are disliked by foreign railway officials and employés.' Lord Houghton and his sister had unwittingly assisted these researches.

I have witnessed many sad instances of ill-bred Englishmen forgetting themselves [wrote D.F.C.], but what I experienced to-day, at the station of the Chemin de Fer du Nord in Paris, induces me to address you, and to give your readers a true sample of the highly improper conduct of which Englishmen . . . may be guilty,

on the Continent. There were but four first-class carriages in the
mid-day train from Paris to Boulogne to-day, the 6th of October.
I had taken a first-class ticket, and was about to seat myself in the
front compartment of carriage No. 205, when I was rudely hustled,
if not jostled, by a burly John Bull of about 55 years of age, wearing
a seedy white hat who had taken into the carriage and was de-
positing above and around his portly person more than a dozen
packages and parcels, besides a bundle containing a dozen of
walking-sticks, parasols and umbrellas. This person told me . . .
that there was 'no room' for me; that he had engaged and paid for
four places in that compartment, and that he expected three ladies.
Discrediting and disregarding his statement, I (an old stager)
coolly took a seat, determined not to vacate it until the said ladies
made their appearance. It turned out that my estimate of the
veracity of my fellow-traveller was well-founded for no other
person joined him, except a stout elderly woman. Between Paris
and Amiens, where he and she quitted the train, my monopolist
fellow-traveller was repeatedly and ostentatiously addressed by his
servants as Lord —— (I won't mention the name, suffice it to say
that it was one of the recent Whig additions to the peerage).
. . . It is just possible that the man who conducted himself in the
above improper manner is an imposter, and not the person who was
last year elevated to the peerage. In that case he will probably
expose the imposture and abuse of his name.

It is seldom gratifying to see ourselves as strangers see us, and
Lady Galway did not relish these descriptions of her brother or
herself. Snatching up her pen, she composed a private missive to
the Editor of the offensive *Standard*:

Lady Galway's attention has been attracted today to a letter in the
Standard [she wrote]. She remembers there was some difficulty
about getting places at Paris and a gentleman kept the two best for
himself and his bag. Lord Houghton had taken *four first class
tickets*. An Englishman who pretends to be a foreigner & wears a
foreign order is always looked on with suspicion, & Lady Galway
supposes the writer of this letter was that person. As she does not
care to know his name the Editor of the Standard had better communicate this note to him, & if he is a gentleman he will no doubt
take the first opportunity of apologizing to Lord Houghton, whose
address he can easily ascertain.

There is no malice in judging Lady Galway's explanation inadequate !

VI

It was while Lord Houghton was at Hyères in August 1864 that
he learned of the death at Spa of his best and oldest friend, Sir
Charles MacCarthy. 'It is strange how the links of life snap as one

goes on,' he wrote to Abraham Hayward; but, though the acquisition of a new friend does not exactly compensate for the loss of an old one, he was always busy forging fresh links. More than three hundred long letters from MacCarthy to Lord Houghton are preserved—a collection only equalled in bulk by those from George Bunsen and from one more recent acquaintance, who by the mid-sixties had become an intimate friend, to some extent replacing MacCarthy in Houghton's life. These letters, one hundred and seven in number, were written between 1861 and 1884 by the Liverpool shipping merchant and littérateur, Henry Bright.

On their mother's side the brothers Henry, Heywood and Hugh Bright were connected with the Milnes family, themselves of merchant stock. In Lord Houghton's grandiloquent phrase the Brights 'belonged to that aristocracy of commerce and finance which is generated by individual industry, probity and enterprise in our great sea-board cities.'[1] Henry and Heywood Bright were partners in their father's shipping business of Gibbs, Bright & Co., an enterprising firm engaged in the South American trade, and responsible for the first regular sea communication between this country and Australia. Sufficiently conscientious in the office, Henry Bright was early criticised by his brother and his cousins for being more interested in literature than in shipping. As time went on Bright, a Liberal and, of course, a Unitarian, educated at Rugby and Trinity College Cambridge, became the recognised leader of literary Liverpool, gradually assuming the position of arbiter of taste for industrial Lancashire held half a century earlier by the learned banker, and historian of the Medici, William Roscoe. Nineteen years younger than Monckton Milnes, and thus virtually belonging to another generation, Bright epitomised in his character and his conduct the fine, intellectual, charitable, Unitarian tradition which he represented in Liverpool, and which his friends and relations, the Gaskells, represented in Manchester. Many passages in his letters, trivial in themselves, suggest the atmosphere in which they lived:

By the way [he writes in 1864] have you seen Mrs. Gaskell's pleasant articles on 'French Life' in Fraser?—I felt sure they were hers, & taxed her with it the other day at Manchester, when we were helping Mr. Stansfield to lay the stone of our heretic 'Memorial Hall.'

In Liverpool as in Manchester this mercantile tradition had produced a quiet, rich, well-bred provincial society, a little heavy, a little high-minded, much bent on good works, their interests

[1] *In Memoriam* of Henry Bright, printed in the final (1884) volume of *The Philobiblon Miscellanies*.

divided between helping the poor and making money for themselves. Henry Bright, himself a prominent philanthropist, had soon succeeded in interesting Milnes in one of his favourite subjects, the 'ship-cruelty question.' This question was how to put a stop to the terrible floggings and other cruelties practised aboard Yankee ships by Yankee captains and Yankee mates. In 1859, over the signature 'A Liverpool Merchant,' Bright published a pamphlet *Cruelties on the High Seas*, with a motto from Scapin on its title-page— *La justice en pleine mer! Vous moquez-vous des gens?* Later in the same year he sent a knuckle-duster used on an American vessel to Monckton Milnes, who took this instrument down to Westminster and, waving it 'in humble imitation of Mr. Burke's revolutionary dagger,' informed a sceptical House of Commons that it had been 'used by one of the incriminated captains for purposes of manslaughter or mutilation.' The campaign of Milnes and Bright against inhumanities reminiscent of those exposed by Herman Melville in *White Jacket*, seemed likely to lead to the setting-up of an Anglo-American Commission of Enquiry, when the outbreak of the Civil War prevented it. Although unable to alleviate conditions on ship-board, Bright continued to work for the improvement of the seaman's lot and for the establishment of Sailors' Homes in English ports. He also involved himself in many other causes, such as the improvement of prison vans, and the bold reforms of Josephine Butler, who, moving to Liverpool in 1866, had there set up the standard of her movement for helping 'fallen women,' and repealing the Contagious Diseases Act. 'Yesterday I went to the Contagious Diseases,' wrote Bright in an altogether typical letter, of September 1870, to Lord Houghton.

The paper was a clear sound mass of unanswerable statistics, quite unimpassioned & badly read. Mrs. Josephine Butler spoke.—I had never seen her properly before;—a slight graceful woman in a black hat & long purple veil & gold cross hanging in front of her black dress.—She has a thin penetrating voice,—but without much power or modulation. . . . She was cheered,—& she deserved it,— for she was spirited & gallant;—but on the whole the meeting was nearly equally divided.

Bright always exercised his judgement over good causes, and was never indiscriminate or fatuous: 'The unconscious cruelty of good people is frightful,' was one of his sensible comments, 'I really believe they do as much harm as bad people.' To all these humanitarian interests, he added others less strictly within the Liverpool tradition, and thus doubly useful there:—an admiration for Balzac, or for Gustave Doré, a passion for collecting autographs equal to Houghton's own, a sympathy with Pre-Raphaelite poetry and painting, a love of flower-gardens (a subject on which he published two popular books), and a turn for literary criticism responsible for his many unsigned articles in *The Examiner* and *The Athenæum*. His shipping connections had carried him to the United States in 1852, where he had become acquainted with the Concord circle, and he had developed an understanding of contemporary American literature almost unique in mid-Victorian England. Bright was also in the unusual position of being the one Englishman of whom Nathaniel Hawthorne when U.S. consul at Liverpool wholeheartedly approved.

'Bright was the illumination of my dusky little apartment as often as he made his appearance there,' wrote Hawthorne, who described how Bright would seldom sit down but liked to stand erect upon the hearth-rug

tall, slender, good-humoured, laughing, voluble; with his English eye-glass, his English speech, and his English prejudices; arguing, remonstrating, asserting, contradicting,—certainly one of the most delightful, and delightfully English, Englishmen that ever lived.

Like Hawthorne's other English friends, Henry Bright detested the garbled versions of her husband's private notebooks which the impoverished Mrs. Hawthorne began publishing after his death: he thought them destructive of Hawthorne's reputation, 'a matter of vexation—& almost of despair,' and told Houghton he regarded the widow as 'grinding up her poor husband's bones for bread.' All the same he was deeply touched by the warm references to himself which he found in Hawthorne's published Journals, and by the knowledge that this gelid New Englander, with his 'strange gnarled & twisted fancies,' had esteemed him so much. 'These few words will be the only thing by which anyone will one day come across my name,' he wrote with pathetic prescience to Lord Houghton in March 1872. 'What must it be for those, who know their name is really stamped on the literary history of their time.' He was correct, for he belonged to that wide category of educated men who are of immeasurable service to their contemporaries, but who do not produce lasting work by which their name survives. *A Year in a Lancashire Garden*, which Houghton lavishly compared with Izaak Walton and with Gilbert White, predicting for it immortality, is a touching little account of the seasonal work in the small garden at Knotty Ash, the 'long red-gabled house, with stone facings,' and a good library, where Bright lived with his wife and children outside Liverpool. This unpretentious little book won popularity when it was first printed; Bright's readers would make pilgrimages to Knotty Ash to see just why the arbutus did not fruit or whether the Julia Lagravière chrysanthemums were doing well on the porch. It is a friendly, informal series of essays, written for successive issues of *The Gardener's Chronicle* of 1874, and then gathered into book form. With its successor, *The English Flower Garden*, an essay originally written for the *Quarterly Review*, *A Year in a Lancashire Garden* is perhaps the earliest example of the kind of desultory gardening notes which we now see in every solid Sunday and weekly newspaper; for Bright's books have neither the minute zestful exactitude of Gilbert White, nor the style of Izaak Walton; they are, in fact, not literature but journalism. Nor are Bright's letters in themselves fascinating, although they show us a simple man of considerable sensibility and good heart. 'I think much of you,' he wrote at the time of Lady Houghton's prolonged and dangerous illness in 1867, '& I sometimes feel as if I had never said half enough of the happiness your & Lady Houghton's friendship has given me for now nearly ten years'; or, again,

when I feel disheartened at the want of strength—& so I suppose the want of firm will—which has caused me to do & be so much less than I would wish—the thought of the friendships I have somehow won, comes upon me more cheerily and pleasantly than I can tell you.

The Houghtons' friendship with Henry Bright had a homely and intimate quality lacking in many of their London contacts, and even those with people whom they saw more often. It was to Lady Houghton that he wrote to describe Mrs. Gaskell's funeral in the tiny sloping graveyard of the old Presbyterian meeting-house at Knutsford, to Lord Houghton that he wrote about the shock of Hawthorne's death; he would tell little Florence Milnes ghoststories, and commiserate with Lady Houghton on the great fire which burned Crewe Hall to the ground one night in 1866. He would send them sweetwater-grapes (an old-fashioned remedy for the gout); Indian corn; white haricot-bean seed; barrels of American apples; and boxes of preserved peaches from New Orleans. Henry Bright was a man quite devoid of social as well as of political ambition: like the other members of the gentlemanly merchant society of Lancashire he would be summoned at certain intervals to Knowsley, and like them he regarded the Derbys as the hereditary social deities of this midland world; but, beyond dining and leaving cards there occasionally, he had no wish to get to know that great house or its owners better. His heart lay in literature, and in the friendship of literary men for which he yearned.

Although so much younger than Lord Houghton, Henry Bright predeceased him; their last meeting was in 1883, at Cannes, where Bright was sent by the doctors for a disease of the lungs. 'In 1883,' wrote Houghton in the memoir of Henry Bright which he just lived to see printed in the final volume of the *Philobiblon Miscellanies*,

I had the sad satisfaction of solacing and diverting Henry Bright's exile at Cannes in company with the learned and kindly Lord Acton, in whose late acquaintance he found much delight. . . . Before another winter came Henry Bright had passed away in his home amid his family and books, and had gone to his rest beneath the wreaths of his own Lancashire garden.

Henry Bright died at Liverpool after spending his final months at Bournemouth. One of the most insular of all Lord Houghton's friends (he had been abroad twice in sixteen years) Bright preferred this odious resort to anything he had seen on the Mediterranean.

I am delighted with the place: [he wrote, after describing the difficulties of English house-hunting] it is so pretty,—*greener* than Cannes, & less dusty.—I like the firtree better than an olive—& [added this most English of Englishmen] I am fond of getting the 'Times' first day!

VII

The fire at Crewe Hall, about which Henry Bright had written, destroyed everything but the four outer walls, the large Dining Hall and the Oak Parlour of this famous old house. Caused by a defective flue, the fire occurred in mid-winter, January 1866, and, like most catastrophes, at night. Lady Houghton, who was awakened by the servants hammering on her bedroom door, Robin Milnes and Mrs. Blackburne were the only people staying in the house. It was to his sister that Lord Crewe owed the preservation of his splendid pictures. Knowing him to be incapable of organising any salvage operations himself, Lady Houghton directed the removal of the Reynoldses to the snow-covered lawn, herself coolly standing in the room adjacent to the great Gallery down which the flames were roaring.

Since her marriage in 1851, when she had left Madeley Manor for good, Lady Houghton had spent part of every year staying with her brother at Crewe. Even for someone of her amiable temperament this was not always an agreeable undertaking. Monckton Milnes, who did his genial best to get along with his brother-in-law, found it at times impossible to do so. But to those not connected with him by blood or marriage, Lord Crewe was a figure of interest.

The English have always liked eccentrics, and as he grew older Lord Crewe's remarkable mannerisms made him well known far beyond the borders of Cheshire.   When he died in 1894 long newspaper obituaries were devoted to anecdotes of his eccentricities. 'Tall, ungainly and painfully diffident in manner,' bearded and very shy, Lord Crewe had never recovered from the boyhood shock of seeing his tutor commit suicide in his presence.   This horrible incident had left him with a fear of seeing people—*Truth* quoted Lord Houghton as having once said that his brother-in-law 'would stick his face in a holly-bush sooner than meet a party of his neighbours'—and a form of religiosity which expressed itself in his preference for clerical company and his habit of going to hear three sermons on a Sunday.   On the Great North-Eastern Lord Crewe was well known for his way of arguing aloud with himself as he sat, his travelling cap on his head, in the public dining-car; while the rare guests at Crewe were never much surprised by anything their host did or said.   He loved strange flowers, and would appear in the evening with a line of orchids, or of 'red-hot pokers' pinned down one side of his coat.   Never married, and with a dislike of children almost as strong as his love of sermons, Lord Crewe had one passion in life—Crewe Hall.   In that active architectural period, when the country-houses of England were being expensively ruined by elaborate Gothic additions, he had set to work to 'embellish' his ancestral seat which, built in 1636, had been one of the finest examples in England of the late Jacobean style.   Beginning by consulting Ambrose Poynter, who had built St. Katherine's Chapel and Hospital in Regent's Park, Lord Crewe ended by relying upon old Edward Blore, who had built Abbotsford for Sir Walter Scott, the young architect George Street, who afterwards designed the Law Courts, and the landscape gardener, Nesfield, who laid out the new gardens beside the artificial lake.   Lord Crewe had already spent a great deal of time and money in 'improving' Crewe Hall, and the fire of January 1866 thus seemed to his relatives especially disastrous.   Lady Houghton was surprised by the calm with which her brother surveyed the blazing ruins of his house. 'Well, Annabel,' he remarked, turning to his sister who stood beside him, 'you have always said Crewe was a cold house, but you can't call it that now.'   Seating himself at a writing-table which had been brought out with other furniture into the snow, he sent for ink and paper, and composed a telegram to George Street, explaining to him that Crewe Hall was burning down and asking him to undertake to build it up again at once.

To all his family and his connections—including Lord Houghton who had hoped that his son would in due time inherit this splendid house—the fire at Crewe seemed tragic; but the owner saw in it an opportunity to commission more building than he had ever been able to do before. Blore was asked to draw up designs for reconstruction, but pleaded his age (he had been born in 1787) and the disappointment that he felt at seeing so much of his own good work at Crewe destroyed. Within a week of the fire Lord Crewe was up in London interviewing other architects: from his house in Hill Street he wrote to his sister Henriett that 'a son of the Celebrated Man—the Late Sir Charles Barry' had been recommended to him. He did in the end choose Edward Barry, who had rebuilt Covent Garden theatre in eight months after the fire of 1857, had just completed the station hotel and Eleanor Cross at Charing Cross, and was then designing for Lord Stradbroke the mustard-yellow block of Henham Hall. The rebuilding of Crewe, which had been completely gutted except for the dining-room, took three years. The result, described in a contemporary architectural journal[1] as 'very elaborate' (in those days a term of praise), was in part an exact reproduction of the Old Hall, in part an epitome of mid-Victorian romantic taste. The stone chimney-pieces were replaced by others of alabaster and marble throughout the house; stained-glass windows with armorial bearings filtered the daylight into the great hall; wrought-iron gaseliers, family busts by the modern sculptor Weekes, plaster-work by Mabey and book-cases supported by carved wooden statuettes of Elizabethan worthies, decorated the new rooms. An attic storey for twenty servants' bedrooms was added, and, as a final piece of judicious planning, the menservants' rooms were divided from those of the womenservants 'by a wall of separation' and approached by separate stairs.

While the superintendence of the work at Crewe Hall gave Hungerford Crewe a full-time occupation, it did not make him any easier to deal with. He would still send churlish notes to Upper Brook Street beginning: 'I fear I cannot let you have my Carriage on Saturday,' or 'I have not a stable full of Carriage Horses eating the bread of Idleness.'

I remember thinking, that after the Peerage, there was not much more for me to do socially & politically [Houghton had written to his wife in 1864], but that I had three objects to look after—your health—my few remaining friends—& keeping well with Crewe . . . : and now you have been very ill, & I have lost the closest friend.I had [Sir Charles MacCarthy] & I have all but had a regular row with your brother—so go human intentions.

---

[1] *The Builder* of 1869 has ground-plans and a description of the new Crewe Hall (pp. 485–486).

Chapter Ten

1867   1874

I

Though it might seem to Richard Monckton Milnes that 'there was not much more' for him to do after his acceptance of a peerage —he used to declare that since he had applied for the Chiltern Hundreds he no longer 'felt like an Englishman,' and it was about this time that he began referring to himself as 'an old gent'—he continued his active help of any cause, however unpopular, which he considered just.   In July 1864, at the very height of the *Essays and Reviews* scandal,[1] he asked the Lord Chancellor in the House of Lords whether he had taken an opinion on the legal right of Convocation to condemn any book, and whether he did not think it unfairly injurious to the careers of Temple, Jowett and the thirteen other authors of the essays denounced by Convocation as heretical to be publicly censured in this way.   It was in reply to this question that the Lord Chancellor, Lord Westbury, enunciated his celebrated definition of a synodical judgement ('a well-lubricated set of words, a sentence so oily and saponaceous that no-one can grasp it; like an eel it slips through your fingers') thus adding insult to injury, enraging the Archbishop of Canterbury and much increasing the difficulties of the situation in which the English bishops had placed themselves.   While not exactly a storm in a tea-cup, the nation-wide *Essays and Reviews* controversy did at length die down.   In 1865 and '66 the country's attention was diverted to the more serious problem of John Bright's agitation for the extension of the franchise.   Lord Houghton was one of the few peers who came out in emphatic support of this far-reaching reform.   He was strongly in favour of Lord Russell's abortive Bill of 1866, and him-

---

[1] The case of *Essays and Reviews*, a volume of essays on modern Biblical criticism and kindred topics, published in February 1860 and widely read throughout England, had dragged on to 1864; the first prosecutions for heterodoxy against two of the contributors, Wilson and Williams, had been conducted before the arches court at Canterbury in the winter of 1861–1862, and appeals and re-hearings of the case continued until 1864.   Apart from increasing dissension inside the Church of England, and bringing Jowett and Temple under suspicion of heresy, the book 'marked the appearance of a very important development of religious and philosophic thought' (Leslie Stephen's *Studies of a Biographer*, vol. ii).

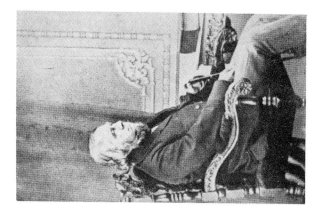

LORD HOUGHTON, CIRCA 1868

self presided over a mammoth Reform meeting in the Cloth Hall at Leeds in April of that year. 'You are one of those who are in earnest about the business,' Gladstone wrote to him, '—I believe an increasing band.' Not content with the new franchise granted under the Reform Act of 1867 (Lord Derby's 'Leap in the Dark'), Lord Houghton went further, and permitted John Stuart Mill to use his name and Lady Houghton's on the General Committee list of the Women's Suffrage Society.

In his extreme youth a nominal Conservative, Houghton was, at sixty, nearly a Radical. The 1867 Reform Bill, a logical continuation of that of 1832, marked the beginning of real democracy in this country, or at any rate represented the greatest step so far taken towards it.

I no more believe that political democracy in England will be compatible with social aristocracy than I do that Colenso is compatible with Christianity [a friend of Milnes wrote in protest to him at this time]. Perhaps an American England may produce a larger average of happiness than the existing system, but it would not be a country for a gentleman, and I for one should be quite strange in it.[1]

To Houghton the ultimate extinction of social aristocracy in England seemed of less importance than the immediate amelioration of shocking industrial conditions, the prevention of working-class crime by the establishment of Juvenile Reformatories, the proper education of mechanics and artisans, and the other urgent causes for which he sincerely cared. Perfectly at home in every coterie of London society, where he had now assumed an even more prominent and eccentric position than before, Houghton had never confined himself to seeing only one class:

I have a weakness for Lord Houghton [wrote a girl to Robert Browning in 1864];[2] there seems to me something manqué about him, which always draws me towards people. I think in those odd omnium gatherum collections of his there is such a curious kind of aspiration after excellence in one walk or another, and then he is content to be 2nd rate himself, which very few people are.

Miss Julia Wedgwood knew of Lord Houghton by hearsay only, or she might have realised that at one time he had very much minded being second-rate. Without being entirely cynical, Houghton had always seen things as they were: he no longer had any illusions

---

[1] G. S. Venables to Lord Houghton, 23 November 1866.
[2] *Robert Browning and Julia Wedgwood—A Broken Friendship as revealed in their Letters*, ed. Richard Curle (Murray & Cape 1937), p. 111.

about his own talents, and he had never made an act of faith in the absolute value of his own class. His comments on that agreeable country-house life which formed an important component of his existence and those of his friends, were always quizzical, always illuminated by mellow gleams:

There are some Tableaux going on at Lady Edward Howard's, which I have not seen [he wrote in 1869, in one of his now frequent letters to his daughter Amy, already seventeen]. I met Lady Sebright at dinner in her costume—a Louis Quatorze dress made out of the pink & yellow one she wore at Fryston & her hair powdered; she was to be mounted up on a swing in a Watteau Picture. Lady Di Beauclerk was to do a water nymph standing with bare feet on a glass which was to do for water. This is all for the distressed Irish.

II

Notable in England as a period of progressive political reform, of orderly agitation culminating in the peaceful extension of the franchise, 1866 and 1867 were on the Continent years of awful portent. The Peace of Prague which followed on the battle of Sadowa, ending the Seven Weeks' war of the summer of '66, had left Prussia triumphant; in Paris, as Lord Houghton found in 1867, a Franco-Prussian war was being openly discussed, with the Empress as alleged leader of the war party. To most observers, French and foreign, it was clear that the Napoleonic regime was tottering: 'The Empire,' wrote Persigny in 1867 'appears, to be collapsing on every side.' As a system of government the Second Empire had by now lost almost all of its adherents. The Emperor, careworn and disillusioned, ageing and tortured by stone in the bladder, was attacked from all sides. Threatened by the alternate dangers of war or revolution, Parisians found relief in a frenzied reign of pleasure for which the Empress and her followers set the tone while the Emperor acquiesced. The Second Empire had always relied on spectacle to beguile its subjects, and in 1867 it provided the greatest one of all. In April of that year was opened, on the Champ de Mars, in a gigantic elliptical building shaped like an inverted pie-dish, the largest, the most comprehensive, the gayest and most showy international exhibition that the century had seen. By its scope alone the 1867 exhibition really merited its proud title of '*L'Exposition Universelle*.' There were more than forty-two thousand exhibitors, and the stands, grouped geographically, offered examples of the arts and industries of every country under the sun, Eastern as well as Western. The exhibits overflowed into the park surrounding the temporary palace; here Norwegian and Swiss châlets, Tartars' tents, Arab mosques, Roumanian pavilions and Yarcoutes' bark huts vied with each other to attract the alert, inquisitive attention of the swarming crowds.

The Universal Exhibition was opened on the scheduled date, 1 April, but in so sadly uncompleted a condition that the English journalist, George Augustus Sala, 'covering' the exhibition for *The Daily Telegraph,*[1] wrote that 'really the next best thing' after the opening ceremony 'would have been to shut up the palace and grounds until the works were finished and the place fit for the inspection of the public.' Packing-cases lay everywhere. Some countries, such as Brazil and Portugal, had not even begun to unpack one object when the Exhibition was declared open. The only section approaching completion was the English one, but even this was imperfect until the last days of April; 'a forest of iron columns' with the crowned initials VR upon their shafts, this section displayed the industrial might of Manchester and Sheffield in all its glory, though the French were tiresomely critical of some exhibits, including a strange item called 'The Test House,' a heterogeneous building designed to show off every form of patent or experimental chimney, cowl, ornamental tile, drain-pipe and other convenience; the French, pretending to admire this bristling cottage as a typical specimen of modern English architecture, christened it 'Le Goddam.' Nevertheless, on the afternoon of the ceremonial opening, the English stands were looking smarter and more tidy than the rest of the Exhibition; at the base of the iron staircase leading up to them a 'handsome green carpet' had been spread, and here the five British Commissioners and the fifteen Jurors stood awaiting the benign advance of the imperial party. The Emperor, dressed entirely in black, with the Empress leaning on his arm, closely followed by the Princess Mathilde and a throng of 'chamberlains, ushers, equerries, and pages, down to footmen and chasseurs,' moved painfully through the corridors of the elliptical palace, amid echoing applause, loudest from the sections of Egypt and the United States. The imperial party had arrived in three calèches with outriders clad in the Houshold liveries of green and gold. They had crossed the Pont de Jéna under a canopy of cashmere powdered with golden bees, had descended at the great doorway of the exhibition and were now making their slow way round. On reaching the English contingent, the Emperor smiled warmly at Mr. Cole, the hated head of the British Commission—'Ce terrible Cole est arrivé,' Marshal Vaillant had said to Lord Cowley in

---

[1] Sala's reports were republished as a book—*Notes and Sketches of the Paris Exhibition* (Tinsley 1868).

Houghton's hearing at the French Embassy—and while the Empress talked to this 'energetic little man,' the Emperor moved on to speak to a short, portly grey-haired personage standing next him, who was both a Juror, and, at the special request of the French Government, President of the Group of Liberal Arts for the whole Exhibition. 'The Emperor evidently recognised Lord Houghton as an old friend,' wrote Sala, 'and after a few more gracious words Cæsar and his fortunes went by.'

The Exhibition is vulgar and speculative [wrote the President of the Group of Liberal Arts to his friend Bunsen]—a congeries of incongruous interests, of real industrial usefulness and the lowest form of gratified curiosity. You see Lord Shaftesbury haranguing between the Chinese dancing girls and the great guns. What it will be in the heat and confusion of summer is unimaginable.

Lord Houghton's position as a President and Juror involved him in a serious amount of toil:

I have been here for some time, and sit with the Conseil Supérieur, making speeches utterly irrespective of tenses and genders. But, as one of the Chamiers said to me 'You are here to look after English interests, not French grammar' [he told Henry Bright].

Lord Houghton had never been daunted by his somewhat indifferent French, one of several weaknesses on which his father had always teased him. Seizing the opportunity of a spring and summer in Paris, he took the Champs-Elysées apartment of his wife's friend Mrs. Symons, and settled down. Since Lady Houghton was too unwell to face the inferno of entertainments to which her husband eagerly looked forward, he had brought his sister Lady Galway over to act as hostess for him. Harriette Galway had become a somewhat unwieldy old lady, as her brother recognised—'Harriette has set her heart on a seal-skin like yours,' he told his wife this summer, 'I fear I cannot get her one large enough'— but she was sensibly determined not to be out of fashion as well.

Aunt Harty is gone to look out for a smart gown to go in to Lady Cowley's to-morrow [Lord Houghton wrote to his daughter]. This is the more necessary as there is a total change in costume, all the ladies being drest like the picture of your Grandmama in the breakfast room & nobody but cooks wearing crinolines.

As so often in Paris, the uncertainty and danger of the political situation expressed itself in an extravagant change of fashion; Lord Houghton noted boots with tassels, skirts not far below the knee, young ladies at balls who 'frizzed' their hair, pushed it low down over their eyes and tied it with a bandeau. The Paris of Haussmann and Renoir was very different from the grey Bourbon city which Richard and Harriette Milnes had first seen together in the late eighteen-twenties, when they would stay with their parents in the Rue Richelieu at the old Hôtel de Bruxelles.

In spite of the 'frying and trying character' of the weather, which had given him 'red blotches' on his face ('to which' he told Amy, 'I have applied cream made of snails which is thought the right thing'), Lord Houghton fitted gleefully into Paris life. No longer a theoretical opponent of the regime, he frequented the Court while it was in Paris, talking politics with the Emperor, visiting Prince Napoleon, sympathising with the Empress over the operation for abscess just performed upon the Prince Imperial's little leg. Typically enough he was also *persona grata* within the circles of the Opposition, where he heard 'L'Espagnole' accused of trying to bring about a war with Prussia; he was told that 'they only wished [the Empress] had been drowned the other day at St. Jean de Luz' and that she 'would come to the same end as L'Autrichienne if she didnt take care.' He was in Paris that October, when the French fleet sailed for Italy to support the Pope against Garibaldi, soon defeated by French troops at the battle of Mentana. Houghton, who later spoke in the House of Lords in a sense favourable to this intervention, incurring the silly accusation of being the 'spokesman of the Emperor,' was much elated by this development. 'It is quite possible that you saw from your windows yesterday morning the French fleet on their way to Italy!' he wrote to his wife, who was quietly residing with their elder daughter at the Hôtel Beau-Site in Cannes.

The news fell like a thunderbolt on the world here—everyone having looked on the affair as being well settled, at least for a short time. Now everyone asks what next? & the agitation is extreme. This is indeed a delightful place to live [he rather ruefully continued], always some confusion & excitement going on.

Apart from the multitude of political and social pleasantries of this sensational summer, Lord Houghton was getting to know a generation of writers in Paris with whom he was not previously acquainted; it seems likely that it was in 1867 that he first met Gustave Flaubert, Zola, and Daudet and renewed contact with Turgenev. Madame Mohl had given this last a note of introduction for Monckton Milnes on one of the Russian novelist's early visits to London, perhaps that of 1859:

This is to introduce to you Ivan Tourguenieff who has written a book called Aventures d'un Chasseur Russe [she wrote] . . . he is a

man to suit you & your house you'll see that with half an eye.   I'm
sure you will like him.   Mérimée is very fond of him.

It seems questionable whether this first meeting had been fruitful,
for two undated notes from Turgenev, who was then staying at an
hotel in Leicester Square, have turned up in a box of unsorted
papers of the years 1857–1859.   One of these notes inauspiciously
begins: 'Cher Monsieur, Il doit y avoir deux entrées à Westminster
Hall—car de mon côté j'ai aussi attendu jusqu'à 5½ h. à la porte
qui fait face à l'Abbaye'; while the other, though expressing formal
gratitude for hospitality, explains that Turgenev had not received
an invitation to eat in Upper Brook Street until he was in Manchester.   The work of Flaubert Lord Houghton already knew
(Swinburne had brought *Salammbô* to his notice in 1863), but
though he may have just met him in Paris in '67, an interesting letter
from a young American friend suggests that he did not expect to be
remembered.   'Dear Lord Houghton,' wrote one of that peer's
most affectionate admirers, Henry James, in a letter simply dated
'April 15th' without any year.

I am most happy to do what you request—in the very small measure
indeed of my ability.   I enclose a note for Gustave Flaubert & one
for Tourguenieff—though I think it very possible you know the
latter (I have left the note open, according to the rules of American
civility—which has more rules than are commonly supposed).   If
you *do* know Tourguenieff (or if you only make his acquaintance
through my note) he will himself be the best possible introduction to
the other man—the Frenchman.   It was through him that I made
Flaubert's acquaintance, who was the only one of *ces messieurs* with
whom I established personal relations.   I am sure the others won't
do me the honor to remember me, though I often used to meet
them at Flaubert's.   The latter is an excellent & interesting fellow,
well worth knowing & worth all the others a hundred times over—
both in genius & personal nature.   He is a great friend of Tourguenieff, & my respectful advice would be that you go first to see the
latter & go with him to Flaubert's—he being an excellent introducer.
He also knows Zola intimately & Daudet (tho' rather less) & would
be most happy to make you know them.

Since Henry James did not return to London from New England
till 1868, when he was twenty-five years of age, this note may
belong to that year, or even a later one; though Lord Houghton's
first biographer declares that it was at the epoch of the Universal
Exhibition that Houghton first met the writers whom James
mentions.   It is natural to assume that Lord Houghton, who
already knew Turgenev, would meet him again that summer at
Madame Mohl's salon in the Rue du Bac; and likely that in that

case he would persuade the Russian to take him to see Flaubert—
for Houghton's passionate interest in genius was quelled neither
by the gout nor by dining frequently at the British Embassy, where
Lord and Lady Cowley had made him free of the house.

'Two Emperors and a Sultan and half a score of Kings came
specially to see it,' Sala wrote of the Exposition Universelle.
'Princes were for months as plentiful in Paris as blackberries.'
Only the Queen of England, the Queen of Spain and the King of
Italy had stayed away.   Lord Houghton, who made a new friend,
Sophia, Queen of Holland, that summer in Paris, also took part in
the great military review in honour of the Emperor of Austria
staged that autumn at Versailles.   His presence, and his uniform,
caused friendly comment:

There was one red coat in the midst of that gay cavalcade [ran an
English newspaper report of the Versailles review]—a red coat
with silver epaulettes and buttons, surmounted by a cocked hat
with white plumes, and supplemented by blue trousers with silver
stripe; and it might be said of Lord Houghton as he sat his steed
among the press of knights, all radiant with stars and crosses and
orders, in that plain, unadorned, and peaceful attire of a Deputy-
Lieutenant of an English county, 'Ma foi! il est bien distingué!'

III

Lady Houghton's wretched health, which had driven her to
seek refuge at Cannes from the fogs of London and the raw mists of
Yorkshire, made it necessary for the whole family to spend the
spring of 1868 in France or Italy.   Her husband's brief survey of
society at Cannes and Nice had convinced him that he would not
'much care' for a real sojourn on that littoral: 'but,' he remarked,
'I should like Rome very much, both to see the dear old place again,
& because at this moment it is full of so much political interest.'

It was at Rome, close on a quarter of a century before, that Milnes
had first set eyes upon his future wife, then a light-hearted, blue-
eyed girl, wearing her dark hair in gleaming ringlets, already
delicate, but fired with an innocent, irresistible zest for living.   Mrs.
Cunliffe Offley and her niece, who had been wandering about
Germany, Austria and Italy since 1833, had taken a Roman
apartment near the Pincio for the winter of 1834, and here, in
March 1835, their young Catholic friend Charles MacCarthy
brought a new acquaintance, Richard Monckton Milnes.

At first Miss Crewe had not liked Mr. Milnes, observing how often
he affronted people by his impertinence.   His gaiety and his goodness soon won her over; from definite dislike she changed to finding

him 'very paradoxical and very amusing,' and soon began 'to take a sort of fancy to MM.' She was sitting for her portrait to the English painter Boxall, a proceeding which, while 'not a penance' since she liked the artist, would speedily have become a bore had it not been for the constant ebullient intrusions of Milnes and Mac-Carthy into the studio, where Annabel Crewe would sit each morning, her pretty, dimpled, amiable face tilted towards the light, her neck stiff from holding it in one position for so long.   In Rome unlike London, it was possible for young men to drive out with girls, and 'drop in' on them in what Miss Crewe called 'an intimate way'; she much enjoyed the easy-going bonhomie of the little clique formed by Milnes and his friends.   They would come and recite their own poetry to her as she sat in Boxall's studio, drink tea or dine with her and Mrs. Cunliffe at the Casa Margherita, conduct her to churches or to view the Coliseum by night.   Milnes and MacCarthy bantered each other in a way she found delightful.   All three of them were young, and only too anxious to be amused or entertained; Mrs. Cunliffe, whose chief pleasures were music and 'fine country' would wistfully complain that in these she was never 'indulged' in her niece's Roman circle, where poetry and dancing formed the staple occupations.   The event of that Roman season had been the marriage of Lord Shrewsbury's daughter Lady Guendoline Talbot to the Prince Borghese's eldest son.   Miss Crewe, who could not conceal a smile at the self-satisfaction with which Lady Guendoline handed the red and gold morocco volume of her own verses round amongst her friends, smugly discussing their merits with Richard Monckton Milnes, rather liked the sonnet which the latter wrote upon the marriage, and which he repeated to her one night as they sauntered quietly beside the moonlit fountains of St. Peter's:

> . . . may the cool northern dew
> Still rest upon thy leaves, transplanted flower!
> Mingling thy English nature, pure and true,
> With the bright growth of each Italian hour.

She did not, however, share her new friend's enthusiasm over the match; Lady Guendoline was to have no separate establishment but would, in the Roman way, merely become an inmate of her father-in-law's palace; half the fun of marrying, would, Annabel Crewe considered, under these circumstances be forfeited.   She was herself attracting several excellent proposals of marriage in these years, and one or two bold attempts at what her aunt called 'heartless flirtations'; but she calmly refused the first, and wittily evaded the second.   This time in Rome was one of the happiest and most carefree of a life which family complications had made difficult and sometimes sad. We may thus imagine with what emotions Lady Houghton returned in 1868 to these scenes of her youth. Her husband took their children to look at the Casa Margherita where their parents had first met; but, though always haunted by the swirling speed with which life rushes by, Lord Houghton never gave himself time to be tortured by nostalgia. He was, in any case, extraordinarily happy in his family, and united to them by bonds of quiet but strong affection. As he stood gazing up at the windows of the Casa Margherita with his three children at his side, he could indeed feel that the relationship started within those walls so many years ago had been for him a lucky one. He had wished to marry Florence Nightingale, he had nearly proposed to the second Lady Ashburton; fate had saved him from both of these hazardous experiments. On this side of his life he had everything to be thankful for, and nothing to regret.

In Rome in 1868 political affairs were full of interest to an observer of Lord Houghton's experience and curiosity. The struggle of Pio Nono, Pope since 1846, to keep the temporal dominions of the Holy See intact had so far been successful, but the integrity of the Temporal Power now depended on the French troops who, triumphant at Mentana in November 1867, were stationed at the Papal port of Cività Vecchia. If these troops should be withdrawn, as they were in the Franco-Prussian war of 1870, the Temporal Power would be doomed; in fact in the September of 1871 an Italian army did enter Rome, and by the summer of the next year the city had been declared the capital of a united Italy. The Pope had retired into voluntary isolation within the Vatican. By 1868 it was evident that the artificial support of the Temporal Power by a French garrison could not last for ever; if the Milnes children were to see the old Rome of the Papacy as their father had seen it in his youth, they should see it soon. This, together with his own wish to chat politics with Cardinal Antonelli, and to re-visit the grave of John Keats, made Lord Houghton opt for Rome.

On the first of February 1868, the party, which had foregathered at Cannes, set off from Nice to Mentone in open carriages. They formed a typically English contingent. An elderly English milord with an invalid wife was a figure well known in Mentone and in Genoa; nor could the nationality of the three fresh-faced children— golden-haired Amy, aged sixteen, the darker Florey, aged fourteen, and little Robin, who was ten—have been mistaken. Lord Houghton himself, who had been judged 'Italianate' in looks and manner in his youth, had gradually undergone a transformation in appearance. Just as those expatriate Americans who have spent their lives upon the continent of Europe seem to revert to their own national characteristics as they age, so the Yorkshire blood in Monckton Milnes was coming out; a 'crusty' if polished and cosmopolitan man of nearly sixty, he looked to many people who met him for the first time a typically North Country figure, though his manners were still at times as Latin as they had been in his early youth. The son of Henry Spencer Ashbee has recorded the surprise of his parents when Lord Houghton, coming to dine at their Bloomsbury house late one night after a debate, went down on one knee to Mrs. Ashbee, 'called her my beautiful lady, and kissed her hand. She was disturbed at the poetic licence,' but Ashbee 'laughed at her scruples and said the poet had drunk too well.'[1] Robin's tutor, young Mr. Wivell, who did not much enjoy the foreign tour, Lord Houghton's valet Charles, Lady Houghton's beloved maid Dawkins, and the girls' old nurse Oliver, completed the party, which rolled into Mentone towards evening, to be welcomed by Louisa Ashburton.

The second Lady Ashburton, now three years widowed, had once more taken the villa at Mentone in which she entertained Carlyle in 1867, shortly after his wife's death. Her little daughter Mary Baring set about showing the Milnes children the beauties of Mentone, which Carlyle describes as

principally built as a street by the seashore, along the diameter of two beautiful semicircular little hollows . . . formed by the mountains which are the airiest wings of rocky peaks and cliffs, all terraced and olive-clad, with sometimes an old castle and village.

They stayed ten days at Mentone and went on to San Remo, leaving Lady Ashburton, her child and its governess. 'This place lost all its charm the day you left,' wrote Lady Ashburton from a 'camp under the trees' above Cap Saint Martin, while Mary and the servants were building a fire to warm their picnic luncheon 'and I have been quite sad without you . . . no-one of any interest has arrived. I will sit as a mother with Mary', she continued, in reply to a request for a carte-de-visite photograph, '& gladly send it or give it in England, at present none exists of me.' From San Remo they made their way by Genoa and Pisa to Rome, halting at each place to allow Lady Houghton to recover. Pisa, though 'charming,' was 'rather oppressive,' and as she lay bedridden in the hotel, she remembered the motto—'Pisa, pesa, che posa'—she had heard

[1] Incident related in C. R. Ashbee's memoir of his mother *Grannie, A Victorian Cameo*, privately printed at the Oxford University Press in 1939. 'My early readings of Keats are inseparably bound up with this scene,' Mr. Ashbee continues, 'and it was Lord Houghton that first led me on that search for the immortals.'

years ago. The twelve-hour rail journey to Rome, on the other hand, was delightful: in a carriage to themselves they could eat, read, talk, and even lean out of the window, since the train was going most beautifully slow. 'Then the last $\frac{1}{2}$ hour there was the immense excitement of catching sight here & there of some ruin or marvel of the Eternal City'; and then there was the arrival, the sense of actually standing at last in Rome, the drive to the Hotel Costanzi in the Roman starlight, and Mr. Wivell's pride at being the first to detect the dim outline of Saint Peter's from the window of their salon. The next day Mrs. Story, wife of the American sculptor who lived in Rome, drove Lady Houghton and her daughters out in her carriage. Meanwhile, Mr. Wivell and Robin making a first expedition in the Roman streets, were rewarded by an encounter with the Pope's own carriage and watched him blessing the passers-by. Everything in Rome was exciting and instructive to the children. Their father determined to take an apartment there for at least two months. He soon found one to his taste in the Via San Basilio near the Piazza Barberini. In securing this apartment, which even had a garden filled with lemon-trees, Lord Houghton relied upon the practical advice of Joseph Severn, since 1860 British Consul in Rome.

Severn, the friend of Keats, had been known to Monckton Milnes some forty years. In 1831 he copied his painting of Keats for this enthusiastic young man who was then one of the very few English people interested in that poet; in the same winter Severn had designed a Greek dress for Milnes' sister to wear at one of the *bals costumés* given by the over-exclusive English society of Rome. In the intervening years he had seen Milnes in London—painting his portrait in '47, giving him some rather contentious information for the *Life* of Keats in '48, and in 1860 appealing to him as one 'famed for your attachment to your old friends & also for a convincing eloquence' to help him to get from the Whig Government the very suitable appointment of British Consul in Rome. The post had fallen vacant through the resignation of the archæologist Charles Newton—'Mr. Charles *Mausoleum* Newton' Severn, who was his father-in-law, called him; Bunsen and Gladstone were trying to persuade Lord John Russell to give Severn the position, and he, hearing that Lord Palmerston was visiting Fryston in October 1860, had written to ask Milnes to 'clinch the consular nail so well driven in by Bunsen & Gladstone' by speaking to the Premier: 'I may hope,' he wrote, 'that with such a *triumvirate of friends* as *Bunsen, Gladstone & Milnes* I may insure indulgence to my claim.' Having secured the job, Severn was executing it admirably, for he had a real love and deep knowledge of Roman life. Then seventy-five, he looked twenty years younger; whereas Milnes, his junior by more than fifteen years, had always looked older than he was. Joseph Severn took the whole family under his wing, writing to compliment Lady Houghton on the 'great beauty & graces of her daughters, who seemed to me like a charming allegory of dear old England.'

Ever since his youth in Rome, when he had been constantly to dine at the Collegio Inglese, then under the direction of Nicholas Wiseman, Milnes had been saner than the majority of his contemporaries on the subject of Roman Catholicism; during the Oxford Movement he had adopted an open-minded, liberal attitude to the pondered conversions of that moment—'*via media vilissima*' as he once wrote of his own point of view. In London he had friends both in the old Catholic society, a somewhat self-absorbed, inbred body who kept the spirit of the Elizabethan Recusants aflame, and among the new converts, some of whose extravagancies at the 'court' of Westminster amused him. 'I had perverts enough to meet him to send Aunt Loo-loo into fits,' Lord Houghton wrote of a luncheon party for the 'puffy and prelatical' Monsignor Talbot (his father's sister, Louisa Milnes, being fanatically Unitarian; and the other noun having still a strictly religious connotation).

We had a really miraculous escape at luncheon—not from fire, at least of a physical nature—but from an explosion! As I went out of the dining-room Dey said a young gentleman had called & he had asked him into the dining-room—but he would not come in & would call another day & had left his cards—*R. Garibaldi*! No human being but would have believed that I had asked him to meet Talbot & what a confirmation it would have been of the wildest stories of my parties!

Lord Houghton was thus less shocked than other non-Catholics by the promulgation of the decree of Papal Infallibility by the Vatican Council in July 1870. He went to Rome for the opening of this Council on 8 December 1869, a day which the *Osservatore Romano* declared to be the 'most eventful day in the history of the world,' and which began with the ceaseless cannonade from five a.m. It was raining heavily on the day the Council opened, and Rome was dark:

It was still, however, very fine to see the seven hundred bishops and patriarchs sitting in seven rows with the Pope in the middle [he wrote to his son]. They were all in white and gold, except the Eastern patriarchs, who wore wonderful costumes. Some of them were quite dark brown.

He told Augustus Hare, who had enjoyed the little dinners for six in the Via San Basilio in 1868, and who saw a good deal of him at Rome in 1870, that Manning had said that to find out what they had been doing at the Council, the Cardinals always read *The Times* next day. The 1870 pronouncement on Infallibility was a contributory cause of the loss of the Papal temporalities: for by alienating the Powers, who suspected in the decree a possible challenge to lay sovereignty, it made certain that no outside protest would be raised against the Italian advance on Rome in that September. When Lord Houghton in old age paid his next, and last, visit to the Eternal City, Rome was different: no longer the silent, ecclesiastical city of Stendhal and of his own youth, a place where you might see the carriage of a Cardinal, or of the Pope himself, in any street, it had become the capital of a new, united, modern country, and the playground of a wealthy American beau-monde.

IV

> Adieu, dear Yorkshire Milnes! we think not now
> Of coronet or laurel on thy brow;
> The kindest, faithfullest of friends wast thou.

This epitaph composed after Lord Houghton's death by William Allingham, one of the many needy poets whom he had helped, stresses the fact that as he aged, Milnes became more and more of a Yorkshireman: kind, gruff, thickly built, his red face fringed with greying whiskers, he almost took on the aspect of a North Country farmer. Perhaps as part of this development, he began to like Yorkshire more. Fryston, in which he had now spent more than thirty years, was bound up with many happy memories of the past. For the first time it began to seem an agreeable residence.

I write alone in the big house, haunted too with your smile and the children's laughter [he wrote in a letter of May 1868 to Lady Houghton, whom he had left in Rome]. This modest place, with its lush and various greens, and the air heavy with white and red may, and the songs of innumerable birds, has a quiet charm even after Italy; not more or less, but one of its own.

Lord Houghton had a busy summer before him, for he was planning to entertain at Fryston the London people who would flock to Yorkshire for the Leeds Exhibition of Fine Arts, opened by the Prince of Wales in May 1868 in a wing of Scott's newly-erected West Riding Infirmary. Lord Houghton, who had lent two Milnes portraits as well as some other pictures to the exhibition, naturally attended the banquet for the Prince held in a ward of the hospital. 'What room is this to be?' asked a neighbour at dinner, glancing round the white-painted walls. 'The dissecting-room, of course,' replied Lord Houghton. 'Will you take a leg?'

The Leeds festivities were 'trying for an old gent,' since parties would go on until four in the morning. The Prince of Wales was 'getting terribly fat' and had a heavy cold in the head. With his detached interest in the absurdities of human behaviour, Lord Houghton was gratified to note that when the Prince complained of the heat in the magnificent long gallery at Temple Newsam, lit entirely by candles in his honour, his eager host had the windows smashed through to give HRH sufficient air. The remainder of 1868 and much of 1869 were passed by Houghton in the ceaseless social round, going to the crowded London parties (which now more than ever resembled Madame de Staël's definition of London as 'une société à coups de poing'), and staying in other people's houses—Madresfield, Stratfield Saye (where he saw a falling beam knock the Duchess over in the Library), Serlby, Hawarden Castle. At his own request he was elected a Fellow of the Royal Society, and in the same autumn, 1868, he organised a dinner for Long- fellow at the Athenæum. In September 1869 he was the guest of the Queen of Holland for the Statistical Congress at The Hague, and in November he steamed across the Mediterranean as the repre- sentative of the Royal Geographical Society at the Khedive's official opening of the Suez Canal.

'It now strikes me as very curious that though I have been in Egypt and Turkey, I never came to a country, within a few hours' steam, full of natural interest and historical associations,' Lord Houghton wrote to Robin from the House in the Wood at The Hague. Holland, as always, was alarmingly cold; like every other visitor to that neat country, Houghton was surprised to find that it so closely resembled the pictures of the Dutch landscape painters. He was also reminded of Turner:

When the steamer came in sight of Dort, I knew exactly what to expect, from Turner's picture at the Fawkeses at Farnley; and the moment I got into the streets, there came Van der Heyden and Teniers all about one. The estuaries are Cuyps all over; and one is always looking out for the white horse of Wouvermans. I have drunk tea with the Queen and her younger son, and she laid herself out to be charming.

Sophia, Queen of Holland, had first taken a fancy to Lord Houghton during the Paris Exhibition of 1867. Staying at the Tuileries, the Queen had soon tired of the frivolous conversation of the imperial circle. She appealed to Madame Mohl (whose

husband Julius Mohl had been a subject of her father, the Prince of
Württemberg), to provide an alternative to Tuileries 'twaddle' by
arranging 'literary and intellectual *meetings*' for her in the Rue du
Bac. 'She is enchanted with *you* . . . & qui ne l'est pas?' wrote the
Queen's old friend Lady William Russell to Lord Houghton. In
the distant past Lord William Russell had been English Minister at
the court of Württemberg, and the Princess Sophia had thus become
acquainted with his wife, who quickly became an intimate friend.

Cher Milord [scribbled Lady William in one of her wild, slapdash
notes], You ask'd me *how* I knew Q of H—— 'diplomatic relations'
are always set on foot *at Legations* amongst the *royal Ladies* & the
diplomatic Ladies . . . as their *Home* entourage is never very amusing
(in *Small Courts*) . . . & so they are glad of the foreign pepper & salt
other Nations *season* their daily Bread with ——?

She went on to explain that Queen Sophia had in this way got to
know Lady Napier, Lady Dumfermline, Lady Cowley, and '"*meine
Wenigkeit*" as *we* say out of humility in German, "*ma petite personne*"';
Lady Grosvenor was another English friend, but most intimate of
all was Lady Westmorland who had 'pass'd a *Summer* at *Ischl* . . .
they walk'd & talk'd & drove & climb'd mountains & *adored* one
another like 2 Mountain Nymphs—about 10 or 12 years ago.' The
Queen of Holland had now brought her talent for engoûment to
bear upon Lord Houghton. She told everyone in Paris that he was
'her kindest friend.' When he came to The Hague she made an
immense fuss of him, placing an overdecorated, four-roomed
apartment in her palace at his disposal, giving him his own carriage,
and taking him out driving with her 'in great state' to a sea resort
on the cold wind-swept Dutch coast. Lord Houghton was a trifle
startled to find how strictly the Queen treated her second son,
Prince Alexander. This youth of eighteen she always addressed as
'Loulou,' sent off to have his lessons, and ordered up to bed at ten
o'clock. There was a talking parrot in the hall of the House in the
Wood, which screamed 'Loulou' all day in such good imitation of
the Queen that Prince Alexander never knew whether he was being
summoned by his mother or mocked at by this irritating bird.

The Statistical Congress had been interesting, but Lord Houghton
left Holland without regret: 'The wild winds of this country are
worse than the South of France, and the windmills rush round and
round like maniacs,' he wrote from the Hotel Amstel in the 'very
handsome town' of Amsterdam. We may suppose that Holland
was a little quiet, and Dutch society a shade provincial for Lord
Houghton's florid taste. He could not even remember whom he

had met there, and, since he liked to keep a record of new friends, he was obliged to write to one of the Queen's ladies-in-waiting for a list.

The names of the people you have met are as far as I can remember as follows [she replied]: Mme van der Oudermeulen, Grande Maîtresse; Count de Randwijck, Grand Maître; Mr. Gevaerts, chambellan; Baron de Hardebrock, ditto; Baron de Pabst, ditto; Baronne de Pabst, première dame de compagnie. . . .

It was a long and very courtly list, but Lord Houghton had been spared something: 'I do not think,' his correspondent added, 'that you saw the Württemberg ladies, Mme Stumpfeder & her daughter who are now staying with the Queen?'

Though he quitted The Hague without repining, Lord Houghton left his new admirer in a wistful, even a reproachful mood:

Nearly a fortnight has passed since you left me, and I have not heard from you [Queen Sophia complained]. . . . Our Congress has passed unobserved and unnoticed. Can you account why the *Times* has not deigned to mention it? Have we undergone the bad will of Mr. Delane? Why?

She told him that she longed to know how he felt after his stay in Holland 'in fine and in bad weather, in sunshine and storm.' Elderly and stout, Lord Houghton had lost none of that volatile, will-of-the-wisp quality which all his life had agitated distant friends. Back in London he was immediately involved in a new series of activities, amongst these the unveiling of a monument to Leigh Hunt—a tasteless block of marble supporting a foolish-looking bust in the big new cemetery at Kensal Green.

V

This ceremony was but one instance of the sort of public function which Lord Houghton was now constantly expected to perform. The days were long past when he had been reproved for muttering during Tom Campbell's interment in the Abbey that he 'had got the Poets' Corner cheap'; he was now the personage to whom the Dean and Chapter of Westminster automatically turned for advice. When Charles Dickens had his fatal stroke at Gadshill in June 1870, Dean Stanley wrote at once to ask Lord Houghton to find out whether the public demand for an Abbey burial was fervent enough to override the novelist's own directions for a simple burial in Kent. *The Times* article which called for Dickens' funeral in the Abbey was inspired and perhaps written by Lord Houghton. After the quiet ceremony, which only the Dickens' family attended, Lord Houghton walked over at night from the House of Lords and looked down into the open grave at the plain elm coffin, faintly illuminated by a lantern which the Stanleys' butler stood holding at his side.

Houghton was now more than ever the ideal medium by which foreigners or obscurer English persons hoped to approach the literary eminent. He would take his friend Mrs. Greville to call on Tennyson at Blackdown or do his best to arrange for American visitors to undergo the awesome ordeal of an interview with George Eliot. G. H. Lewes and 'Mrs. Lewes' were long-standing friends of Lord Houghton, and had been often entertained at Upper Brook Street where Lady Houghton with her excellent manners treated them as man and wife. Yet when Lord Houghton tried to arrange for the Connecticut authoress Louise Chandler Moulton to call at The Priory, North Bank, Regent's Park, in April 1878, his suggestion was not well received. Mrs Moulton, a 'melancholy' poetess, and writer of travel books, short biographies and tales for children, had breakfasted with Houghton and had there met George Eliot. Eager to cement the acquaintances, she had asked their host's help.

Dear Lord Houghton [came the austere, polite reply, tidily written in violet-coloured ink], I had a little chat with Mrs. Moulton the morning I met her under your kind auspices, & I think we came to the understanding that I preferred the breach to the observance of such flattering attentions as calls from 'Strangers.' I have been so constantly declining to accept proposed visits of that kind from American ladies, that it would be invidious on my part to make an exception unless it were warranted by the prospect that I could render some needed service. . . . Visits from friends, & from those who are likely to become friends, I am very fond of, but I have a horror of being 'interviewed' & written about, & though I would not impute an intention of that sort to Mrs. Moulton, my experience in relation to other American ladies has confirmed me in my churlish habits. Pray interpret me charitably.

Besides his supervision of the *Philobiblon Miscellanies*, and his own contributions to these volumes, Houghton continued to write occasional notices of literary works for the serious reviews. Thus he composed articles on *Lothair* or on *Endymion*, as well as on *Atalanta in Calydon* or *Chastelard*. The *Edinburgh* was his usual vehicle; and in this he published, in 1868, a long notice of George Eliot's *Spanish Gypsy*, and, in 1872, an essay on her supreme achievement, *Middlemarch*. So far as the *Spanish Gypsy* was concerned, Lord Houghton sensibly urged the authoress to cease attempting poetry and to return to prose; when reviewing *Middlemarch* he suggested that the verse experiment of the *Gypsy* had done considerable damage to the texture of George Eliot's prose-writing, making it even heavier than before. He condemned the 'abundance of aphorism and weight of wit' which 'burdened' this great novel, while praising its 'healthy tone and honest purpose.' Some of the psychology—particularly the motives which made Mr. Casaubon alter his will—seemed to him unconvincing, while he declared that the picture of provincial society in the book as a whole was anachronistic, and belonged to an earlier epoch than the Reform Bill period which George Eliot had avowedly set out to describe. As a contemporary record of the impact of this masterpiece upon contemporary readers, Houghton's article is not without interest. He tries to analyse the mounting excitement with which each volume of *Middlemarch* had been received, and he deduces from certain indications in the work itself that the authoress' intentions had been drastically revised as the book progressed. In an enlightening passage which shows how a novel which to us seems the epitome of the beauties and virtues of mid-Victorian fiction at its best appeared when it was first published, he compares George Eliot's position in literature to that of John Everett Millais in painting.

. . . We must remark that all observers of the progress of the art of landscape-painting in this country must have noticed a great change of late years in the choice of its subjects, of which Mr. Millais' 'Chill October' may be taken as a decisive specimen. It is not merely the absence of any such central effect as gives to the Sun itself in Turner's greatest works a painful monotony of treatment, but it is the desire to give the impression of a simple fragment of Nature, taken out of the whole scene not for any special grace or merit, or for the purpose of leaving on the mind of the spectator any stirring particular remembrance, but to stand on its own deserts as a faithful representation of an ordinary aspect of the material world about us. With the same 'intention' our artist in fiction takes a quiet country-town of forty years ago, and a squire's house lying near it, with just the people whom we know were there at that time, and places them before us with very little apparatus or detail of surrounding events, and says, 'Here is my novel.'

He compares George Eliot's treatment of her country characters with the 'descriptive minutiae' of Miss Mitford's *Our Village* and the 'semi-serious, semi-comic' characterisations of Mrs. Gaskell in *Cranford*. He concludes that it is the very commonplace quality of George Eliot's characters, people 'whom we might have met any day,' combined with her superlative 'skill of moral machinery' and 'power of mental delineation,' that gives *Middlemarch* its importance as a work of art. 'It is,' he carefully explains, 'another "Chill October."'

In 1873 Lord Houghton published a selection of his old essays under the title *Monographs: Personal and Social*, promising John Murray's (who also produced a collected edition of his poems in two volumes in 1876) that he would provide them with a companion volume, *Monographs: Political and Literary*. The first book went into two editions, and achieved a fair popularity. The projected sequel, which would presumably have contained reprints of such articles as that on Alexis de Tocqueville from the *Quarterly* of October 1861, was never compiled, and except on certain public occasions—as for instance the opening of the Albert Hall, when massed choirs sang a *Workmen's Choral Song* nimbly adapted by Lord Houghton from the Dutch—he now also abstained from writing verse; a self-restraint which his published lines upon the death of Livingstone, entitled *Ilala—May 1873*, can only make one feel was merciful, as well as justified.

> The swarthy followers stood aloof,
>> Unled—unfathered;
> He lay beneath that grassy roof,
>> Fresh-gathered.
>
> He bade them, as they pass the hut,
>> To give no warning
> Of their still faithful presence, but
>> 'Good Morning.'
>
> .   .   .   .   .
>
> Morning o'er that weird continent
> Now slowly breaking—
>
> .   .   .   .   .
>
> Morning of sympathy and trust
>> For such as bore
> Their Master's spirit's sacred crust
>> To England's shore.

His songs were still popular, and at London balls he would find his daughters' friends (moustachio'd guards officers; wasp-waisted girls in tight skirts and with their hair in a 'bang') waltzing to the tune of *Strangers Yet*. Modern composers were just as anxious to set his songs to music as Lady Blessington's friend Mrs. Kate Maberley had been in the remote days of Gore House. 'I have just set some charming words of Lord Houghton, "A fair little girl sat under a tree," and now the author's permission is requisite ere we can publish it,' wrote Henry Leslie in July 1869 to Effie Millais, whose husband was collaborating with him to produce illustrated albums of children's songs:

Do you know his Lordship? I have no doubt you do, so perhaps you will kindly ask for the desired authority. At the same time you might enquire if he has more of the like kind. We ought to have subjects that the childish heart can hug and caress—such as 'The Kitten'—'Robin Redbreast'—and it is quite possible that Lord Houghton may have written such things. . . . I have already sent you two of the songs—'Round and round and round we go' and 'How much I love my happy home.'

Such permission Lord Houghton gladly gave.

Although Houghton had ceased writing poetry himself, and had allowed his prerogative of editing Keats to pass to the conscientious care of William Rossetti, he was willing (as we have seen in the signal instance of Swinburne) to do everything he could to help young and unrecognised genius. Concurrently with his discovery of Swinburne, he had been trying to save the life of another young poet, condemned by consumption, and by his own febrile temperament, to an early and despairing death. This youth was the Scots poet, David Gray, the writer of a long poem on the Glasgow river the Luggie, and of several other pieces posthumously published in 1862, with a preface by Richard Monckton Milnes. In 1865 a monument to Gray had been unveiled, in Lord Houghton's presence, in the 'burying ground' at Kirkintilloch. An obelisk of white Wigtown Bay granite, with a wreathed harp upon its summit, this monument bore a short and human epitaph composed by Houghton, who continued to help Gray's widowed mother and his two brothers until as late as 1879. The brief and tragic tale of David Gray is one which shows Houghton at his best. It may equally be judged to show some aspects of Victorian England at their worst.

VI

In January 1838, a year which Richard Monckton Milnes had spent finding his feet in the House of Commons and in the drawing-rooms of London, a Mrs. Gray, wife of a young hand-loom weaver living eight miles from Glasgow, gave birth to her first child, a son. Called David after his father, the boy was the eldest of eight children whom the Grays reared in a tiny, damp, one-storied cottage with a slate roof at Kirkintilloch. The cottage had three rooms —the work-room, devoted to the looms; the kitchen, paved with stone; the cabin-like bedroom with one piece of carpet on the floor. The ten members of the Gray family slept in 'extraordinary mural recesses' and lived and ate in the kitchen; the children

played along the banks of the local stream, the Luggie, and on the
nearby Campsie fells.   Seven Grays, boys and girls alike, were
brought up to follow their father's trade; of their first-born, David,
the Gray parents, dour and undemonstrative but high-minded and
well-intentioned, hoped for greater things.   David's exceptional
powers of concentration and his general intelligence had persuaded
them to back him in his wish to go to Glasgow University, whence
he returned to work as a pupil-teacher in his own home town.   By
1859, when David was twenty-one, his time as pupil-teacher was up.
His own conscience (and his parents) clearly indicated that he must
earn his living, and here the cleavage between David Gray and his
relatives began: for while they had secretly clung to the conviction
that he was destined for what seemed the highest of all offices to
their simple, earnest minds, that of Minister in the Church of
Scotland, David was equally convinced that he was born to be a
poet—and not merely a great poet, but the greatest poet of his
generation.   He had for some time been contributing verses to
The Glasgow Citizen under a pseudonym, and he was always working
upon the draft of the long Thomsonian poem on which his reputation rests.   Long after his son's death, Gray's father confided
to an enquirer that the family had often wished *The Luggie* 'in
the fire'; but with an absolute tenacity of purpose David Gray
continued to work at his poetry, postponing or evading any decision
about the Ministry.   His tenacity was that of a fanatic; had he
lived longer and developed his remarkable gift we might to-day
recognise it as that of a genius.   'I am a poet: let that be understood distinctly,' he once wrote to a stranger; and according
to Lord Houghton, who has described him as strongly resembling a
cast of Shelley in his youth, David Gray's face, of which no portrait
or photograph exists, bore the stamp of the poet.   Light, well-built,
with a slight stoop, black curling hair and dark lustrous eyes, Gray
had a mouth that struck observers as 'feminine' and the skin and
complexion of a beautiful girl.   By temperament he was hysterical,
but self-confident: bashful in person, he was 'bold' on paper,
writing long letters in which pride, despair, self-pity, the conviction of genius and requests for money alternated one with
another.

   Scottish literary history offers many instances of poets of peasant
stock, whose gifts have blossomed in hovels like that of Burns's
father at Alloway.   Robert Burns himself is the most obvious
example: but the cowherd Robert Nichol, who died at twenty-four,
the stone-breaker John Bethune, who died before he was thirty, and
the weaver William Thom of Newtyle are all lesser examples of the
species.   Gray himself, who died at twenty-three, was certainly

greater than these last, and had he lived he might perhaps have fulfilled even his own lofty expectations. These expectations he pitched high, partly in reaction to his parents' opposition, partly from the natural excitement of a self-educated man who discovers his own talents, partly because he feared he might not live. In the busy port of Glasgow—in the words of Gray's friend Buchanan, that 'most hideous of cities, wherein the very clangour of church bells is associated with abominations'—Gray acquired his thirst for fame. It never left him. 'My whole short life,' he wrote to Monckton Milnes from his death-bed, 'has been set to the tune of that line from Cowley—"What shall I do to be for ever known?"'

Like many other obscure youths with literary aspirations, Gray soon began to ask for help and advice from those who had succeeded in this field. Pathetically, all he wanted was that someone should read *The Luggie*: he wrote to Disraeli, to G. H. Lewes, to Professor Masson of Miltonic fame, to Professor Aytoun editor of the *Lays*. None took the slightest notice. Gray next wrote to Sydney Dobell, who responded warmly, and they exchanged letters. In the spring of 1860 he wrote, enclosing some verses and explaining his origins, to Richard Monckton Milnes.

We know that David Gray's letter was one of many such missives which piled up on Milnes' writing-table in Upper Brook Street. Milnes might have been justified in answering as the others did or, like some of them, in not answering at all. Instead, 'struck with the superiority of the verses to almost all the productions of self-taught men' that he had ever seen, he answered Gray at length, praising his verse, but begging him not to try to build his career on poetry or to 'make the perilous venture of a London literary life.' In David Gray's lonely and overwrought state Milnes' letter seemed like a summons from Heaven; seizing his carpet-bag, and accompanied by his Glasgow friend the journalist Buchanan (from whom he separated on his arrival) Gray caught the express for London, and, after drifting about the streets of the metropolis in a mazy state, he settled on a lodging-house in Deveril Street on the Dover Road and wrote to Milnes:

You promised to read my poem. I travelled from Glasgow to give it you, and to push my fortune. Looking two days before me I see starvation. Shall I *send* or *bring* it? I know that you do not wish to be troubled with people of my sort coming about you: that is what makes me ask. Whatever you do—do it *quickly* in God's name.

He followed this up with a personal visit, or more probably he had brought the note by hand.

I was dismayed at this unexpected result of my advice [wrote Houghton in his *Introductory Note* to Gray's posthumous poems],[1] and could do no more than press him to return home as soon as possible. I painted as darkly as I could the chances and difficulties of a literary struggle in this great city. . . . 'No—he would not return.' I determined in my own mind that he should do so before I myself left town for the country, but at the same time I believed he might derive advantage from a short personal experience of hard realities. He had a confidence in his own powers, a simple certainty of his own worth, which I saw would keep him in good heart and preserve him from base temptations. He refused to take money, saying he had enough to go on with; but I gave him some light literary work.

The work was copying, and Milnes also arranged for him to act as a part-time amanuensis to Laurence Oliphant, just back from Tokyo. Gray called again, and Milnes and he 'went over' some of his writing together. When Milnes told him he was 'an undeniable poet,' Gray felt intoxicated, but when his new friend tried to get Thackeray to print *The Luggie* in the Cornhill, it was refused, and Gray found the disappointment hard to bear. About this time Milnes seems to have presented him with a copy of his *Life* of Keats. Gray devoured this book, and suddenly perceived a dangerous similarity between his own situation and that of John Keats; shortly afterwards he arrived at Upper Brook Street 'apparently under the influence of violent fever,' saying that (being 'insufficiently clothed') he had caught cold from the rain in Hyde Park, and had fallen ill, but had not wanted to bother anyone. Milnes immediately sent him back to his lodgings, despatched the excellent Dr. Tweed to look after him, and frequently visited him himself with food and drink from Upper Brook Street, his only regret being 'that imperative circumstances' did not permit him to instal the boy in his own house. It was soon clear that David Gray's lungs were affected. On learning this, he knew himself to be doomed.

From his first illness in London in the spring of 1860, until his painful death in December 1861, David Gray's life became a torment. The sense of unfulfilled renown and a terror of dying, both much aggravated by the relentless course of his consumption, tortured him. 'I fear not death or a future existence: but O how I fear dying,' he wrote to Milnes in December 1860 from a nursing home at Richmond where some London friends had sent him while he was waiting admission to a hospital at Torquay, which Milnes was

---

[1] *The Luggie and Other Poems* by David Gray, appeared after the poet's death in 1862, with a Memoir by James Hedderwick and a 'prefatory notice' by Milnes. The poems were again published in 1874.

trying to arrange through his Torquay aunts, and at his own expense. In the meanwhile, Gray had been back to Kirkintilloch and had told his father that Milnes had said things to him that had been 'worth coming to London for alone': 'You told me once that to be a brave *man* was above being a *poet*,' he wrote. Like all abnormally sensitive people, poor David Gray was difficult to handle, but Milnes never flinched. He noticed that Gray's boastful 'over-confidence' gave way when 'he knew he was really appreciated and cared for,' and that he began comparing his own achievements with those of others, and to draw lessons therefrom.

I know how easy a thing it is to give counsel, and how poor is consolation [Milnes wrote most feelingly to his young friend]; but still I must expect you to be brave and resigned. . . . There is much in this world far sadder and crueller than the thought of leaving it; and the old Greeks counted every man happy who died young.

Of course I am sorry at the failure of the Torquay venture [he wrote later]. . . . I knew the conditions of hospital life would be painful and embarrassing to you; but I hoped that the medical advice, the climate, and the scenery would have proved compensations . . . but it is not for one in health and comfort to analyse the feelings of one in your position.

'The Torquay venture,' Milnes' well-intentioned plan to have David Gray admitted as a patient at the 'water-hospital' there, had ended lamentably. After a few hours in the place Gray had 'escaped' to a Torquay hotel, where he kept to his room in a state of hysterical fear lest the hospital officials should ferret him out and drag him back to their verminous wards. Those who have formed the habit of regarding the Victorian period with nostalgia, and of investing it with all the virtues of a Golden Age, should read extracts from the long letter in which David Gray described to his benefactor the reasons for his flight from the water-hospital at Torquay. Before perusing this letter, which is dated January 1861, it is instructive to recall that since 1853 Torquay had been the chief seaside resort of wealth and fashion in this country, comparable to Brighton in the days of the Regency. Huge villas—the largest of them being Baroness Burdett-Coutts' palace, 'Ehrenburg'—had been constructed; the yachts of foreign royalties lay out on the smooth waters of the bay; London carriages, carriage-horses, powdered footmen and coachmen in livery were transported from the capital for the Torquay season, as well as London's favourite clergymen, to preach. Yet in the hospitals of this sophisticated and salubrious town there prevailed conditions of filth and squalor that would have surprised almost every contemporary except perhaps Milnes' friend Miss Nightingale.

Now that my brief struggle for life is past [David Gray began his letter from Kirkintilloch], and I am once more at home, let me write you this last letter. And let me explain to you why I am here. After receiving a note from Mr. Pollard the Hony Secy saying that I could get into the Hospital immediately, I started next day by the earliest train, and arrived in Torquay at 4 o'clock PM. Taking a cab I drove to the Institution. . . . Driving along the seashore I was most happy. I looked forward to five months of agreeable companionship and easy labour with my book. . . . Arriving at the door of the Hospital I was met by a nurse who . . . led me without saying a single word thro' long not-very-clean corridors; then thro' a lobby where the clothes of the patients were stuffed in open boxes and ticketed as in a pawnshop. How it smelt! Then thro' a large room with 8 or 10 beds in it: through another with 6 or 8 beds and pointing to one at the corner said 'This is your bed.' I asked if it was not necessary for me to see the physician or the matron. It was not. Having taken off my overcoat . . . I enquired where I should go now. She said she would take me where 'the rest' sat, and repassing the same lobby and corridor I was introduced to my fellow sufferers—23 of them. I could have borne everything but what I saw here. Not one of them was *clean*. They all sat round a fire, and loud empty laughter was heard at every vulgar joke. One man about 30 years of age was roasting some piece of meat with a spit and as I entered held it up to me with some rude remark and then the loud laughter rose again. Two young fellows were evidently very far gone, and they were assisting each other to walk across the room; while their poor weak attempts at walking were greeted with loud shouts of 'Quick march!' There were no easy chairs for persons in this condition—no quiet corner to think of home . . . no comfort but sleep—and how much of that would they have? I sat among them for some time, but the constantly recurring thought that I was to *live here* was too much and my heart overcame me till I fainted.

When he recovered he appealed to a nurse, and then to the Matron, for permission to sit in a room alone for an hour or two till he felt better—a request roughly refused. Gray next demanded to see the Honorary Secretary who curtly sent him about his business. 'They are all poor *uneducated* men here,' the Matron remarked. If he stayed, she told him, he must behave like his fellows. Waiting till the Matron's back was turned, he fled from the hospital, to an hotel room in the town.

On returning from our drive [wrote Milnes' aunt Caroline, who, with her two sisters, still lived at Fryston Lodge, Torquay], I find a note enclosing this wild epistle from David Gray. What steps are to be taken to maintain him, as he writes from the expensive Hotel below, where he was before & expressed so little thankfulness for the

attentions & very small charge they made? The man can scarce be
in a sound state of mind . . . probably he would not be a pleasant
inmate anywhere.

The Misses Milnes were known throughout Torquay for their
persistent church-going and their zeal in good works, but excellent
though these ladies were they were not equipped to understand
the neurotic behaviour of Richard's protégé. To them David
Gray appeared as the ungrateful working-class recipient of their
brother's bounty. No doubt they felt that Gray should have
stayed in the water-hospital, and that Richard Milnes had done
enough.

Worldly people are lavish in their praise of some slight act of duty
or affection, of some faint aspiration towards beneficence. By
magnifying the effort involved in the most trivial and natural act of
human kindness, they contrive to make more strenuous exertions
seem impossible, greatly reduce the standard of potential self-
sacrifice, and thus insulate themselves from disturbing or exacting
demands. Like Florence Nightingale, who was invariably implored by her family and friends to 'do less' and to 'rest' and to
'give it all up,' Richard Monckton Milnes was born and bred among
such people. It is to his eternal credit that he was never influenced
by them, and that he was never deterred by conventional worldly
considerations from doing what he thought right in difficult or
thankless circumstances. So far as David Gray was concerned,
Milnes was as disinterested as he was solicitous. He had early
conceived a moderate opinion of Gray's talents. He had not the
glorious illusion that he was saving a second Keats; he knew that he
was merely doing what he could to alleviate the close of a sad young
life.

What would David Gray have done without you? [a friend wrote to
Milnes in January 1864]. Is it not a deep satisfaction to you to feel
that you contributed to that poor boy's happiness & that he blessed
you when he died? If you had been Horace Walpole, he might have
met the fate of Chatterton.

Milnes, however, reproached himself for not having done more for
Gray earlier on: he told his wife that had he thought of buying him an
overcoat on his first trip to London, the boy might never have
caught consumption at all.

After Gray's death, Lord Houghton did everything in his power
to help his family and to increase his fame. He wrote an introduction to the collection of Gray's poetry published by Macmillan
in 1862; from time to time he quietly sent money to Gray's parents,

two of whose other children were 'sinking' from tuberculosis in the dank little house beside the Luggie; and he personally gave nearly half the sum required to raise the monument in the Auld Aisle Burying Ground on the hill above Kirkintilloch, as well as composing for it an inscription which he hoped would have gratified the 'poor boy,' its subject.

> This Monument of Affection, Admiration, and Regret, is erected to DAVID GRAY, The Poet of Merkland, By friends from far and near, Desirous that his grave should be remembered amid the scenes of his rare genius and early death, and by the 'Luggie,' now numbered with the streams illustrious in Scottish song.

VII

In an impressive passage of Eckermann's *Conversations*, under date February 1827, Goethe is reported as declaring, with all his customary prescience, that three massive geographical tasks awaited mankind—the cutting of the Isthmus of Panama, the junction of the Danube and the Rhine, and the creation of a canal from Port Said to Suez. Forty-two years later, after a decade of engineering work hampered by lack of money and by political opposition, Lesseps' Canal to Suez was at length inaugurated in November 1869. The newspapers of Europe solemnly declared this to be the greatest feat of man since the discovery of the American continent. Even the English press, which had shared the hostile attitude of the City of London to this tremendous project, acclaimed its completion, and grudgingly sent journalists to attend the opening: 'In spite of some personal discomforts endured by the less privileged visitors who were too numerous to be properly accommodated on this occasion, the opening of the Suez Canal was, the *Illustrated London News* admitted, 'a great success.' The Indian Mutiny had shown the urgency of being able to reach our Indian territories quickly. 'It will be a curious feeling to steam for the first time from the Mediterranean to the Red Sea. Even Alexander the Great could not do that,' Lord Houghton wrote to his son.

Lord Houghton, who said that he had been one of Lesseps' earliest supporters in London when the Suez plan was being opposed 'by the commercial classes and political opinion of this country'—'Vous étiez de nos amis quand les amis étaient rares,' Lesseps told him at Ismailia—was an obvious guest to ask to the Khedive's international festivities for the opening of the Suez Canal, and in spite of his rather tricky health he readily accepted the invitation. Lord Houghton appeared at Cairo, however, in an unexpected capacity—that of special envoy from the Royal Geographical Society, to which body he gave a contentious, extempore, and also rather inaccurate, account of the proceedings on his return to London. Travelling with Lord Dudley and 'three cousins' in a half-empty P & O steamer, the *Delta*, he had a comfortable journey to Alexandria, the only drawback being that they had passed between Scylla and Charybdis after dark. At Alexandria they were transferred to a 'magnificent yacht' nominally reserved for 'persone di distinzione,' but this vessel was suddenly invaded by 'all the riff-raff not otherwise provided for.' After losing his wife's wedding present to him, a gold watch, in the general confusion, Lord Houghton hastily transferred himself and his baggage to the English yacht *Hawk*, where he found pleasant and instructive company. The spectacle, or rather the suite of spectacles, connected with the opening of the Canal did much to compensate for the very marked discomfort of the Egyptians' arrangements: 'The organisation of everything here is bad,' wrote Houghton, 'but the profusion like a fairy tale.' Anxious to miss no episode of the strange adventure, Lord Houghton trudged on foot to watch the ceremonial blessing of the Canal locks by clergy of the Mohammedan, Greek, Coptic and Roman Catholic churches, saw the illuminations at Port Said (where the rigging of every ship was festooned with little lights) and went back to the *Hawk* to take part in the procession of forty vessels, headed by the Empress of the French on board the *Aigle*, which entered the Suez Canal soon after dawn had broken on November 16th.

A striking moment it was, and to my mind . . . the grandest of the whole [Lord Houghton told the Geographers]. The entrance of that quiet and solemn procession of ships into the desert, on that bright, beautiful Egyptian morning. [The whole of that day they] traversed the silent desert. I don't know whether it was done on purpose, with that sense of art which the French so curiously exemplify in all their great manifestations [he continued], but every sign of life seemed to be withdrawn from the banks. There was not a dwelling, there was hardly a wandering Arab. In this place, which had been the sepulchre of so many lives—which had been the hive of humanity for the last ten years—there was perfect, desolate stillness. On went the vessels through the marsh, through the sand —as it were, new animals invading that solitude—until we arrived at Lake Timseh.

We are fairly in the Canal which is to join two worlds [he wrote in some excitement to his wife at 3 p.m. on 17 November]. The boat, the motion, everything, reminds me of my Nile of twenty-seven years ago. The Empress led the way . . . and we follow at some four hours' distance, but hope to reach Ismailia in the evening.

At Ismailia Lord Houghton presented the compliments of the Royal Geographical Society to the Khedive, and then took part in the great evening fête, which was said to be costing two hundred thousand pounds. 'You saw the Royalties of Europe in the midst of 100,000 Arabs,' he wrote, '. . . a most curious spectacle.'

The Royalties of Europe—who included the Emperor of Austria, the Empress Eugénie, the Crown Prince of Prussia, one Dutch and several other German princelings—were in holiday mood. They behaved in sportive and unexpected ways. The Emperor of Austria forgot the stringent etiquette of the court of Vienna and allowed himself to be hauled up the Great Pyramid by his arms like any common tourist, while at Ismailia the Empress of the French left the Khedive's palace by a back door, and riding on a camel. With that unerring sense of the theatrical which made her husband's court seem so unroyal, the Empress had appeared for the solemn blessing of the Canal (which was followed by a public eulogy of herself from her almoner, the florid Jewish monsignore, Bauer) in a simple walking dress of lavender silk, with white lace fichu, a black hat with a black feather, a black veil and a black lace fall. She had worn no jewellery whatever, a carefully planned contrast to her shimmering appearance at the Ismailia ball. The Suez festivities were the Empress's last great international appearances. In less than a year Europe witnessed the smash-up of the Napoleonic empire, and the disappearance from Europe for ever of that delicious atmosphere of sumptuous, second-rate gaiety and show in which the Emperor and the Empress had lived for fifteen years—the hunts at Compiègne, the Courts of Love at Fontainebleau, the frivolous conversations at the Tuileries which visiting royalties condemned as 'twaddle.' In Egypt that winter the Empress was at her most fascinating and amiable: she told Lord Houghton that she felt disappointment 'at finding so few friends' from England at Port Said—she had expected 'the Sutherlands and Manchesters.' Her one regret, she explained to him, was not to be able to go on to India, which 'had been the dream of her life.' 'Ah!' she cried, 'how can your Queen have such a delightful dominion and not go there ? If it was ours, I should be there over and over again.' Here, in a nutshell, was the unroyal, parvenu attitude to power which stolid, dyed-in-the-wool royalties resented, and which made them feel that Napoleon and Eugénie were somehow as spurious as Second Empire versions of Louis Seize furniture seem to us to-day. To the Empress of the French, India would be a jewelled paradise, with infinite possibilities for amusement and ostentation. To Queen Victoria it was a sombre duty, one vast and grim responsibility the more.

Lord Houghton did not see the Empress again until after the battle of Sedan. 'The Empress came over from Trouville, in a small sailing vessel, with a lady and M. Lesseps and without a maid,' he wrote to his wife in September 1870, in words almost identical with those he had used of the flight of Louis Philippe and Queen Amèlie in March 1848. 'She was wet through, and had difficulty in getting into an hotel at Ryde.'

VIII

When the Franco-Prussian war broke out in July 1870, Lord Houghton stoutly took the German side. Writing to tell Henry Bright that the war was preventing his going to the Passion Play at Oberammergau—'the chief person is taken off to serve in the artillery, with Judas Iscariot as his superior officer'—he added:

What is called society here is wholly French. . . . I am Prussian to the backbone, which is a pure homage to principle, as they are the least agreeable people in the world.

This atrocious invasion of Germany by the French seems likely to meet with its appropriate punishment [he told Amicia three weeks after war had been declared]. I wish it only fell on its iniquitous authors & not on the comparatively innocent French people. If you live to a long life you will to the last, I believe, hear it spoken of as the most unjustifiable war in history.

Which was the first cry, 'A Berlin!' or 'Zu Paris!'? he wrote somewhat pugnaciously to Lady Galway, who was pro-French.

If the French were not now punished for their wilful vanity, they would be murdering and pillaging the quiet inoffensive Germans in Germany, who never thought of touching a hair of a Frenchman's head.

Accustomed as we have become to the idea of Germany as an aggressor nation, it is easy to forget that it was in fact the French who embarked upon the Franco-Prussian war.

England's official neutrality pleased neither of the combatant nations, while the anti-French tone of the London press caused fierce annoyance in France. The English, too, were busily thriving on the export of coal and weapons of war to both sides: Lord Houghton reported that the French ambassador had told Lady William Russell that he had never believed till now that the English were a nation of shopkeepers. 'And I,' Lady William sharply answered, 'have always believed till now that the French were a nation of soldiers.' The Germans were equally irritated:

For us Anglomaniacs in Berlin it is sad & painful to observe how utterly the attitude of England is regarded with mistrust & aliena- tion [George Bunsen wrote to Lord Houghton in a letter extolling the war fever of the Rhenish provinces]. 'England is an Asiatic power,' 'England is ludicrously afraid of a French invasion,' 'there is no man in England whom the prestige of Napoleon III or his skill do not seem to overshadow.' . . . Having inherited a warm affection for England and the belief that she is the flower of the Universe, I feel this estrangement intensely, & should wish it to be removed by open acts of condemnation & commination performed by England *before*, not *after*, we have had occasion to fight.

From the Château de Herry, where Lord Houghton had taken his sister to stay six years before, Duvergier de Hauranne wrote twice to his English friends during the September invasion of France : 'Je reste à Herry,' wrote the old man, 'pour y attendre les Prussiens s'il leur prend fantaisie de passer la Loire.' He upbraided England bitterly for its failure to appreciate the significance of the loss of Alsace and Lorraine. Always a steadfast opponent of the Second Empire, Duvergier welcomed the establishment of the Republic, but felt that France was being punished unduly for past sins.

J'ai souvent dit plus d'une fois depuis 18 ans que la destinée des Bonapartes était de livrer la France à l'étranger, après l'avoir opprimée, exploitée, émasculée ; mais je ne croyais pas si bien dire. Ce que l'oncle avait fait en 15 ans, le neveu plus expéditif l'a fait en 15 jours. Le premier avait enlevé à la France les conquêtes de la république ; le second va peut-être lui enlever les conquêtes de Louis 14 & de Louis 15. Certes la France est bien coupable d'avoir toléré pendant 18 ans le gouvernement de cette odieuse famille ; mais le châtiment dépasse la faute.

Prussia might seize Alsace-Lorraine, but France would have them back again in time, even at the price of an alliance with Russia and a general war. 'Ce ne sera pas la paix, mais une trêve plus ou moins longue, et l'Europe entière finira par être entrainée dans le tourbillon.' He found the English inability to understand France's viewpoint inexcusable, and told Houghton that his compatriots were now most unpopular throughout France ; English residents were not maltreated, he thoughtfully explained, unless they happened to be mistaken for Germans. An August edict of the Ministry of the Interior directed against what would now be called Fifth Column activities had led to much confusion : in the Dordogne a landowner had been roasted alive by his peasants on suspicion of pro-German sympathies, while poor old Duvergier himself had actually been accused of taking money to the Germans when he left Herry for a few days to go and visit a daughter-in-law at

Trouville. His two sons were actively engaged in the War, one as captain in the *Garde Mobile*, the other organising *francs-tireurs* along the Loire. His daughter-in-law and her children were in Normandy, prepared to flee across the Channel if need be, and to throw themselves upon the hospitalities of Fryston and of Serlby.

As so frequently before in Lord Houghton's lifetime, London was full of refugees from France, some of them, like Walewski and Persigny, men who had already spent their youth in exile in this country as supporters of Louis Napoleon: 'Madame Walewski is at Brown's Hotel; Princess Metternich in Half Moon Street. I shall call on them to-morrow.' At the Rothschilds', who were stoically enduring an influx of their French relatives, Lord Houghton heard that the Emperor had written to the Queen of Holland from Metz 'in a tone of despair, saying the position was irretrievable and that he had been deceived by everybody.' In London some of the most eminent statesmen of the late regime went about denouncing the Emperor and each other: 'The Duc de Persigny abused the Emperor and Empress so brutally at the Rothschilds' that they turned him out of the room. The whole tone of the French here is most degrading.' After condemning the Emperor for his surrender, the refugees turned to criticising the Parisians for not capitulating. People who made last-minute escapes from the French capital, were spreading the most alarming rumours all over London: at Holland House Lord Houghton met a friend who had been one of the last to get away from Paris before the bridge at Creil was blown up, and who told him that the whole Bois de Boulogne had been cut down and turned into a cattle farm, and that the forests of Compiègne and Fontainebleau were scheduled for immediate destruction. From Cold Overton Hall, where she had sought refuge, Madame Mohl wrote bewailing the possible loss of her 'Penates' in the Rue du Bac:

The killed and wounded soldiers whom I don't know I can bear very well [wrote this singular old woman], for they each went with the hope of killing others and had no business to go. But I am troubled for so many others and for the town I so love. . . . L.N's vanity [she added in a venomous postcript] is such that I am convinced the immense noise this makes comforts him very much.

The German behaviour at the siege of Paris, as well as other stories of the 'Teutonic' invasion of the French countryside, began to swing Lord Houghton's feelings against Prussia.

With all my German proclivities [he wrote in October 1870 to Mary Augusta, Lady Holland], I think this siege of Paris not only wrong but unnecessary. I believe every reasonable object would have been effected if, after the capitulation of Sedan, Prussia had confined her campaign to Alsace and Lorraine. . . . There is no use in humiliating men, women or nations.

Lord Houghton was as much alarmed as most other people of property in England by the Paris Commune and the terrible fighting of April and May 1871 inside the French capital. 'There are a very large number of foreigners, even English and German, in the rebel force at Paris, so that all the world will gain by their defeat,' he wrote to Henry Bright on 5 April, recalling that in 1848 one of 'the roughs' he had seen in Paris had said 'Nous aussi voulons tâter la chair blanche,' and fearing that the whole city might be burned down. Lord Houghton regarded the Commune as a local manifestation of a new and sinister political and social trend.

I am no alarmist [he wrote in September to Mr. Gladstone], but it is undeniable that a new and thoroughly false conception of the relations of work and wealth is invading European society, and of which the Paris Commune is the last expression. Therefore any word from such a man as you implying that you look on individual wealth as anything else than a reserve of public wealth, and that there can be antagonism between them, is infinitely dangerous . . .; a certain encouragement is now given by some thoughtful men, not only to the envy of the superior material well-being of others, which is bad enough, but to a jealousy of intellectual eminence, and a dislike of culture itself.

He feared Gladstone was becoming not a demagogue but a 'demophile.'

The Commune overthrown, his old bespectacled acquaintance Thiers firmly installed as President of the Third Republic, Lord Houghton determined to revisit Paris in July 1872 to see how it had changed. Architecturally, a good deal, including the palace of the Tuileries, had been destroyed. The streets seemed 'more still,' and 'the gabble less continuous,' but otherwise life was going on as before; the Rothschilds were re-installed in their Bois de Boulogne villas, the Deputies were gesticulating in the Assembly, and the French people generally seemed to him to be resiliently recovering from 'calamities that would have crushed England ten times over.' Lord Houghton took his younger daughter, Florence, now eighteen, to Paris with him, where they dined several times with the President and Madame Thiers, who lived in what Florey thought 'a beautiful house, and guarded by soldiers in quite a royal manner.' From Paris Lord Houghton proceeded to Vichy, then joined his wife in Switzerland and set off thence with his sister for a short tour of Italy including Venice.

Your aunt Harriette and I have been revisiting the scenes of our youth, and trying to get out of the motions of a gondola the emotions of thirty-six years ago [he told his son]. I have found only one old friend here, and he is totally blind; he said he should have known me by my voice.

Here everything is nearly unchanged since eight-and-thirty years ago. Harriette said philosophically, 'We have had bad and good days since, but more good than bad on the whole; and we should be thankful for that,'

he wrote to his wife, whom he had left trying the experiment of a few weeks in a small house in the village street of the newly-discovered Alpine health resort, Saint Moritz. Lady Houghton's health was now declining visibly. With quiet determination, and wholly for the sake of her husband and of her three young children, she was waging a long and losing battle to stay the slow, unfaltering advance of death.

IX

With that passion for flowers, which had made Henry Bright wish to dedicate to her his *Lancashire Garden,* and her love of natural scenery—a taste her husband only partly shared—Annabel Houghton adored her summer in the Engadine. 'Besides the grand mountains, there is the colour of the mosses, & wild flowers & little scarlet leaves among grey stones—I wish I were more alive to it all,' she wrote in the summer of 1872, in one of the loving notes, signed with a heart, which she had been faithfully sending to her sister Henriett all their lives long. In spite of the 'sedulous care' of her husband and her children and of innumerable doctors, English and foreign, Lady Houghton could not get well. Every fresh journey was an effort to her. For her family's sake she held on, striving to do all that she could.

Do not ever think I do not know how ill you are [Lord Houghton wrote to her in 1870], and how much I value your fight for life, for others more than yourself. Please remember this, and when we think of the multitudes in France dying in lonely agony or miserable tumult, there may be thankfulness even for quiet sorrow, and for suffering alleviated if possible by science and sympathy.

Although Lady Houghton, who had been born in 1814, was not yet sixty, her sufferings made her look older than her age; and as we may observe in the photograph, taken about 1873, of the Houghtons, their daughters and Hungerford, Lord Crewe, on the steps of Fryston Hall which is reproduced in this volume, she had at

OUTSIDE FRYSTON HALL, CIRCA 1873

times a melancholy air. But she was still capable of her most charming gaiety, and strove to take her daughters about in London. In March 1870, the renewed lease of the 'dear old house' at Sixteen Upper Brook Street had fallen in. Henceforth when in London the family lodged at Almond's Hotel in Clifford Street, or in a house which they took furnished, number twenty-seven Berkeley Square. Here, during the last London season of her life, that of 1873, Lady Houghton did her best to amuse Amy, who was 'out,' and Florence, who had not yet been presented. She planned Amy's clothes, taking her to the Queen's Drawing-room on one occasion in 'pale green and white, decked with white narcissus,' on another in a dress of faint lilac colour decorated with sprigs of white lilac flowers. On the latter occasion she herself wore a dress of white, yellow and brown satin, which was acclaimed by all the family as being 'a Vandyke picture.' She would also take the girls about to draughty country-houses—to stay with the Fitzwilliams in 'the grand and gloomy Wentworth,' or to Trentham, and of course to Crewe. One day she drove Florence over from Crewe for her first sight of Madeley Manor, walking with her nineteen-year-old daughter round the Bryn where she herself had walked each morning before breakfast as a girl. At Fryston (still subject to white fogs which did not lift till mid-day and in winter were so thick that you could not see an inch before you, and when out riding the girls would lose each other in the woods ; and where the frost blackened the geraniums in the garden) Lady Houghton gave up her big cold bedroom and settled cosily in her boudoir on a 'sofa-bed.'

In January 1874, at the Liberal Prime Minister's request, the Queen dissolved Parliament. In the subsequent election a curious Conservative revolution took place, and the Liberals were decisively defeated after what Gladstone, in his own election manifesto, described as holding 'the main direction of public affairs' for 'a period of forty-three years.' The Tory victories were distributed over the whole country. In mid-February, a few days after the election, certain leading Yorkshire Liberals gathered at Fryston to discuss this astounding state of affairs with each other and with their host. Thomas Wemyss Reid, who for some reason was a member of the house-party, records that Lady Houghton played her part in entertaining these local friends; he particularly remembered her amusing reminiscences of Charles Dickens' grandmother, who had been housekeeper at Crewe Hall half a century before and had been beloved by the Crewe children for her storytelling powers. But Yorkshire in February had never suited Lady Houghton, and she caught a cold. When the Liberals had left and she was alone with her husband, her daughters and the Torquay aunts, she developed pneumonia. Physicians from Leeds and Pontefract could do nothing. 'I have little hope myself, but try to keep up the girls', Lord Houghton wrote hurriedly in a note informing Henry Bright of his anxiety; a few hours later he added to it a postscript: '3 p.m. I had written this in the morning. She has just passed away without pain. She was a perfect woman. Pity us all!' Robert, who was devoted to his mother, arrived from Harrow too late to see her alive.

The burial of Lady Houghton took place at Fryston the same week—a black cortège moving with all the heavy pomp of nineteenth-century funeral processions down the long elm avenue in the freezing winter weather, out through the lodge gates and on to Ferry Fryston, a 'board of feathers' borne before the hearse. The coffin was lowered into the Milnes vault outside the walls of the little Norman church of St. Andrew. The mourners sorrowfully retraced their steps to the great empty house, and to that weary sense of inexplicable absence that death brings.

I was the other day present at a funeral here [wrote Alfred Tennyson from Farringford, in a letter of condolence], and one of the chief mourners reached me her hand silently almost over the grave, and I as silently gave her mine. No words were possible; and this little note, that can do really nothing to help you in your sorrow, is just such a reaching of the hand to you, my old college comrade of more than forty years' standing, to show you that I think of you. . . . I may say that I think I can see as far as one can see in this twilight that the nobler nature does not pass from its individuality when it passes out of this one life. If you could believe as much it would be a comfort to you, and perhaps you do.

Although Lord Houghton felt that the worst loss of all was to his son, he himself was never the same after his wife had died. Even in illness, she had exercised an influence at once wise, cheerful and restraining on him, and though he now came to depend upon his daughter Amy, he never ceased to miss and mourn his wife. 'Do you remember that pretty sentence against anniversaries that dearest Mamma was so fond of, and where it came from?' he asked his daughter in a letter one July, the day before his marriage anniversary, 'I shall hear her saying it to me to-morrow.'

The place is haunted [he wrote from Vichy where he was once more gone in the summer of '74 to do a cure], and the happiest recollections—such is the perversity of the human mind—are the worst. That little tour in the Cautel is a kind of closing epoch: she climbing half-way up the Puy de Dôme, & you & the young French poet all the way: the drive in the omnibus through that curious basaltic country from Riom & she walking up the hills—so well— never so well again!

'He owes it all to his dear mother,' he wrote when Robert won the award for the prize poem at Harrow, 'who knew Shakespeare by heart in all senses.' Lady Houghton was a human being to whom the adjective irreplaceable could exactly be applied.

Chapter Eleven

1875   1885

I

With the hope of comforting or distracting his children in the autumn of the year their mother died, Lord Houghton took Amy and Robert with him to Scotland, for a few quiet visits to old friends like Louisa, Lady Ashburton, who spent this portion of each year in the Gothic-revival lodge which her predecessor had had constructed amongst the birch woods on the banks of Loch Luichart.

Robert . . . is getting some shooting (a puerile diversion becoming his age, but which I believe some poor incompetent persons carry on into mature life) and [Amy] is regaining health and spirits. I am still too lame to do more than poke about on a pony,

the old man wrote in September to his constant correspondent Henry Bright. Bright had shocked him at this moment by his bigoted attitude to the religious topic of the hour, Lord Ripon's public conversion to Catholicism. 'What earthly or heavenly right have you or I to find fault with a man who attaches himself to the faith held by nineteen-twentieths of the Christian world?' Houghton told him, with characteristic tolerance, in another letter from the Highlands. '. . . All my friends who have embraced Popery have done better than those who have embraced wives.' 'It is as well to remember,' wrote Stirling of Keir to Lord Houghton about this conversion, '. . . that a little more or less of some unknown ingredient, which might appear or disappear in or from our blood or brain, and the same thing might happen to you or me.' Stirling, to whom Houghton had sent a copy of the last photograph taken of his wife, was writing to thank him for this 'relic of goodness and kindness that are gone, but not forgotten' and told him that the historian John Lothrop Motley and his wife were at Keir. Like every other American literary man who came to England, Motley knew Lord Houghton. He loved Fryston, a place which he said held for him 'very tender associations' and where Mrs. Motley and their daughter had 'been sheltered' at the outbreak of the American Civil War. Easily the most popular man in England with visiting

238

Americans, Richard Monckton Milnes had long wished to travel in the United States, and 'as old age approached, a desire had entered his breast to turn his footsteps once towards the setting sun.' This pompous but probably authentic phrase occurs in the newspaper report of an interview which Lord Houghton granted to an eager journalist in the month of September 1875. This interview, in date just one year after the placid visit to the Highlands, took place in Lord Houghton's hotel room in the raw, new, noisy, mid-West City of Saint Louis, Missouri, U.S.A.

There was more than a normal curiosity about the aspect of the other hemisphere in Lord Houghton's determination to see the American Continent, though 'See Niagara, and die' had become his own version of the hackneyed phrase on Naples. Houghton was deeply and thoroughly acquainted with American literature, as well as with those of its authors who had come to London during the last forty years—Emerson, Longfellow, Motley, 'Mark Twain,' Nathaniel Hawthorne, Herman Melville, Mrs. Beecher Stowe, Margaret Fuller, and many lesser luminaries of the transatlantic scene. Early in the 'seventies he had made particular friends with the thirty-year-old Joaquin Miller, that wild romantic figure, 'the Byron of Oregon,' who was sweeping all before him in London, where he would stride about dressed in an open-necked red shirt, a sombrero hat, trousers tucked into his boots and held up by a flowing sash. 'The greatest liar living', young Miller was immensely good company, with his stirring autobiographical yarns of Sioux Indian attacks on caravans, of pony expresses and gambling hells, and all the stock paraphernalia and incident of the Wild West, then quite novel to English ears.[1] In London, with the help of Lord Houghton and of two Irish friends, Miller prepared and printed his *Songs of the Sierras* which, conventional and Scott-like in treatment, were stirring in theme. Lord Houghton, who knew good poetry when he saw it, and had admired Whitman before anyone else in London had heard his name, did not perhaps take Miller's work too seriously, though he allowed a volume to be dedicated to himself; but he and his children found 'Joaquin' extremely refreshing, and he would listen sympathetically while this brash young bandit told him that he was 'timid' in company— 'the truth is I had rather meet a whole tribe of savages than a parlor full of strangers'—and confessed to a romantic attachment for an orphaned connection of Lady Houghton's, a lonely Miss Crewe, who answered his impassioned letters tersely, and sent his tentative proposal of marriage to her guardian.

[1] See, for an account of Miller, Van Wyck Brooks' *The Times of Melville and Whitman* (Dent & Co. 1948).

239

It does not say much for the poet's favour with fashionable society that he dined the other day with Lord Houghton [the gossip-column of a London daily, announcing Miller's return from San Francisco, declared], for it is a matter of course that an American notability in London receives the hospitalities of that graceful poet and entertainer. Indeed a notion prevails amongst some of our Transatlantic cousins that Lord Houghton was raised to the peerage on the understanding that he would promote kindly feelings between the great Republic and the 'Old Country' by giving breakfasts and dinners to celebrities in London hailing from the other side of the great ocean.

In 1869, at Suez, Lord Houghton had renewed acquaintance with William Henry Hurlbert, editor of the *New York World*, and friend of Landor (who had once, Hurlbert told Houghton, defined London to him as 'a huge sponge full of soot'). Hurlbert, whom he had first met in 1856, had often urged Milnes to come to the United States, but first the Civil War, and then Lady Houghton's illness had made the journey impracticable. Lord Houghton now realised that it would be a stimulating change for himself, as well as a diverting and instructive one for Robert Milnes, if he made a trip to North America with his son. On 5 August 1875, attended by the Fryston house-steward, Day, they embarked on a Sarmatian steamer for Quebec.

By 1875 a tour in the United States had become a routine part of the burden of celebrity shouldered by really famous English men of letters. As enjoyable then as it is to-day, a visit to America was also exceedingly exacting. In the very month in which Lord Houghton set his face westward, Canon Charles Kingsley returned to England, worn down by the racketing about and the constant lecturing he had been doing in the United States; he died next January. There is good reason to suppose that Dickens' second visit to America in 1867 hastened his death, for his constitution suffered terribly from the demands made upon him in New York, Boston and other cities; when told that the people of Chicago would 'have a fit' if he did not rush off there at once, he replied that he would rather they had a fit than he did. Lord Houghton, who was in imperfect health when he started, found his four months in Canada and the United States delightful but debilitating: 'This tour of mine has had its difficulties,' he wrote in November, 'and I have never been quite well for a single day.' 'I have been troubled with neuralgia ever since I have been in America, and it is little consolation to be told it is the malady of the nation,' he told Henry Bright in a letter from Emerson's house in the quiet haven of shady Concord, 'It has damped all my pleasure, and a week of medicine in New York has only made it worse.' Lord Houghton's open support of the North during the Civil War had made his name popular in the Northern States. Wherever he went he was given huge receptions, and wined and dined on a positively gargantuan scale. He moved about so much that Samuel Ward (the original of 'Uncle Sam'), would refer to his progress as that of 'Ulysses,' nicknaming him 'Lord of Ithaca.' American reporters found him ready to talk and very courteous and simple in his manner. One of them wrote with some enthusiasm in his newspaper that Lord Houghton was 'as easy and plain as an old shoe.'

II

Landing in Canada on 16 August after an 'unprecedentedly' peaceful crossing, Lord Houghton and Robert spent ten days there, visiting Quebec, Montreal, Toronto and Niagara. The Canadian public men were kind and welcoming, but not especially interesting, and the great natural phenomenon of the Niagara Falls impressed Lord Houghton somewhat less than he expected, while the Lachine Rapids were distinctly disappointing. On the way across the Atlantic they had passed floating icebergs which looked much as he had anticipated they would, one 'huge one' resembling a 're-cumbent mastiff or sphinx' and others seeming like 'solemn statuary islands.' From Niagara they went down to Buffalo in a Pullman car which though roomy was hot; the Pullmans did not 'quiver' and 'oscillate' as much as European railway carriages but they could be 'very bumpy.' From Buffalo they proceeded to Chicago for one week, and to St. Louis for another. The U.S. Minister in Brussels, General Badeau, had given Lord Houghton a letter of introduction to General Sherman in St. Louis, and both he and the 'city authorities' showed them round the new city and its parks. Lord Houghton was judged 'the livest Englishman St. Louis has ever seen.'

He is surely a gentleman of refinement and culture [General Sherman wrote to General Badeau, adding], You may safely send any of your friends to me here, and I will endeavour to redeem any promise you may make them. Generally strangers want to go out on the plains when an army acquaintance is indispensable.

Lord Houghton had no ambition to go out on the plains: he wanted politics, gossip and literature, and to seek these he hurried on to Washington, up to New York and then, early in October to New England—Quincey, Cambridge, Concord, Boston. At Cambridge Longfellow entertained him, and at Concord Emerson begged him to stay in his house for as long as he liked.   Here, in this tranquil centre of all that was finest in the literary traditions of the Eastern states, Lord Houghton spent three very happy days, visiting Hawthorne's 'Old Manse' and his grave in the sloping cemetery, sometimes called 'the Westminster Abbey of America.' He approved the monument of the Minute Man on the bridge at Concord, and another to two English soldiers killed fighting the Rebellion.

Emerson is very well [he wrote], and easy to talk with, but, he says, unable to write.   I had two charming days at Cambridge— Longfellow full of tenderness.   I am afraid he is ill, and so is Lowell.   I dine to-morrow with Holmes, who is very sprightly, and like his books.   On Monday I go to Albany and down the Hudson, intending to remain in New York till the end of the month.

In New York, where he paid two long visits during his four months in America, Lord Houghton stayed at the fashionable Brevoort House hotel on Fifth Avenue, near Washington Square. Here he was literally hounded by hospitable acquaintances, and by those who wanted to become so.

Few English noblemen have endured with like patience all that Lord Houghton suffered at the hands of our tuft hunters [ran a New York paper's valedictory on his departure in November], Yet he never lost his temper, never gave a hint of disgust and bore with a cheerful countenance the young editors' speeches and the obtrusive attentions of that wondrous menagerie of brain workers, the Lotos Club.   Lord Houghton must be a man of iron constitution and unexampled self-control.
    It can never be said [another newspaper correspondent remarks] that he failed to do justice to the hospitalities which were offered to him—he has 'dined out' to an extent which only long training, a strong constitution, and a clear conscience could have enabled him to support.

The Century Club, the Union Club, the unpopular Lotos Club— 'a club whose members are writers by profession and snobs by practice' as one newspaper called it—vied with each other to give him breakfasts, 'déjeuners' and dinners: there were parties at Delmonico's organised by Cyrus Field and by William Cullen Bryant, and a mass of invitations from what Hurlbert called

the leading lights of literature, society, negro minstrelsy, and the Cause (with a capital C) of Humanity (with a capital H).   I never attended one of these things in my life [Hurlbert continued] but I judge, from what I have heard of them, that they must be very edifying to the 'Stranger in our midst,' who is their subject at once

& object. Kingsley, I believe, judiciously got drunk before he submitted to the ordeal; Froude took it all in deadly earnest. . . . Forster threw his hosts into spasms of fury by appearing in a morning jacket and red cravat, while they were all point device in white chokers and patent pumps.

Old friends who knew Lord Houghton in London were apprehensive about the pace of his New York activities. Amongst these was Annette W. W. Hicks, the widow of Thomas Hicks the painter. In New York Mrs. Wilco Wilkens Hicks, who had known Lady Houghton, lived, as her startlingly embossed writing-paper proclaimed in letters of blue and silver, of scarlet and gold, at number ten West Fourteenth Street. Here she gave several dinner-parties for Lord Houghton, as well as a number of more intimate tea-time receptions.

Don't let N. Y. kill you with kindness, dear friend [wrote Mrs. Hicks]. You looked worn and weary at the reception this ev'g & for the sake of our dear mutual friends in old England—I take liberty to beg you *to hold up*, as we say—& not do *too* much. Remember the climate with its sudden changes, our exhausting gas-lights & ways of living are a strain & you must *seek rest*. I hear the City will show you attentions *Thursday*—that means fatigue, body & mind. In the evening you will meet twenty at dinner at my house, every one an admirer & acquaintance. . . . Some of our *best* people are still at their country homes—Please do not consider me officious when I ask you not to over-do yourself.

When Lord Houghton at last sailed for England at the end of November, after postponing his departure twice, he found in his state-room a large hamper of edibles such as foie-gras and ginger biscuits, as well as bottles of 'delicate sherry' and 'choice old brandy' thoughtfully sent by kindly Mrs. Hicks, who also gave into his charge some dried autumn leaves for the 'dear girls.' Mrs. Hicks had varnished the leaves herself; 'they will retain their colour,' she explained, 'for years.'

It is not surprising that Lord Houghton's first biographer found himself choosing for the chapter following that called *Visit to United States* the ominous title *Failing Health*.

III

On getting back to London, Lord Houghton set about preparing one of his last *Quarterly* articles, an essay on a number of American genealogical works, *Social Relations of England and America*, and only notable for the shrewd comment, 'Americans are growing daily more like one another' followed by the more disputable assertion 'and all more like Europeans.' Unfortunately Lord Houghton had made no notes upon his conversations at Concord and at Cambridge, or of a meeting which he seems to have had with Walt Whitman.

I am very glad to hear from you that you had seen Whitman & that he showed interest in my recognition of his genius [wrote Algernon Swinburne from Holmwood on 21 January 1876]. I wish you could have brought him over to shake hands with his English admirers, among whom there are plenty of sober & rational judges like myself, apart from the ultras or Whitmaniacs who regard him as the father—anything certainly but the 'silent father—of our Kings to be' in the world of song.

This was the month in which the news of the Turks' Bulgarian massacres began to reach England. Excitement tore up and down the country, and set political passions flaming; the anti-Turkish agitation did not slacken for many months. In May, Disraeli's cabinet turned down an invitation to England to join the Powers in the promulgation of the Berlin Memorandum, an instrument insisting on Turkish reforms; the Prime Minister made public speeches hinting at a pro-Turkish war with Russia, while in September Gladstone swung the country against the Government's policy by his celebrated pamphlet demanding the total withdrawal of Turkey from the provinces of Bulgaria, Bosnia and Herzegovina. This pamphlet, *The Bulgarian Horrors and the Question of the East*, was compared by admirers to Burke's *On a Regicide Peace* and to Milton's sonnet *On the Late Massacre in Piedmont*. Algernon Swinburne's attitude to the massacres would have pained Mr. Gladstone; in the same letter in which he wrote of Lord Houghton's meeting with Whitman, Swinburne continued in an even gayer vein:

I don't know whether you agree with Pythagoras or with Malvolio as to the doctrine of metempsychosis; but no disbelief could hold out against the evidence supplied in the Constantinople correspondence of the Times, of the reappearance of a famous man of time past in identity of *name* as well as nature, of nature as well as name, with only his conventional title altered from the Christian dignity of Marquis to the Turkish dignity of Bey. What infidel can question this identity when he reads that 'one man, Sadick Bey, goes from village to village violating Bulgarian girls (sic),' of whom more than a hundred have fallen victims? Various tortures not unknown to the Justinian Code are further enumerated in the same paragraph; & any little appearance of error or improbability as to sex will vanish if we consider that 'a Bulgarian girl' may be plausibly taken as a delicate periphrasis for the word 'boy'—seeing that in a quarter of Europe whose name has become a proverb, a boy would naturally take the place, in speech as in fact, elsewhere reserved for a girl. And certainly B-g-a is the precise quarter where a new Avatar of such a Vishnu might, if anywhere, have been confidently looked for. All these probabilities must be weighed against the one possibility that the Bey may be an emanation of the correspondent's brain, fired by residence in the city of Justinian—a name which wd. naturally recall Sadic memories.

Lord Houghton had actually travelled in Turkey, which Gladstone had not, and had never at any time shared his old friend's innocent faith in the kindliness of human nature or his odd belief in the essential virtue of some nations and the innate criminality of others: for Gladstone had written of the Turks as 'the one great anti-human specimen of humanity,' the only people capable of 'fell satanic orgies,' and declared that there was 'not one criminal in an European gaol' nor 'a Cannibal in the South Sea Islands' whose indignation would not rise at accounts of what was being done in Bulgaria. He wrote to Gladstone, pointing out that to turn the Turks out and give over the Province to non-Moslem rule would be fatal, yet what he termed 'the failure of forty years of Greek independence' plainly showed that these areas were not capable of autonomy: 'I do not see,' he wrote from the Rosses' at Birr Castle, 'the conditions of Tenant Right or Home Rule in Bosnia or Bulgaria.' Gladstone replied that Greek independence had not failed; and that the Provinces might perhaps require 'a little foreign nursing' before they could manage for themselves. 'I said in a speech yesterday,' he concluded, 'I had now just one friend who did not see the need of decisive measures; I hope you do not make two.' To this letter Lord Houghton sent a wise rejoinder. As in 1860 he had told David Gray there were sadder and crueller things about this world than leaving it, so in 1876 he told Gladstone that there were worse fates for nations than an occasional massacre, and one of them was the suggested Russian 'protection':

I am a member of the Polish Association, and thus my prejudice against Russian occupation. I know her violation of engagements and 'massacre' of mind. Material cruelty is short to suffer; semi-civilised political oppression is a lifelong torture; a century of Warsaw is worse than a week of Batak.

IV

In the third week of November 1876 Lord Houghton was staying at the Shelbourne Hotel in Dublin, on his leisurely homeward way from Birr. Here on the 17th of that month he was handed a telegram. Despatched by the housekeeper at Fryston, it told him that the Hall was at that very moment being destroyed by fire.

The fire at Fryston was of unknown origin. It had been discovered at half past ten at night. The Pontefract fire-engine, which came rattling out to Ferrybridge behind its horses, was short of hose, and what hose it had was full of holes. An additional fire-engine, sent to Knottingley by the railway, arrived too late to prevent the whole front part of the house from being gutted. The pictures and the library had been moved twice, the place was a seething babel of local farm-hands and tenants trying to help. Nobody was killed, but one of the most famous collections of books in England lay in sodden mounds all over the lawn.

Leaving his son in Dublin, Lord Houghton rushed home to examine the damage. He was curiously brave about this destruction of the collections of a lifetime and the house of his youth.

I will not call it a calamity, but it is as great a trouble as could well happen to one [he told Lady Holland]. The morning room is open to the morning sun [he wrote] and the evening sky. *All* the front is gone—that is, all the best rooms. . . . I dare not yet look over the books. Most are saved; but wetted, knocked about. . . . The people about worked night and day—quite a demonstration, intensified by the wish that somebody else's house had been burnt instead of mine. . . . The loss would have been of hundreds, not thousands, had the Pomfret engine been effective; but it would not work, and the hose was as rotten as the ancient borough.

The confusion after the fire was increased by swarms of sightseers, (for the conflagration had been reported in every newspaper), and these people were suspected of carrying off mementoes of the fire. 'My best books will *not* turn up; they tell me they were saved, but I should like to see them,' Lord Houghton wrote to Bright.

I find my books still more disordered than I expected [he wrote again in April 1877], hardly any large series complete, and the number of broken volumes most annoying. My Dante and Froissart have turned up, but Charles I's Spenser is still missing.

There was enough left of the back rooms at Fryston for the family and one or two literary friends to live in if they wished—'a sort of lay parsonage'—and, like his brother-in-law Crewe in 1866, Lord Houghton set to work to build his house up again. But it was weary work for an old man, and expensive too.

The foundations are turning out so bad that there will be a very heavy expense in renewing them [he told his daughter Florence]. The architect must have been thinking of Venice, for the whole front is built on a wooden base which has gradually decayed, and there are heaps of rotten wood taken out. Placknett says the drawing-room side might have come down with a run. In which of Wilkie Collins's books is the disappearance of a whole house and its contents in a landslip?

In January 1877 Lord Houghton journeyed north to Glasgow to unveil a statue of Robert Burns in the presence of one hundred thousand people. In June he had a nasty accident in Hyde Park, when the loose curb rein of 'a Miss Farquhar' caught his leg in the jam of riders and dragged him off his pony: he fell on his face and retired to bed for a week, later emerging in a carrying chair to dine at the Roxburghe Club. In 1877 his sister's husband, Galway, died and in the first days of 1878 Lord Houghton was further saddened by the death at Venice of Sir William Stirling-Maxwell. This last loss he described as 'a desolation,' describing in a private letter himself, Stirling-Maxwell and Bright, as the 'only real men of letters in Great Britain.' 'I use the term "man-of-letters" designedly, in distinction from that of scholar or writer,' Lord Houghton stated in the obituary notice of William Stirling which he contributed to *The Academy*.

Sir William's scholarship was that of the ordinary liberal education of our time, retained and cultivated in maturer years. His style of writing was not especially good, and exhibited little, if any, of the wit and liveliness which distinguished his conversation; but as a man who made literature the employment, the pleasure and the consolation of his life, who used his great wealth and free time in collecting interesting material to be used by himself and others in accurate representation of the history of the past; and who loved to associate with men of intellectual culture in . . . relations of perfect equality and mutual respect . . . his loss will be severely felt, not only in his own country, where literary tastes are so widely diffused, but in all our most important departments of letters and art.

In certain ways, and excising the phrase 'great wealth,' this passage might be read as descriptive of Lord Houghton himself, and of his own most civilised career.

The friends not only of Lord Houghton's youth but also of his middle life were swiftly disappearing: 'You and I and Mr. Kinglake are all that are left of the goodly band that used to come to St John's Wood,' wrote old Mrs. Procter, who had abandoned her house in that neighbourhood to live what Swinburne called 'up a lift' in Queen Anne's Mansions. Lord Houghton indeed was joining those persons 'to whom' (in a memorable phrase which in his youth he had heard Samuel Rogers coin) 'the streets of London

have become a range of inhabited tombs.' 'Alas for Stanley!'
James Anthony Froude wrote to Lord Houghton in July 1881 after
the death of the Dean of Westminster.

'. . . The other place is rapidly absorbing all those whom we knew
and valued most and we shall have no objection to join them.
The next generation may be as good (better for all I know) but I
cannot fit myself into the ways of them.—Carlyle, Spedding,
Stanley, all within a few months gone. C. had a vague hope that
there might be something beyond. Spedding distinctly none.
For Stanley I cannot say.

Thomas Carlyle had died in February of 1881, having given what
Froude regarded as absolute and binding instructions for the
immediate publication of his *Reminiscences,* that book of ruthless
self-revelation which Longmans published, under Froude's editorship, later the same year. In the row which the first appearance of
this volume caused, Lord Houghton very sanely and calmly sided
with Froude—one of the only friends of the Carlyles to do so. He
evidently wrote to Froude in this sense, for the historian, who had
retired to Norway to recover from his amazement at the attacks
launched on him in the reviews by fanatical admirers of Carlyle,
sent him a long letter from Christiania on 31 July 1881.

It was very welcome to me [Froude wrote gratefully of Lord
Houghton's note], showing as it does that at least *one* of Carlyle's
friends can recognize the real nature of the Reminiscences and my
duty in respect of them. I could do nothing but what I did. It
was with his own full approval. His own account of himself was &
is the only possible real basis for any accurate judgement about him.
As to the *time* of publication which you naturally considered
premature the motive was really so simple that nobody thought of
it. He himself foresaw that when he died there would be much
written & said about him. He wished the world to have something
authentic to go upon & it was therefore arranged that the book
should appear as soon as possible after his death. This was one
reason. Another was that I supposed that Mary Carlyle & her
husband would be in some straits when first left to themselves &
therefore that the money from the book would be useful to them.
I have had to learn that people do not like to be placed under
obligations. I told C. that I would treat Mary Carlyle as if she was
my own daughter. She had no wish to be treated as my daughter.
She concluded, I suppose, that I should not have given her a large
sum of money unless I knew that she had a legal right to it, and
therefore she had stood and stands upon her rights, and Stephen
and I are doing what we can to unravel the knots which she has
contrived to tie. He may have succeeded I hope while I am out of
the way. *Mrs. Carlyle's* letters are a far more difficult problem

. . . I *ought* to write and publish *his* Life before I publish them, but this too Mary Carlyle's action has complicated. I shall see when I get home.

As a truthful exposition of Froude's point of view in the sorry wrangle over Carlyle's literary bequest this letter, hitherto unprinted, seems not only lucid and earnest, but convincing.

V

'Your old friend grows feeble,' wrote another figure of Milnes' youth to him in May 1877. At eighty-five Harriet Grote confessed herself

compelled to renounce general society, as well as the life-long pleasures of visiting Exhibitions of Art & the musical performances in public places. How you contrive to hold on your wonted activity, & to figure on the stage in so many 'parts' surprises, whilst it pleases me. But then you are still in the prime of life!

Mrs. Grote had reason to be surprised at Lord Houghton's activity. In fairly constant pain from gout, much hampered by the disabilities of age emphasised in his case by a lifetime of good living, Lord Houghton was still to be seen at every notable social, political or literary function in London. He still organised his 'omnium-gatherum' literary parties in some house which he would hire for the season. He was still alert to help new talent—Hall Caine, for instance—or to meet the new fashionable writers like Miss Rhoda Broughton or the perfumed, orchidaceous Louise de la Ramée, who wrote under the name of 'Ouida' (and in 1880 produced her most popular volume, *Moths*). He still sometimes spoke, and very frequently voted, in the House of Lords. He still went for his health to Torquay and Vichy, and was perfectly prepared to go at a moment's notice farther afield. In 1882 he was only thwarted in a project for going to India by his doctors, who gave a lengthy explanation 'resolvable,' Lord Houghton told his son, 'into four words—"you are too old"—very disagreeable, but unanswerable.' 'He says the doctors will not let him go this winter to India,' wrote Lord Ronald Gower in his diary for June 1882 (of an encounter with Lord Houghton at Lady Holland's house at Chertsey), 'and that if he does, he will never return, and that he does not wish to come back—that he is tired of Europe, and of life'.[1] Yet Houghton still entertained valiantly: in January 1879 Fryston

---

[1] *Old Diaries 1881–1901* by Lord Ronald Sutherland Gower (John Murray 1902), p. 14.

had been reconstructed and a great dinner-party in the new drawing room, attended amongst others by the aged Mrs. Procter and
by Houghton's Cambridge contemporary Venables, celebrated the
renaissance of the house.

The object of deep affection to his own friends, of curiosity to those
of his children, Richard Monckton Milnes was now become a gouty,
stooping old man, with white whiskers, and fronds of white hair
curling out from under the black skull-cap worn well back on his
head—'the dance, and Lord Houghton in a skull-cap, were both
successful and picturesque,' wrote an acquaintance who met him
at a fancy-dress dance at Lowther Lodge in the summer of 1881.[1]
Benevolent, humorous, anecdotal, he was also very short-tempered,
and had a tendency to go suddenly to sleep. He had always
been gluttonous—he was indeed the author of the well-known
witticism 'my exit will be the result of too many entrées'—and this
characteristic, like his love of wine, became the solace of his old age.
The very young no longer understood him. They did not like
his paradoxes, nor his habit of quizzing their remarks: for in
age Lord Houghton continued his life-long occupation of watching
the idiosyncracies of others with those shrewd grey eyes which
Lehmann has well portrayed in the last portrait of him, and of
commenting on them in his irreverent way. In the autumn of
1882 he and Mrs. Procter were both staying at Dunnichen in For-
farshire with the Frederick Lehmanns, whose son has left a description of this visit. 'During the day,' writes Mr. R. C. Lehmann,[2]
'while we were attempting to secure partridges, Lord Houghton
used to drive about the country or saunter in the garden. After
dinner, when the ladies had departed to their beds he arrayed himself in a voluminous smoking-gown and a red fez, and joined us
in the smoking-room, where he kept us all alive with anecdotes and
stories drawn from the great storehouse of his experience. One
evening, I well remember, he played an active part in helping us to
organize and carry through a series of "dumb crambo" performances'. Writing a 'Collins' to his host from Aberdeenshire, Lord
Houghton showed himself as alert and inquisitive as ever: who
had written *Vice Versa* ('Of which I am unworthy'). Was it true
the author only got ten pounds for it? Could he have a letter from
James Payn for his collection of autographs? 'Tired of Europe
and of life' he was still possessed of an inexhaustible curiosity.

A few persons still living can recall Lord Houghton in his final
phase; most of these are now themselves well past the age he had

[1] *Old Diaries 1881–1901*, p. 8.
[2] Letter printed in part in *Memories of Half a Century: A Record of Friendships*,
edited by R. C. Lehmann, M.P. (Smith, Elder 1908).

LORD HOUGHTON IN 1883

reached then, and with one solitary exception their memories of him are neither striking nor succinct. The exception is that of a grand-daughter of his wife's chaperon and cousin, Mrs. Blackburne, who recalls receiving much kind attention from Lord Houghton in Rome in 1885, when she was a young girl. Miss Blackburne would often breakfast with Lord Houghton and his sister Lady Galway, and she quickly came to love and respect this remarkable old man. On one occasion Lord Houghton drove her to Saint Peter's. Leading her into the basilica, he conducted her to a certain place upon the flagstones before the Stuarts' tombs. 'Stand there, my dear,' he said to her. 'Now I want you always to remember that where you stand now *I* saw Sir Walter Scott standing when *I* was a boy.' It had been in April 1832 that Milnes' cousin Sir William Gell had conducted the infirm old Scott to see the tombs of the Stuarts in Saint Peter's; Richard Monckton Milnes, aged twenty-two, had been of the party, and had commemorated the sight in jingling verses (afterwards published in his *Memorials of Many Scenes*), of which the last stanza goes:

> There lie the Stuarts!—There lingers Walter Scott!
> Strange congress of illustrious thoughts and things!
> A plain old moral, still too oft forgot,—
> The power of Genius and the fall of Kings.

His profound belief in the omnipotence of genius was something that Milnes never, throughout his life, forgot.

In the summer of the year 1879, Lord Houghton's son Robert Milnes became engaged to Miss Graham of Netherby, a grand-daughter of the old Duchess of Somerset (the ravishing heroine of the Eglinton Tournament, now a stout old lady) and great-niece of Mrs. Norton. The extreme youth of the bride and bridegroom struck many of Lord Houghton's friends, and amongst the letters of congratulation he received was a strange lugubrious epistle from the person he had himself wished to marry when he was young.

My dear Friend [wrote Miss Florence Nightingale in May 1880], I *will* give you joy, I *do* give you joy . . . on your boy's marriage. . . . On the other hand [Miss Nightingale continued after some remarks upon serving one's apprenticeship to hard work] there is something very inspiring in the faithful love, the early and the late, when two always say 'we.' I remember when I was a girl, Madame Hoche in Paris, widow of General Hoche, after the first year of marriage (far away be the omen!) to her dying day always said 'nous,' she never called him to her only child 'ton père.' I think one has known such instances of two in one through a long life together, God in both and both in one; but then the wife must help

the husband in work, not prevent him.   May such a life be given
to our young pair; may all true blessings be theirs, and may it be
theirs to be a blessing to many in these the most stirring times of
this or any day! And after these are over may it be given them
'world beyond world to visit and to bless' together. Can one
wish them more? What worlds there are even in this world! [she
went on].   There is India . . . what have we done for the people of
India?   There is a country farther away from us than India.   In one
end of London there are whole lands unvisited and unblessed by us
in England.   There is Ireland, there is Liverpool, and the big
towns; there is education, there is pauperism. . . .   But this is a
strange 'Wedding March.' Believe that I would, if I could,
contribute the sweetest music to inspire the footsteps of the beautiful
marriage pair. My love, please, to the two daughters from the
bottom of my heart. You kindly ask after me. After twenty-
three years of overwork and illness. . . .   I am quite broken down,
more than I knew myself, and have had to go away twice for a little
silence.   Alas, how work halts! I think I am 'done' as to work.

Miss Nightingale, in fact, lived on, senile and useless, until nineteen
hundred and ten.

Robert Milnes' marriage took place in 1880.   In the next year
both his sisters married, leaving Lord Houghton now quite alone.
Amicia selected Mr. Gerald FitzGerald, a Catholic Irishman
in the Indian Civil Service, whom she had met in Cairo during a
tour in the Middle East with her aunt the year before.   Florence
married the third son of Lord Henniker, and, having inherited her
father's literary tastes, became a successful novelist of the London
'nineties, a friend of Thomas Hardy, with whom she combined to
produce a joint work of fiction, and authoress of such lively, ephemeral *études de mœurs* as *Foiled* and *Scarlet and Grey*.

While Amicia had been travelling in Palestine and Egypt with
her Aunt Harriette, her father had embarked upon a last journey to
Germany.   At Oberammergau he saw the Passion Play—'there is
nothing dramatic about it', he wrote, 'though the actors are fairly
good, but it is wonderfully pictorial, and you see Van Eyck, and
Rubens, and Raphael, in life.'   From there he went up to Berlin to
stay with George Bunsen, to examine the new museum of classical
antiquities, and to be present, in his scarlet Deputy-Lieutenant's
uniform, at a great September parade before the German Emperor.
Seated in the Bunsens' carriage, Lord Houghton watched the
Emperor, spry and upright at eighty-three, review fifty thousand
troops.   He chatted with the Empress and met Von Moltke, and
had an earnest, intimate political conversation with the Crown
Prince of Austria, Rudolf, the future victim at Mayerling.   This
last occasion was marred by one of those indiscretions for which

Milnes had always been notorious, and which had prevented first Peel and later Palmerston from giving him public office. 'What passed between them,' Lord Houghton's biographer loyally recorded of this interview, 'was mentioned by Lord Houghton only to a few persons in whom he had confidence, and that merely in a casual manner.' All the same the conversation, in which the Crown Prince, charmed by Lord Houghton's winning manner, had been exceptionally outspoken, promptly appeared upon the front pages of the Cologne Gazette. It caused embarrassment to all concerned.

No English editor would have reproduced a private conversation without the permission of the conversee [wrote Lord Houghton stiffly], and I fear that the consequences to me will be serious in my intercourse with both Austrian and Belgian diplomatists. I am never likely [he added] to go again to the Court of Berlin or Vienna, so that that does not much matter.

Though he never went again to Germany, which he had loved since boyhood, Houghton did make a bold journey as far as Cairo to see his daughter Amy in 1882. He planned to come back by way of Athens and Rome; but no sooner had he settled in a room with a view of the Acropolis from the window than he had a bad heart-attack 'which might', he wrote cheerfully to his son, 'have ended all.' His family came to Athens and took him home:

I am now sorry I did not carry out my Roman plan at all risks [he told Severn]. At the worst, Keats would have lain very pleasantly between his friend and his biographer, with a wreath of fresh Athenian violets over his head.

Lord Houghton took angina as easily as he took most things. 'Let me know where your hotel is, and whether it has a lift,' he instructed Henry Bright, whom he wished to join at Cannes in '83, 'That is a serious matter for my weak heart, for if I run up a long stair, I may find the Elysian fields at the top.'

After visiting Cannes, and Rome in 1883, Lord Houghton spent most of 1884 in England, sorting papers and arranging what the Fryston fire had left of his books. He knew that he had not long to live. One day, in the Fryston library, he complained of feeling ill. 'What is the matter with you?' a friend enquired. Lord Houghton looked up quickly. 'Death,' he replied. 'That is what is the matter with me. I am going to die. I am going over to the majority, and you know I have always preferred the minority.'

In the early spring of 1885 Lord Houghton was once again in Rome, in high spirits. 'This makes you the seventh Lady Fitz-Gerald,' he wrote to Amicia, whose husband had just been knighted, 'according to the Red Book, & as you cannot affix the Hon. you might put *of Cairo* like Lord Wolseley.' The hero of the hour, Lord Wolseley, back from the 'relief' of Khartoum, was given a tremendous popular reception in London in August 1885: Lord Houghton, set on witnessing this triumph, pottered out alone into the milling crowd, where he was rather knocked about and whence he returned shaken and tired. Two or three days after this he set off to join his sister at Vichy, where he arrived on the eighth of August. He began to look about him for acquaintances and company.

VI

In the May before he came to Vichy Lord Houghton had taken part in two ceremonies of a literary character: he had spoken at the unveiling of the Coleridge bust in Westminster Abbey (recalling that that great man had received him 'as Goethe or Socrates might have done' when he and Arthur Hallam had been to pay him their trembling homage nearly sixty years before), and later in the same month he had himself unveiled, at Pembroke College, Cambridge, the bust of the poet Thomas Gray. In July he had addressed the sixth annual meeting of the new Wordsworth Society, assembled to hear him in the drawing-room of his sister's house in Rutland Gate. Referring modestly to the part he and his Cambridge contemporaries—Charles, Frederick and Alfred Tennyson, Arthur Hallam, Stafford O'Brien, James Spedding, the Lushington brothers, mad Sunderland, Venables—had played in popularising the poetry of Wordsworth, in making that of Keats and Shelley widely known, he told his hearers that, whenever asked to write the title of 'the greatest poem in the language' in a lady's album he always wrote Wordsworth's *Ode on the Intimations of Immortality*. 'It comprehends,' said Lord Houghton, 'the life of man.'

It is the life of man and not his death that matters to us; for we are ourselves, in our turn, making the experiment of living. Richard Monckton Milnes died suddenly at Vichy on the night of 11 August 1885. He was seventy-six. His body was brought back across France and southern England to the family vault in the little marshy churchyard at Ferry Fryston, where it was laid beside the coffins of his father and his wife. The many thousand letters in his private papers were sorted by his executors' orders, and stored away. The dusty residue of a lifetime of relationships genial and ardent, subtle, jocular or sad, these letters are all that now remain to conjure up a personality which, while achieving little of permanent historical or literary importance, yet seems to us more vital than that of many of Lord Houghton's celebrated contemporaries and friends.

The two days which Lord Houghton had spent at Vichy with his sister, before his fatal seizure upon a night of storm and heavy rain in which no doctor would come to his hotel, had been conversible and happy. As a friend, philanthropist and talker, even as a poet, Milnes had consistently proclaimed his quiet, Liberal belief in the moral value of felicity. Enjoying his own life hugely, he had invariably tried to help other people to enjoy theirs. 'I will not contradict anything you say except the *general usefulness* of suffering,' he wrote a few days before his death, addressing a somewhat fervid High Anglican friend. 'I admit that it is so to the higher natures—but it is my decided experience that the mass of mankind are better for being happier. I am sure I am.'

APPENDIX

The following are the two holographs of Algernon Swinburne, referred to in the course of Chapter Eight:

(1). Undated love-song, evidently an early work, and without a title.

(2). '*Charenton en 1810*': verses inspired by the incarceration of the Marquis de Sade in the asylum at Charenton, and written before Swinburne had read his works.

I

Say, is it day, is it dusk, in thy bower,
　Thou whom I long for, who longest for me?
O be it night, be it light, 'tis love's hour,
　Love's that is fettered as love's that is free.
Free love has leaped to that innermost chamber,
　O the last time & the hundred before;
Fettered love, motionless, can but remember,
　Yet something that sighs from him passes the door.

2

What were my prize could I come to thy bower,
　This day, tomorrow, at eve or at morn?
Large lovely arms & a neck like a tower,
　Bosom then heaving that now lies forlorn:
Deep in warm pillows (the nun's bed is colder!)
　Thy sweetness all near me, so distant to-day,
My hand round thy head & my hand on thy shoulder,
　My mouth in thy neck as the world melts away.

3

What is it keeps me afar from thy bower,
　My spirit, my body, so fain to be there—
Waters engulfing or fires that devour,
　Earth heaped against me or death in the air?
Nay, but in day-dreams, for terror, for pity,
　The trees wave their heads with an omen to tell:
Nay, but in night-dreams, throughout the dark city,
　The hours, clashed together, lose count in the bell.

4

Shall I not one day remember thy bower—
　One day when all days are one day to me?
Thinking 'I stirred not, & yet had the power'—
　Yearning 'Ah God, if again it might be!'
Peace, peace! such a small lamp illumes on this highway,
　So dimly so few steps in front of my feet,
Yet shows me that her way is parted from my way—
　Out of sight, beyond light, at what point shall they meet?

Charenton en *1810*

En ce temps-là c'était un vieillard calme et fort :
Il avait le front grave et l'œil serein : la Mort
Avait peur à l'aspect du satyre sublime ;
Et la Douleur qui ronge et mord comme une lime
Se tordait sous son pied comme un chien écrasé.
Parfois il débordait de son cœur évasé
Quelque parole amère, effroyable, cynique ;
Tout se courbait devant ce vieillard titanique,
La Haine avec l'Amour, le Mal avec le Bien ;
On sentait, à le voir rire et songer, que rien,
Ni le Désir dont l'œil éblouissant étonne,
Ni l'Homme qui rugit, ni Dieu qui trompe et tonne,
Ni l'affreuse Vertu, gouge au cœur ulcéré,
N'avait su mettre un pli sur ce front vénéré.
Il vit le monde énorme et vide où rien ne bouge ;
Gomorrhe lui jetait des reflets d'un feu rouge,
Et l'horrible Capri flamboyait sous ses yeux ;
Il contemple ; et sa main semble avoir dans son creux
Tout ce grand siècle éteint qui n'est qu'un brouillard pâle ;
Sporus tout nu couché près d'Héliogabale,
Et le plaisir caché dans la profonde horreur,
Et les bains effrayants de ce sombre empereur
Qui livrait sa chair nue aux morsures craintives
Des enfants violés et des filles plaintives,
Et saignait les garçons pour sucer les plus beaux ;
Le succube qui rôde et rit dans les tombeaux ;
Sémiramis pâmée au milieu de l'étable,
Et la Luxure auprès du Meutre assise à table,
La fauve Lesbienne au corps brûlé de feux,
Et l'abîme, et l'amour sans forme et sans aveux,
Et Venus Aphacite, effroi de la nature ;
Toute la flamme avec toute la pourriture ;
Et de Retz aspirant la cendre avec les chairs,
Et la fumée humaine éparse dans les airs :
Ce qu'un faune impudique en ses vêtements cache ;
Et cette reine, ayant des appétits de vache,
Haletante, et l'œil plein d'une affreuse douceur,
Mère du Minotaure et de Phèdre sa sœur :
Cimgras appuyé sur les seins de sa fille ;
Tout ce qui vibre, émeut, rugit, frissonne et brille ;
La terre en fièvre, monstre aux ébats furieux ;
Le ciel, lupanar fait d'azur luxurieux,
Où s'échappe et jaillit le jet d'un dieu phallique
Qui laisse aller ses jus en un flot métallique ;
Où la lune erre et cherche un assouvissement ;
Où le grand soleil entre au lit cyniquement
Et répand, rouge et nu, sans pudeur et sans trêve,
Le débordement vaste et sanglant de sa sève ;
Car les rayons sont tous des souillures ; l'envers
Du ciel, c'est le gros ventre ouvert de l'univers.
Il marchait l'œil pensif, grave ; et toute Sodôme
Vivait, flambait, rêvait, hurlait dans ce grand homme.

Il touchait au bon temps, au siècle antique, aux dieux;
A le voir, on sentait un frisson aux cheveux;
Sa mâchoire avait l'air d'une faim titanique;
Il avait la candeur superbe et satanique;
Quand il baisait, sa bouche avait la soif du sang;
Son rire était un grand rictus éblouissant;
Son haleine était comme un souffle plein de rage;
Il semblait le Priape assis sous le feuillage
Qui ronge à belles dents sa nymphe au cou bruni;
Cet homme était le noir cadet de l'infini.

Il revoyait, plissant son sourcil plein de rides,
Marseille et la fureur des âpres cantharides,
La barrière d'Arcueil, les onguents, le canif,
La chair trouée et rouge et qu'il taillait à vif.

Un dédain sombre enflait sa poitrine nageuse.
L'empire l'avait pris dans sa griffe fangeuse,
Il souriait. Cet homme avait des dieux à lui.
Il vit tout, mais jamais il ne fut ébloui.
Un appétit grouillait dans son âme profonde
Plus grand que Bonaparte et plus grand que le monde.

Or, un soir, un jeune homme âgé de vingt-quatre ans
Vit ce front blême et fier chargé de cheveux blancs,
Ces yeux noirs, cette bouche impérieuse et fine;
Il frissonna.

L'enfant lisait ce jour *Justine*;
Il levait ses regards, comme on fait en priant,
De la page proscrite au vieillard souriant.
Enfin, pensif, il dit: 'Qu'est-ce donc que cet homme?
Je voudrais bien savoir, pardieu, ce qu'il se nomme.
On se rappelle, à voir les gestes de sa main,
Les sublimes ébats du vieux monde romain;
Tous ceux qui furent grands et qu'on appelle infâmes,
Femmes de leurs maris et maris de leurs femmes;
Tout l'éblouissement au sein des nuits rentré;
Le gladiateur bruni dans l'arène éventré,
L'empereur qui lui tient son talon sur la nuque
Et flatte de sa lèvre immonde un bel eunuque;
Tout ce que la nature abhorre, et ce que Dieu,
Jaloux, craintif, noya dans un grand flot de feu;
Ce qui revit; ce qu'on dérobe à sa colère: ·
Ce que rêvait Socrate et ce que fit Tibère;
Tous les festins, tous les combats, tout l'inouï;
Tout ce qu'on entrevoit dans l'ombre épanoui;
Ce qu'un satyre errant venait apprendre au pâtre,
Et ce que la vertu funeste efface et châtre;
La cynique mamelle où boit le monde entier,
Et l'emblème aperçu du côté du sentier;
Et le sang jaillissant de la chaude ruelle;
Les alcôves; la femme abominable et belle,
Et le rire de l'homme assouvissant ses dents
Sur l'épaule nacrée et sur les seins ardents,
Tout cela flotte et fuit dans sa prunelle vive,
Dans la crispation de sa bouche lascive.
Qui donc es-tu, vieillard? d'où viens-tu? qui t'a fait

Cet air triste d'un dieu qui frappe et qui se tait?
Quelle main surhumaine a posé ce sourire
Sur ta lèvre orgueilleuse et pâle? Que veut dire
Cette flamme allumée au fond noir de tes yeux
Comme un éclair du soir qui passe, et, radieux,
Dore et ravive toute une morne façade?

—Enfant, dit le viellard, je m'appelle de Sade'

Dimanche, 27 octobre, 1861.

Note: In composing what Lord Houghton chose to call 'this physiological extravaganza' it is clear that Swinburne was deliberately imitating the style of Victor Hugo, a poet whom he earnestly admired. Compare the opening lines of *La Terre sous le troisième César* in Hugo's *La Judée*, a second book of *La Fin de Satan*:

En ce temp-là, le monde était dans la terreur;
Caiphé était grand-prêtre et Tibère empereur;

etc. etc.

INDEX

Aberdeen, Lord, 27–8, 71
Academy, The, 247
Acton, Lord, 197
Adams, Charles Francis, Junr., 45
Adams, Mrs. C. F., 45, 167
Adams, Henry, and Swinburne, 138, 140–1; at Fryston, 138–41; respect for Milnes, 166, 167; quoted, 52, 130, 166
Adams, James, 166–7
Aidé, Charles Hamilton, 141 *and n.*
Albany, Duke of, 41
Albert, Prince Consort, lectures on science, 28 *n.*; patron of Philobiblon Society, 40–1; Milnes' criticism of behaviour, 41; reserved manner, 44; visits Ireland, 66; unpopularity, 70; death, 162, 168
Alexander, Prince of Holland, 215
Alexandra, Princess, *see* Wales, Princess **of**
Alford, Lady Marion, 99–100, 106
Alice, Princess, marriage, 169
Allingham, William, epitaph on Houghton, 213
Almack's, 52
Almond's Hotel, 235
Amazon (steamboat) disaster, 23, 24
America, Houghton's visit to (1875), 239–43
American Civil War, 162, 165–8, 238; Milnes' support of the North, 139, 165, 189, 241
American literature, Houghton and, 239–40
Americans, in England: ridicule of, 35–6; Milnes' views on, 36–7, 165, 168
Ampthill, Lord, 94
Ampthill Park, 4, 18
Antonelli, Cardinal, 209
Arlès-Dufour, M., 191
Arnim, Bettina von, 13
Arnold, Matthew, 137
Ashbee, Henry Spencer, 118 *and n.*, 119 *n.*, 120, 210 *and n.*
Ashburton, Harriet Lady, estimates of her personality, 18–19; her 'printers,' 60–1; railway carriage incident with Mrs. Carlyle, 101–2; death, 101–3; Milnes' essay on, 102; to have been godmother to Milnes' son, 105; quoted, 14, 18, 59; mentioned, 3, 4, 7, 20, 32

Ashburton, Lady Louisa, marriage, 103; daughter born, 103; mentioned, 209, 210, 238
Ashburton, Lord, 14, 101; second marriage, 103
Ashridge, 99–101
Athenæum, The, 57, 135, 195
Athenæum Club, 51
Auerbach, Berthold, 17
Augustenburg, Duke and Duchess of, 14
Aumale, Henri Duc d', 40, 43
Austria, Milnes' tour of (1851), 12, 15–17; position in 1851, 13; Milnes' attitude to, 163
Austria, Emperor of, 207, 229
Authors, Milnes' solicitude for, 62–6, 220
Autographs, Milnes' collection of, 25, 38, 113, 194–5, 250

Bacon, Miss Delia, 60
Badeau, General, 241
Baring, Mary, 210
Barrett, Elizabeth, *see* Browning, Mrs.
Barrot, Odilon, 183, 189
Barry, Edward, 199
Bates, Joshua, 44–5
Bawtry, 3, 4, 108
Beauclerk, Lady Di, 202
Bedford, Duke of, 19, 94
Belgium, Throne of, 44
Berkeley Square, house in, 235
Berry sisters, 53–6
Bessborough, Lady, 69
Bidwell, Lady Selina, 187
Billiards, Milnes' attitude to, 112
Birching, Swinburne's references to, 146, 149, 150–1, 157, 158 *n.*
Bismarck, Prince, 162, 163, 176, 179
Blackburne, Miss, 251
Blackburne, Mrs., 5, 105, 197
Blackburne, Emma, 9, 10 *n.*
Blackwood's Magazine, 142
Blake, William, Milnes' collection of works, 151; Swinburne's interest in, 151–2
Blanc, Louis, 22
Bland, Tom, 181–2
Blessington, Marguerite, 48
Bloomer, Mrs. Amelia, 17 *n.*
Blore, Edward, 198, 199
Bolte, Amely, 13

Index

Index

Index

Index

Planché, lines about pronunciation of 'Houghton,' 172
Planet, M., 188–9
Poet Laureateship, 56–7
Pontefract, volunteers, 22; represented by Richard Monckton Milnes, 27, 94
Poynter, Ambrose, 198
Prague, Peace of, 202
Praz, Mario, cited, 117, 132–3
Pre-Raphaelites, 15, 95, 133 n., 135, 195
Prescott, quoted, 47
Princess Royal, engagement to Prince William of Prussia, 95
Prison vans, improvement of, 194
Procter, Mrs., 6, 19, 247, 250; lines on Milnes' peerage, 172
Prussia, in 1851, 13; Milnes' attitude to, 13, 163, 176, 230, 232; inevitability of war, 179; in 1866, 202
Pugin, A. N., 68–9
Punch, 35

Quarterly Review, 49, 196; Milnes' contributions, 49, 99, 124, 130, 219, 243

Raglan, Lord, 72–4
Redcliffe, Lord Stratford de, 50, 71
Redesdale, Lord, 32
Reeve, Henry, 33 and n., 34
Reform Act, 1867, 201
Reformatories, Juvenile, 62, 178, 201
Reid, Sir Thomas Wemyss, ix–x, 180, 235; quoted, 6, 68; cited, 66
Rémusat, 189
Rheindorf, 177, 179
Rio, A. F., 13, 81
Ripon, Lord, conversion to Catholicism, 238
Ritchie, Lady (Anne Thackeray), 138, 144–5
Rock Cottage, Tunbridge Wells, 74
Roebuck, J. A., 2
Rogers, Samuel, 29, 46, 247; refuses Poet Laureateship, 56
Rome, 207–13
Roscoe, William, 193
Rosen, Baron de, 175
Rosse, Lord and Lady, 69
Rossetti, D. G., 129, 134
Rossetti, William, 151, 152, 220
Rothschilds, The, 186, 232, 233
Royal Geographical Society, 214, 228, 229
Royal Society, Houghton elected Fellow, 214

Rudolf, Crown Prince of Austria, Houghton's conversation with, 252–3
Ruskin, Effie, 32
Ruskin, John, 65
Russell, Arthur, 94, 105
Russell, Lady John, 85
Russell, Lord John (later Earl Russell), 19, 32, 72, 200
Russell, Lady William, 92–4, 215, 230
Russell, Sir William Howard, 74
Russia, transformation of, 164; hints of war with, 244; Houghton's view of Russian 'protection,' 245; *see also* Crimean War

Sade, Marquis de, 114–15, 117; alleged influence of works on Swinburne, 115, 128, 134, 146–50
Sadists, English, 117–22: Milnes' collection of books on sadism, *see* Erotic
Sailors' Homes, establishment of, 194
St. Germans, Lady, 67 n.
St. Germans, Lord, 67
St. Maur, Lady, 14
Saint-Victor, 117, 118, 121
Sala, George Augustus, 203 and n., 204, 207
Sand, George, 188–9
Schleswig-Holstein duchies, ownership question, 173
Schwarzenberg, Prince Felix zu, 13–14 and n.
Scots Education Bill, 95
Scott, Sir Walter, 251
Sebright, Lady, 202
Sellwood, Emily, *see* Tennyson, Emily
Serlby, 3, 27
Severn, Joseph, 211–12
Seymour, Lady, *see* Somerset, Duchess of
Seymour, Sir Hamilton, 36
Shakespeare Tercentenary, 187–8
Sherbrooke, Lord, 112–13
Sherman, General, 241
'Ship-cruelty question,' 194
Simeon, Sir John, 42, 58, 95
Sinclair, Sir George, 60
Slavery, Milnes' attitude to, 165, 168
Smith, Sydney, 86
Smith, Vernon, 80
Smythe, George, *see* Strangford, Lord
Society, London seasons, 32–3, 39, 95; changes, 51–3; effect of marriage of Prince of Wales, 173–4
Somerset, Duchess of (Lady Seymour), 48, 251
Somerset, Lord Fitzroy, *see* Raglan, Lord

Index